To Tell the Truth

Practice and Craft in Narrative Nonfiction

Connie D. Griffin
University of Massachusetts Amherst

PEARSON
Longman

New York San Francisco Boston
London Toronto Sydney Tokyo Singapore Madrid
Mexico City Munich Paris Cape Town Hong Kong Montreal

Senior Acquisitions Editor: Vivian Garcia
Executive Marketing Manager: Joyce Nilsen
Production Manager: Savoula Amanatidis
Project Coordination, Text Design, and Electronic
    Page Makeup: PrePress PMG
Cover Design Manager: Nancy Danahy
Cover Designer: Nancy Sacks
Cover Photo: Copyright © Guy Cali/Stock Connection
Senior Manufacturing Buyer: Dennis J. Para
Printer and Binder: R. R. Donnelley and Sons Company—Crawfordsville
Cover Printer: R. R. Donnelley and Sons Company—Crawfordsville

For permission to use copyrighted material, grateful acknowledgment is made to
the copyright holders on pp. 314–316, which are hereby made part of this
copyright page.

Library of Congress Cataloging-in-Publication Data

Griffin, Connie D.
  To tell the truth : practice and craft in narrative nonfiction / Connie D. Griffin.
      p. cm.
  ISBN 978-0-205-60549-1
  1. Reportage literature—Technique. 2. Narration (Rhetoric) I. Title.
  PN3377.5.R45G76 2009
  808'.042—dc22

                                                                                    2008032832

Please visit us at www.pearsonhighered.com

ISBN-13: 978-0-205-60549-1
ISBN-10: 0-205-60549-4

1 2 3 4 5 6 7 8 9 10—DOC—11 10 09 08

for Shawn

Contents

Preface

We commonly do not remember, that it is, after all, always the first person that is speaking.

—HENRY DAVID THOREAU, WALDEN

*C*an nonfiction writing be creative? Can creative writing be factual? Can anyone write creative nonfiction? This book responds to such questions with a resounding "yes" as it sits down with the writer and bends over the task at hand, providing a conversational tone, generous guidance, abundant examples, and numerous models for analysis. *To Tell the Truth: Practice and Craft in Narrative Nonfiction* presents strategies for practice; prompts for generating new material, and creative approaches to research that both beginning and experienced narrative nonfiction writers will find useful. Lively essays on craft by major writers in the field address the most pressing concerns facing writers of the genre today, thus creating an intimate colloquium for readers and writers.

In roughly two decades of teaching narrative nonfiction in college and university courses, writing conferences and institutes, as well as other writing workshop settings, I have observed that writers of narrative nonfiction tend to arrive believing in the verisimilitude between life and narrative. The frequently cited defense for poorly crafted prose—but that's *exactly* how it happened—suggests one of the key challenges teachers of narrative nonfiction writing face: helping writers integrate fact and creativity. Unlike fiction, poetry, and drama, which writers consciously approach as art forms, narrative nonfiction writers walk a fine line, negotiating the technical challenges of transforming *life as lived* into *literary representation*, while remaining true to lived experience. Because it is a creative act, the art of writing narrative nonfiction is learned primarily through practice; thus, *To Tell the Truth* will enhance both the process and the product for writers engaged in the creative process of literary truth-telling. For, by entering into the metaphorical medium of language, creative nonfiction writers transform lived experience into art—fact becomes artifact.

Market

In *A Writer's Guide to Nonfiction*, Elizabeth Lyon observes that 30,000 new nonfiction books are published in the United States each year. Eight books of nonfiction appear for every book of fiction, according to Annie Dillard in her introduction to *In Fact: The Best of Creative Nonfiction*, edited by Lee Gutkind. Not all of these are creative nonfiction, of course, but many are, and this is in addition to newspapers, magazines, journals, and a plethora of new media, many of which publish literary journalism. The past couple of decades have seen the growth of journals exclusively dedicated to its publication, such as *Creative Nonfiction*, *The Fourth Genre*, and *River Teeth*, as well as numerous contests and awards. The National Endowment for the Arts, as well as many state arts agencies and private foundations, now recognize the genre in providing fellowship awards and research grants. In response to this productivity, growing interest and need, colleges and universities are developing more courses in narrative nonfiction that draw on students not only from creative writing programs, but also communication, education, sociology, journalism, and other disciplines and fields. Writing institutes, scholarly conferences, and professional societies incorporate the genre into their platforms, and low residency MFA programs have come to emphasize creative nonfiction along with fiction, poetry, and screen writing. Some universities now offer doctorates in creative nonfiction. The genre is flourishing across the disciplines of literature, creative writing, journalism, and media studies, and also history and the social sciences. Scholarly inquiry into the field is growing and instructors such as myself are in need of comprehensive texts that address not only the practice and craft of narrative nonfiction, but also engage in analytical discussions about the genre.

Organization

Approaches to creative nonfiction writing are varied, depending on the writer as well as the instructor. With this in mind, the apparatus remains flexible throughout, allowing for the book to be followed linearly, or for a reference-styled approach to those chapters, sections, and subsections that suit a particular project. **Part 1, "Creativity and Nonfiction Writing,"** includes four chapters: **Chapter 1** provides an introduction to creativity, to the writing process, and addresses how different writers approach storytelling, as well as why some writers choose to be writers. **Chapter 2** provides an overview of the field of narrative nonfiction (a term used interchangeably with creative nonfiction) and details some of the differences and commonalities of the various subgenres. **Chapter 3** explores how writers work and encourages student writers to develop a writing practice, while demystifying the myth that professional writers write when they feel like it, or only when the muse descends. This chapter introduces writers to effective ways to keep a writing journal, as well as the importance of prewriting techniques in generating ideas and getting to the first draft of a story. **Chapter 4** approaches considerations of story structure and examines how active reading of early drafts provides the writer with effective guidance for revision, while stressing that revision is an organic part of the writing process, not a correction of a faulty piece.

Part 2, "Craft Matters: Techniques for Practice," proceeds with Chapters 5 through 9. **Chapter 5** works with scene, setting, and summary, imagery, metaphor, and theme. **Chapter 6** looks at the particular challenges of working with characters who are real people. **Chapter 7** explores narrative persona, voice, and current debates about narrative art, imagination, and truth. **Chapter 8** lifts the discussion to the level of theme and explores how thematic resonance becomes the point of the story. And **Chapter 9** provides a healthy coverage of approaches to research, public records, ethical and legal concerns, as well as tips for effective interviewing.

The book's chapters include references to the models provided at the end of the chapters. The in-text analyses focus on a particular aspect of the model based on the chapter topic, while leaving other techniques and motifs, as well as literary interpretation, up to the instructors' and students' discretion for further discussion. Each chapter on craft contains segments addressing research and practice strategies that include prewriting prompts, and pointers to avoid potential pitfalls.

Special Features

To Tell the Truth: Practice and Craft in Narrative Nonfiction engages in current conversations in the popular field of creative nonfiction, incorporating discussions and contemporary selections of memoir and autobiography, the essay in its many guises, including the lyric and segmented or collage essay, and literary journalism (itself an extensive field whose rubric includes features, profiles, immersion, investigative, and narrative journalism). Due to the increasing interest in the short and the prose poem, these too are included. Designed to meet the growing needs resulting from the burgeoning interest in narrative nonfiction, this book emphasizes key elements common to all three major branches of the genre. It assists nonfiction writers in developing a writing practice specifically modeled to their unique needs. It addresses the practical task of applying techniques of craft in the actual process of generating and shaping material. And it includes contemporary models that represent the range and diversity of the genre.

A key feature of the text, one seldom found in books on the subject, is the inclusion of a significant number of essays on the practice and process of the craft, which reveal known nonfiction writers' imaginative processes—that quirky quality we call creativity—bringing in writers' revelations about individual efforts at foiling the inner critic, applying specific elements of craft, and approaches to research. A special feature of the book is the author's engagement with major voices in the field, both within the book's narrative and through careful selection of essays that bring a variety of approaches and points of view to bear on the subject of narrative nonfiction. For example, the book includes discussions about the fine line between fact and fiction, memory and imagination, and the imperative of the nonfiction writer's credibility.

Additional features include guidance on developing narrative persona, dealing with point of view, as well as strategies for applying literary techniques such as characterization, setting and scene, imagery and metaphor, as well as thematic resonance. *To Tell the Truth* breaks down the recursive writing process of generating, composing, and revising into manageable stages and stresses the effectiveness of working in drafts to create exemplary narrative nonfiction.

Acknowledgments

I am deeply indebted to my life partner, Shawn de Jong for her work alongside me in the development of this project, for her tireless communication with publishers, agents, and authors for permissions, and for her thoughtful suggestions and support at every step along the way. I could not have done this project without her. I want to extend my heartfelt gratitude to my community of friends who have shared in this, as well as all of life's endeavors. I am particularly appreciative of students, colleagues, and other writers who understand the pleasure, the passion, and the pain of translating thought, feeling, and idea into words on the page, and who find in the story sustenance of the deepest sort. I would also like to thank Erika Berg, who assisted me in the early stages of developing the ideas and organization of the book, Matthew Wright, who later took on the project, and Vivian Garcia, who carried it to completion. A special thanks to Haley Pero, editorial assistant extraordinaire, and to Kristy Zamagni, for constant and immediate assistance throughout the production process. Thank you to those individuals who took the time to provide reviews of the project in process. Your constructive criticism has served as a healthy dose of challenge and support.

—Connie D. Griffin, Ph.D.
University of Massachusetts Amherst

About the Author

Connie D. Griffin has been a member of the creative writing faculty at Boston College for many years. She leads workshops in memoir writing in the Blue Hills Writing Institute, Curry College, and teaches narrative journalism and feature writing for the journalism program of the University of Massachusetts Amherst. Dr. Griffin is an Assistant Professor at Commonwealth College, the honors college of the University of Massachusetts Amherst. She received her B.A. from the University of Tulsa, her M.A. from Boston College, and her Ph.D. from the University of Massachusetts Amherst. She has published essays, articles, reviews, features, and profiles in numerous venues. She lives in western Massachusetts. Visit her website at www.conniedgriffin.com.

PART I

Creativity and Nonfiction Writing

CHAPTER 1

An Introduction to Storytelling...

Every child is an artist! The problem is how to remain an artist once we grow up.

— PABLO PICASSO

An Invitation to Creativity

As children we are alive with awareness; our sensory, perceptual, imaginative capacities are vitally engaged. The world is a place of discovery and unless we are sleeping we are actively engaged with it. Children live fully in the present moment, giving it their undivided attention. Watch children at play on the beach, for example, deeply engrossed in building a sandcastle replete with shells and rocks, moats and turrets. They're not concerned that the next high tide will wipe away all of their hard work—because they're not working; they are at play, serious and vigorous though it may be. And if high tide doesn't sweep the castle away, the children themselves are likely to. I spent an afternoon once with a little boy meticulously building a magnificent sandcastle only to have him stand back and gaze on it, clapping his hands in delight as he took a running leap, landing right in the middle of it. Flinging himself about in the sandcastle, he took as much pleasure turning it back into a beach again as we had taken in creating it in the first place. I think Picasso was onto something. Children create for the sheer pleasure of it. They aren't thinking about what they will do with it when it's done—at least not young children, say preschool age. While I'm not suggesting that you shred your creative work, the freedom to consider it just might liberate you from some of the constraints writers often feel when faced with the blank page.

Sometimes a sense of self-consciousness descends upon us when we sit down to write. At other times, we forget ourselves and become lost in the process. Like public speaking, writing brings us face to face with our own personal voice in ways that we seldom feel when chatting with friends. Because both writing and public speaking bring us into contact with an audience, perhaps it is the fear of criticism that makes the composing process fraught with anxiety. Of course we

3

want to have an awareness of audience when we write; if we're not considerate of those who take the time to read our work, we are likely to be misunderstood. The problem comes when we become overly focused on our readers before we even begin to write. Or, when we begin by trying to write the final product. In other words, being overly goal oriented early on in the composing process can short-circuit the creative process altogether. It can be helpful to find ways to overcome the stage fright of a blank page and children are our most unselfconscious teachers at this point in the creative endeavor.

Creativity and the Unconscious

What is this quirky thing we call creativity? Interest in the creative process is far from a new development. Both Plato and Aristotle took up the subject and over the millennium others have had something to say about it as well. Certainly it intrigued the Romantic poets—Shelley and Keats, Wordsworth and Coleridge, Blake. Those most advantageously situated to observe and comprehend—philosophers and psychologists, scientists and artists—have provided a plethora of studies of the phenomenon. It is for practical purposes, too, that we explore the creative processes, for such an endeavor can assist in making our creative practice more efficient, as well as its outcome, the product, itself, more effective in the long run. Individual approaches to creativity vary widely and if you're serious about writing, you will want to understand a bit about your own creative process. By becoming aware of how you approach the stages of writing, generating ideas, gathering data, shaping narrative, rewriting toward an overall unity of organization and theme, you will be far more capable of bringing forth your best ideas and manifesting them in the form of a story.

While many believe that creativity cannot be taught, and this very well may be true, we do know that some environments are more conducive than others. I worry when a student writer tells me that she writes when she feels moved to do so and that developing a daily writing habit would kill her creativity. I worry because I know from my own experience and from talking with and reading about the writing habits of others that the myth of the muse is alive and well, while the muse tends to be fickle at best.

Over the years of teaching writing workshops I have become aware of an initial tendency to fear creativity, or the state of mind conducive to its realization, even though there is a sense of exhilaration once students and I find ourselves further along in a creative project. Schooled in critical modes of knowledge, it appears that our logical, linear, analytical thinking has become more developed as we have advanced in our formal educations. This is not necessarily a bad thing, but an overly critical eye can subvert the creative process if it is permitted to predominate in the generative stages of producing creative work. The process of writing creatively is a complexly dynamic one, drawing as it does on various aspects of the psyche: the subconscious as well as the conscious, the creative as well as the critical, the associative as well as the linear. Unfolding through a series of stages, the generative stage is much more likely to be successful if we find ways to set aside the conscious, critical, discriminating aspects of the mind. A critical eye is essential and will be brought to bear on the process later on, but in the early stages of getting your ideas onto the page you want to approach the endeavor with a serious playfulness, a focused awareness that is nonjudgmental and forgiving. By breaking down the three key stages of writing into manageable parts— prewriting, writing, and rewriting—you may be surprised to discover that each stage becomes far more productive than when you try to do them all at once.

Telling Our Stories

The desire to shape our experience into stories is an innate human drive, motivated by our need to understand, to find meaning in our lives and the world around us. We are all storytellers shouting our existence from the time we can say, "Look Mom! Look at me!" And with a big grin on our faces we demonstrate our amazing agility for climbing the monkey bars or zipping down the slide, pleased and proud of ourselves for such an accomplishment. Although with age the chest beating settles down for most of us, still we share the big things and the little as we move through our everyday lives.

And then there are those who want to write it all down—well, not all of it, but certainly the high points and the low. Jane Bernstein, whose essay, "How and Why" is included in this chapter, thinks about writing as a mulling state of mind, one she enters into when she runs, a time when she lets herself ask questions about the things, both large and small, that life brings our way. Indeed, contrary to what we may have learned about writing in our early years—beginning with an outline, for example, or having a clear sense of direction and conclusion, or knowing what we want to say before we say it—most of the writers who share their personal practice in this book approach writing as a question, as a way of exploring what it is that they are curious about, not what they already know. As Annie Dillard suggests in *The Writing Life* we must give voice to our own astonishment, follow our own sensitivities. It isn't enough, however, to write from the inside out; we must also know the field within which we work, warns Dillard; we must know its limits "the way a tennis player knows the court." It is only then that we can enjoy the excitement of playing the edges.

Based on the premise that anyone who has a deep desire to write creatively can do so and do it well, this book provides a foundation for knowing the field of narrative nonfiction and for developing an effective writing practice. It offers numerous prompts for generating raw material, creative approaches to research, and strategies for approaching your work in progress with the creatively critical eye required for revision, including incorporating workshop feedback from peer reviews. Bringing to the discussion numerous writers who share their thoughts on the practice and craft of narrative nonfiction, as well as how they approach this quirky thing we call creativity, *To Tell the Truth* provides a broad spectrum of approaches, reminding us that there is no one way to become a writer.

In addition, the readings presented here by way of examples of the craft represent a rich diversity of voices, styles, subject matter, structural approaches, and subgenres. It is my hope that the book will provide a range of methods sufficiently broad that you, the reader, may find those that work best for your own particular needs, permitting you to begin by knowing the court and then to move on into playing the edges.

Getting Started

The seemingly paradoxical nature of the term creative nonfiction derives from a growing body of literature that links life as lived and the representation of life in language. We want to believe in the verisimilitude between narrative and life. And, of course, there is a relationship. But, the two aren't a seamless fit. Writing a good story isn't merely a matter of transcription; if it were, many more people would be writers and successful ones at that. A good story is a work of art; its creator draws on the skillful knowledge and application of techniques to create the story's illusion of reality. I say illusion because language is a symbolic medium. Through it we represent life. The story is itself an experience, both in the writing and in the reading. As an artifact, however, it represents experience and is not the actual experience itself.

One reason we come to believe in the verisimilitude between life and story may be because the medium we use for storytelling is the same medium that we use in going about our daily lives. Language, as a functional part of the practical world in which we live our daily lives, is a familiar element, so we are less inclined to approach it as an artistic medium. This isn't true for the pianist, the painter, or the dancer. If we decide we want to become a pianist, we approach the piano expecting to learn musical notes, to practice our scales on the piano, to begin with simple pieces and gradually develop the skills to take on more complicated songs. Even the realist painter knows she must learn to translate what she sees with the eye through a malleable medium—paint—to the canvas, something that will take years of dedication and practice before she can do it well. The dancer, too, begins with diligent exercises and a few specific steps, which he will repeat rigorously on a daily basis and over a long period of apprenticeship before he feels confident to go before an audience.

Approaching creative writing is like that, and it can be helpful to break down the complex process in which any creative writer engages so that we come to understand that there are specific and essential elements of craft. Practicing the craft of creative nonfiction asks that we do the equivalent of the novice pianist practicing her scales, the dancer practicing his steps, the painter working, not only with perspective, but also with paint, colors, texture, application, and so on. In creative nonfiction, the elements of craft include, among other things, scene, setting, and summary; imagery and metaphor; character and complication; plot and pacing; dialogue and dramatic action. Creative nonfiction writers find themselves developing a narrative persona—the writer's presence through voice, made up of stylistic devices, diction, syntax, the turn of a phrase. And point of view becomes apparent through the process of writing—that position from which the writer views things, the perspective that you and only you can offer to the subject at hand. This is what you have come to do. While there are many more elements to the craft of creative nonfiction, which we will get to as we go along, for now simply start by suspending your self-criticism and self-doubt. Approach your writing with an attitude of trust. Trust that you, your writing, and your relationship to your writing are all that you need to get started.

Writing as a Process

Often misconstrued as "writer's block," the discomfiture with which the novice writer faces the unknown of beginning is a familiar feeling for longtime writers. Longtime writers know that the beginnings of any writing project are fraught with uncertainty, false starts, and experimentation, and they will have to wing it until a particular phrase or image or tone strikes an inner chord and leads them into the story that wants to be told.

We cannot be reminded too often that stories do not flow from the mind to the page fully formed and crystal clear. Writing isn't something we do *after* gaining clarity; it is a recursive process through which we *gain* clarity, a process most productively carried out in stages—prewriting, writing, and rewriting. "How can you know what it will be?" wrote the avant-garde American writer Gertrude Stein. "If you know it, it will be dictation, not creation." The writer, immersed in the process of writing, is not thinking about being a writer but about getting it right.

Sometimes we don't even know what form it will take. Will it be a personal essay? Memoir? A travel narrative? Literary journalism? Perhaps it will face the confusing challenge of fitting comfortably under the rubric of a number of sub-categories of narrative nonfiction. More than likely this will be the case. One of the most interesting, if disconcerting, aspects of creative nonfiction is its ambiguity—ambiguity of form, of genre boundaries, even ambiguity around truthfulness. A personal essay may just as well be a memoir; a travel essay may just as likely be considered nature writing. Biographical portraits often slip into what I describe as auto/biography (the slash intended), as the writer becomes intimately involved, not simply in the production of the biographical portraiture, but fully as a character in the narrative itself. Even literary journalism may find itself spilling over into the realm of the personal essay as the journalist brings her own insights and point of view to bear on the subject. In living with this genre over the past 25 years, it has been a pleasure to discover just how unwieldy narrative nonfiction can be. So, while I believe it's important to have models, in fact it's essential, I have found all my attempts to categorize narrative nonfiction have only served to give me a deeper respect for the genre's rich diversity, its fluidity and dynamic play at the edges of the field. As it does so, new voices join in. Thus, the field itself is vitally alive and in a continual state of redefinition. What a wonderful endeavor in which to participate.

Thinking Like a Writer

I have learned through writing that what is most personal is, in fact, what binds us together as human beings.

—TERRY TEMPEST WILLIAMS

Writers have a way of experiencing life twice: the event itself and the reconstruction of the event for story. Thinking like a writer asks that we not only view events and experiences in a fresh way, but that we also become inquisitive about the tensions, difficulties, and questions that life brings our way. Instead of brushing aside complexities and contradictions with narratives of easy resolve, instead of offering the obvious answer to the questions that come up in your writing, take this as an opportunity to examine them closely, turning them this way and that to see what lessons they might have to teach. Often it is more than one. Writers seem more likely than most to follow the question and take their time when they find themselves circling within the labyrinth of multiple choices and paradox.

To what purpose do we write? What motivates writers to spend long hours shaping sentences and paragraphs into stories that recapture moments from their lives? Writers are often considered an odd lot; but then again, friends, family—the public, in general—tend to look askance at the working writer prior to success and recognition. What is frustrating and challenging, but ultimately rewarding—the process of creativity itself—is frequently overlooked by those who marvel at the finished product. They see only the final result of an experience that is as real to the writer as daily life is to the nonwriter.

Are you familiar with fractals? While the complexity of natural phenomena may refuse to be stripped down to something simple and straightforward, patterns do appear within the rich profusion of the natural world. These are called fractals. In *Fractals: The Patterns of Chaos*, John Briggs posits that even an "individual tree is the result of a vast, shifting set of unique circumstances, a kaleidoscope of influences such as gravity, magnetic fields, soil composition, wind, sun angles, insect hordes, human harvesting, and other trees." An individual life, like the tree, is also made up of numerous and constantly changing circumstances. When we begin the process of writing about ourselves, about others, and the world at large, we enter into what sometimes appears to be complete chaos—the chaos of unmediated life experience. As writers we pause, put pen to paper, and self-consciously move into the promise of the narrative arc—discovering patterns of meaning in our own existence.

The task of the writer, then, becomes one of mediation. Not an aggressive imposition of order onto experience, but a search for patterns that might suggest a meaningful coherence; only then can we coax meaning into being. This is the creative part. This is what the writer has in common with the painter, photographer, musician, the dancer. The pleasure in finding patterns, in giving expression to our experience—through composition—in meaningful, aesthetic form: this is sufficient motivation to keep the artist creating.

Even if you don't aspire to become a published writer, creative experimentation with language will lead to the discovery and development of a means of self-expression that is uniquely yours. Drawing on your own rich storehouse of experiences and emotions, memories and observations, questions and concerns, you will come to a deeper awareness of your own sensibility, while cultivating a capacity for the metaphorical nature of language. You aren't really cultivating an entirely new ability; the qualities that will imbue your work with originality have been within you from childhood, even if they have lain dormant. As children we had a strong relationship with our own imagination and its interdependence with language. Whether it was "pretend games" (which we called "play-like" when I was a child), or the simple spontaneity and pleasure of the work of childhood—engaging in play—the curiosity and wonder of childhood discovery are unmatched at any other time in our lives. The running questions of "why?" and "how?" the plaintive cries of "watch me," the sheer virtuosity of the child's eager engagement with life and learning—all are stunning for their richness, range, and immediacy.

In her influential book, *Writing the Natural Way*, exploring left and right brain engagement in the process of creative writing, Gabriele Rico draws on a number of linguistic findings suggesting that a fundamental act of early childhood is "storying." The term, put forth by psychologist Renee Fuller, relates to what she describes as children's innate aesthetic activity involving discovery and the fashioning of experience into narrative forms. This process occurs at the "most formative stage of intellectual development," according to Fuller. For example, children are drawn to rhythm and rhyme, patterns and repetition, vivid imagery, and a sense of what Fuller refers to as "wholeness." Writers often refer to this as **organic unity** in a written piece. "Storying," then, "expresses an innate human need to make mental connections, to perceive patterns, to create relationships among people, things, feelings, and events—and to express these perceived connections to others," Rico notes. There you have it. We are hard wired from childhood to shape our experience into story form. We can't help ourselves.

As you move through this book please follow the suggested prompts, do the short exercises, and apply the proposed range of research strategies. Merely reading them will do little good. Books that offer instruction in the art of photography, physical exercise, or self-help of any sort may be interesting to read, but readers will not benefit from them unless they apply the concepts. This book is no different. Following the cumulative effects of the exercises, you will be moving through a series of stages of creative writing—prewriting, writing, and revising—as you do so, you will find yourself making connections, first with yourself and then with others. You will find yourself *telling the truth* through the fine art of *storying*.

Readings

Writers on Writing

"How and Why," Jane Bernstein

"Writing Personal Essays: On the Necessity of Turning Oneself Into a Character," Phillip Lopate

Lyric Essay

"On the Street: Nobody Watches, Everyone Performs," Vivian Gornick

Literary Journalism

"A Boy of Unusual Vision," Alice Steinbach

The Short

"Volar," Judith Ortiz Cofer

Prose Poem

"Two Hearts," Brian Doyle

How and Why
Jane Bernstein

*M*ost important is that I run. This is not merely an item culled from a list of my extracurricular activities, nor a boast meant as evidence that I am health conscious, but a beginning, a connection: if I did not run, I would not write essays. These two profoundly different activities are woven together for me: one physical, mindless enough so that dogs, rhinos, and rats do it, the other—How else can you say it?— cerebral, an activity reserved for the only animals capable of despair, delight, and reflection. I think therefore I am.

My body is an engine, a middle-aged engine, admittedly. The start-up is often rough; the beginning of the run, if I turned it into words, would be a litany of complaints. But inevitably, I get comfortable on the road, and shift into a kind of cruise control, in which my body moves forward of its own accord. A kind of forgetting washes over me then. It's not only that I forget the road, my beating heart, and tender knees, but what I think of as my daily self, the mother-teacher-datebook-keeper-member-of-the-community self. When this self is shed, my mind, another machine, begins to hum. The voice of my truest, most private self surfaces, and I drift into a kind of mulling state, a state in which I worry things. Not worry about them, the more sedentary, less productive activity done by my daily self. But "worry" as defined by Webster's Third: "to bite at or upon . . . to touch, poke, or disturb . . . To subject to persistent or nagging attention or effort . . ."

"Why?" I ask, when I am out on the road. In this mulling state, I cannot will myself to address problems or think through things. I am dreamy and utterly unselfconscious, drifting through the easiest most trivial dilemmas—enough broccoli for stir fry? brown shoes or black?—until bigger things begin to rise.

Sometimes the *why* that surfaces is merely a question, not yet embodied. Or the *why* might be an image that continues to reappear, as if asking to be studied. Sometimes the why is embedded in a conversation that I replay or invent, a kind of auditory hallucination. Some of this mulling dissipates on these runs; the questions rise, float, and pop, ephemeral as soap bubbles. Other issues are played out later in conversation. But some of what surfaces on these runs keeps rising, demanding to be further mulled. These questions or voices become irritations, splinters beneath my skin.

Why

I am running one day, wondering why running and mulling are so inseparable for me, when it occurs to me that even as a small child, I felt compelled to mull, to "subject to . . . nagging attention" questions that did not seem to plague others in my family. Long after the toddler years, I was still bugging my parents with why questions.

Three miles into my run, I remember the cemetery we drove past on our weekly visit to my ancient grandmother, how I looked out the car window each time and asked:

"Why do we die?"

I imagine my parents exchanging one of those oh-no-not-again looks in the front seat, my mother, bored, saying, "That's the way we're made."

"But why?"

"Because our bodies wear out."

"Why?"

My questions deemed a verbal tic, an attention-getting device. But, no, the need was real, the dismissive answers intolerable, even then.

Wearily: "Because that's the way it is."

"Why do they wear out?"

"Because I said so."

Several miles into my run, the questions I worry about are often just as unanswerable. I ponder the fact that the world has so little patience for mullers. There is no room for our questions on an ordinary day in the domestic world or the world of commerce. We are the object of fun if we voice our cosmic concerns too often. Cuckoos. Navel-gazers. Obsessed.

"Because," the world tells us.

"Is and always was," it says.

"Because I said so."

"Just because."

Back on the road, motor purring, I wonder why I wonder and think of my dog, a terrier, from the Latin *terre*, earth. He does not point or retrieve, could not pull a sled. But he needs to dig, this earth dog, at times so intent upon digging up a rock from beneath the soil that nothing can stop him once he starts. Passionate and fervent are the words that come to mind when I watch him dig. Is he looking for the rock of his dreams? Routing out the rock from hell? On the road I wonder if I am like my dog, born to dig. There is photographic evidence that this might be the case. Look! Here I am, in a photo at two years old, covered in mud, a literal digger. Perhaps there is a genie for mulling, the way some people feel there might be genes for patriotism and shyness. Maybe there's a strange trisomy that dooms the genetically challenged victim to ask and ask, incapable of accepting "because."

The teenage years: I did not outgrow it.

"Better not to dwell on such things," said my parents. "Leave well enough alone."

"Looking for trouble," my mother called my speculations. When my tenacity, my relentless digging, really irritated her, she would say, "Stop already. Stop analyzing everything!"

A second theory: Mulling in opposition to the style of the rest of my family, as a protest against the heavy door of "because," the wall of "stop analyzing."

How

And so: I am the kind of person who is predisposed to writing (and reading) essays and has found a way to shake free of the worldly stuff and hear the voice of my true self. What do I worry? What problems are persistent and irritating enough that I take them from the road to the desk? I'd like to say that my range of subjects is limitless, but in reality, much of my work fits into what essayist Nancy Mairs only half facetiously calls "the literature of personal disaster." To baldly list the disasters is an embarrassment to me—murder, senility, disability. But as Mairs points out, serious writers whose work fits into this genre don't write about adversity as a single monolithic event, the disaster as a disaster. While the adversity might become the background, the heart of the essay comes from one of what Mairs calls "the welter of little incidents" that make up the whole.

When I write about my daughter Rachel, who is blithely categorized by the world at large as a "special needs child," I don't write about her retardation itself. Nor do I replay secondhand sentiments that come in lockstep beside the word *retarded*. For instance, I neither write (nor think) of her as "one of God's Special Children." I don't write about how fortunate I am to be her mother, or how much she has taught me. I do not adhere to the party line by claiming that adversity has made me a better person. (It hasn't.) I write about my daughter competing in Special Olympics or about the times I regret her birth. My daughter is fundamentally unknowable, because she lacks the language to describe her own moods, desires, and dislikes. She lives in a world she cannot understand, and that often fails to accommodate what I believe to be her needs.

What I believe . . . "I am Rachel's interior voice," I tell people, as if there is something amusing in this. In fact, I take this quite seriously. If writing essays is a clear assertion of one's voice, I supposed I could say that I write about Rachel to make her voice heard, and in opposition to the sentiments that diminish her as an individual, make her an indistinguishable member of a fuzzy, barely human category.

But often, when I am mulling on the road, it occurs to me that there is something audacious and obnoxious in my presumption. Who am I to claim to be the keeper of Rachel's consciousness? And yet, if not me, then who?

This is the kind of tension that cannot be resolved on a run, that makes me want to take to my desk, to shape what is hazy and unformed into something comprehensible. Once I begin to transfer my vague mulling into words on paper, everything changes radically. The private act of removing the splinter becomes an attempt to wrench meanings from my shapeless pondering. It is at my desk that I recall the French root from which *essay* is derived. *Essaier*, to try. I will try not to solve the problem I wish to work out on paper, since the most vexing problems escape tidy solutions, but to work through it in a way that makes my tale of interest to people I have never met.

An Example

Some years ago, I found myself rather excessively mulling over the word *pleasure*, wondering as I ran what pleasure was for a child whose responses were muted, who never expressed what she wanted, never complained when deprived of what she had seemed to enjoy. First the word itself: pleasure. syn: delight, joy. Why was I stuck on this? I asked myself.

An image formed in my head one day, a picture of pure joy: my daughter, shrieking and flapping her arms in a swimming pool. Without question, the water was something she loved. All I had to do was provide the opportunity for her to swim, to put her in the water, and I could say, "Rachel knows pleasure." But a problem was locked inside this seemingly perfect picture, for her physician thought that swimming induced her seizures, and suggested that perhaps I keep her away from the water. If we no longer took her swimming, would she recall that she had lost something she loved? Would she experience deprivation? Or did experiences, even pleasurable ones, simply vanish without any traces? Was the evidence of her pleasure worth the possible risk that she might have the kind of dangerous, intractable seizures that once she'd had in a swimming pool?

How best to tell this modest tale? I did not aim to write a philosophical inquiry into the nature of human happiness. I wanted to tell a small story with larger questions embedded inside it, a story about one child, unable to speak up for herself, a well-meaning physician, and a mother caught between wanting her child to have pleasure and providing for her safety. I used the techniques of fiction for this piece when I opted to give the reader a glimpse of our life, to show Rachel in the pool, to set off the drama between the characters.

When the form of this piece made itself known, I began to draft away, flush with grandiosity, convinced that my tale would be meaningful to others. Then one day, in the midst of what seemed to be a final draft, I found myself clutched by modesty and terror. What a puny, deeply insignificant story it suddenly seemed.

"Who was I?"

"My trivial life!"

"Who could possibly care?"

"How could I presume?"

A struggle that I now realize is inevitable for me, permanent, sometimes crippling, and yet of value, too, for it creates a tension, twists my self-effacement ("Who am I?") into a fierce desire to get the story right ("I am no one, but I must be heard!").

Perhaps if I were bolder or quicker, if I could tug on someone's sleeve and say exactly what I meant, I would not need to punch through my modesty on paper. But I cannot do it in person, and therefore depend upon my written words to say to the reader, "This is what it's like" and "This is what I think. This is my daughter. This is me. This is how we traveled in our search for accommodation."

The rewards: no fame, not much in the way of recognition, but the immense satisfaction of a single reader who says, "You found the words for me." Or, "This is my life, too."

My satisfaction feels permanent when I hear this, my need to question feels forever quenched.

And it is, until I lace up my shoes and hit the road again.

Writing Personal Essays:
On the Necessity of Turning Oneself Into a Character
Phillip Lopate

*I*n personal essays, nothing is more commonly met than the letter *I*. I think it a perfectly good word, one no writer should be ashamed to use. Especially is first person legitimate for this form, so drawn to the particulars of character and voice. The problem with "I" is not that it is in bad taste, but that fledgling personal essayists may think they've said or conveyed more than they actually have with that one syllable. In their minds, that "I" is swarming with background and a lush, sticky past, and an almost too fatal specificity, whereas the reader, encountering it for the first time in a new piece, sees only a slender telephone pole standing in the sentence, trying to catch a few signals to send on. In truth, even the barest "I" holds a whisper of promised engagement, and can suggest a caress in the midst of more stolid language. What it doesn't do, however, is give us a clear picture of who is speaking.

To do that, the writer needs to build herself into a character. And I use the word *character* much the same way the fiction writer does. E.M. Forster, in *Aspects of the Novel*, drew a famous distinction between "flat" and "round" characters—between those fictional personages seen from the outside who acted with the predicable consistency of caricatures, and those whose complexities or teeming inner lives we came to know. But whether the writer chooses to present characters as flat or round, or a combination, the people on the page—it scarcely matters whether they appear in fiction or nonfiction—will need to become knowable enough in their broad outlines to behave "believably," at the same time as free willed enough to intrigue us with surprises. The art of characterization comes down to establishing a pattern of habits and actions for the person you are writing about and introducing variations into the system. In this respect, building a character is a pedagogic model, because you are teaching the reader what to expect.

So how do you turn *yourself* into a character? First of all, you need to have—or acquire—some distance from yourself. If you are so panicked by any examination of your flaws that all you can do is sputter defensively when you feel yourself attacked, you are not going to get very far in the writing of personal essays. You need to be able to see yourself from the ceiling: to know, for instance, how you are coming across in social situations, and to assess accurately when you are charming, and when you seem pushy, mousy, or ridiculous. From the viewpoint of honest essay writing, it is just as unsatisfactorily distorting to underrate yourself all the time, and think you are far less effective than you actually are, than to give yourself too much credit. The point is to begin to take inventory of yourself so that you can present that self to the reader as a specific, legible character.

A good place to start is your quirks. These are the idiosyncrasies, stubborn tics, antisocial mannerisms, and so on that set you apart from the majority of your fellowmen. There will be more than enough time later to assert your common humanity, or better yet, to let the reader make the mental bridge between your oddities and those of everyone else. But to establish credibility, you would do well to resist coming across at first as absolutely average. Who wants to read about that bland creature, the regular Joe? The mistake many beginning essayists make is to try so hard to be likable and nice, to fit in, that the reader, craving stronger stuff (at the very least, a tone of authority), gets bored. Literature is not a place for conformists, organization men. The skills of the kaffeeklatsch— restraining one's expressiveness, rounding out one's edges, sparing everyone's feelings—will not work as well on the page.

The irony is that most of us suspect—no, we *know*—that underneath it all we *are* common as dirt. But we may still need to maximize that pitiful set of quirks, those small differences that seem to set us apart from others, and project them theatrically, the way actors work with singularities in their physical appearances or vocal textures. In order to turn ourselves into characters, we need to *dramatize* ourselves. I don't mean inventing or adding colorful traits that aren't true; I mean positioning those that are already in us under the most clearly focused, sharply defined light. It's a subtractive process: You need to cut away the inessentials, and highlight just those features in your personality that lead to the most intense contradictions or ambivalence.

An essay needs conflict, just as a short story does. Without conflict, your essay will drift into static mode, repeating your initial observation in a self-satisfied way. What gives an essay dynamism is the need to work out some problem, especially a problem that is not easily resolved. Fortunately, human beings are conflicted animals, so there is no shortage of tensions that won't go away. Good essayists know how to select a topic in advance that will generate enough spark in itself, and how to frame the topic so that it will neither be too ambitious nor too slight—so that its scale will be appropriate for satisfying exploration. If you are serenely unconflicted when you first sit down to write an essay, you may find yourself running out of steam. If you take on a problem that is too philosophically large or historically convoluted, you may choke on the details and give up.

Still, these are technical issues, and I am inclined to think that what stands in the way of most personal essays is not technique but psychology. The emotional preparedness, if you will, to be honest and open to exposure.

The student essayist is torn between two contrasting extremes:

A. "I am so weird that I could never tell on the page what is really, secretly going on in my mind."
B. "I am so boring, nothing ever happens to me out of the ordinary, so who would want to read about me?"

Both extremes are rooted in shame, and both reflect a lack of worldliness. The first response ("I am so weird") exaggerates how isolated one is in one's "wicked" thoughts, instead of recognizing that everyone has strange, surreal, immoral notions. The second response ("My life is so boring and I'm so boring") requires a reeducation so that the student essayists can be brought to acknowledge just those moments in the day, in their loves and friendships, in their family dynamics, in their historical moments, in their interactions with the natural world, that remain genuinely perplexing, vexing, luminous, unresolved. In short, they must be nudged to recognize that life remains a mystery—even one's own so-called boring life. They must also be taught to recognize the charm of the ordinary: that daily life that has nourished some of the most enduring essays.

The use of literary or other models can be a great help in invoking life's mystery. I like to remind myself, as well as my students, of the tonal extremes available to us. It is useful to know we can rant as much as Dostoyevsky's Underground Man or Céline's narrators, that we can speak—as the poet Mayakovski says—"At the Top of My Voice." That we can be passionate as Hazlitt and Baldwin, or even whine, the way Joan Didion sometimes does, albeit with self-aware humor. It is useful to remind students, enamored of David Lynch or Quentin Tarantino movies, that some of that bizarre sensibility can find a place in their essays—that "outlaw" culture does not have to be left outside the schoolhouse. At the same time, it is necessary to introduce them to the sane, thoughtful, considered, responsible essayists like George Orwell or E.B. White. From both sets of models we can then choose how reasonable or hysterical we want to come across at any time: in one piece, seem the soul of reason; in another, a step away from the loony bin.

Mining our quirks is only the beginning of turning ourselves into characters. We are distinguished one from another as much by our pasts, the set of circumstances we are born into, as by the challenges we have encountered along the way, and how we choose to resolve them, given our initial stations in life. It means something very different to have been born the second-oldest boy in an upper-middle-class Korean family that emigrated from Seoul to Los Angeles than to have been born the youngest female in a poor Southern Baptist household of nine.

Ethnicity, gender, religion, class, geography, politics: These are all strong determinants in the development of character. Sometimes they can be made too much of, as in the worst sort of "identity politics," which seeks to explain away all the intangibles of a human being's destiny by this or that social oppression. But we must be bold in working with these categories as starting points: be not afraid to meditate on our membership in this or that community, and the degree to which it has or has not formed us.

When you are writing a memoir, you can set up these categories and assess their importance one by one, and go on from there. When you write personal essays, however, you can never assume that your readers will know a thing about your background, regardless of how many times you have explained it in previous essays. So you must become deft at inserting that information swiftly and casually—"I was born in Brooklyn, New York, of working-class parents"— and not worry about the fact that it may be redundant to your regular readers, if you're lucky enough to have any. In one essay, you may decide to make a big thing of your religious training and very little of your family background; in another, just the opposite; but in each new essay, it would be a good idea to tell the reader both, simply because this sort of information will help to build you into a character.

In this sense, the personal essayist must be like a journalist, who respects the obligation to get in the basic orienting facts—the who, what, where, when, and why—as close to the top of every story as possible.

So now you have sketched yourself to the reader as a person of a certain age, sex, ethnic and religious background, class, and region, possessing a set of quirks, foibles, strengths, and peculiarities. Are you yet a character? Maybe not: not until you have soldered your relationship with the reader, by springing vividly into his mind, so that everything your "I" says and does on the page seems somehow— oddly, piquantly—characteristic. The reader must find you amusing (there, I've said it). Amusing enough to follow you, no matter what essay topic you propose. Whether you are writing this time on world peace or a bar of soap, readers must sense quickly from the first paragraph that you are going to keep them engaged. The trouble is that you cannot amuse the reader unless you are already self-amused. And here we come to one of the main stumbling blocks placed before the writing of personal essays: self-hatred.

It is an observable fact that most people don't like themselves, in spite of being, for the most part, decent enough human beings—certainly not war criminals—and in spite of the many self-help books urging us to befriend and think positively about ourselves. Why this self-dislike should be so prevalent is a matter that would require the best sociological and psychoanalytic minds to elucidate; all I can say, from my vantage point as a teacher and anthologist of the personal essay, is that an odor of self-disgust mars many performances in this genre and keeps many would-be practitioners from developing into full-fledged professionals. They exhibit a form of stuttering, of never being able to get past the initial, superficial self-presentation and diving into the wreck of one's personality with gusto.

The proper alternative to self-dislike is not being pleased with oneself—a smugness equally distasteful to the reader—but being *curious about* oneself. Such self-curiosity (of which Montaigne, the father of the essay, was the greatest exemplar) can only grow out of that detachment or distance from oneself about which I spoke earlier.

I am convinced that self-amusement is a discipline that can be learned; it can be practiced even by people (such as myself) who have at times a strong self-dislike or at least self-mistrust. I may be tired of myself in everyday life, but once I start narrating a situation or set of ideas on the page, I begin to see my "I" in a comic light, and I maneuver him so that he will best amuse the reader. My "I" is not me, entirely, but a character drawn from aspects of myself, in somewhat the same way (less stylized or bold, perhaps) that Chaplin drew the Little Fellow or

Jerry Lewis modeled the arrested-development goofball from their experiences. I am willing to let my "I" take his pratfalls; maintaining one's dignity should not be a paramount issue in personal essays. But first must come the urge to entertain the reader. From that impulse everything else follows.

There is also considerable character development in expressing your opinions, prejudices, half-baked ideas, etc., etc., provided you are willing to analyze the flaws in your thinking and to entertain arguments against your hobbyhorses and not be too solemn about it all. The essay thrives on daring, darting flights of thought. You must get in the habit of inviting, not censoring, your most far-fetched, mischievous notions, because even if they prove cockeyed, they may point to an element of truth that would otherwise be inaccessible. When, for instance, I wrote my essay "Against Joie de Vivre," I knew on some level that it was an indefensible position, but I wanted to see how far I could get in taking a curmudgeonly stance against the pursuit of happiness. And indeed, it struck a chord of recognition in many readers, because lots of us are "so glad to be unhappy," at least as much as we "want to be happy." (To quote two old songs.)

Finally, it would do well for personal essayists to follow another rule of fiction writers, who tell you that if you want to reveal someone's character, actions speak louder than words. Give your "I" something to do. It's fine to be privy to all of "I's" ruminations and cerebral nuances, but consciousness can only take us so far in the illumination of character. Particularly if you are writing a memoir essay, with chronology and narrative, it is often liberating to have the "I" step beyond the observer role and be implicated crucially in the overall action. How many memoir pieces suffer from a self-righteous setup: the writer telling a story in which Mr. or Ms. "I" is the passive recipient of the world's cruelty, the character's first exposure to racism or betrayal, say. There is something off-putting about a nonfiction story in which the "I" character is right and all the others wrong, the "I" infinitely more sinned against than sinning. By showing our complicity in the world's stock of sorrow, we convince the reader of our reality and even gain his sympathy.

How much more complicated and alive is George Orwell's younger self, the "I" in "Such, Such Were the Joys," for having admitted he snitched on his classmates, or James Baldwin's "I" in "Notes of a Native Son," for acknowledging how close he came to the edge with his rages about racism in restaurants. Character is not just a question of sensibility: There are hard choices to be made when a person is put under pressure. And it's in having made the wrong choice, curiously enough, that we are made all the more aware of our freedom and potential for humanity. So it is that remorse is often the starting point for good personal essays, whose working-out brings the necessary self-forgiveness (not to mention self-amusement) to outgrow shame.

I have not touched on some other requirements of the personal essay, such as the need to go beyond the self's quandaries, through research or contextualization, to bring back news of the larger world. Nor have I spoken of the grandeur of the so-called formal essay. Yet even when "I" plays no part in the language of an essay, a firm sense of personality can warm the voice of the impersonal essay narrator.

When we read Dr. Johnson and Edmund Wilson and Lionel Trilling, for instance, we feel that we know them as fully developed characters in their own essays, regardless of their not referring personally to themselves.

The need thus exists to make oneself into a character, whether the essay uses a first- or third-person narrative voice. I would further maintain that this process of turning oneself into a character is not self-absorbed navel gazing, but rather a potential release from narcissism. It means you have achieved sufficient distance to begin to see yourself in the round: a necessary precondition to transcending the ego—or at least writing personal essays that can touch other people.

On the Street: Nobody Watches, Everyone Performs
Vivian Gornick

A writer who lived at the end of my block died. I'd known this woman more than twenty years. She admired my work, shared my politics, liked my face when she saw it coming toward her, I could see that, but she didn't want to spend time with me. We'd run into each other on the street, and it was always big smiles, a wide embrace, kisses on both cheeks, a few minutes of happy unguarded jabber. Inevitably I'd say, "Let's get together." She'd nod and say, "Call me." I'd call, and she'd make an excuse to call back, then she never would. Next time we'd run into each other: big smile, great hug, kisses on both cheeks, not a word about the unreturned call. She was impenetrable: I could not pierce the mask of smiling politeness. We went on like this for years. Sometimes I'd run into her in other parts of town. I'd always be startled, she too. New York is like a country, the neighborhood is your town, you spot someone from the block or the building in another neighborhood and the first impulse to the brain is, What are *you* doing here? We'd each see the thought on the other's face and start to laugh. Then we'd both give a brief salute and keep walking.

Six months after her death I passed her house one day and felt stricken. I realized that never again would I look at her retreating back thinking, Why doesn't she want my friendship? I missed her then. I missed her terribly. She was gone from the landscape of marginal encounters. That landscape against which I measure daily the immutable force of all I connect with only on the street, and only when it sees me coming.

At Thirty-eighth Street two men were leaning against a building one afternoon in July. They were both bald, both had cigars in their mouths, and each one had a small dog attached to a leash. In the glare of noise, heat, dust, and confusion, the dogs barked nonstop. Both men looked balefully at their animals. "Yap, yap, stop yapping already," one man said angrily. "Yap, yap, keep on yapping," the other said softly. I burst out laughing. The men looked up at me, and grinned. Satisfaction spread itself across each face. They had performed and I had received. My laughter had given shape to an exchange that would otherwise have evaporated in the chaos. The glare felt less threatening. I realized how often the street achieves composition for me: the flash of experience I extract again and again from the endless stream of event. The street does for me what I cannot do for myself. On the street nobody watches, everyone performs.

Another afternoon that summer I stood at my kitchen sink struggling to make a faulty spray attachment adhere to the inside of the faucet. Finally, I called in the super in my building. He shook his head. The washer inside the spray was too small for the faucet. Maybe the threads had worn down. I should go to the hardware store and find a washer big enough to remedy the situation. I walked down Greenwich Avenue, carrying the faucet and the attachment, trying hard to remember exactly what the super had told me to ask for. I didn't know the language, I wasn't sure I'd get the words right. Suddenly, I felt anxious, terribly anxious. I would not, I knew, be able to get what I needed. The spray would never work again. I walked into Garber's, an old-fashioned hardware store with these tough old Jewish guys behind the counter. One of them—also bald and with a cigar in his mouth—took the faucet and the spray in his hand. He looked at it. Slowly, he began to shake his head. Obviously, there was no hope. "Lady," he said. "It ain't the threads. It definitely ain't the threads." He continued to shake his head. He wanted there to be no hope as long as possible. "And this," he said, holding the gray plastic washer in his open hand, "this is a piece of crap." I stood there in patient despair. He shifted his cigar from one side of his mouth to the other, then moved away from the counter. I saw him puttering about in a drawerful of little cardboard boxes. He removed something from one of them and returned to the counter with the spray magically attached to the faucet. He detached the spray and showed me what he had done. Where there had once been gray plastic there was now gleaming silver. He screwed the spray back on, easy as you please. "Oh," I crowed, "you've done it!" Torn between the triumph of problem-solving and the satisfaction of denial, his mouth twisted up in a grim smile. "Metal," he said philosophically, tapping the perfectly fitted washer in the faucet. "This," he picked up the plastic again, "this is a piece of crap. I'll take two dollars and fifteen cents from you." I thanked him profusely, handed him his money, then clasped my hands together on the counter and said, "It is such a pleasure to have small anxieties easily corrected." He looked at me. "Now," I said, spreading my arms wide, palms up, as though about to introduce a vaudeville act, "you've freed me for large anxieties." He continued to look at me. Then he shifted his cigar again, and spoke. "What you just said. That's a true thing." I walked out of the store happy. That evening I told the story to Laura, a writer. She said, "These are your people." Later in the evening I told it to Leonard, a New Yorker. He said, "He charged you too much."

Street theater can be achieved in a store, on a bus, in your own apartment. The idiom requires enough actors (bit players as well as principals) to complete the action and the rhythm of extended exchange. The city is rich in both. In the city things can be kept moving until they arrive at point. When they do, I come to rest.

I complain to Leonard of having had to spend the evening at a dinner party listening to the tedious husband of an interesting woman I know.

"The nerve," Leonard replies. "He thinks he's a person too."

Marie calls to tell me Em has chosen this moment when her father is dying to tell her that her self-absorption is endemic not circumstantial.

"What bad timing," I commiserate.

"Bad timing!" Marie cries. "It's aggression, pure aggression!" Her voice sounds the way cracked pavement looks.

Lorenzo, a nervous musician I know, tells me he is buying a new apartment.

"Why?" I ask, knowing his old apartment to be a lovely one.

"The bathroom is twenty feet from the bedroom," he confides, then coughs self-consciously. "I know it's only a small detail. But when you live alone it's all details, isn't it?"

I run into Jane on the street. We speak of a woman we both know whose voice is routinely suicidal. Jane tells me the woman called her the other day at seven ayem and she responded with exuberance. "Don't get me wrong," she says, "I wasn't being altruistic. I was trying to pick her up off the ground because it was too early in the morning to bend over so far. I was just protecting my back."

My acquaintanceship—like the city itself—is wide-ranging but unintegrated. The people who are my friends are not the friends of one another. Sometimes—when I am feeling expansive and imagining life in New York all of a piece—these friendships feel like beads on a necklace loosely strung, the beads not touching one another but all lying, nonetheless, lightly and securely against the base of my throat, magically pressing into me the warmth of connection. Then my life seems to mirror an urban essence I prize: the dense and original quality of life on the margin, the risk and excitement of having to put it all together each day anew. The harshness of the city seems alluring. Ah, the pleasures of conflict! The glamour of uncertainty! Hurrah for neurotic friendships and yea to incivility!

At other times—when no one is around and no one is available—I stare out the window, thinking, What a fool you are to glamorize life in the city. Loneliness engulfs me like dry heat. It is New York loneliness, hot with shame, a loneliness that tells you you're a fool and a loser. Everyone else is feasting, you alone cannot gain a seat at the banquet. I look down at the street. I see that mine is a workhorse life. As long as I remain in harness I am able to put one foot in front of the other without losing step, but if anything unbalances me I feel again the weight of circumstance hanging from my neck, a millstone beneath which I have taught myself to walk upright.

The day is brilliant: asphalt glimmers, people knife through the crowd, buildings look cut out against a rare blue sky. The sidewalk is mobbed, the sound of traffic deafening. I walk slowly, and people hit against me. Within a mile my pace quickens, my eyes relax, my ears clear out. Here and there, a face, a body, a gesture separates itself from the endlessly advancing crowd, attracts my reviving attention. I begin to hear the city, and feel its presence. Two men in their twenties, thin and well dressed, brush past me, one saying rapidly to the other, "You gotta give her credit. She made herself out of nothing. And I mean nothing." I laugh and lose my rhythm. Excuse me, my fault, beg your pardon. . . . A couple appears in the crowd, dark, attractive, middle-aged. As they come abreast of me the man is saying to the woman, "It's always my problem. It's never your problem." Cars honk, trucks screech, lights change. Sidewalk vendors hawk food, clothing, jewelry. A man standing beside a folding table covered with gold and silver watches speaks quietly into the air. "It's a steal, ladies and gentlemen," he says. "A real steal." Another couple is coming toward me, this time an odd one. The woman is black, a dwarf, around forty years old. The man is Hispanic, a boy, twelve or fourteen. She looks straight ahead as she walks, he dances along beside her. As they pass she says in the voice of a Montessori mother, "It doesn't matter what he thinks. It only matters what you think."

My shoulders straighten, my stride lengthens. The misery in my chest begins to dissolve out. The city is opening itself to me. I feel myself enfolded in the embrace of the crowded street, its heedless expressiveness the only invitation I need to not feel shut out.

There are mornings I awake and, somehow, I have more of myself. I swing my legs over the side of the bed, draw up the blind, and, from my sixteenth-floor window, feel the city spilling itself across my eyes, crowding up into the world, filling in the landscape. Behind it, there in the distance, where it belongs, is the Hudson River and, if I want it, the sky. But I don't want it. What I want is to take this self I now have more of down into those noisy, dirty, dangerous streets and make my way from one end of Manhattan to the other in the midst of that crowd that also may have more of itself. There is no friend, lover, or relative I want to be with as much as I want to swing through the streets being jostled and bumped, catching the eye of the stranger, feeling the stranger's touch. In the street I am grinning like an idiot to myself, walking fast at everyone coming my way. Children stare, men smile, women laugh right into my eyes. The tenderness I encounter in that mood! The impersonal affection of a palm laid against my arm or my back as someone murmurs, "Excuse me," and sidles skillfully past my body: it soothes beyond reasonable explanation. I feel such love then, for the idea of the city as well as the reality. And everyone looks good: handsome, stylish, interesting. Life spills over without stint and without condition. I feel often that I am walking with my head tipped back, my mouth thrown open, a stream of sunlight on water pouring into my throat. When I consider the days on which I find myself looking into one gargoyle face after another—everyone in front of me old, ugly, deformed, and diseased—I have to realize the street gives me back a primitive reflection of whatever load of hope or fear I am carrying about with me that day.

Nothing heals me of a sore and angry heart like a walk through the very city I often feel denying me. To see in the street the fifty different ways people struggle to remain human until the very last minute—the variety and inventiveness of survival technique—is to feel the pressure relieved, the overflow draining off. I join the anxiety. I share the condition. I feel in my nerve endings the common refusal to go under. Never am I less alone than alone in the crowded street. Alone, I imagine myself. Alone, I buy time. Me, and everyone I know. Me, and all the New York friends.

A Boy of Unusual Vision

Alice Steinbach

May 27, 1984

*F*irst the eyes: They are large and blue, a light, opaque blue, the color of a robin's egg. And if, on a sunny spring day, you look straight into these eyes—eyes that cannot look back at you—the sharp, April light turns them pale, like the thin blue of a high, cloudless sky.

Ten-year-old Calvin Stanley, the owner of these eyes and a boy who has been blind since birth, likes this description and asks to hear it twice. He listens as only he can listen, then: "Orange used to be my favorite color but now it's blue," he announces. Pause. The eyes flutter between the short, thick lashes, "I know there's light blue and there's dark blue, but what does sky-blue look like?" he wants to know. And if you watch his face as he listens to your description, you get a sense of a picture being clicked firmly into place behind the pale eyes.

He is a boy who has a lot of pictures stored in his head, retrievable images which have been fashioned for him by the people who love him—by family and friends and teachers who have painstakingly and patiently gone about creating a special world for Calvin's inner eye to inhabit.

Picture of a rainbow: "It's a lot of beautiful colors, one next to the other. Shaped like a bow. In the sky. Right across."

Picture of lightning, which frightens Calvin: "My mother says lightning looks like a Christmas tree—the way it blinks on and off across the sky," he says, offering a comforting description that would make a poet proud.

"Child," his mother once told him, "one day I won't be here and I won't be around to pick you up when you fall—nobody will be around all the time to pick you up—so you have to try to be something on your own. You have to learn how to deal with this. And to do that, you have to learn how to think."

There was never a moment when Ethel Stanley said to herself, "My son is blind and this is how I'm going to handle it."

Calvin's mother:

"When Calvin was little, he was so inquisitive. He wanted to see everything, he wanted to touch everything. I had to show him every little thing there is.

A spoon, a fork. I let him play with them. The pots, the pans. *Everything*. I showed him the sharp edges of the table. 'You cannot touch this; it will hurt you.' And I showed him what would hurt. He still bumped into it anyway, but he knew what he wasn't supposed to do and what he could do. And he knew that nothing in his room—*nothing*—could hurt him.

"And when he started walking and we went out together—I guess he was about 2—I never said anything to him about what to do. When we got to the curbs, Calvin knew that when I stopped, he should step down and when I stopped again, he should step up. I never said anything, that's just the way we did it. And it became a pattern."

Calvin remembers when he began to realize that something about him was "different": "I just figured it out myself. I think I was about 4. I would pick things up and I couldn't see them. Other people would say they could see things and I couldn't."

And his mother remembers the day her son asked her why he was blind and other people weren't.

"He must have been about 4 or 5. I explained to him what happened, that he was born that way and that it was nobody's fault and he didn't have to blame himself. He asked, 'Why me?' And I said 'I don't know why, Calvin. Maybe there's a special plan for you in your life and there's a reason for this. But this is the way you're going to be and you can deal with it.'"

Then she sat her son down and told him this: "You're *seeing*, Calvin. You're just using your hands instead of your eyes. But you're seeing. And, remember, there is *nothing* you can't do."

It's spring vacation and Calvin is out in the alley behind his house riding his bike, a serious looking, black and silver two-wheeler. "Stay behind me," he shouts to his friend Kellie Bass, who's furiously pedaling her bike down the one-block stretch of alley where Calvin is allowed to bicycle.

Now: Try to imagine riding a bike without being able to see where you're going. Without even knowing what an "alley" looks like. Try to imagine how you navigate a space that has no visual boundaries, that exists only in your head. And then try to imagine what Calvin is feeling as he pedals his bike in that space, whooping for joy as the air rushes past him on either side.

And although Calvin can't see the signs of spring sprouting all around him in the neighboring backyards—the porch furniture and barbecue equipment being brought out of storage, the grass growing emerald green from the April rain, the forsythia exploding yellow over the fences—still, there are signs of another sort which guide him along his route:

Past the German shepherd who always barks at him, telling Calvin that he's three houses away from his home; then past the purple hyacinths, five gardens away, throwing out their fragrance (later it will be the scent of the lilacs which guide him); past the large diagonal crack which lifts the front wheel of his bike up and then down, telling him he's reached his boundary and should turn back—past all these familiar signs Calvin rides his bike on a warm spring day.

Ethel Stanley: "At 6, one of his cousins got a new bike and Calvin said 'I want to learn how to ride a two-wheeler bike.' So we got him one. His father let him help put it together. You know, whatever Calvin gets he's going to go all over it with those hands and he knows every part of that bike and what it's called. He learned to ride it the first day, but I couldn't watch. His father stayed outside with him."

Calvin: "I just got mad. I got tired of riding a little bike. At first I used to zig-zag, go all over. My cousin would hold on to the bike and then let me go. I fell a lot in the beginning. But a lot of people fall when they first start."

There's a baseball game about to start in Calvin's backyard and Mrs. Stanley is pitching to her son. Nine-year-old Kellie, on first base, has taken off her fake fur coat so she can get a little more steam into her game and the other team member, Monet Clark, 6, is catching. It is also Monet's job to alert Calvin, who's at bat, when to swing. "Hit it, Calvin," she yells. "Swing!"

He does and the sound of the ball making solid contact with the bat sends Calvin running off to first base, his hands groping in front of his body. His mother walks over to stand next to him at first base and unconsciously her hands go to his head, stroking his hair in a soft, protective movement.

"Remember," the mother had said to her son six years earlier, "there's *nothing* you can't do."

Calvin's father, 37-year-old Calvin Stanley, Jr., a Baltimore city policeman, has taught his son how to ride a bike and how to shift gears in the family's Volkswagen and how to put toys together. They go to the movies together and they tell each other they're handsome.

The father: "You know, there's nothing much I've missed with him. Because he does everything. Except see. He goes swimming out in the pool in the back yard. Some of the other kids are afraid of the water but he jumps right in, puts his head under. If it were me I wouldn't be as brave as he is. I probably wouldn't go anywhere. If it were me I'd probably stay in this house most of the time. But he's always ready to go, always on the telephone, ready to do something.

"But he gets sad, too. You can just look at him sometimes and tell he's real sad."

The son: "You know what makes me sad? *Charlotte's Web*. It's my favorite story. I listen to the record at night. I like Charlotte, the spider. The way she talks. And, you know, she really loved Wilbur, the pig. He was her best friend." Calvin's voice is full of warmth and wonder as he talks about E.B. White's tale of the spider who befriended a pig and later sacrificed herself for him.

"It's a story about friendship. It's telling us how good friends are supposed to be. Like Charlotte and Wilbur," he says, turning away from you suddenly to wipe his eyes. "And when Charlotte dies, it makes me real sad. I always feel like I've lost a friend. That's why I try not to listen to that part. I just move the needle forward."

Something else makes Calvin sad: "I'd like to see what my mother looks like," he says, looking up quickly and swallowing hard. "What does she look like? People tell me she's pretty."

The mother: "One day Calvin wanted me to tell him how I looked. He was about 6. They were doing something in school for Mother's Day and the kids were drawing pictures of their mothers. He wanted to know what I looked like and that upset me because I didn't know how to tell him. I thought, 'How am I going to explain this to him so he will really know what I look like?' So I tried to explain to him about facial features, noses and I just used touch. I took his hand and I tried to explain about skin, let him touch his, and then mine.

"And I think that was the moment when Calvin really *knew* he was blind, because he said, 'I won't ever be able to see your face . . . or Daddy's face,'" she says softly, covering her eyes with her hands, but not in time to stop the tears. "That's the only time I've ever let it bother me that much."

But Mrs. Stanley knew what to tell her only child: "I said, 'Calvin, you *can* see my face. You can see it with your hand and by listening to my voice and you can tell more about me that way than somebody who can use his eyes.'"

Provident Hospital, November 15, 1973: That's where Calvin Stanley III was born, and his father remembers it this way: "I saw him in the hospital before my wife did, and I knew immediately that something was wrong with his eyes. But I didn't know what."

The mother remembers it this way: "When I woke up after the caesarean, I had a temperature and couldn't see Calvin except through the window of the nursery. The next day a doctor came around to see me and said that he had cataracts and asked me if I had a pediatrician. From what I knew, cataracts could be removed so I thought 'Well, he'll be fine.' I wasn't too worried. Then when his pediatrician came and examined him he told me he thought it was congenital glaucoma."

Only once did Mrs. Stanley give in to despair. "When they knew for certain it was glaucoma and told me that the cure rate was very poor because they so seldom have infants born with glaucoma, I felt awful. I blamed myself. I knew I must have done something wrong when I was pregnant. Then I blamed my husband," she says, looking up from her hands which are folded in her lap, "but I never told him that." Pause. "And he probably blamed me."

No, says her husband. "I never really blamed her. I blamed myself. I felt it was a payback. That if you do something wrong to somebody else in some way you get paid back for it. I figured maybe I did something wrong, but I couldn't figure out what I did that was that bad and why Calvin had to pay for it."

Mrs. Stanley remembers that the doctors explained to them that the glaucoma was not because of anything either of them had done before or during the pregnancy and "that 'congenital' simply means 'at birth.'"

They took Calvin to a New York surgeon who specialized in congenital glaucoma. There were seven operations and the doctors held out some hope for some vision, but by age 3 there was no improvement and the Stanleys were told that everything that could be done for Calvin had been done.

"You know, in the back of my mind, I think I always knew he would never see," Mrs. Stanley says, "and that I had to reach out to him in different ways. The toys I bought him were always toys that made a noise, had sound, something that

Calvin could enjoy. But it didn't dawn on me until after he was in school that I had been doing that—buying him toys that would stimulate him."

Thirty-three-year-old Ethel Stanley, a handsome, strong-looking woman with a radiant smile, is the oldest of seven children and grew up looking after her younger brothers and sisters while her mother worked. "She was a wonderful mother," Mrs. Stanley recalls. "Yes, she had to work, but when she was there, she was with you every minute and those minutes were worth a whole day. She always had time to listen to you."

Somewhere—perhaps from her own childhood experiences—Mrs. Stanley, who has not worked since Calvin was born, acquired the ability to nurture and teach and poured her mothering love into Calvin. And it shows. He moves in the sighted world with trust and faith and the unshakable confidence of a child whose mother has always been there for him. "If you don't understand something, ask," she tells Calvin again and again, in her open, forthright way. "Just ask."

When it was time to explain to Calvin the sexual differences between boys and girls, this is what Mrs. Stanley said: "When he was about 7 I told him that when you're conceived you have both sexes. It's not decided right away whether you're going to be a boy or a girl. And he couldn't believe it. He said, 'Golly, suppose somebody gets stuck?' I thought, 'Please, just let me get this out of the way first.'"

"And I tried to explain to him what a woman's sexual organs look like. I tried to trace it on the table with his fingers. I said, well you know what yours look like, don't you? And I told him what they're called, the medical names. 'Don't use names if you don't know what they mean. Ask. Ask.'"

"When he was little he wanted to be Stevie Wonder," says Calvin's father laughing. "He started playing the piano and he got pretty good at it. Now he wants to be a computer programmer and design programs for the blind."

Calvin's neatly ordered bedroom is outfitted with all the comforts you would find in the room of many 10-year-old, middle-class boys: a television set (black and white, he tells you), an Atari game with a box of cartridges (his favorite is "Phoenix"), a braille Monopoly set, records, tapes and programmed talking robots. "I watch wrestling on TV every Saturday," he says. "I wrestle with my friends. It's fun."

He moves around his room confidently and easily. "I know this house like a book." Still, some things are hard for him to remember since, in his case, much of what he remembers has to be imagined visually first. Like the size and color of his room. "I think it's kind of big," he says of the small room. "And it's green," he says of the deep rose colored walls.

And while Calvin doesn't need to turn the light on in his room he does like to have some kind of sound going constantly. *Loud* sound.

"It's 3 o'clock," he says, as the theme music from a TV show blare out into his room.

"Turn that TV down," says his mother, evenly. "You're not *deaf*, you know."

From the beginning, Ethel and Calvin Stanley were determined their blind son would go to public school. "We were living in Baltimore county when it was time for Calvin to start school and they told me I would have to pay a tuition for him to go to public school, and that really upset me," Mrs. Stanley says. "I had words with some of the big honchos out there. I knew they had programs in schools for children with vision problems and I thought public education should be free.

"We decided we would move to Baltimore city if we had to, and I got hold of a woman in the mayor's office. And that woman was the one who opened all the doors for us. She was getting ready to retire but she said she wasn't going to retire until she got this straight for Calvin. I don't know how she did it. But she did."

Now in the fourth grade, Calvin has been attending the Cross Country Elementary School since kindergarten. He is one of six blind students in Baltimore city who are fully mainstreamed which, in this context, means they attend public school with sighted students in a regular classroom. Four of these students are at Cross Country Elementary School. If Calvin stays in public school through the 12th grade, he will be the first blind student to be completely educated within the regular public school system.

Two p.m., Vivian Jackson's class, Room 207.

What Calvin can't see: He can't see the small, pretty girl sitting opposite him, the one who is wearing little rows of red, yellow and blue barrettes shaped like airplanes in her braided hair. He can't see the line of small, green plants growing in yellow pots all along the sunny window sill. And he can't see Mrs. Jackson in her rose-pink suit and pink enameled earrings shaped like little swans.

("Were they really shaped like little swans?" he will ask later.)

But Calvin can feel the warm spring breeze—invisible to *everyone's* eyes, not just his—blowing in through the window and he can hear the tapping of a young oak tree's branches against the window. He can hear Mrs. Jackson's pleasant, musical voice and, later, if you ask him what she looks like, he will say, "She's nice."

But best of all, Calvin can read and spell and do fractions and follow the classroom work in his specially prepared braille books. He is smart and he can do everything the rest of his class can do. Except see.

"What's the next word, Calvin?" Mrs. Jackson asks.

"Eleven," he says, reading from his braille textbook.

"Now tell us how to spell it—without looking back at the book!" she says quickly, causing Calvin's fingers to fly away from the forbidden word.

"E-l-e-v-e-n," he spells out easily.

It all seems so simple, the ease with which Calvin follows along, the manner in which his blindness has been accommodated. But it's deceptively simple. The amount of work that has gone into getting Calvin to this point—the number of teachers, vision specialists and mobility instructors, and the array of special equipment is staggering.

Patience and empathy from his teachers have played a large role, too.

For instance, there's Dorothy Lloyd, the specialist who is teaching Calvin the slow and very difficult method of using an Optacon, a device which allows a blind person to read a printed page by touch by converting printed letters into a tactile representation.

And there's Charleye Dyer, who's teaching Calvin things like "mobility" and "independent travel skills," which includes such tasks as using a cane and getting on and off buses. Of course, what Miss Dyer is really teaching Calvin is freedom; the ability to move about independently and without fear in the larger world.

There's also Lois Sivits who, among other things, teaches Calvin braille and is his favorite teacher. And, to add to a list which is endless, there's the music teacher who comes in 30 minutes early each Tuesday to give him a piano lesson, and his home room teacher, Mrs. Jackson, who is as finely tuned to Calvin's cues as a player in a musical duet would be to her partner.

An important part of Calvin's school experience has been his contact with sighted children.

"When he first started school," his mother recalls, "some of the kids would tease him about his eyes. 'Oh, they're so big and you can't see.' But I just told him, 'Not any time in your life will everybody around you like you—whether you can see or not. They're just children and they don't know they're being cruel. And I'm sure it's not the last time someone will be cruel to you. But it's all up to you because you have to go to school and you'll have to deal with it.'"

Calvin's teachers say he's well liked, and watching him on the playground and in class you get the impression that the only thing that singles him out from the other kids is that someone in his class is always there to take his hand if he needs help.

"I'd say he's really well accepted," says his mobility teacher, Miss Dyer, "and that he's got a couple of very special friends."

Eight-year-old Brian Butler is one of these special friends. "My *best* friend," says Calvin proudly, introducing you to a studious-looking boy whose eyes are alert and serious behind his glasses. The two boys are not in the same class, but they ride home together on the bus every day.

Here's Brian explaining why he likes Calvin so much: "He's funny and he makes me laugh. And I like him because he always makes me feel better when I don't feel good." And, he says, his friendship with Calvin is no different from any other good friendship. Except for one thing: "If Calvin's going to bump into a wall or something, I tell him, 'Look out,'" says Brian, sounding as though it were the most natural thing in the world to do when walking with a friend.

"Charlotte would have done it for Wilbur," is the way Calvin sizes up Brian's help, evoking once more that story about "how friendship ought to be."

A certain moment:

Calvin is working one-on-one with Lois Sivits, a teacher who is responsible for the braille skills which the four blind children at Cross Country must have in order to do all the work necessary in their regular classes. He is very relaxed with Miss Sivits, who is gentle, patient, smart and, like Calvin, blind. Unlike Calvin, she was not able to go to public school but was sent away at age 6, after many operations on her eyes, to a residential school—the Western Pennsylvania School for the Blind.

And although it was 48 years ago that Lois Sivits was sent away from her family to attend the school for the blind, she remembers—as though it were 48 minutes ago—how that blind 6-year-old girl felt about the experience: "Oh, I was so *very* homesick. I had a very hard time being separated from my family. It took me three years before I began getting used to it. But I knew I had to stay there. I would have given anything to be able to stay at home and go to a public school like Calvin," says the small, kind-looking woman with very still hands.

Now, the moment: Calvin is standing in front of the window, the light pouring in from behind him. He is listening to a talking clock which tells him, "It's 11:52 a.m." Miss Sivits stands about 3 feet away from him, also in front of the window holding a huge braille dictionary in her hands, fingers flying across the page as she silently reads from it. And for a few moments, there they are as if frozen in a tableau, the two of them standing in darkness against the light, each lost for a moment in a private world that is composed only of sound and touch.

There was another moment, years ago, when Calvin's mother and father knew that the operation had not helped, that their son was probably never going to see. "Well," said the father, trying to comfort the mother, "we'll do what we have to do and Calvin will be fine."

He is. And so are they.

Volar

Judith Ortiz Cofer

At twelve I was an avid consumer of comic books—*Supergirl* being my favorite. I spent my allowance of a quarter a day on two twelve-cent comic books or a double issue for twenty-five. I had a stack of *Legion of Super Heroes* and *Supergirl* comic books in my bedroom closet that was as tall as I. I had a recurring dream in those days: that I had long blond hair and could fly. In my dream I climbed the stairs to the top of our apartment building as myself, but as I went up each flight, changes would be taking place. Step by step I would fill out: my legs would grow long, my arms harden into steel, and my hair would magically go straight and turn a golden color. Of course I would add the bonus of breasts, but not too large: Supergirl had to be aerodynamic. Sleek and hard as a supersonic missile. Once on the roof, my parents safely asleep in their beds, I would get on tip-toe, arms outstretched in the position for flight and jump out my fifty-story-high window into the black lake of the sky. From up there, over the rooftops, I could see everything, even beyond the few blocks of our barrio; with my X-ray vision I could look inside the homes of people who interested me. Once I saw our landlord, whom I knew my parents feared, sitting in a treasure-room dressed in an ermine coat and a large gold crown. He sat on the floor counting his dollar bills. I played a trick on him. Going up to his building's chimney, I blew a little puff of my super-breath into his fireplace, scattering his stacks of money so that he had to start counting all over again. I could more or less program my Supergirl dreams in those days by focusing on the object of my current obsession. This way I "saw" into the private lives of my neighbors, my teachers, and in the last days of my childish fantasy and the beginning of adolescence, into the secret room of the boys I liked. In the mornings I'd wake up in my tiny bedroom with the incongruous—at least in our tiny apartment—white "princess" furniture my mother had chosen for me, and find myself back in my body: my tight curls still clinging to my head, skinny arms and legs and flat chest unchanged.

In the kitchen my mother and father would be talking softly over a café con leche. She would come "wake me" exactly forty-five minutes after they had gotten up. It was their time together at the beginning of each day and even at an early age I could feel their disappointment if I interrupted them by getting up too early. So I would stay in my bed recalling my dreams of flight, perhaps planning my next flight. In the kitchen they would be discussing events in the barrio. Actually, he would be carrying that part of the conversation; when it was her turn to speak she would, more often than not, try shifting the topic toward her desire to see her *familia* on the Island: *How about a vacation in Puerto Rico together this year, Querido? We could rent a car, go to the beach. We could . . .* And he would answer patiently, gently, *Mi amor, do you know how much it would cost for the all of us to fly there? It is not possible for me to take the time off . . . Mi vida, please understand . . .* And I knew that soon she would rise from the table. Not abruptly. She would light a cigarette and look out the kitchen window. The view was of a dismal alley that was littered with refuse thrown from windows. The space was too narrow for anyone larger than a skinny child to enter safely, so it was never cleaned. My mother would check the time on the clock over her sink, the one with a prayer for patience and grace written in Spanish. A birthday gift. She would see that it was time to wake me. She'd sigh deeply and say the same thing the view from her kitchen window always inspired her to say: *Ay, si yo pudiera volar.*

Two Hearts
Brian Doyle

Some months ago my wife delivered twin sons one minute apart. The older is Joseph and the younger is Liam. Joseph is dark and Liam is light. Joseph is healthy and Liam is not. Joseph has a whole heart and Liam has half. This means that Liam will have two major surgeries before he is three years old. The first surgery—during which a doctor will slice open my son's chest with a razor, saw his breastbone in half, and reconstruct the flawed plumbing of his heart—is imminent.

I have read many pamphlets about Liam's problem. I have watched many doctors' hands drawing red and blue lines on pieces of white paper. They are trying to show me why Liam's heart doesn't work properly. Blue lines are for blood that needs oxygen. Red lines are for blood that needs to be pumped out of the heart. I watch the markers in the doctors' hands. Here comes red, there goes blue. The heart is a railroad station where the trains are switched to different tracks. A normal heart switches trains flawlessly two billion times in a life; in an abnormal heart, like Liam's, the trains crash and the station crumbles to dust.

There are many nights just now when I tuck Liam and his wheezing train station under my heart in the blue hours of the night and think about his Maker. I would kill the God who sentenced him to such awful pain, I would stab Him in the heart like He stabbed my son, I would shove my fury in His face like a fist, but I know in my own broken heart that this same God made my magic boys, shaped their apple faces and coyote eyes, put joy in the eager suck of their mouths. So it is that my hands are not clenched in anger but clasped in confused and merry and bitter prayer.

I talk to God more than I admit. Why did you break my boy? I ask. I gave you that boy, He says, and his lean brown brother, and the elfin daughter you love so. But you wrote death on his heart, I say. I write death on all hearts, He says, just as I write life. This is where our conversation always ends, and I am left holding the extraordinary awful perfect prayer of my second son, who snores like a seal, who might die tomorrow, who did not die today.

Practice Strategies

1. Now that you've read "Volar," reflect on some meaningful memories from your childhood. Do you remember particular scenes or situations in which you drew on imaginative play, creating fantasies of yourself in a different, perhaps happier or more exciting situation? What kind of games did you play as a child? Did you have an imaginary friend or pet? On the left side of a sheet of paper, jot down the memories that surface as you reflect on your childhood. After you have a list, take some time to place these memories within the context of what was going on at the time around you and your family. Jot down these *situations* on the right side of the same piece of paper. Some things you might consider: Were you the oldest child? The youngest? Somewhere in between? Did your family move to a new neighborhood or town? Did your parent or parents work at jobs outside of the home? Was a grandparent involved in your childhood? If so, why?

From these two columns, select the imaginative play scenes and the family situation(s) that seem most connected to one another, or from which you can create parallels (like Cofer does with the notion of flying).

Write a brief story, no more than about three pages, depicting the scenes of childhood play woven into the family situation you decide to work with. Try not to reflect on or explain the memory, just recreate it as vividly as possible. Don't forget to *show* the action, including descriptive, sensory details. We'll practice this more specifically in Chapter 5, where we focus on scenes. And in Chapter 6 we will work on developing characters, so don't be overly concerned with that for this exercise. Just consider some specific circumstances in which your family was situated and your experiences, perspective, and feelings as a child within those circumstances. From there try to reconstruct specific scenes that begin to capture and reveal both the micro and the macrocosm of your life at that time.

As you do this exercise keep in mind that you will be working with smaller scenes that come together to create a larger whole, as Cofer does in "Volar." From the situation, the scenes will become apparent, and as you work with situation and scenes, the story's deeper themes should become apparent.

2. At least once a week try to go somewhere and observe what is going on around you and write about it in your journal. Of course, you may do this as a part of your daily life, as well, observing those around you as you run your errands, attend meetings, lectures, and so forth. Write a sketch of the scenes and settings you observe. These might include:

- a hospital waiting area or emergency room
- a police station
- a playground or park
- a town meeting
- a court trial
- an urban pedestrian setting
- a theatre during intermission

Simply describe what you see. Notice the sounds around you. Do you overhear bits of conversation? What kinds of smells do you notice? What is the texture of the bench or chair on which you are sitting, the table under your notebook, the feeling of the banister as you came up the stairs. Be specific. Keep writing until you get beyond the obvious. Go deeper into your description by making associations between what you see and how you are feeling. Stay focused until you feel yourself becoming more aware of the subtleties of both aspects of the experience—seeing and feeling. Stay with the writing for 10 to 15 minutes or more without editing or deleting anything. Don't stop to see what you have written.

When you have accumulated a considerable amount of material from different scenes and settings, consider drawing on them as Gornick does in her lyric essay, "On the Street: Nobody Watches, Everyone Performs." How might some of the scenes connect thematically?

3. One of the most challenging emotions to write about is grief. It is easy to overdo it, but you also want to give it the emotional weight it deserves. You have to find a balance. Through a close reading of "Two Hearts," explore how Doyle writes about grief, focusing especially on his analogies. If you decide to write about an experience of grief, how might you reconstruct your experience in descriptive narrative—not focusing on tears or crying, but trying to get at what lies behind that expression of pain?

CHAPTER 2

Narrative Nonfiction: Distinguishing Among Forms

Reading As A Writer

The past becomes the present on the page. In the act of reading, words touch our hearts, relationships are forged, we breathe a book alive.
— TERRY TEMPEST WILLIAMS

"Like most—maybe all—writers," writes Francine Prose in *Reading Like a Writer*, "I learned to write by writing and, by example, by reading books." Very few writers write in a vacuum. Most have their favorites, their mentors, those who have led the way. Sometimes these are works the writers have read as children, adolescents, or young adults. More likely, they are writers whose work has spoken to them as they began to see themselves as writers.

Reading for information, or pleasure, for that matter, is quite a different experience from reading as a writer. Of course we want to read for pleasure and to be informed. But, as we study the craft of writing, we will greatly benefit from approaching works more analytically, deconstructing the piece for the very elements that culminate in story: the turn of a phrase, peculiar to each of us; syntax and diction; the interweaving and balance of scene and summary; the painting of detail, as well as how and when character and story are moved along through dialogue. To read as a writer is to approach stories as an ongoing initiation into the art of storytelling. Writers read, not just for *what* is written—a work's content—but *how* it is written—always keeping a keen eye open for technique, style, and innovation. Allowing ourselves to fully experience the *act* of reading, the reading writer inhabits a narrative, consciously charting the technical accomplishments of the story, asking questions such as the following:

- What is the structure of the narrative and how does structure interact with storyline and theme?
- What is the tone of the piece and how does the tone affect theme?
- Which images are used? How are they used? How do the images interact with and help create thematic resonance?

- What is the theme? Is it substantial or does it render a superficial treatment of its topic? Does it provoke deep thought, make you smile, laugh, or cry?
- How does narrative persona affect your response to the piece?

Woven throughout this book are fine examples of narrative nonfiction representing its primary subgenres—memoir and auto/biography, the lyric essay, literary journalism, the increasingly popular short, and prose poems. As you read, look carefully at works to which you find yourself particularly drawn. What is it about them that truly compels you? Explore their narrative infrastructure. Analyze their literary devices. Notice word choice, sentence structure and rhythm, even how punctuation is used. Peruse the pieces for all those decisions the writer has made, major and minor. Take pleasure in these private conversations between you and the writer. Let the readings provide enjoyment, as well as guidance.

Narrative Nonfiction: History and Form

The true writer knows that feeling must give way to form.

—JEANETTE WINTERSON

In narrative nonfiction the story emerges as much from scene, setting, imagery, and characterization as from a writer's exposition, analysis, and reflection. The primary distinction I make between narrative nonfiction and nonfiction in general is the *evocation* rather than the *explanation* of meaning.

Growing exponentially over the past quarter of a century, the branch of literature that the term narrative nonfiction has come to define—a term used interchangeably with creative or literary nonfiction—is actually a confluence of disparate traditions. Variations on the fundamental elements of creative nonfiction create a variety of subgenres, which range across memoir, auto/biography, the essay (in its various guises), and literary journalism. Literary journalism, in turn, ranges across the profile, the feature, cultural commentary, travel, and nature writing. Even this list is not exhaustive; editorial columnists and investigative journalists today bring literary elements to their commentary and reportage.

While much ado has been made about the genre's codification as a negative, that is, that creative nonfiction is *not* fiction, one of the strengths of the genre, in my view, is its unwieldy, web-like tendency to bridge and incorporate various subgenres. Indeed, the very difficulty we have in categorizing narrative nonfiction attests to its dynamism and versatility. Perhaps the somewhat controversial term—*nonfiction*—derives from the fact that narrative nonfiction incorporates devices of dramatic storytelling traditionally associated with fiction. Basing its subjects on the stuff of real life, the genre has incorporated the fictional maxim, "show, don't tell," but with a difference. While the emphasis is on the construction of scenes, delineation of character, associations with sensory detail, imagery, and metaphorical resonance, narrative nonfiction writers rely on a strong narrative presence. In fiction the imagined, or fictional, characters subsume this presence. In nonfiction, aspects of the writer's own self draw forth this presence. Such a dynamic creates a process of merging and separating between the writing self—the author—and the self whose presence appears on the page—a narrative persona.

Generally speaking, creative nonfiction falls into three main categories: memoir, the essay, and literary journalism. After this, it gets much trickier. The memoir, for instance, may incorporate literary elements often associated with the essay, such as meditation and reflection, or, the essay, in its various guises, may incorporate a strong sense of narrative persona, thus bringing elements often associated with memoir to bear on the essay. Literary journalism and the essay are frequently interchangeable, but there are a few distinctions that tend to tilt the scale in one direction or another. For example, the extensive use of quotations to reveal character might push a piece more toward literary journalism and the profile than toward the essay. On the other hand, the essay is widely used today in journalistic formats, including newspapers, magazines, radio broadcasts, web logs (blogs), and so on. You can see why there might be confusion and debate around the genre and its various subgenres. In "The Art of Memoir," Mary Clearman Blew writes, "The boundaries of creative nonfiction will always be as fluid as water."

A helpful distinction between the personal essay and memoir is provided by Janet Burroway in *Imaginative Writing: Elements of Craft*, suggesting that it is more a matter of degree than anything else that may make the difference between one category and another. "A memoir," Burroway writes, "is a story retrieved from the writer's memory, with the writer as protagonist—the I remembering. **Memoir** tends to place the emphasis on the story, and the 'point' is likely to emerge, as it does in fiction, largely from the events and characters themselves, rather than primarily through the author's speculation or reflection. The **personal essay**, on the other hand, usually has its origin in something that has happened in the writer's life, but it may have happened yesterday afternoon, or it may represent an area of interest deliberately explored, and it is likely to give rise to a meditation on some subject that the experience suggests." **Literary journalism** has a tendency to push back away from the table of memory, get up, and leave the room, setting off into the world and other people's lives to find its stories. In *Contemporary Creative Nonfiction: I & Eye*, B. Minh Nguyen and Porter Shreve explore turning inward and outward in creative nonfiction, as is suggested by the phrase "I & Eye." Of course, both are woven in all of the subgenres, so, once again, it is more a matter of emphasis than exclusivity. And although the "I" is always fully present in literary journalism, it may be the "eye" that is telling the story.

Brushing aside the debates and controversy over terminology and using the descriptive term, literary nonfiction, Stephen Minot states in *Literary Nonfiction: The Fourth Genre* that readers and writers are "needlessly confused about how to define this genre. It's simpler than one might think," he argues. "Literary nonfiction is distinguished by three basic characteristics: It is based on actual events, characters, and places; it is written with a special concern for language and it tends to be more informal and personal than other types of nonfiction writing." Case closed.

In any case, it is always striking to me just how many caveats come to bear on any conversation about narrative nonfiction. So, while the following categories emphasize distinctions, there will be numerous opportunities as we move through the text to explore elements the subgenres have in common.

Memory, Meaning, and Memoir

My debt, in short, was to memory. And its persistence.
— BERNARD COOPER

In "Memory and Imagination," Patricia Hampl points out that "for the memoirist, more than for the fiction writer, the story seems already there, already accomplished and fully achieved in history." Writing the memoir as a matter of "dutiful transcription," however, is an impossibility Hampl warns, as any early draft will amply illustrate with its "jumble of crossed-out lines, false starts, confused order." Memoir as a creative art might be likened to a poetics of memory, drawing, as it does, on selection and arrangement, subordination and emphasis, syntax and diction, as well as the ever-present "I" that shapes any art form. Memoirists are presented with a particular challenge, however, since they are writing about events that actually happened. And this is why it is tempting to say, "But that's the way it happened," and presume we have successfully defended a poorly constructed story. We haven't.

Like other forms of creative nonfiction, memoir doesn't have a structure into which you pour your memories, feelings, and thoughts. Rather, the story you are trying to tell will take shape from your memories and ideas as you work with the narrative, cutting and pasting, trying out this angle and that, until you achieve a design that serves a particular story. By the time you have done that, you will have written the story, since story and structure are interactive.

Joan Didion, journalist, essayist, memoirist, and novelist, writes that the best memoirs forge their own forms, whether they are constructed from what Margaret Fuller calls the "mosaic method"—the piecing together of seemingly unrelated fragments, images, and scenes to create a larger whole—or are written more traditionally, as a linear unfolding of event and thematic thought.

Mosaic Memoir

The mosaic memoir is a particularly intriguing form, suggesting the movement of memory as associative moments, scene juxtaposed by scene, image by image, even. Memory is an odd phenomenon with a mind all its own. It may flash back to fifth grade (for example) to a specific incident on a specific day, say the day you were chosen to sing the solo for the school chorus, or the day you didn't make the cut for the little league team, only to trigger an association from that incident with the award or trophy you won in seventh grade. And then the mind is off on another train of thought, perhaps the fact that your grandmother couldn't make the awards ceremony because she was ill and in the hospital. Suddenly you are struck by the illusions of control that we live by and you feel a sense of fear, or despair even. Memory doesn't offer up its treasures in linear fashion, nor does it remain neatly inside the lines. It runs about, leaping among associations and memories, spilling over set boundaries and creating chaos, often just when you want to get hold of something and make sense of it. Scott Russell Sanders describes this experience as being "ambushed by memory." How might we best "grasp the slippery world," he asks, and "divide up this vast panorama into thinkable chunks? " Memoir writing can be a messy thing. "Any description of the world is a net thrown over a flood; no matter how fine the mesh, the world leaks through."

Written in vignettes of compressed, often lyrical narrative, the sectional parts of a mosaic memoir take on a cumulative effect, so that the whole is greater than the sum of its parts. When it all comes together, its meaning resonates well beyond any particular anecdote, but each part accumulates into an organic whole. One of the most beautiful examples of this structuring device that I have encountered is Sandra Cisneros's *The House on Mango Street*, which I do not include here because, although it is autobiographically based, it is, nonetheless, fiction.

It is the elevation of the personal to a larger truth that moves memoir beyond mere recollection to a higher literary status. When we lift memoir writing to the status of literature, it is not only we who are nurtured by our travels into the past, but our readers who, according to William Zinsser, "will be nourished by the journey," bringing along associations of their own. Literary nonfiction, like any good literature, deepens our capacity for understanding experience, ours as well as others; it gives us a fuller comprehension of what it means to be human. As Zinsser notes in *Inventing the Truth: the Art and Craft of Memoir*, it is through memoir that "we try to make sense of who we are, who we once were, and what values and heritage shaped us."

The Essay

The essay can do everything a poem can do, and everything a short story can do—everything but fake it.

—ANNIE DILLARD

The essay tradition is a long and venerable one, traditionally traced back to the sixteenth-century French writer Michel de Montaigne whose collection of experimental, personal prose was titled *Essais* in 1580. His works were written in an informal voice, revealing intimately personal experience, and moving among ideas and experiences associatively rather than logically and linearly. Robert Atwan, founder and editor of the successful series, *The Best American Essays*, first published in 1986, writes that when Montaigne realized that "his efforts fit no conventional category—they could not be termed letters, or memoirs, or treatises—he simply referred to them by the French word *essais*, meaning attempts, trials, or experiments." Modern and pre-modern writers who have enlivened the essay form include Virginia Woolf, E. B. White, Ralph Waldo Emerson, Henry David Thoreau, among others. Although contemporary writers of the essay are far too numerous to list, some who have relied on the essay as their primary form of written self-expression include Annie Dillard, Terry Tempest Williams, Gretel Ehrlich, Barry Lopez, and Scott Russell Sanders. The stylistic model is a rich one that encourages an openness to form and an unfolding point of view that takes shape as the essay progresses. Essayists rarely come to a final or ultimate conclusion. Instead they consider themselves to be *trying out* different ways of thinking about the subject or experience at hand. There is, however, a sense of wholeness and organic unity to any effective essay; you don't want to leave your readers wondering what you were trying to accomplish in the piece.

Although personal in nature, experimental in form, casual or elegant in style, the essay form may derive from the French verb meaning "to try," but this doesn't mean the essay's standards are sloppy or its structure lazy. On the contrary, we do ourselves a disservice when we offer the "leaps and gambels" of a Montaigne as a model without also emphasizing the importance of structure and form, unity and coherence. What may appear to be effortlessly penned in reality has been the result of hours, days, weeks (dare I say months and years?) of pondering and tinkering, arranging and rearranging for shape and pattern. Design is as intricate an endeavor as content. Robert Atwan describes the basis on which essays are considered for publication in the series he edits as one of "literary achievement," that is "they must be admirably written and demonstrate an awareness of craft as well as a forcefulness of thought."

The Segmented Essay

Perhaps the segmented essay is most suited to postmodern life, representing, as it does, the fragmented, episodic, quick takes that contemporary culture seems to demand of us.

Like the mosaic memoir, the segmented essay provides a way to break out of chronology, eliminates the need for transitions, and permits the narrative to make leaps across time, focusing instead on thematic unity and resonance. In his essay "Beyond Linearity: Writing the Segmented Essay," Robert Root, Jr. notes that while organizational schemes such as chronological sequence come easily, they can interfere with the need to compress and focus a scene and subject.

The segmented essay may signal its structural device in a number of ways, for example, through groups of asterisks, textual breaks of white space, subheadings, or the weaving of differing fonts. Whether they are called collage, montage, mosaics, or go by some other term, segmented essays are not without structure, although their organizing principle is experimental and unique to their subject. Like other forms of narrative nonfiction, the segmented essay finds its form as the writer goes along.

The Lyric Essay

The lyric essay situates itself in relation to the poem, specifically the lyric poem, which in ancient times was sung while accompanied by the lyre. Bringing together the ruminative capacities of the essay and the metaphoric power of the poem, the lyric essay values the careful use of language and artfulness; the writer of a lyric essay is being as selective in the use of language as any poet would be, while also keeping an eye on rhythm, patterns, and repetition. A lyric essay is evocative rather than expository, suggestive rather than definitive. It is likely to pose questions while allowing the reader much interpretative latitude. The lyric essayist rarely insists on imposing finality of thought.

The lyric essay often progresses more associatively than logically, and relies on imagery more than analysis. Like the Greek poet Sappho's lyric poems, which come down to us from ancient times in mere fragments, the lyric essay may accumulate through fragmentary weavings and juxtapositions, its cumulative power deriving from imagery, metaphor, and thematic resonance.

Deborah Tall, editor, and John D'Agata, associate editor, for lyric essays for the *Seneca Review* describe the lyric essay in the following fashion:

> *Loyal to that original sense of essay as a test or a quest, an attempt at making sense, the lyric essay sets off on an uncharted course through interlocking webs of idea, circumstance, and language—a pursuit with no foreknown conclusion, an arrival that might still leave the writer questioning. While it is ruminative, it leaves pieces of experience undigested and tacit, inviting the reader's participatory interpretation.*

Lyric essays tend not to explain themselves. Lyric essays invite readers to bring their own responses to the imagery, rhythm, and form that infuse narrative with meaning. In lyric essays we ask our readers not to passively consume, but to actively participate in a mutual process of meaning-making between writer and reader.

Sometimes lyric essays are made up of short sections capable of standing on their own, while also culminating, mosaic-like, in a larger whole. An excellent example of this is Marjorie Agosín's *Cartographies*, whose "A Map of My Face" is included in Chapter 5.

Literary Journalism

> *Readers look to writers of creative nonfiction for the same reason they looked to Shakespeare's histories and dramas, to flesh out and bring to compelling life the events and people we experience from a distance.*
>   —MARK BOWDEN

Literary journalism has become increasingly popular in creative writing and journalism programs as well as among the general public. Having built on the innovative work of the New Journalism of the sixties—a term Tom Wolfe coined, whose impatience with strictly factual reporting led him to describe traditional journalism as pale and beige in tone—literary journalism sets aside traditional reporting conventions of keeping the "I" under wraps while the "eye" covers the story from an objective point of view. Inviting a strong narrative presence, literary journalism has come to insist on the journalist's personal involvement in the event or subject being covered.

Writers such as Joan Didion, Tracy Kidder, John McPhee, Calvin Trillin, Truman Capote, Jane Kramer, Mark Kramer, and Susan Orlean, among others, have contributed to the form's richness of range, as well as its popularity. As Norman Sims points out in "The Art of Literary Journalism," "Literary journalists write narratives focused on everyday events that bring out the hidden patterns of community life as tellingly as the spectacular stories that make newspaper headlines," bringing to journalism what Susan Orlean has called "the dignity of ordinariness."

So what makes it literary, rather than merely journalistic? In addition to narrative point of view and personal engagement with the subject, literary techniques that traditionally have been associated with fiction have come to be used quite liberally in the genre. In response to accusations of nonfiction writers' appropriation of fictional devices, Tracy Kidder responds: "Those techniques, except for invention of character and detail, never belonged to fiction. They belong to storytelling."

"Those techniques," to which Kidder refers, include characterization, an eye for descriptive detail, the development of scene, those symbolic resonances found equally in fact, as in fiction, the narrative voice and persona of the writer, as mentioned earlier, and, of course, accuracy of research and reportage—an adherence to the truth. Indeed, in his book, *The Art of Creative Nonfiction*, Lee Gutkind argues that literary journalism must be "as accurate as the most meticulous reportage—perhaps even more accurate because the creative nonfiction writer is expected to dig deeper into a subject, thereby presenting or unearthing a larger truth."

Literary journalism's appeal, as Norman Sims summed up "has grown from the solid foundations of the form—immersion reporting, narrative techniques that free the voice of the writer, and high standards of accuracy."

The Short

In a moving essay entitled "The Disproportionate Power of the Small," Bernard Cooper describes a trip he makes to the Museum of Modern Art in New York City because he wants to view Salvador Dali's *The Persistence of Memory*. He has seen reproductions of the work, which he describes as including a landscape with distant cliffs, sulphurous light, elongated shadows, and a watch draped over the limb of a tree. The "engulfing, dreamlike perspective" of the reproductions had so impressed Cooper he was expecting to find a huge canvas, and so he passed the tiny painting several times, believing that only a work of art on the scale of a mural could contain "the sense of the infinite" he had come to associate with Dali's masterpiece.

This moment lived on in Cooper, although more subconsciously than consciously, perhaps, until one day one of his own nonfiction works found its form in a four-page narrative. The piece combined what he describes as the memory of memoir, the reflection of the personal essay, and the compression and intensification of the "short." "To write short nonfiction requires an alertness to detail, a quickening of the senses, a focusing of the literary lens," notes Cooper, "until one has magnified some small aspect of what it means to be human."

Three collections of nonfiction Shorts over the past decade attest to the growing popularity of the form. Judith Kitchen and Mary Paumier Jones, editors of *In Short* and *In Brief*, describe the development of the **Short** as part of a wider cultural trend toward experimentation in the burgeoning field of creative nonfiction. While more traditionally-minded writers may feel obligated to provide transitions among shifts in scene and summary and fully developed plot and character, writers of the Short—perhaps influenced by the quick takes of today's media and technology—are just as likely to take Dali's approach and paint the miniature instead of the mural.

In her third and most recent collection, *Short Takes*, Kitchen describes the Short as "succinct, but not slight," her selections representing a variety of forms that range across the formal and the lyric essay, memoir writing, and even journal entries, each only two or three pages in length. Density, depth, and wholeness are qualities essential to the Short. And whatever its thematic exploration, the Short is complete in itself.

The Prose Poem

Only a house quiet as snow, a space for myself to go, clean as paper before the poem.

— SANDRA CISNEROS, *THE HOUSE ON MANGO STREET*

Prose poems rely on images, which take on metaphorical qualities. Such imagery, whether **similes** or **metaphors**, provides comparisons between the **concrete** (things we can see, touch, hear, taste, or smell) and the **abstract** (ideas, feelings), thereby enlarging the image's meaning.

In the epigraph above, as the two similes (quiet as snow; clean as paper) demonstrate, the metaphorical image relies on the quality of something we know and understand being applied to something we don't. Working with imagery in this way helps us come to understand something about the unknown in light of the known. Cisneros shares her desire for the solitude and silence of a home of her own by comparing it to the quality of snowfall and to a clean piece of paper before the poem. The comparison suggests that her clean, quiet house will provide a space of solitude, a solitude that is conducive to creativity—to the production of poetry even. A home that can be a writer's haven.

To draw on imagery in a figurative way, then, is to represent one thing by another. A **figure of speech** may be a concrete image, but it informs as a result of its nonliteral representation. For example, a bird in the hand is worth two in the bush. When a comparison is repeated and extended throughout a narrative or poem (with repeated instances of imagery), the comparison becomes an extended metaphor. In this way poetry, and literary prose, draw on **figurative language**.

Judith Ortiz Cofer explores the writer's emotional relationship to both poetry and prose in "But Tell It Slant: From Poetry to Prose and Back Again," and I believe her insights can help us in our understanding of how prose poems work, as well. Writing about the same event as both a poem and a story, Cofer acknowledges that the poem is closer to her emotional memory of the incident, while the prose is the result of an extrapolation that begins with the facts. It is in writing the poem, notes Cofer, that she finds "the neural pathways to a deeply felt memory-generated emotion." This is how she knows "it is the Truth (not to be mistaken by the Fact)." Like many narrative nonfiction writers, Cofer distinguishes between truth and fact, basing her notion of truth on deeply felt memory, rather than absolute, verifiable fact.

Cofer suggests that we first try writing in poetic form in our search for a meaningful subject, or "that which is worth writing about." Comparing the poetry-to-prose technique to the intensive revision process of experienced writers, Cofer proposes the technique in hopes of helping the less experienced prose writer come to terms with the cutting and compression required for good writing, a reality the poet has been required to confront immediately. Perhaps the greatest lesson such selectivity can offer is the consequence of the kind of care with which literary writers use language, as well as the importance of being as technically proficient with prose as one is with poetry. Deeply felt memory, after all, when taken from the imagination and placed on the page, is transformed from truth to story, from fact to artifact.

Fluidity and Form

As I have cautioned before and as the reading selections of this book aptly demonstrate, narrative nonfiction ebbs and flows across numerous boundaries, including but not limited to, memoir, the essay, and literary journalism, creating a dynamic form that is more inclusive than exclusive, whose permeable boundaries are perhaps its greatest strengths. For example, the memoir and the personal essay often are strengthened by historical research and interviews, while literary journalism is often characterized by the incorporation of personal point of view and a unique sensibility embedded in its narrative voice and style.

Nature writing, travel writing, cultural commentary, all these often show up as literary journalism, especially if the piece primarily turns outward. When the same subgenres, however, journey inward, revealing as much of the self as the outer world, the pieces are just as likely to be lyric essays. And, if they rely heavily on childhood moments, they may be grouped with memoir. Narrative nonfiction, however, is a far larger phenomenon than any combination of canons or categories might suggest. In addition to those disciplines and genres typically associated with narrative nonfiction—literature, journalism, and creative writing—the fields of history, education, sociology, and psychology have come to recognize and incorporate nonfiction narrative.

Remember Mary Clearman Blew's insight with which I began this chapter? It is significant enough to conclude with it, so here it is again: "The boundaries of creative nonfiction will always be as fluid as water."

CHAPTER 3

How Writers Work: Developing a Writing Practice

For the poem is not nailed together, or formed from one logical point to another . . . it is created through work in which the interweavings of craft, thought, and feeling are intricate, mysterious, and altogether "mortal."

— MARY OLIVER

Demystifying the Myth of the Muse

The Myth

A story pops into your head and you are compelled to rush to your desk and begin to transcribe your thoughts directly to the page. Your ideas come with such force and clarity, and in just the right order, so that when you have gotten them down, from beginning to end, you have a finished story.

The Reality

A story is never finished on the first draft. Writers are always writing. We weave our writing into our daily lives. We keep journals by the bed for the midnight flash of inspiration, jot notes on cocktail napkins and on the backs of restaurant checks. We carry post-it notes or 3×5 cards for the random idea that pops up at the most inconvenient times, the significance of which will become apparent only later. We eavesdrop. We scribble ideas for our next story in our notes during lectures and meetings and while waiting for doctor's appointments. Writers are always writing. And when we are feeling out of sorts and uninspired we still go to our writing desks, faithfully, regularly, in order to keep our writing practice alive.

Novice writers begin by composing, and when a first draft is done, more often than not, deem the writing task complete. Writers who are more seasoned have come to realize that it is much better to begin with the prewriting stage—doodles and jottings, associations and leaps, freewriting and clustering. This makes the beginning of the writing process easier, lighter, more playful, and tells your writing self that you know that you are trying out different ideas and approaches, getting down scenes and images, sketching out character and tinkering with details. This tells your writing self that it's okay to write poorly, that writing well at this stage is not what it's about. This approach will take you places in your writing that a premature focus on getting it right will most surely circumvent.

No one else knows what works best in your writing practice than you. More importantly, especially early on in developing a writing practice, neither do you. And since you don't yet know what will work best for you, you will want to experiment with different approaches. How best to honor your desire to tell stories? How best to tap into the flow of ideas, disjointed and chaotic though they may be, in order to gather your thoughts in a useful way? How best to move through the inevitable state of *not knowing* so that your writing can begin to accumulate meaning and form? This is the most difficult part of the writing process and the point at which most writers give up. So, you must be patient. It's a stop and go process at first. If you stay with it, eventually, inevitably, clarity will begin to shine through the confusion.

As you make progress in developing a regular writing practice you'll find that you work better at certain times of the day than at others. This may be first thing in the morning before you move into your day. It may be as a mid-day break. Or, perhaps you enjoy writing at the conclusion of the day, as it winds down. As you find what works best for you, try to become consistent about writing at this time of the day. Like jogging, or working out, or developing any new skill, you want the issue to be *when* we do it each day, not *whether* you do it. You should think of your writing time as *your* time, time for you to gather your thoughts, express yourself, play with ideas, do free-writing exercises, try out literary techniques you've noticed while reading someone else's work that you admire. Like any disciplined artist or athlete or academic, being punctual about your practice is simply engaging in a serious way in what it is that you do—write.

Courtship and Creativity: A Date Best Kept

Creativity isn't something that can be commanded, rather, like any good relationship, it needs to be respected and generously cultivated.

Developing a disciplined practice of writing is not so different from the love affair between, for example, Romeo and Juliet, observes Mary Oliver in *A Poetry Handbook*. Describing one's writing practice as a "possible love affair between something like the heart (that courageous but also shy factory of emotion) and the learned skills of the conscious mind," Oliver proposes that if these parts of the writerly self make appointments with each other, and they keep those appointments, then something will begin to happen. However, if they make appointments, but are fickle and fail to keep them, count on it, she warns, nothing is going to happen.

Three caveats from Oliver, a Pulitzer prize-winning poet:

> "It learns quickly what sort of courtship it is going to be."
> "It won't involve itself with anything less than a perfect seriousness."
> "Anything else is only a flirtation."

Practice and the Journal: Diamonds in the Dust Heap

Story ideas are just that—ideas. And as mentioned earlier they come from the unlikeliest places and at the most inconvenient times—while jogging, showering, attending a family gathering, riding the subway. You should try to have a portable journal so that when inspiration strikes it will not be a passing thought lost to the wind. Jot it down and evaluate it later. Life is full of good story ideas and journal jottings will provide a rich source of material from which to draw when you are ready to focus on a particular story. Virginia Woolf calls these journal notes "diamonds in the dust heap." Although many of these notes will never end up in your stories, some will. And you will be grateful for the diamonds even as you realize that most of your journal jottings will end up in the dust heap.

Your journal is a private space for you. It is meant for all your prewriting efforts and anything else that finds its way into it: your thoughts about things other than your writing, your hopes and plans, your observations as you go through your daily life, memories and reflections, fears and hurtful things, perhaps even your lunch plans or the recipe for this weekend's dinner date. The journal is for generating raw material through free association exercises as well as getting observations down on paper in the very moment of observing; it is for copying down quotations that speak to you when you are reading other writers' work. No one should read your journal without your permission and under no circumstances should anyone critique the writing in your journal.

You also should keep a writing journal that is more substantial than your portable one. One's journal is a deeply personal thing. For some it's a leather-bound journal penned in careful ink. For others it's a three-ring binder. Many writers use spiral notebooks. I have found that a sketchbook serves my purposes for the very reason that it has no lines, no real beginning and no end, really. I can write anywhere in the book, anywhere on the page, and at any angle that I prefer at any given moment. My journals are truly mosaics made up of many moments' ponderings. I usually have my journal and a pen nearby when I read, as I find that reading inspires my inner murmurings.

Weaving her writing practice into her love of being in nature, Oliver writes of having carried a small notebook with her for 30 years or more in which she jots down what she calls "sand dabs," some of which will be the beginnings of what will eventually become poems and essays. By the time she needs a new one her journal has become blurred from the wear and tear of accompanying her everywhere and in all kinds of weather, because as a poet who finds inspiration in nature, her entries are mostly made somewhere out-of-doors. In her essay, "Pen and Paper and a Breath of Air," she describes journal jottings as associations that help return her "to the moment," to the "felt experience, whatever it was" at the time she made the entry.

In her classic essay, "On Keeping a Notebook" (in the "Writers on Writing" section toward the end of this chapter), the journalist and essayist Joan Didion writes that "the point of keeping a notebook has never been, nor is it now, to have an accurate factual record," but rather to "remember what it was to be me." Didion's notebook is a space where she can be in relationship with herself, over time, her present self "keeping in touch" with past selves. She provides a helpful admonition for anyone, but certainly the writer when she writes: "I think we are well advised to keep on nodding terms with the people we used to be, whether we find them attractive company or not."

Keeping a notebook or journal is a way to acknowledge, respect, and engage with the creative unconscious in all its various ways of working—from idea to completion. After all, our minds are always in motion, working hard for us—even as we sleep. And catching the fleeting thought, the overheard phrase, the dream image, the vividly remembered scene from ages ago that comes forth in cinematic color as a result of a simple scent carried on the wind during an evening walk, that flash of an image that makes you think: I should write that down. This is the stuff of stories. It isn't a tidy process, obediently waiting for you to get to your writing desk. Implicit in the act of keeping a journal is the understanding that it is often the intuitive kinds of knowing, the perceptive flashes, the felt memories that set our stories in motion. As Marshall Cook notes in "Training Your Muse: Seven Steps to Harnessing Your Creativity," "Write it down now or risk remembering *later* only that you had a great idea but not what that great idea was."

When you are writing in your journal you want to toss out any notions of goal-oriented writing. A writer's journal is a place for building sandcastles that may be kept or not. It is for attitudes of serious and not so serious play. It is a place for unabashed nakedness. There will be plenty of time later on for clothing your narrative so that you may send it confidently out into the world.

Practice and Prewriting Techniques

Beginning a creative work is one thing, but carrying it to completion is another. Completing a creative writing project involves a recursive process that brings into play all aspects of one's being, from the imaginative free play of the early stages to scanning for patterns, from the close reading for details and discovery to the critical analysis of what you have written. From the emotional to the intellectual, free association to logical, deductive thinking, all your mental skills will be brought to the creative process. The problem arises when we get the cart before the horse, the critical voice attacking the creative endeavor. Let's consider how this works.

The process of prewriting provides "a multitude of choices from a part of our mind where the experiences of a lifetime mill and mingle," writes Gabriele Rico in her book *Writing the Natural Way*. Rico emphasizes the importance of incorporating a prewriting stage into our writing practice. This allows us to approach writing as a process that invites wondering and not knowing, even as we begin to write. Gradually we map out a landscape of ideas as patterns and meaning begin to emerge. It is an opening to the unknown; it is an attitude that asks, "I wonder where this is taking me?" It is learning to follow the story.

A regular practice of prewriting, Rico notes, reminds us that "it's okay to start writing not knowing exactly what, where, who, when, and how. Most writers acknowledge that this is how it is anyway." Gertrude Stein knew this when she wrote that if we knew what it was going to be before we began it would be "dictation, not creation." As did Woolf, who approached her writing journal with a galloping pace, intended, among other things, to outrun the critic; only later would she return to find those valuable "diamonds in the dustheap."

Clustering

Because creative writing is a complex symbolic activity, clustering offers a kind of shorthand for what happens in writing. It jump-starts the creative juices and takes the writer from wondering what to write about to having many potential topics with which to work. To begin a cluster you should write a word or phrase—anything will do—in the middle of a clean page. Draw a circle around it and then let yourself begin to free associate from the initial word or phrase; jot down whatever pops into your mind and then let your mind leap among associations. (This is why it's called free association; it's really a word association process.) As you follow along with your associations, simply try to keep up with your mental leaps, scribbling all over the page and filling it up. You want this to be a spontaneous process—don't edit or censor things that pop into your mind. Clustering may take you far from the subject with which you began and that's okay. Or, it may take you more deeply into a subject through an association with a memory or a felt response. Clustering may take three minutes or 30. You may do it while waiting for the dentist, traveling on an airplane, or relaxing in a coffee shop. It can be particularly effective upon waking, when you are less focused on the external world and haven't shifted into the pragmatic routine of your day.

Rico, who was researching and writing her dissertation on creativity and right-brain techniques for greater expressiveness in the early 1980s, introduced the clustering concept and its usefulness in generating material and finding focus and direction in creative writing. She describes clustering as a powerful inspirational and organizational tool, which always assures us that we have something to say, even if we don't know how to go about saying it yet. Best of all, she notes, a cluster unfolds effortlessly making available a rich array of choices so that at this stage the writer doesn't have to worry about sequence or syntax.

Mapping

Like nature, which operates by profusion, clustering makes conscious a natural, unconscious process "through a nonlinear spilling out of lightning associations that allows patterns to emerge," Rico explains. So it is only after you have finished clustering (you will find that you can only sustain free association for so long, although the duration varies with the individual) that you will want to take a few moments to scan the page and map out what you have come up with. Are there any patterns emerging? If so—and there may be more than one—circle words and phrases that seem related and draw lines among them so that they are connected. The cluster will look something like a web and this mapping technique may provide you with the heart of a story, or several stories. If you don't see patterns taking shape, that's fine. Simply circle those words or phrases that stand out for some reason (on different days different words might be of interest). After you have done this, pause and scan the circled words and phrases and select one to three of them to work with for now. Flip to a clean journal page, jot one of them down at the top of the page, and prepare to do another prewriting technique called "freewriting."

Freewriting

It is the heart, "the guardian of intuition with its secret, often fearful intentions," writes Patricia Hampl, "whose commands the writer obeys." This is especially important in the early stages of writing, when ideas float about, ruminative, largely inchoate, but charged fragments—seeking, perhaps, but not yet having narrative form.

Poets use the term "free verse" to describe poems that are free of traditional, metrical form. In developing a prewriting practice we also free ourselves from form, move outside considering form, even. When freewriting we give ourselves permission to meander and browse, take detours, get lost in our ideas, thoughts, and feelings. If you approach writing as a linear process—beginning to end, first word to last—not only will you be unable to write, but your writing will lack the quickening pulse of originality that comes when we engage in discovery, surprising even ourselves. Freewriting, like clustering, engages the mind in free association, but it is a process of writing in sentences and longer phrases rather than words and short phrases. Again, you simply want to follow where your thoughts lead you, jotting them down as they arise. You should try not to evaluate or reconsider or reorder your thoughts as you write them down. Don't erase. Don't delete. Think of your hand as simply taking notes from your thoughts. Do this until the thoughts begin to dribble rather than flow in, then wind down and take a deep breath. After a pause to rest your mind, you should take a moment to scan and map the page and see what you have written. Once again, are there any patterns emerging, any ideas or images, reflections or scenes that feel like they may have potential for development?

Incorporating prewriting techniques—clustering, mapping, freewriting—into your writing practice allows an attitude of play between language and the creative unconscious; it generates a flow of ideas and images and draws on both recent and buried memories. Prewriting brings into dynamic relationship the conscious and unconscious aspects of the mind. Working associatively, rather than logically, prewriting exercises create a link between emotion and language, meaning and symbol, image and memory. Itself a kind of lively outline, it will take you much more deeply into your ideas than beginning with a traditional outline.

Getting to the First Draft

Once you find your way into your narrative through prewriting techniques, your creative energy and concentration should increase and you will begin to find focus and feel a sense of momentum. You can usually trust this feeling and let it carry you like the crest of a wave enjoying your progress, until the wave tosses you to shore. Then you simply begin the process over again, working with a cluster, mapping out where the ideas then take you, delving back into the freewriting mode if you need to get new material to fill out an unfolding narrative. After all, the process of writing is a recursive one, spiraling out and back again through various stages of prewriting, writing, and revising as the story takes shape.

Prewriting, composing, and revising are actually organic, recursive elements of the writing process. But, it's helpful to break down the stages of writing until you can come to them in an easy, comfortable way, knowing that not knowing and discovery go hand in hand. Coming to understand that the anxiety of beginnings can be reframed as anticipation and excitement. This is easier to do after you have a track record.

Just as it is helpful to break down the stages of writing, it also can be instructive to approach a narrative through its parts: scene, situation, summary, imagery, character, setting, theme, narrative persona, to name a few. But as the parts come together they will begin to achieve an organic whole. Each part interacts with other parts and you will find yourself working with all aspects at once. As you mature in your writing practice you will find yourself moving back and forth between generating new material and editing the extraneous, clarifying, developing, expanding, polishing and pruning, as well as enlarging. Revision will become a central part of this process as you will see in Chapter 4 where we explore how the story takes shape, particularly how reading, writing, and revision are all woven into a dynamic process that we refer to as "writing." For example, you will find yourself moving back and forth from the part to the whole—from the scene to its suggestive qualities, from the image to its symbolism, from thematic resonance back to concrete image, and so on. Whereas inexperienced writers think they have written the story or essay when the first draft is complete, the experienced writer knows that first drafts tend to skim the surface or unevenly develop inappropriate aspects of a given subject. Seasoned writers know that the first draft is simply a blueprint and that to return to a draft is to begin to see the possible directions in which the piece may want to go. Once you have a solid draft, you can see a story's potential.

Writing as Discovery

What we call "writer's block" usually isn't really writer's block at all, but a misunderstanding of what the writing process is all about. As you make a conscious choice to write the first draft for yourself alone, to write for the richly rewarding experience of self-expression and personal discovery, a surprising thing happens—you begin to explore unmapped inner terrain, delving into areas that you may not have thought of writing about before.

Writing that it "still comes as a shock" to realize that she doesn't write about what she knows, but "in order to find out," Hampl describes the "lovely illusion" we have when *reading* a well-written work, whose words "appear to have been written exactly as they appear, rhythm and cadence, language and syntax, the powerful waves of the sentences laying themselves on the smooth beach of the page one after another faultlessly." Hampl reminds us that for the writer putting the words on the page the experience is quite different; there is an "enormous degree of blankness, confusion, hunch and uncertainty lurking in the act of writing."

Your Inner Critic and Your Writing Practice

Making time for writing, getting to one's writing desk and actually writing is a challenging task. And the one who will succeed as a writer is the one who does just that—writes. If the successful writer is the one who stays in the chair—writing—then surely we must find a way to outfox the inner critic who will do everything in its power to propel us from the writing chair to do something that is seemingly far more important. What is an inner critic? It's that voice that tells us that our writing isn't going anywhere, that tells us our writing isn't interesting, that tells us we don't know how to write. It is the voice that tells us after months of research that we don't know enough yet about our subject to write about it, and furthermore, that someone else has written about it already and done a far better job of it than we could ever do. If the insufficient research ploy doesn't work, the inner critic becomes a great fidgeter. It compels us to get up to adjust the crooked print on the wall, or to fix the curtains, which aren't hanging just right. Then it announces, the birds are low on seed, just as we sit down for the third time to settle in to our morning's work. We hear the inner critic seem to say: "It's 20 degrees outside and the birdfeeder must be refilled *right now*."

How to quiet the inner critic who likes to fidget and distract us:

It is understandable that we might avoid getting to the actual task of writing; after all, writing is journeying into the unknown and this journey, which takes us into the disorderliness of our lives—our thoughts and feelings, memories and forgetfulness—can be disconcerting, even to the most accomplished writer. It's a time that can be rife with doubts and second-guessing, and so all narrative takes shape through the courageous act of peering past our own blind spots to scrutinize the unknown—or perhaps, even more challenging, the courage of opening to the known. In "Courting the Muse" (included in this chapter), Diane Ackerman shares some of the quirkier approaches writers take to get the muses going. From gardening to rotten apples, baths, naps, and sex (not necessarily in that order), writers who write find a way to get started on a regular basis.

Discussing the challenges Rick Bragg faced in finally writing about his life, the Pulitzer Prize-winning journalist writes in his memoir, *All Over but the Shoutin'*: "I have been putting this off for ten years, because it was personal, because dreaming backwards can carry a man through some dark rooms where the walls seem lined with razor blades. I put it off and put it off until finally something happened to scare me, to hurry me, to make me grit my teeth and remember." The prompt that pushed Bragg into writing his memoir was the death of his grandmother. "All her songs and sayings, all the beautiful things that filled her, warmed her, were quiet." Still, having honed his writing skills as a journalist, Bragg was uncertain whether he could apply those skills to his life. "It is easy to tell a stranger's story," he notes. "I didn't know if I had the guts to tell my own."

Although I don't necessarily agree that it is easy to tell a stranger's story, I do understand what Bragg is getting at concerning the challenge of turning the investigative lens inward. Whether this difficulty is prompted by perfectionism, the pathos of painful memories, or the anxiety of not knowing where a particular line of thought is going to take us, the situation is similar. When our inner critic isn't dismissing the very idea of a story, it is embarrassed and therefore disparaging of the roughness of the story's beginnings. Rejecting the notion that narrative takes shape in stages and must be constructed from the inside out, the inner critic kindly releases the writer from the difficult challenge that the culmination of any successful story will surely be by shifting the writer's attention to something else that requires immediate attention. In the short run the shift is a relief; in the long run it is forfeiture. In "Watcher at the Gate" (included in this chapter) Gail Godwin describes just such an inner critic with whom she is on deeply intimate terms. "Punctual to a fault," her critic always seems to arrive ahead of her in her study, there it is ready to pounce, insinuate, undermine, distract.

Readings

Writers on Writing

"*Watcher at the Gate*," Gail Godwin

"*Courting the Muse*," Diane Ackerman

"*On Keeping a Notebook*," Joan Didion

Memoir

"The Root of My Mother's Powers," Audre Lorde, from *Zami: A New Spelling of My Name*

Lyric Essay

"What Can't Be Spoken," K. Gregg Elliott

Short

"In the Beginning," Leila Philip, from *A Family Place*

Prose Poem

"Traces," Marjorie Agosín

Watcher at the Gate
Gail Godwin

K afka put down his pen, and went to play with his hair in the mirror, and washed his hands three times . . . and returned to record in his diary: "Complete standstill . . . incapable in every respect . . . have achieved nothing."

Who is this critic within us who keeps assuring us we have glimpsed neither swallow nor angel, and even if we imagine we have, it's not worth recording because it would be only ours?

Let me introduce him to you. Or rather, let me introduce you to *my* inner critic, so that you may recognize from him some aspects of your own. I call him my Watcher at the Gate, and have written about him in an essay by that title.

I first realized I *had* a Watcher when I was leafing through Freud's *Interpretation of Dreams* some years ago. Ironically, it was my Watcher who had sent me to Freud in the first place. A character in my novel was having a dream and I lost confidence in my ability to give her the dream she needed, so I rushed to "an authority" to check out whether she ought to have such a dream. And, thanks to my angel, I found instead the following passage.

Freud is quoting from the poet Schiller, who is writing a letter to a friend. The friend has been complaining to Schiller about his own lack of creative power. Schiller tells him it's not good when the intellect examines too closely the ideas pouring in at the gates. In isolation, Schiller explains, an idea may be quite insignificant, and venturesome in the extreme, but it may acquire importance from an idea *which follows it.*

"In the case of a creative mind, it seems to me," Schiller goes on, "the intellect has withdrawn its watchers from the gates, and the ideas rush in pell-mell, and only then does it review and inspect the multitude. You are ashamed of the momentary and passing madness which is found in all real creators, the longer or shorter duration of which distinguishes the thinking artist from the dreamer . . . you reject too soon and discriminate too severely."

So that's what I had: a Watcher at the Gate. I decided to get to know him, and I have. I have written notes to him and he has replied. I even drew a portrait of him once.

Punctual to a fault, he always arrives ahead of me and is waiting for me in my study. The touching thing is, he's on my side. He doesn't want me to fail. He couldn't bear it. It would be so humiliating for both of us. So he is constantly cautioning me against recklessness and excesses, some of which might lead to brilliance. He is partial to looking out the window, looking for a wrinkle in the rug, looking up words. He adores looking up things, any kind of research. And before I had my computer, he was always advising me to stop in the middle of a typewritten page and type it over. "The neatness will re-establish the flow," he explained to me solemnly, wringing his hands—a favorite gesture of his.

That's my daily regular, who has been with me, looking exactly the same, since I first drew his portrait in 1976 (rather than get on with that morning's work). He's thin, with a willowy, ethereal stance; his hands are clasped tightly before him; he has abnormally round eyes, gazing slightly to his right—my left—bushy eyebrows, a fastidious little mustache and prissy lips. He has all his hair and it's still black. It's beginning to worry me that it's still so black, because he's somewhere between fifty and sixty and it would embarrass me to think he dyes it. He wears a black suit and a black tie. The only *sportif* note is the tightly buttoned collar of a dark plaid shirt peeping out above his lapels. I used to wonder whether he might be a clergyman, but couldn't settle on what denomination. More likely he's a bachelor scholar, with a neat little house full of antiques, who reads edifying books with his supper, committing to memory instructive passages to intimidate or slow me down the next day.

I don't know what this says about me, but I have become rather fond of my Watcher and sometimes think I have learned to work so well *in spite of him* that I wouldn't know what to do if he failed to show up one morning.

The other presence who inhabits the mysterious space in which we go to write is, of course, the angel. I first heard about another person's angel from the late painter Philip Guston. I asked him what he did on the mornings he didn't feel inspired. He said he usually went to his studio anyway. "And then I'll find myself thinking, well, I've got some of this pink paint left, so I'll brush some of it on and see what happens. And sometimes the angel comes. But what if I hadn't gone to my studio that day, and the angel *had* come?"

In my experience, the angel *does*, almost always, come. If I keep faith. On some days, keeping faith means simply *staying there*, when more than anything else I want to get out of that room. It sometimes means going up *without hope* and *without energy* and simply acknowledging my barrenness and lighting my incense and turning on my computer. And, at the end of two or three hours, and *without hope* and *without energy*, I find that I have indeed written some sentences that wouldn't have been there if I hadn't gone up to write them. And—what is even more surprising—these sentences written without hope or energy often turn out to be just as good as the ones I wrote *with* hope and energy.

So for me, the angel presides in that mysterious slice of time between when *I don't know what I'm going to write that day* and when I'm looking afterward at the evidence of *what I did write that day.*

Sometimes the best thing you can do is say: I've gone as far as I can. I'm empty. You might even pick up your diary and write, as Kafka did: "Complete standstill. Incapable in every respect." Or your own version of the above. "I can go no further," perhaps.

And then wait.

The German poet Rilke wrote two of his *Duino Elegies* and then lapsed into an almost decade-long depression. And then suddenly "utterance and release" came to him again. In only eighteen days he wrote the *Sonnets to Orpheus* and the remaining eight of his *Duino Elegies*. In the *Elegies*, the predominant symbol is the angel. The angel, for Rilke, as he explained to his Polish translator, is that creature in whom the actual and the ideal are one. Being in the angel's presence, for Rilke, meant being able to give the highest possible significance to our moments as they pass. And works of art, he further testifies, "are always products of having been in danger. Of having gone to the very end of an experience, to where one can go no further."

To where one can go no further. That is often the very point at which we issue our most irresistible invitation to the angel.

Courting the Muse
Diane Ackerman

*W*hat a strange lot writers are, we questers after the perfect word, the glorious phrase that will somehow make the exquisite avalanche of consciousness sayable. We who live in mental barrios, where any roustabout idea may turn to honest labor, if only it gets the right incentive—a bit of drink, a light flogging, a delicate seduction. I was going to say that our heads are our offices or charnel houses, as if creativity lived in a small walk-up flat in Soho. We know the mind doesn't dwell in the brain alone, so the where of it is as much a mystery as the how. Katherine Mansfield once said that it took "terrific hard gardening" to produce inspiration, but I think she meant something more willful than Picasso's walks in the forests of Fontainebleau, where he got an overwhelming "indigestion of greenness," which he felt driven to empty onto a canvas. Or maybe that's exactly what she meant, the hard gardening of knowing where and when and for how long and precisely in what way to walk, and then the will to go out and walk it as often as possible, even when one is tired or isn't in the mood, or has only just walked it to no avail. Artists are notorious for stampeding their senses into duty, and they've sometimes used remarkable tricks of synesthesia.

Dame Edith Sitwell used to lie in an open coffin for a while before she began her day's writing. When I mentioned this macabre bit of gossip to a poet friend, he said acidly: "If only someone had thought to shut it." Picture Dame Edith, rehearsing the posture of the grave as a prelude to the sideshows on paper she liked to stage. The straight and narrow was never her style. Only her much-ridiculed nose was rigid, though she managed to keep it entertainingly out of joint for most of her life. What was it exactly about that dim, contained solitude that spurred her creativity? Was it the idea of the coffin or the feel, smell, foul air of it that made creativity possible?

Edith's horizontal closet trick may sound like a prank unless you look at how other writers have gone about courting their muses. The poet Schiller used to keep rotten apples under the lid of his desk and inhale their pungent bouquet when he needed to find the right word. Then he would close the drawer, although the fragrance remained in his head. Researchers at Yale University discovered that the smell of spiced apples has a powerful elevating effect on people and can even stave off panic attacks. Schiller may have sensed this all along. Something in the sweet, rancid mustiness of those apples jolted his brain into activity while steadying his nerves. Amy Lowell, like George Sand, enjoyed smoking cigars while writing, and in 1915 went so far as to buy 10,000 of her favorite Manila stogies to make sure she could keep her creative fires kindled. It was Lowell who said she used to "drop" ideas into her subconscious "much as one drops a letter into the mailbox. Six months later, the words of the poem began to come into my head. . . . The words seem to be pronounced in my head, but with nobody speaking them." Then they took shape in a cloud of smoke. Both Dr. Samuel Johnson and the poet W. H. Auden drank colossal amounts of tea—Johnson was reported to have frequently drunk twenty-five cups at one sitting. Johnson did die of a stroke, but it's not clear if this was related to his marathon tea drinking. Victor Hugo, Benjamin Franklin, and many others felt that they did their best work if they wrote in the nude. D. H. Lawrence once even confessed that he liked to climb naked up mulberry trees—a fetish of long limbs and rough bark that stimulated his thoughts.

Colette used to begin her day's writing by first picking fleas from her cat, and it's not hard to imagine how the methodical stroking and probing into fur might have focused such a voluptuary's mind. After all, this was a woman who could never travel light, but insisted on taking a hamper of such essentials as chocolate, cheese, meats, flowers, and a baguette whenever she made even brief sorties. Hart Crane craved boisterous parties, in the middle of which he would disappear, rush to a typewriter, put on a record of a Cuban rumba, then Ravel's *Boléro*, then a torch song, after which he would return, "his face brick-red, his eyes burning, his already iron-gray hair straight up from his skull. He would be chewing a five-cent cigar which he had forgotten to light. In his hands would be two or three sheets of typewritten manuscript. . . . 'Read that,' he would say, 'isn't that the *grrrea*test poem ever written!'" This is Malcolm Cowley's account, and Cowley goes on to offer even more examples of how Crane reminded him of "another friend, a famous killer of woodchucks," when the writer "tried to charm his inspiration out of its hiding place by drinking and laughing and playing the phonograph."

Stendhal read two or three pages of the French civil code every morning before working on *The Charterhouse of Parma*—"in order" he said, "to acquire the correct tone." Willa Cather read the Bible. Alexandre Dumas *père* wrote his nonfiction on rose-colored paper, his fiction on blue, and his poetry on yellow. He was nothing if not orderly, and to cure his insomnia and regularize his habits he went so far as to eat an apple at seven each morning under the Arc de Triomphe. Kipling demanded the blackest ink he could find and fantasized about keeping "an ink-boy to grind me Indian ink," as if the sheer weight of the blackness would make his words as indelible as his memories.

Alfred de Musset, George Sand's lover, confided that it piqued him when she went directly from lovemaking to her writing desk, as she often did. But surely that was not so direct as Voltaire, who used his lover's naked back as a writing desk. Robert Louis Stevenson, Mark Twain, and Truman Capote all used to lie down when they wrote, with Capote going so far as to declare himself "a completely horizontal writer." Writing students often hear that Hemingway wrote standing up, but not that he obsessively sharpened pencils first, and, in any case, he wasn't standing up out of some sense of himself as the sentinel of tough, ramrod prose, but because he had hurt his back in a plane crash. Poe supposedly wrote with his cat sitting on his shoulder. Thomas Wolfe, Virginia Woolf, and Lewis Carroll were all standers; and Robert Hendrickson reports in *The Literary Life and Other Curiosities* that Aldous Huxley "often wrote with his nose." In *The Art of Seeing*, Huxley says that "a little nose writing will result in a perceptible temporary improvement of defective vision."

Many nonpedestrian writers have gotten their inspiration from walking. Especially poets—there's a sonneteer in our chests; we walk around to the beat of iambs. Wordsworth, of course, and John Clare, who used to go out looking for the horizon and one day in insanity thought he found it, and A. E. Housman, who, when asked to define poetry, had the good sense to say: "I could no more define poetry than a terrier can a rat, but I thought we both recognized the object by the symptoms which it provokes in us. . . . If I were obliged . . . to name the class of things to which it belongs, I should call it a secretion." After drinking a pint of beer at lunch, he would go out for a two- or three-mile walk and then gently secrete.

I guess the goal of all these measures is concentration, that petrified mirage, and few people have written about it as well as Stephen Spender did in his essay "The Making of a Poem":

> There is always a slight tendency of the body to sabotage the attention of the mind by providing some distraction. If this need for distraction can be directed into one channel—such as the odor of rotten apples or the taste of tobacco or tea—then other distractions outside oneself are put out of the competition. Another possible explanation is that the concentrated effort of writing poetry is a spiritual activity which makes one completely forget, for the time being, that one has a body. It is a disturbance of the balance of the body and mind and for this reason one needs a kind of anchor of sensation with the physical world.

This explains, in part, why Benjamin Franklin, Edmond Rostand, and others wrote while soaking in a bathtub. In fact, Franklin brought the first bathtub to the United States in the 1780s and he loved a good, long, thoughtful submersion. In water and ideas, I mean. Ancient Romans found it therapeutic to bathe in asses' milk or even in crushed strawberries. I have a pine plank that I lay across the sides of the tub so that I can stay in a bubble bath for hours and write. In the bath, water displaces much of your weight, and you feel light, your blood pressure drops. When the water temperature and the body temperature converge, my mind lifts free and travels by itself. One summer, lolling in baths, I wrote an entire verse play, which mainly consisted of dramatic monologues spoken by the seventeenth-century Mexican poet Sor Juana Ínez de la Cruz; her lover, an Italian courtier; and various players in her tumultuous life. I wanted to slide off the centuries as if from a hill of shale. Baths were perfect.

The Romantics, of course, were fond of opium, and Coleridge freely admitted to indulging in two grains of it before working. The list of writers triggered to inspirational highs by alcohol would occupy a small, damp book. T. S. Eliot's tonic was viral—he preferred writing when he had a head cold. The rustling of his head, as if full of petticoats, shattered the usual logical links between things and allowed his mind to roam.

Many writers I know become fixated on a single piece of music when they are writing a book, and play the same piece of music perhaps a thousand times in the course of a year. While he was writing the novel *The Place in Flowers Where Pollen Rests*, Paul West listened nonstop to sonatinas by Ferruccio Busoni. He had no idea why. John Ashbery first takes a walk, then brews himself a cup of French blend Indar tea, and listens to something post-Romantic ("the chamber music of Franz Schmidt has been beneficial" he told me). Some writers become obsessed with cheap and tawdy country-and-western songs, others with one special prelude or tone poem. I think the music they choose creates a mental frame around the essence of the book. Every time the music plays, it re-creates the emotional terrain the writer knows the book to live in. Acting as a mnemonic of sorts, it guides a fetishistic listener to the identical state of alert calm, which a brain-wave scan would probably show.

When I asked a few friends about their writing habits, I thought for sure they'd fictionalize something offbeat—standing in a ditch and whistling Blake's "Jerusalem," perhaps, or playing the call to colors at Santa Anita while stroking the freckled bell of a foxglove. But most swore they had none—no habits, no superstitions, no special routines. I phoned William Gass and pressed him a little.

"You have no unusual work habits?" I asked, in as level a tone as I could muster. We had been colleagues for three years at Washington University, and I knew his quiet professorial patina concealed a truly exotic mental grain.

"No, sorry to be so boring," he sighed. I could hear him settling comfortably on the steps in the pantry. And, as his mind is like an overflowing pantry, that seemed only right.

"How does your day begin?"

"Oh, I go out and photograph for a couple of hours," he said.

"What do you photograph?"

"The rusty, derelict, overlooked, downtrodden parts of the city. Filth and decay mainly," he said in a nothing-much-to-it tone of voice, as casually dismissive as the wave of a hand.

"You do this every day, photograph filth and decay?"

"Most days."

"And then you write?"

"Yes."

"And you don't think this is unusual?"

"Not for me."

A quiet, distinguished scientist friend, who has published two charming books of essays about the world and how it works, told me that his secret inspiration was "violent sex." I didn't inquire further, but noted that he looked thin. The poets May Swenson and Howard Nemerov both told me that they like to sit for a short spell each day and copy down whatever pours through their heads from "the Great Dictator," as Nemerov labels it, then plow through to see what gems may lie hidden in the rock. Amy Clampitt, another poet, told me she searches for a window to perch behind, whether it be in the city or on a train or by the seaside. Something about the petri dish effect of the glass clarifies her thoughts. The novelist Mary Lee Settle tumbles out of bed and heads straight for her typewriter, before the dream state disappears. Alphonso Lingis—whose unusual books, *Excesses* and *Libido*, consider the realms of human sensuality and kinkiness—travels the world sampling its exotic erotica. Often he primes the pump by writing letters to friends. I possess some extraordinary letters, half poetry, half anthropology, he sent me from a Thai jail (where he took time out from picking vermin to write), a convent in Ecuador, Africa (where he was scuba-diving along the coast with filmmaker Leni Riefenstahl), and Bali (where he was taking part in fertility rituals).

Such feats of self-rousing are awkward to explain to one's parents, who would like to believe that their child does something reasonably normal, and associates with reasonably normal folk, not people who sniff rotten apples and write in the nude. Best not to tell them how the painter J. M. W. Turner liked to be lashed to the mast of a ship and taken sailing during a real hell-for-leather storm so that he could be right in the middle of the tumult. There are many roads to Rome, as the old maxim has it, and some of them are sinewy and full of fungus and rocks, while others are paved and dull. I think I'll tell my parents that I stare at bouquets of roses before I work. Or, better, that I stare at them until butterflies appear. The truth is that, besides opening and closing mental drawers (which I picture in my mind), writing in the bath, beginning each summer day by choosing and arranging flowers for a Zenlike hour or so, listening obsessively to music (Alessandro Marcello's oboe concerto in D minor, its adagio, is what's nourishing my senses at the moment), I go speed walking for an hour every single day. Half of the oxygen in the state of New York has passed through my lungs at one time or another. I don't know whether this helps or not. My muse is male, has the radiant silvery complexion of the moon, and never speaks to me directly.

On Keeping a Notebook
Joan Didion

" 'T hat woman Estelle,' " the note reads, " 'is partly the reason why George Sharp and I are separated today.' Dirty crepe-de-Chine wrapper, hotel bar, Wilmington RR, 9:45 a.m. August Monday morning."

Since the note is in my notebook, it presumably has some meaning to me. I study it for a long while. At first I have only the most general notion of what I was doing on an August Monday morning in the bar of the hotel across from the

Pennsylvania Railroad station in Wilmington, Delaware (waiting for a train? missing one? 1960? 1961? why Wilmington?), but I do remember being there. The woman in the dirty crepe-de-Chine wrapper had come down from her room for a beer, and the bartender had heard before the reason why George Sharp and she were separated today. "Sure," he said, and went on mopping the floor. "You told me." At the other end of the bar is a girl. She is talking, pointedly, not to the man beside her but to a cat lying in the triangle of sunlight cast through the open door. She is wearing a plaid silk dress from Peck & Peck, and the hem is coming down.

Here is what it is: the girl has been on the Eastern Shore, and now she is going back to the city, leaving the man beside her, and all she can see ahead are the viscous summer sidewalks and the 3 a.m. long-distance calls that will make her lie awake and then sleep drugged through all the steaming mornings left in August (1960? 1961?). Because she must go directly from the train to lunch in New York, she wishes that she had a safety pin for the hem of the plaid silk dress, and she also wishes that she could forget about the hem and the lunch and stay in the cool bar that smells of disinfectant and malt and make friends with the woman in the crepe-de-Chine wrapper. She is afflicted by a little self-pity, and she wants to compare Estelles. That is what that was all about.

Why did I write it down? In order to remember, of course, but exactly what was it I wanted to remember? How much of it actually happened? Did any of it? Why do I keep a notebook at all? It is easy to deceive oneself on all those scores. The impulse to write things down is a peculiarly compulsive one, inexplicable to those who do not share it, useful only accidentally, only secondarily, in the way that any compulsion tries to justify itself. I suppose that it begins or does not begin in the cradle. Although I have felt compelled to write things down since I was five years old, I doubt that my daughter ever will, for she is a singularly blessed and accepting child, delighted with life exactly as life presents itself to her, unafraid to go to sleep and unafraid to wake up. Keepers of private notebooks are a different breed altogether, lonely and resistant rearrangers of things, anxious malcontents, children afflicted apparently at birth with some presentiment of loss.

My first notebook was a Big Five tablet, given to me by my mother with the sensible suggestion that I stop whining and learn to amuse myself by writing down my thoughts. She returned the tablet to me a few years ago; the first entry is an account of a woman who believed herself to be freezing to death in the Arctic night, only to find, when day broke, that she had stumbled onto the Sahara Desert, where she would die of the heat before lunch. I have no idea what turn of a five-year-old's mind could have prompted so insistently "ironic" and exotic a story, but it does reveal a certain predilection for the extreme which has dogged me into adult life; perhaps if I were analytically inclined I would find it a truer story than any I might have told about Donald Johnson's birthday party or the day my cousin Brenda put Kitty Litter in the aquarium.

So the point of my keeping a notebook has never been, nor is it now, to have an accurate factual record of what I have been doing or thinking. That would be a different impulse entirely, an instinct for reality which I sometimes envy but do not possess. At no point have I ever been able successfully to keep a diary; my approach to daily life ranges from the grossly negligent to the merely absent, and on those few occasions when I have tried dutifully to record a day's events, boredom has so overcome me that the results are mysterious at best. What is this business about "shopping, typing piece, dinner with E, depressed"? Shopping for what? Typing what piece? Who is E? Was this "E" depressed, or was I depressed? Who cares?

In fact I have abandoned altogether that kind of pointless entry; instead I tell what some would call lies. "That's simply not true," the members of my family frequently tell me when they come up against my memory of a shared event. "The party was *not* for you, the spider was *not* a black widow, *it wasn't that way at all.*" Very likely they are right, for not only have I always had trouble distinguishing between what happened and what merely might have happened, but I remain unconvinced that the distinction, for my purposes, matters. The cracked crab that I recall having for lunch the day my father came home from Detroit in 1945 must certainly be embroidery, worked into the day's pattern to lend verisimilitude; I was ten years old and would not now remember the cracked crab. The day's events did not turn on cracked crab. And yet it is precisely that fictitious crab that makes me see the afternoon all over again, a home movie run all too often, the father bearing gifts, the child weeping, an exercise in family love and guilt. Or that is what it was to me. Similarly, perhaps it never did snow that August in Vermont; perhaps there never were flurries in the night wind, and maybe no one else felt the ground hardening and summer already dead even as we pretended to bask in it, but that was how it felt to me, and it might as well have snowed, could have snowed, did snow.

How it felt to me: that is getting closer to the truth about a notebook. I sometimes delude myself about why I keep a notebook, imagine that some thrifty virtue derives from preserving everything observed. See enough and write it down, I tell myself, and then some morning when the world seems drained of wonder, some day when I am only going through the motions of doing what I am supposed to do, which is write—on that bankrupt morning I will simply open my notebook and there it will all be, a forgotten account with accumulated interest, paid passage back to the world out there: dialogue overheard in hotels and elevators and at the hat-check counter in Pavillon (one middle-aged man shows his hat check to another and says, "That's my old football number"); impressions of Bettina Aptheker and Benjamin Sonnenberg and Teddy ("Mr. Acapulco") Stauffer; careful *aperçus* about tennis bums and failed fashion models and Greek shipping heiresses, one of whom taught me a significant lesson (a lesson I could have learned from F. Scott Fitzgerald, but perhaps we all must meet the very rich for ourselves) by asking, when I arrived to interview her in her orchid-filled sitting room on the second day of a paralyzing New York blizzard, whether it was snowing outside.

I imagine, in other words, that the notebook is about other people. But of course it is not. I have no real business with what one stranger said to another at the hat-check counter in Pavillon; in fact I suspect that the line "That's my old football number" touched not my own imagination at all, but merely some memory of something once read, probably "The Eighty-Yard Run." Nor is my concern with a woman in a dirty crepe-de-Chine wrapper in a Wilmington bar. My stake is always, of course, in the unmentioned girl in the plaid silk dress. *Remember what it was to be me*: that is always the point.

It is a difficult point to admit. We are brought up in the ethic that others, any others, all others, are by definition more interesting than ourselves; taught to be diffident, just this side of self-effacing. ("You're the least important person in the room and don't forget it," Jessica Mitford's governess would hiss in her ear on the advent of any social occasion; I copied that into my notebook because it is only recently that I have been able to enter a room without hearing some such phrase in my inner ear.) Only the very young and the very old may recount their dreams at breakfast, dwell upon self, interrupt with memories of beach picnics and favorite Liberty lawn dresses and the rainbow trout in a creek near Colorado Springs. The rest of us are expected, rightly, to affect absorption in other people's favorite dresses, other people's trout.

And so we do. But our notebooks give us away, for however dutifully we record what we see around us, the common denominator of all we see is always, transparently, shamelessly, the implacable "I." We are not talking here about the kind of notebook that is patently for public consumption, a structural conceit for binding together a series of graceful *pensées*; we are talking about something private, about bits of the mind's string too short to use, an indiscriminate and erratic assemblage with meaning only for its maker.

And sometimes even the maker has difficulty with the meaning. There does not seem to be, for example, any point in my knowing for the rest of my life that, during 1964, 720 tons of soot fell on every square mile of New York City, yet there it is in my notebook, labeled "FACT." Nor do I really need to remember that Ambrose Bierce liked to spell Leland Stanford's name "£eland $tanford" or that "smart women almost always wear black in Cuba," a fashion hint without much potential for practical application. And does not the relevance of these notes seem marginal at best?:

In the basement museum of the Inyo County Courthouse in Independence, California, sign pinned to a mandarin coat: "This MANDARIN COAT was often worn by Mrs. Minnie S. Brooks when giving lectures on her TEAPOT COLLECTION."

Redhead getting out of car in front of Beverly Wilshire Hotel, chinchilla stole, Vuitton bags with tags reading:

MRS LOU FOX
HOTEL SAHARA
VEGAS

Well, perhaps not entirely marginal. As a matter of fact, Mrs. Minnie S. Brooks and her MANDARIN COAT pull me back into my own childhood, for although I never knew Mrs. Brooks and did not visit Inyo County until I was thirty, I grew up in just such a world, in houses cluttered with Indian relics and bits of gold ore and ambergris and the souvenirs my Aunt Mercy Farnsworth brought back from the Orient. It is a long way from that world to Mrs. Lou Fox's world, where we all live now, and is it not just as well to remember that? Might not Mrs. Minnie S. Brooks help me to remember what I am? Might not Mrs. Lou Fox help me to remember what I am not?

But sometimes the point is harder to discern. What exactly did I have in mind when I noted down that it cost the father of someone I know $650 a month to light the place on the Hudson in which he lived before the Crash? What use was I planning to make of this line by Jimmy Hoffa: "I may have my faults, but being wrong ain't one of them"? And although I think it interesting to know where the girls who travel with the Syndicate have their hair done when they find themselves on the West Coast, will I ever make suitable use of it? Might I not be better off just passing it on to John O'Hara? What is a recipe for sauerkraut doing in my notebook? What kind of magpie keeps this notebook? "*He was born the night the Titanic went down.*" That seems a nice enough line, and I even recall who said it, but is it not really a better line in life than it could ever be in fiction?

But of course that is exactly it: not that I should ever use the line, but that I should remember the woman who said it and the afternoon I heard it. We were on her terrace by the sea, and we were finishing the wine left from lunch, trying to get what sun there was, a California winter sun. The woman whose husband was born the night the *Titanic* went down wanted to rent her house, wanted to go back to her children in Paris. I remember wishing that I could afford the house, which cost $1,000 a month. "Someday you will," she said lazily. "Someday it all comes." There in the sun on her terrace it seemed easy to believe in someday, but later I had a low-grade afternoon hangover and ran over a black snake on the way to the supermarket and was flooded with inexplicable fear when I heard the checkout clerk explaining to the man ahead of me why she was finally divorcing her husband. "He left me no choice," she said over and over as she punched the register. "He has a little seven-month-old baby by her, he left me no choice." I would like to believe that my dread then was for the human condition, but of course it was for me, because I wanted a baby and did not then have one and because I wanted to own the house that cost $1,000 a month to rent and because I had a hangover.

It all comes back. Perhaps it is difficult to see the value in having one's self back in that kind of mood, but I do see it; I think we are well advised to keep on nodding terms with the people we used to be, whether we find them attractive company or not. Otherwise they turn up unannounced and surprise us, come hammering on the mind's door at 4 a.m. of a bad night and demand to know who deserted them, who betrayed them, who is going to make amends. We forget all too soon the things we thought we could never forget. We forget the loves and the betrayals alike, forget what we whispered and what we screamed, forget who we were. I have already lost touch with a couple of people I used to be; one of them, a seventeen-year-old, presents little threat, although it would be of some interest to me to know again what it feels like to sit on a river levee drinking vodka-and-orange-juice and listening to Les Paul and Mary Ford and their echoes sing "How High the Moon" on the car radio. (You see I still have the scenes, but I no longer perceive myself among those present, no longer could even improvise the dialogue.) The other one, a twenty-three-year-old, bothers me more. She was always a good deal of trouble, and I suspect she will reappear when I least want to see her, skirts too long, shy to the point of aggravation, always the injured party, full of recriminations and little hurts and stories I do not want to hear again, at once saddening me and angering me with her vulnerability and ignorance, an apparition all the more insistent for being so long banished.

It is a good idea, then, to keep in touch, and I suppose that keeping in touch is what notebooks are all about. And we are all on our own when it comes to keeping those lines open to ourselves: your notebook will never help me, nor mine you. "*So what's new in the whiskey business?*" What could that possibly mean to you? To me it means a blonde in a Pucci bathing suit sitting with a couple of fat men by the pool at the Beverly Hills Hotel. Another man approaches, and they all regard one another in silence for a while. "So what's new in the whiskey business?" one of the fat men finally says by way of welcome, and the blonde stands up, arches one foot and dips it in the pool, looking all the while at the cabaña where Baby Pignatari is talking on the telephone. That is all there is to that, except that several years later I saw the blonde coming out of Saks Fifth Avenue in New York with her California complexion and a voluminous mink coat. In the harsh wind that day she looked old and irrevocably tired to me, and even the skins in the mink coat were not worked the way they were doing them that year, not the way she would have wanted them done, and there is the point of the story. For a while after that I did not like to look in the mirror, and my eyes would skim the newspapers and pick out only the deaths, the cancer victims, the premature coronaries, the suicides, and I stopped riding the Lexington Avenue IRT because I noticed for the first time that all the strangers I had seen for years—the man with the seeing-eye dog, the spinster who read the classified pages every day, the fat girl who always got off with me at Grand Central—looked older than they once had.

It all comes back. Even that recipe for sauerkraut: even that brings it back. I was on Fire Island when I first made that sauerkraut, and it was raining, and we drank a lot of bourbon and ate the sauerkraut and went to bed at ten, and I listened to the rain and the Atlantic and felt safe. I made the sauerkraut again last night and it did not make me feel any safer, but that is, as they say, another story.

The Root of My Mother's Powers
from *Zami: A New Spelling of My Name*
Audre Lorde

*G*renadians and Barbadians walk like African peoples. Trinidadians do not. When I visited Grenada I saw the root of my mother's powers walking through the streets. I thought, this is the country of my foremothers, my forebearing mothers, those Black island women who defined themselves by what they did. "Island women make good wives; whatever happens, they've seen worse." There is a softer edge of African sharpness upon these women, and they swing through the rain-warm streets with an arrogant gentleness that I remember in strength and vulnerability.

My mother and father came to this country in 1924, when she was twenty-seven years old and he was twenty-six. They had been married a year. She lied about her age in immigration because her sisters who were here already had written her that americans wanted strong young women to work for them, and Linda was afraid she was too old to get work. Wasn't she already an old maid at home when she had finally gotten married?

My father got a job as a laborer in the old Waldorf Astoria, on the site where the Empire State Building now stands, and my mother worked there as a chambermaid. The hotel closed for demolition, and she went to work as a scullery maid in a teashop on Columbus Avenue and 99th Street. She went to work before dawn, and worked twelve hours a day, seven days a week, with no time off. The owner told my mother that she ought to be glad to have the job, since ordinarily the establishment didn't hire "spanish" girls. Had the owner known Linda was Black, she would never have been hired at all. In the winter of 1928, my mother developed pleurisy and almost died. While my mother was still sick, my father went to collect her uniforms from the teahouse to wash them. When the owner saw him, he realized my mother was Black and fired her on the spot.

In October 1929, the first baby came and the stockmarket fell, and my parents' dream of going home receded into the background. Little secret sparks of it were kept alive for years by my mother's search for tropical fruits "under the bridge," and her burning of kerosene lamps, by her treadle-machine and her fried bananas and her love of fish and the sea. Trapped. There was so little that she really knew about the stranger's country. How the electricity worked. The nearest church. Where the Free Milk Fund for Babies handouts occurred, and at what time—even though we were not allowed to drink charity.

She knew about bundling up against the wicked cold. She knew about Paradise Plums—hard, oval candies, cherry-red on one side, pineapple-yellow on the other. She knew which West Indian markets along Lenox Avenue carried them in tilt-back glass jars on the countertops. She knew how desirable Paradise Plums were to sweet-starved little children, and how important in maintaining discipline on long shopping journeys. She knew exactly how many of the imported goodies could be sucked and rolled around in the mouth before the wicked gum arabic with its acidic british teeth cut through the tongue's pink coat and raised little red pimples.

She knew about mixing oils for bruises and rashes, and about disposing of all toenail clippings and hair from the comb. About burning candles before All Souls Day to keep the soucoyants away, lest they suck the blood of her babies. She knew about blessing the food and yourself before eating, and about saying prayers before going to sleep.

She taught us one to the mother that I never learned in school.

Remember, oh most gracious Virgin Mary, that never was it known that anyone who fled to thy protection, implored thy help, or sought

*thy intercession, was ever left unaided. Inspired with this confidence I
fly unto thee now, oh my sweet mother, to thee I come, before thee I
stand, sinful and sorrowful. Oh mother of the word incarnate, despise
not my petitions but in thy clemency and mercy oh hear and answer
me now.*

As a child, I remember often hearing my mother mouth these words softly,
just below her breath, as she faced some new crisis or disaster—the icebox
door breaking, the electricity being shut off, my sister gashing open her
mouth on borrowed skates.

My child's ears heard the words and pondered the mysteries of this mother
to whom my solid and austere mother could whisper such beautiful words.

And finally, my mother knew how to frighten children into behaving in public. She knew how to pretend that the only food left in the house was actually a
meal of choice, carefully planned.

She knew how to make virtues out of necessities.

Linda missed the bashing of the waves against the sea-wall at the foot of
Noel's Hill, the humped and mysterious slope of Marquis Island rising up from
the water a half-mile off-shore. She missed the swift-flying bananaquits and the
trees and the rank smell of the tree-ferns lining the road downhill into Grenville
Town. She missed the music that did not have to be listened to because it was always around. Most of all, she missed the Sunday-long boat trips that took her to
Aunt Anni's in Carriacou.

Everybody in Grenada had a song for everything. There was a song for the
tobacco shop which was part of the general store, which Linda had managed
from the time she was seventeen.

3/4 of a cross
and a circle complete
2 semi-circles and a perpendicular meet . . .

A jingle serving to identify the store for those who could not read T O B A C C O.

The songs were all about, there was even one about them, the Belmar girls,
who always carried their noses in the air. And you never talked your business too
loud in the street, otherwise you were liable to hear your name broadcast in a
song on the corner the very next day. At home, she learned from Sister Lou to
disapprove of the endless casual song-making as a disreputable and common
habit, beneath the notice of a decent girl.

But now, in this cold and raucous country called america, Linda missed the
music. She even missed the annoyance of the early Saturday morning customers
with their loose talk and slurred rhythms, warbling home from the rumshop.

She knew about food. But of what use was that to these crazy people she
lived among, who cooked leg of lamb without washing the meat, and roasted
even the toughest beef without water and a cover? Pumpkin was only a child's

decoration to them, and they treated their husbands better than they cared for their children.

She did not know her way in and out of the galleries of the Museum of Natural History, but she did know that it was a good place to take children if you wanted them to grow up smart. It frightened her when she took her children there, and she would pinch each one of us girls on the fleshy part of our upper arms at one time or another all afternoon. Supposedly, it was because we wouldn't behave, but actually, it was because beneath the neat visor of the museum guard's cap, she could see pale blue eyes staring at her and her children as if we were a bad smell, and this frightened her. *This* was a situation she couldn't control.

What else did Linda know? She knew how to look into people's faces and tell what they were going to do before they did it. She knew which grapefruit was shaddock and pink, before it ripened, and what to do with the others, which was to throw them to the pigs. Except she had no pigs in Harlem, and sometimes those were the only grapefruit around to eat. She knew how to prevent infection in an open cut or wound by heating the black-elm leaf over a wood-fire until it wilted in the hand, rubbing the juice into the cut, and then laying the soft green now flabby fibers over the wound for a bandage.

But there was no black-elm in Harlem, no black oak leaves to be had in New York City. Ma-Mariah, her root-woman grandmother, had taught her well under the trees on Noel's Hill in Grenville, Grenada, overlooking the sea. Aunt Anni and Ma-Liz, Linda's mother, had carried it on. But there was no call for this knowledge now; and her husband Byron did not like to talk about home because it made him sad, and weakened his resolve to make a kingdom for himself in this new world.

She did not know if the stories about white slavers that she read in the *Daily News* were true or not, but she knew to forbid her children ever to set foot into any candystore. We were not even allowed to buy penny gumballs from the machines in the subway. Besides being a waste of precious money, the machines were slot machines and therefore evil, or at least suspect as connected with white slavery—*the most vicious kind*, she'd say ominously.

Linda knew green things were precious, and the peaceful, healing qualities of water. On Saturday afternoons, sometimes, after my mother finished cleaning the house, we would go looking for some park to sit in and watch the trees. Sometimes we went down to the edge of the Harlem River at 142nd Street to watch the water. Sometimes we took the D train and went to the sea. Whenever we were close to water, my mother grew quiet and soft and absent-minded. Then she would tell us wonderful stories about Noel's Hill in Grenville, Grenada, which overlooked the Caribbean. She told us stories about Carriacou, where she had been born, amid the heavy smell of limes. She told us about plants that healed and about plants that drove you crazy, and none of it made much sense to us children because we had never seen any of them. And she told us about the trees and fruits and flowers that grew outside the door of the house where she grew up and lived until she married.

Once *home* was a far way off, a place I had never been to but knew well out of my mother's mouth. She breathed exuded hummed the fruit smell of Noel's

Hill morning fresh and noon hot, and I spun visions of sapadilla and mango as a net over my Harlem tenement cot in the snoring darkness rank with nightmare sweat. Made bearable because it was not all. This now, here, was a space, some temporary abode, never to be considered forever nor totally binding nor defining, no matter how much it commanded in energy and attention. For if we lived correctly and with frugality, looked both ways before crossing the street, then someday we would arrive back in the sweet place, back *home*.

We would walk the hills of Grenville, Grenada, and when the wind blew right smell the limetrees of Carriacou, spice island off the coast. Listen to the sea drum up on Kick'em Jenny, the reef whose loud voice split the night, when the sea-waves beat upon her sides. Carriacou, from where the Belmar twins set forth on inter-island schooners for the voyages that brought them, first and last, to Grenville town, and they married the Noel sisters there, mainlander girls.

The Noel girls. Ma-Liz's older sister, Anni, followed her Belmar back to Carriacou, arrived as sister-in-law and stayed to become her own woman. Remembered the root-truths taught her by their mother, Ma-Mariah. Learned other powers from the women of Carriacou. And in a house in the hills behind L'Esterre she birthed each of her sister Ma-Liz's seven daughters. My mother Linda was born between the waiting palms of her loving hands.

Here Aunt Anni lived among the other women who saw their men off on the sailing vessels, then tended the goats and groundnuts, planted grain and poured rum upon the earth to strengthen the corn's growing, built their women's houses and the rainwater catchments, harvested the limes, wove their lives and the lives of their children together. Women who survived the absence of their sea-faring men easily, because they came to love each other, past the men's returning.

Madivine. Friending. Zami. How Carriacou women love each other is legend in Grenada, and so is their strength and their beauty.

In the hills of Carriacou between L'Esterre and Harvey Vale my mother was born, a Belmar woman. Summered in Aunt Anni's house, picked limes with the women. And she grew up dreaming of Carriacou as someday I was to dream of Grenada.

Carriacou, a magic name like cinnamon, nutmeg, mace, the delectable little squares of guava jelly each lovingly wrapped in tiny bits of crazy-quilt wax-paper cut precisely from bread wrappers, the long sticks of dried vanilla and the sweet-smelling tonka bean, chalky brown nuggets of pressed chocolate for cocoa-tea, all set on a bed of wild bay laurel leaves, arriving every Christmas time in a well-wrapped tea-tin.

Carriacou which was not listed in the index of the *Goode's School Atlas* nor in the *Junior Americana World Gazette* nor appeared on any map that I could find, and so when I hunted for the magic place during geography lessons or in free library time, I never found it, and came to believe my mother's geography was a fantasy or crazy or at least too old-fashioned, and in reality maybe she was talking about the place other people called Curaçao, a Dutch possession on the other side of the Antilles.

But underneath it all as I was growing up, *home* was still a sweet place some-where else which they had not managed to capture yet on paper, nor to throttle and bind up between the pages of a schoolbook. It was our own, my truly private paradise of blugoe and breadfruit hanging from the trees, of nutmeg and lime and sapadilla, of tonka beans and red and yellow Paradise Plums.°

What Can't Be Spoken
K. Gregg Elliott

A "guest journal" reveals the inner life of friends made along the road.

I was being swept along by the other passengers debarking the Gibraltar ferry to Tangiers. They were mostly tall thin men wearing flowing djallabas and burdened with all sorts of packages. Immediately upon my arrival, a tout ignored my steadfast refusal and escorted me into the cool den of a Moroccan shop, where I sat drinking mint tea and admiring each richly-colored carpet rolled out for my inspection. "*Mais, je n'ai pas beaucoup d'argent! Je n'ai pas l'espace!*" I said, mainly to convince myself, as my hosts exchanged knowing glances and refilled my glass to the brim.

The next day, clad in a beautiful new kilim-weave coat, I set out for the Rif Mountains, famous for both their remoteness and their thriving trade in hashish. I was in search of the former. For days I wandered through narrow cobblestoned streets, past whitewashed adobe houses trimmed in violet and lemon. Each morning, as the sun rose higher in the sky, the immaculate dwellings suffused the air with blue-white light, mirroring the surrounding snow-capped peaks. Barefoot children pushed wheelbarrows of fragrant loaves of bread—still warm—through the cool streets, jostling foot traffic, goats, and bicycles. Steep twisting alleys beckoned with the promise of new surprises at every turn. In the tiny village of Chouan I met an American woman who introduced me to the Turkish baths, where we joined the village women in pouring extravagant buckets of hot water over one another's lathered heads and bodies. Back outside the baths, these same women turned anonymous, hidden behind the folds of their veils.

People do it all the time, but what is the reason for traveling, for backpacking alone to a remote and foreign place? I suppose I wanted to escape the heavily

---

°Years later, as partial requirement for a degree in library science, I did a detailed com-parison of atlases, their merits and particular strengths. I used, as one of the foci of my project, the isle of Carriacou. It appeared only once, in the *Atlas of the Encyclopedia Brit-tannica*, which has always prided itself upon the accurate cartology of its colonies. I was twenty-six years old before I found Carriacou upon a map.

touristed Iberian coast and have my own personal experience of the exotic. I wanted the conversations I had with strangers to yield shards of meaning. I wanted to apply my travel journal to the road, like a pickax to a vein of gold, sifting the dust of my journey for a wider comprehension of the world.

In Rabat, where many of the Muslim women simply wore headscarves rather than a face covering, I finally met a young Moroccan woman eager to speak with me. She was a university student. Saida had a round intelligent face, a ready smile, and spectacles. She was filled with ambition, pursuing a career in teaching. But her future included no plans for a family.

"I will not get married," she told me, gazing into the distance. This seemed to explain everything. I had begun soliciting guest entries in my journal. I proffered a blank page to Saida:

"J'observe partout. . ." she wrote, "I observe everywhere in Morocco that wealth plays a very important role, provoking a comparison between rich and poor. Our society has little means of constructing factories for improving life or eliminating unemployment. Unemployment is the state of young Moroccans, and jealousy reigns everywhere." That same day, after lunch at a sidewalk café, I watched as a frayed man in a filthy djallaba slipped onto the patio where I sat alone in the late afternoon sun. He hurried up to an uncleared table, snatched up a half-full glass, and drank rapidly and a little unsteadily. A bread crust disappeared into the folds of his garment. Once he paused and glared straight into my eyes. I could not hold his gaze. He continued until he had consumed the remains in every glass and on each plate, then disappeared as quickly and quietly as he had entered. I sat in stillness afterward for a long time.

One morning in Rabat I visited the medina, the old market quarter that sits at the center of every Moroccan city. I purchased a round of freshly-baked bread and began eating, tearing off huge chunks as I inched my way through the bazaar. A piece slipped from my fingers. Instantly a tall Moroccan youth with a mustache and penetrating eyes was at my shoulder offering me the bread. *"Tu l'as perdu."* You've lost this, he said.

"*Non, merci*, I dropped it."
"Take it," he said.
"I don't want it, thank you."
"Are you English?" he asked.

"No, American." His eyes narrowed and immediately I became the subject of a piercing inquisition during which my interrogator loudly announced his antipathy for the American government. I managed to blunt his hostility somewhat by agreeing with many of his criticisms then asking him to explain his politics.

He paused in mild astonishment, then answered, "That will take some time."
"Time," I said, "is precisely what I've got."

We spent the day walking through the city, discussing politics and philosophy, consulting my French-English dictionary to look up the big words. By mid-afternoon, having made short shrift of Moroccan history, we had begun tackling Western versus Muslim attitudes toward women. Abdelkhalik spoke with conviction, but when I asked if he would marry he became silent.

At some point I must have passed an indefinable test, because Abdelkhalik looked at me with new eyes and invited me for supper, saying I'd have to spend the night because it would be too dangerous to make my way to the pension after dark. I was young and struggling to know the world. This was pre-9/11. He was not after the usual prize, of that I was certain. My intuition gave a nod, so I accepted.

Abdelkhalik was from Salé, the slum across the river from Rabat, home to the majority of Moroccans who work in the capital city. The narrow, grimy streets overflowed with garbage and people hurrying home from work. Abdelkhalik stopped and bought two tomatoes and an onion from a sidewalk vendor. I offered to pay, in return for his offer of hospitality for the night, but he refused.

Most dwellings in Salé were of corrugated sheet metal with dirt floors. Abdelkhalik led me to a small room at the end of a decaying building. The room had cement walls, a concrete slab floor, and one barred window high on the wall. One cot and a sleeping mat on the floor, a tiny gas cookstove, a few kitchen implements, and two scarred wooden chairs were its total contents. Pictures of beautiful women from *Elle* magazine were taped over cracks in the wall. A latrine consisting of a hole dug into the bare ground in a dank closet leaked the smell of urine and human waste.

We ate our meal of sauteed tomatoes and onions over rice, and I invited Abdelkhalik to make an entry in my journal. He took the pen, paused, set the tip to paper, paused again. When the words finally came, he wrote quickly. He handed back my journal with the intricately scrolled serifs of Arabic flowing across the page.

"What does it say?"

"You will find out," he answered.

After supper, Abdelkhalik offered me his sleeping mat. He would sleep on the floor.

"Who is the other bed for?" I asked.

"I can't afford to live here without a roommate."

"Where is he?"

"I don't know. He usually returns late." Sensing my unease, he added, "Do not worry."

Too exhausted to ask more questions, I mastered my distaste, used the latrine, and we fell asleep as the murmurs of the city beyond the concrete walls faded. I awoke to the sound of a man bellowing in anguish. With wide-open eyes I strained to see through the cavelike darkness. I smelled alcohol and heard an unfamiliar voice spew an incomprehensible stream of angry Arabic. I froze in fear. I lay awake the rest of the night as Abdelkhalik's roommate snored in his cot, occasionally shouting or moaning his alcoholic rage. I thought of Abdelkhalik's lively intellect, hobbled by lack of opportunity in the hard, narrow track of his life. I recalled his reluctance in speaking of a future with family, and his reticence no longer seemed such a riddle. When dawn outlined the window bars against the purple sky I arose, gave Abdelkhalik a hug of thanks, and taking care not to rouse the swarthy middle-aged man sprawled on the cot, I left—simply because I could.

Memories of Salé faded in the sultry desert air of Marrakesh. For several days I explored the labyrinthine medina and gorged on succulent dates after being taught how to first pull them open to check for the worm that sometimes lives inside. From the taxi drivers, I gathered travel tips and decided to head next to Essaouira, a small town on the coast south of Marrakesh.

After three years of drought, February rains had resuscitated the withered landscape, which overflowed gratefully with buttercups and tiny flowers the color of blue and white porcelain. I found an *auberge* located four kilometers from town amid budding acacias and succumbed to the beguiling rhythm of desert life. Each morning began with the sensual aroma of *café au lait* served in an outsized ceramic bowl with a handle on either side. The soft susurration of the windmill blades above the well pump accompanied morning bird song. Next I would meander toward the ocean, lost in the beauty of the resurrected desert. Once I stumbled upon a shepherd boy helping to birth a lamb. I watched until he was vigorously rubbing down the newborn, a wide grin on his face. The lamb's tottering first steps toward its mother's teats and the shepherd's careful ministrations imparted a biblical quality to the scene. There was no need to speak.

The beach was the widest sweep of sunburnt sand I had ever seen, and utterly deserted. One afternoon, I was invited to tea by some local fishermen. These men were Berber, the original natives of Morocco prior to Arab colonization. They had brown, deeply lined, handsome faces and arresting sky-blue eyes. They explained to me the significance of the mint tea imbibed so regularly throughout Morocco. The tea is prepared in three rounds using the same tea leaves, but adding fresh mint and sugar with each draught.

"The first draught," said the old man preparing the tea, "is bitter, like life. The second draught is sweet, like love." He continued stirring the tea as he impaled me with his impossible eyes, "and the third is gentle," he said, "like death." I realized, with something akin to shame, that for me life had never seemed bitter, and I wondered whether death would ever seem a thing of mercy.

I slept fitfully on the night bus returning to the departure port of Tangier, awaking at each stop. Once, very late, we arrived at a cantina in a tiny village. The yellow light of gas lamps illuminated four men with traditional flowing headdress playing cards, and a dog lying half-hidden and motionless behind the men's feet. People began exiting the bus and with dawning horror I saw the dog was not a dog at all, but an emaciated man without legs. He used his arms and hands to drag himself with surprising dexterity through the mud to beg for a few dinhas. The tableau through the window was silent, but I could see him speaking rapidly, one arm outstretched toward his fellow men. Passengers walked by, absorbed in conversation. The gentlemen at the table dealt another round of cards.

In the ferry queue I made my last random Moroccan acquaintance. I don't remember how we met, perhaps Hassan was watching me observe the surreal stream of people laden with Western goods disembarking from the ferry. Somehow this particular place revealed the nonsensical nature of international borders: A person like every other, born into the struggle for survival, steps over an imaginary line on the earth. Suddenly he has to worry that customs will disallow his meager load, purchased for resale to help support a hungry family.

Hassan was a sophisticate who had lived and worked in Paris for years. His long thin face was always arranged in an attitude of merriment and his laugh was very attractive. Hassan's journal entry reads: "Traveling, for me, is discovering what is important in life. Thanks to travel, you know that life is short. Try to make it happy by seeing through to the truth of things."

I requested a translation of the Arabic script that Abdelkhalik left in my journal. Hassan read to me one and a half pages of geopolitical rant that ended with these words: "I do not know the political secrets of war. I can explain to you the rich and the poor. Me, I am poor. And truthfully, I do not want to tell you my feelings after all."

Hassan and I traveled together for several more weeks until we reached Paris. Years later, we are still friends. We correspond and even talk on the phone occasionally, in a mixture of French and English. But it is Abdelkhalik who speaks to me, across a gulf of hardship and unfathomable poverty, wordlessly.

In the Beginning
from *A Family Place*
Leila Philip

Before me stood Talavera, but all around was darkness. Light was spewing out from so many of the tall windows that the house could have been a ship sailing the night sea. But instead of feeling cheered by what I saw, I felt frozen. Talavera, that grand vessel of the past, how much of it was illusion, a house of cards, precarious, hostage to the slightest breeze?

Even now I could shut my eyes and see each room as it had been. On the uppermost floor in the west room sat the mahogany cradle that had rocked generations. My sister and I had found it a perfect place to nurse the baby rabbits that we sometimes found abandoned in the fields after the mower had gone by. Determined to save them from the dogs and the cats, we wrapped them in old sweaters and nursed them with tiny droppers of milk, feeding them every two hours. The rabbit kits never lived more than a few days, but we would always try, stroking their impossibly small ears and frail, quivering bodies with a finger until they fell still, asleep in our palms.

In that same room was the strange armadillo basket, a Victorian horror made from an armadillo shell, the nose wired to the long tail to form a handle.

Boredom was never possible on rainy days at Talavera. It was an adventure merely to open the huge old doors and wander through these rooms. Each was filled with strange old things to finger and collect or just to stare at from a wary distance. Downstairs the curio cabinets were stocked with prehistoric and Mohican arrowheads collected each season in the upturned plow furrows. I loved to look at them and at the shelves of relics from an ancestor's travels. Medals, bits of stone, a tiny shoe with a message written on the sole, a stone lantern, a piece of Roman tile, the broken edge of an old relief, a square of embroidered fabric, a pile of coins, a strange torpedo-shaped Civil War bullet: so many things that each time you looked you could find something new.

My family saved everything, a habit that would make my search possible when it came to digging up the past. I loved the funny silver and porcelain thimbles, the faded, falling-apart packets of needles and thread and blanket binding, the old quill pens and nibs and the glass inkwells that I painstakingly strove to use when I was twelve, blotching ink all over the white pages of my leather-bound journal. The books were old; the wastebaskets were old; the drapes were old; even the bottles of alcohol and Pepto-Bismol in the medicine closet were from a time long before I was born. Once I went looking for a Band-Aid and pried open the rusting metal box only to find that the Band-Aids inside had withered. I dumped out a dozen yellow strips that crackled and broke to the touch like dried cicada shells.

Talavera was not just a house and not just the past. It was not just my father's dream, and it was not just my aged rival. Somehow Talavera had absorbed my own childhood, becoming me. Once I walked out of the house, across the lawns and onto the farm's land, time would conflate, and I was not just the age I was then but all the ages I had ever been. I was five years old and climbing on, then falling off our Shetland pony. I was nine years old and riding my first new bicycle, down the big hill faster and faster until my wheel caught in a rut and I came to a stop, smack against the boxes of a beehive. I was twelve years old and proudly backing up a tractor and trailer. Then sixteen and racing my horse, faster and faster without a saddle or a bridle, across the meadow.

I walked slowly back up to the house and crossed the north porch. All around me the tall Corinthian columns spired up, echoing the tripartite structure of the house with its north and south wings and its central pavilion, designed to appear as if a temple lost within a grove. I reached out to open the door. Beneath my fingers the brass door handle felt solid, reassuringly smooth and cool. But as soon as I began to turn the knob, I felt myself grow weak. The knob turned and turned, but the door would not open. Broken, the inside mechanism separated from the catch. A simple matter, but at that moment my insides split into panic. I couldn't get in, I couldn't get away.

I thought back to the psalm that my mother and I had chosen for my father's funeral: "You sweep us away like a dream; we fade away suddenly like the grass." Then, as if on cue, the knob on the front door caught and turned. I pushed the door forward and walked in, listening to my footsteps echo in the now-darkening house.

Traces

Marjorie Agosín

*T*raveling creates a desire to write, like a passionate urge to speak or the crazy impulse to lull a word to sleep. Traveling is like paradise, when I find unexpected words. Writing is like traveling in perpetual amazement. The unexpected, what is left to chance, is like a key that I find then misplace, a sunflower made of glass, and always like the pleasure of touching the sky with my feet and my hands.

Prewriting Practice Strategies

We are not merely who we are today, but the sum of our experiences from the time of infancy to now. We have within us everything we need to begin to tell the stories that define who we have become; indeed, who we are still becoming. It may not be the subject we are the most comfortable writing about, but it is what we know the most about. And although we may have doubts about the amount of raw data we can cull from our live's experiences, as writers we quickly realize that there exists a deep reservoir waiting to be discovered.

By beginning with your own memories, which by the way are alive and kicking within, you can amass a surprisingly rich range of material. In your dust heaps are some diamonds just waiting to be discovered and polished. Here is an exercise that will help find them:

1. Take a piece of notepaper and divide it into thirds, either by drawing lines across the page or folding the paper. Now, in your mind's eye, divide your life into thirds, based on what you would consider to be the three major periods of your life. It may be as simple as childhood, adolescence, and adulthood. Or, it may be based on major events that mark turning points in your life. It doesn't matter. This prewriting exercise is meant to get a lot of raw material into your journal so that you may draw on it later. Select one section of your paper and begin to cluster within that section, allowing your mind to wander through that period of your life for 5 to 15 minutes. Jot down everything that comes into your mind. Do this in words and phrases, not sentences, and remember it's a messy process, not tidy and neat. Scribble all over the section of paper in which you are working. Don't stop and think about what you're writing. Don't stop to read what you have written. And don't go back and correct anything. Just keep your pen steadily moving for the time you have set

aside for this exercise. After you've completed all three sections, go back and scan each one in turn, underlining or circling words and phrases that attract your attention. Circle about five within each section. Now select one of these circled words or phrases and put it at the top of a clean piece of paper and begin to freewrite from that word. Again, you are allowing your mind to free associate; you're not composing, just seeing what finds its way onto paper for now. Do this for each section. Once you've finished, set this aside to return to later.

2. Have you ever tried writing with your "other" hand? This exercise can be fun and generates a lot of smiles and laughter, but it isn't merely for amusement. Writing with your nondominant hand connects you with the part of the brain that tends to be more dormant in your writing process. For example, if you are right-handed, you will work with your left hand, connecting to the parts of the right side of the brain associated with creativity and intuition.

   Using your nondominant hand, write about a significant childhood event. If you are right-handed, use your left; if you are left-handed, use your right. If you are ambidextrous, this exercise won't work as well for you. And use crayons or markers and maybe even a Big Chief pad. This exercise can serve to return you to a childlike state of mind as your writing becomes practically illegible and your pace, as in childhood, slows to a crawl. The smell and texture of these implements and the lack of dexterity, together with using a different part of your brain, will nudge your brain into a younger place, which may help make the memories even more vivid as you recall them.

3. Take a few moments to describe your inner critic. For example: My inner critic doesn't want to write unless I have the whole day stretching in front of me. My critic tells me that I will not be able to write with any depth if I have to shift my attention in a few hours to something else. Why not wait until the weekend when I'll really have time to write? When the weekend comes, my inner critic has other reasons I shouldn't write: I should be more social, entertain guests, get out and see the latest independent films, go see that performance that will only be here for another week. Surely that will inspire me and *then* I'll write even *better*.

   What are some of the ways your inner critic subverts your writing process and saps your creativity? Set a timer for five minutes and write everything that comes into your mind about your critic. When you have finished, you may want to type up a few simple bulleted statements that "talk back." Print these in a strong, bold font, and place them in full view of your writing desk. When your critic begins mumbling in your ear, simply chase it away by reading the posted statements.

Pointers and Potential Pitfalls

Careful composing in the early stages of writing is deadly. It slows your thoughts down and dampens your voice. When you return to an early draft later, you will read it with a critical eye, but not now. Think of each draft as fulfilling its potential for that stage of the writing process, rather than something to be perfected. Be patient. Keep writing through the confusion. Clarity will soon come.

CHAPTER 4

The Story Takes Shape: Reading and Writing for Story

Artifacts are alive. Each has a voice. They remind us what it means to be human—that it is our nature to survive, to create works of beauty, to be resourceful, to be attentive to the world we live in.

— TERRY TEMPEST WILLIAMS

The Shape of the Story

Writers draw on a range of analogies and metaphors to describe the process of storytelling. Some describe it architecturally, as building blocks; others more as an art form, for example, as a tapestry, replete with patterns, movement, design. Still others describe it as a birth—the subconscious growth and development of an idea birthed into story—its own kind of labor.

In any case, creative writing is never simply a matter of connecting the dots, coloring inside the lines, or pouring our content into an all-purpose, five-paragraph essay. A narrative isn't complete simply because it has accurately described a scene or vividly represented a situation. It is a relationship that develops between the writer and the work. As Jayne Anne Phillips notes in *Conversations with American Women Writers*: "Many times you're not aware of what you're working with until you get deeply into the material. The material itself instructs, compels, mesmerizes the writer—just as the resulting book teaches the reader how to 'read' the world of that book."

The importance of reading as a writer, also emphasized in the discussion on forms of narrative nonfiction in Chapter 2, is especially important as you begin to consider what shape a particular story is taking. Like Phillips, most writers describe narrative structure as something that can't be imposed from the outside, but rather discovered from within the narrative. Should the story's timeline unfold chronologically? Might the narrative incorporate a **braided effect** by weaving disparate narrative strands? Might the narrative leap about among scenes, time frames, voices, or point of view creating a **narrative collage**? Or, perhaps the narrative needs a **frame**—an opening and closing scene or reflection that holds the body of the piece together, like bookends. The approach of blending scene, summary, and reflection with **flashbacks** into one complexly interwoven whole may best serve the story.

In the early stages of writing, you have to trust that your fits and starts, sketches and impressionistic ideas will coalesce into a coherent whole, eventually taking shape as story. Your story may not have revealed itself yet. No need to worry. Stories become clearer as they take shape. Your beginnings will launch your stories, but you may no longer need your beginnings once the story takes off. Now that you know what your story is really about, you need to be willing to tear up the runway, as Annie Dillard puts it, because it was only meant to help you get going. This can be a difficult decision, because in order to be true to your story, you may have to part with portions of it that you hold dear to your heart. Finding the ideal form for any narrative requires that you be flexible and willing to experiment with varying approaches.

Sometimes, when writers are lucky, the structure of a piece becomes apparent in the initial drafting stages. More frequently, in the early drafts it isn't clear what the patterns are or what the order of things should be. As the story takes shape, however, so will its form. Form and content, structure and idea, these work in concert with one another, creating an interactive dynamic that results in a larger, unified whole. As you immerse yourself in the process of writing you will find yourself moving back and forth between the idea of the completed work and its various parts. Structural possibilities are endless, of course, as the varied and numerous models presented in this text so eloquently reveal. You should feel free to emulate their structural approaches, while experimenting with new and varied forms of your own making. As you do this you will realize that structure is inextricable from content.

Reading, Writing, and Revision

Revision isn't something writers do after they have written a piece. It isn't editing. It isn't polishing. Revising is as significant to the writing process as prewriting, and it begins soon after the first draft. In fact, revising *is* writing. For instance, if an early draft is largely literal, holding to scene and situation, then reentering it will involve development of theme. If an early draft is largely thematic, then revision may involve constructing scenes that interact with and anchor theme in a dramatic way. When you revisit a draft, if you discover an image that has metaphorical potential, you may decide to work with that image more, developing it so that it takes on greater significance and begins to resonate more fully. As you work with an image you may realize that it is deeply connected with your developing story's thematic possibilities. This may take you in a different direction than originally intended, but it may feel so intuitively right that you have to follow its lead.

In an interview in *The Writer's Chronicle*, southern writer Bobbie Ann Mason said that she begins to get a sense of the narrative—the storyline—by about the sixth draft. Even then she said she finds herself still wondering: "What is this all about?" At this point she gets a notebook and combs through the writing, creating "categories of images and sounds and references and details and just bits of things." This process may bring with it a number of helpful surprises. For example, in reviewing one of her works in progress Mason noticed that imagery about dancing kept coming up: angels dancing on the head of a pin, for example, or people dancing to an old big band song. Like most writers, this was not something she had been conscious of when she was writing. But the narrative was telling her something, and if she followed it perhaps it would lead her toward what the narrative wanted to say.

Eventually you will find yourself paying attention to all matters of craft at once, from the minutiae of descriptive detail and the way a particular image takes on metaphorical resonance, to the **narrative arc** of story and theme. *However*, if you have done it well, only you will know what you've accomplished. Your readers will read a seamless story. To draw on the image of the writer as weaver, the final tapestry will have no threads dangling, no raw seams showing; all its parts will be woven into a beautifully textured whole.

How Writers Help Each Other: A Writer's Workshop

When immersed in a writing project, it is difficult to gain distance and one of the ways that writers gain perspective is by having others read it. Most writers prefer to have others read their work only after they've written a number of drafts, at which point they often find they have lost objectivity. Outside feedback can be a helpful thing to have along the way, as long as you don't take others' response to your work as absolute. Most writing courses have built into them a workshop structure for giving and receiving feedback on work in progress.

A workshop structure provides participants with an opportunity to write in a community with other writers, with imposed structure, external guidance, encouragement, critique, and built-in deadlines. One invaluable result of having readers respond to a work-in-progress—honestly and constructively—is the discovery that there is no ideal reader. You will realize that every reader "reads" your work in a different way, depending on individual aesthetics, ability, and even reasons for reading. Perhaps most importantly, a writing workshop, if effective, will provide an opportunity for you to realize that the process of writing can be a more satisfying experience than you thought possible, especially as you come to realize that your readers aren't the harsh critics you had always feared, but that they actually want to understand what it is you have to say.

One of the advantages of being in a writing workshop, rather than working alone, besides the structure and guidance that you receive, is the greater critical awareness that develops from reading and discussing others' work. By sharing in this process with peers you not only come to understand that all writers strike out into the unknown, every time they write, but you also will be exposed to a range of various narrative strategies, structures, and subjects. In discussing peers' writing, you come to appreciate, for example, how writers build on their strengths, some writers preferring dialogue, while others are more drawn to the use of internal monologue. Varieties of voice, style and syntax, the unconscious use of personal imagery and symbolism, the unique perspective any given individual writer has to offer—these are some of the gifts of a good workshop.

We are given an opportunity to read regularly the work of peers in a workshop environment; this is a rare and revealing thing, as interests, experiences, and abilities vary widely within any given writing group. A writing workshop provides writers with the privilege of peering behind the tapestry of works-in-progress, to see the seams and dangling threads as they become woven into the pattern that will shape the final piece. Being a part of this progression is a reminder that writing *is* a process after all, and that the product is what we arrive at when we have finished. Perhaps most importantly, writers in a workshop begin to see that *all* writing begins in uncertainty, proceeds through various stages of clarification, and culminates—when we are both diligent and lucky—in a meaningful story. Once again, meaning has been carved out of life's apparently random experiences.

What Peer Readers Offer the Writer

Responding to peer writing and receiving peer response may feel uncomfortable at first, but that will dissipate as you give and receive "readings" of one another's writing in progress. You might remind yourself that you are not being asked to be a critic, but rather a "reader." What is most helpful to writers is to hear *how* a reader read their work. What you *like* and *don't like* is really irrelevant in this milieu. Peter Elbow, whose work has become a mainstay of many progressive, process-oriented compositional courses, describes the workshop reader's role as "giving movies of your mind." Stories affect us emotionally, aesthetically, and intellectually and our role as readers in a writing workshop is to tell the writer *how* the writing in front of us affected us. Getting comfortable in this role takes some time and you will find yourself responding with what you liked most; that's okay. You just need to be sure to follow your emphasis on what you like with *why* you like it. Explore the piece in front of you to show *how* it has achieved its effects—emotionally, aesthetically, and intellectually.

Motivated by any number of things, writers in a workshop pause, pen in hand, seeking to find words for those meaningful moments in our lives, to shape those moments in language so as to hold onto them, to get them down in a form that will keep them alive before they fade from our memory. We also pause to actively listen to one another's stories, to take in this art form we call narrative. Representing life through the abstraction of language we move into the promise of story. We are all on a journey together. You will find that reading and responding to others and listening to others talk about your work will dramatically improve your ability to approach your writing *as a reader*, which will in turn make you a better writer.

The instructor will set the terms of the workshop, its guidelines and ground rules. Usually the workshop is an opportunity for writers to hear how others are responding to their work. Usually readers will carry on a conversational critique, or "reading" of the work under discussion while the writer listens in on this conversation. While it may be tempting to step in to explain an important point that you feel is being misunderstood, it's important that you not do so. If you intervene in the discussion you will forfeit an invaluable opportunity to "listen in" while others respond and react to your work. Just take what your readers have to say with an open mind and a grain of salt. Take notes. Only later will you decide whether you will make changes based on peer feedback. After the discussion has slowed down or come to a close—everyone has said what they have to say about the work—the writer is usually invited to ask any questions about the work in progress. This is your chance to clarify any questions you may have about particular comments or aspects of the work that haven't been addressed in the discussion.

Becoming an Effective Reader for Others (and Yourself)

Put the red ink pen, and it's attitude of correction, away for the writer's workshop; you're not an editor and you're not correcting your peers' papers. You're offering yourself to the writer as a *reader*, providing observations and constructive feedback about what works and doesn't work *for you* in the piece under discussion. One of the most helpful ways you can help a writer is to ask questions. Questions about the story, not the writer, that have come to mind while you were reading. Questions may suggest confusion, but they also express interest. If you focus on the more complex elements of craft that we have been discussing, rather than spelling, grammar, and punctuation, you will help the writer hear how you "read" the work in progress. Since there are no ideal readers, there are only readers, you will be providing a service for the writer that will move along the process of a work in progress.

Prompts

Here are a few prompts that you may find helpful in providing a constructive peer critique:

> The tone of the piece suggests . . .
> The narrator appears to . . .
> There is tension around . . .
> Is this an essential element to the story?
> This scene sets up an expectation in me that . . .

This image makes me wonder if . . .
As a reader, I want to know more about . . .
I'm confused about . . .
The rhythm of the sentences are . . .

Questions

Here are some questions to ask of our (and others') stories:

1. Are there key images? What about scenes? These may recur, or an image or scene may seem weighted. Sometimes such an image or scene gets picked up again and becomes a significant strand woven into the piece, its meaning made resonant through repetition and development.

2. Where are the key points of tension in the narrative? These are points of potential, although they may not have been fully explored yet. Take the time to do that now. In Terry Tempest Williams's "Sanderlings" (not included here, but available in her memoir, *Refuge*), a single observation becomes a window on a lifetime:

> *Her hands remain unchanged, becoming more beautiful, more expressive each day. Her fingers seem to lengthen and her nails grow long. We hold each other's hands, and I see and feel the years of my mother's nurturing: the hands that cradled me, cuddled me, stroked my head at birth; the hands that bathed me, disciplined me, and combed my hair as a child; the hands that called me, prepared my food, wrote me letters, and loved my father's body; the hands that worked in the garden on long summer days planting marigolds for fall.*
>
> *These hands even at death are beautiful.*

3. Does the opening paragraph draw the reader in and make him want to continue reading? Usually a beginning is a throat-clearing attempt at getting going. Dillard advises that we not waste time polishing this, because, more than likely we'll "just have to take a deep breath and throw it away anyway," once we've finished the work and "have a clearer sense of what it is about." Here is the opening paragraph to "Sanderlings," from Terry Tempest Williams's *Refuge*:

> *"Close the door," Mother said. "I've been waiting for you to get here all morning." She held out her hand. "Something wonderful is happening. I'm so happy. Always remember, it is here, in this moment, and I had it."*
>
> *I didn't understand.*

Notice how this opening puts the reader in the same position as the narrator. Williams doesn't open her narrative with an explanation, nor does she summarize, based on what she now understands in hindsight, but takes us back to the original moment when she walked through that door and did not understand what it was that her mother was about to share.

4. Do the beginning and ending paragraphs interact with one another? Is it necessary that they interact? What is important to consider about the beginning and ending paragraphs? Some pieces have a circular structure, which bring the reader back to the beginning, but with new information or insights. Other pieces may provide a final flourish that brings the piece to completion. In any case, you should try to avoid tidy, perfect endings. They feel controlled and contrived and they close down the story rather than leave room for the reader to participate in the concluding moments of the piece in an active, interpretive way.

5. Some endings veer from the beginnings, pulling the reader along the narrator's journey of exploration, settling finally in a different place altogether where one must pause, look back, and reflect on the meaning of it all. *Uphill Walkers: Memoir of a Family*, by Madeleine Blais, recounts the struggles and survival of her close-knit Irish Catholic family in a small town in Western Massachusetts during the fifties and sixties following the death of her father. In "Serviam," an excerpted chapter from that book (included in this chapter), Blais demonstrates that shaping of the story we have been discussing here. Although only a chapter from her larger book, this piece provides a wonderful opportunity to examine beginnings and endings that perhaps seem miles apart from each other, yet perhaps, in the end, are deeply connected. For now, notice the contrast. Here, in the beginning, Blais introduces us to the Catholic school she attended, Ursuline Academy:

> *We were, in a way, saved by the nuns.*
>
> *My mother had driven me to Ursuline for Mission Day, a chaste little carnival that had in my opinion only two advantages: classes were canceled, and we could wear normal civilian clothes. Throughout the day a girl in a white dress, wearing a crown, circulated the gym, dispensing robotic hellos. She was our Mission Day Queen, elected solely on the basis of her goodness, which meant she had, during private consultations about her spiritual future, let it be known that a religious vocation was not entirely out of the question and, also, that her favorite color was blue, the same as the Blessed Mother's.*

In the ending, Blais writes about John F. Kennedy's assassination, having first heard about it over the loudspeaker at school, and the meaning it held for her:

> *My sisters and I did what insecure people so often do in the face of overwhelming external events that have no clear link to their lives: we found a connection. As fatherless children, John-John and Caroline were now, on some level, like us, a blood brother and blood sister. Our feelings were mixed. While it was heady to be considered in their category, it also made us less singular. They would know, as we did, death's great contradiction: the profound presence of those who are forever absent.*

There is an evident shift in tone here. What was rather humorous has given way to the solemn events surrounding President Kennedy's assassination. What do you make of this as you consider beginnings and endings? Read "Serviam" in its entirety at the end of this chapter. How does this ending change the meaning of this excerpt? Find the place where Blais separates the Kennedy story from the rest of the piece. She uses white space here, shaping this chapter in her book in a way that says, yes, this is humor, and you may laugh. But wait. This experience of shared Catholicism and of shared tragedy was something else altogether, something larger, with implications for the Blais sisters that reached far beyond the school grounds. In her shaping of this chapter, in her attention to both witty storytelling and careful delivery of a larger meaning, Blais leads us on a journey that is both light-hearted and at the same time inescapably poignant. This is what shaping a story means.

Writers, Listen to Your Readers

When you workshop a piece and a reader doesn't understand something, especially if this is corroborated by more than one reader, then you may need to work more with it. You should not have to explain your story to your readers in workshop; it should explain itself. Of course, there is always room for ambiguity and writers often find it fulfilling (and enlightening) to hear how various readers respond to their work, each bringing differing interpretations to the scenes, images, and descriptions of the story. You want the heart of the piece, however, to be understood more or less in line with your intentions, and if it is not, revision will be in order. This is why we workshop. This is why we revise. This is—isn't it—why we write?

As writers, we must listen to what our readers have to say, take notes, and try not to respond to questions. Instead use them to think about possible revisions.

After your work has been read and discussed in a workshop you will want to go back to your writing desk and reflect on how the story might become stronger and more effective, given how your readers have responded to it. There will have been conflicting responses, so you will be left with the final task of deciding which "readings" are the most helpful in terms of your narrative's potential.

Trusting Your Practice

Now that your practice has begun to take shape, you will have learned how best to approach your writing—what works and what doesn't. You will have discovered more about how you approach early drafts as well as the work of development and revision. How you approach a narrative, of course, varies with any particular project. Working writers say that every new beginning is like starting all over as a writer. But, a track record does provide a writer with a sense of the process, the danger points, ways to get you going, and ways to keep going.

You now know better how to look for those places where the narrative needs to be broken open and explored more deeply, as well as those scenes needing only a bit of tinkering. You also know by now that sometimes a work needs to be put away for a while because you're just too close to it.

Trusting the Story

Revision may mean ruthless cutting of what doesn't move the story forward. It may mean cutting and pasting and shuffling parts around. Or, it may mean happy discoveries of intricate parts that invite expansion and emphasis. Whatever the case, revising is an organic part of the writing process and will lead you more deeply and more meaningfully into your story. Patricia Hampl writes in her essay "Memory and Imagination" (included in the readings for this chapter) that writing is a "relationship." The first draft, she writes, is "a little like meeting someone for the first time. I come away with a wary acquaintanceship, but the real friendship (if any) and genuine intimacy—that's all down the road. Intimacy with a piece of writing, as with a person, comes from paying attention to the revelations it is capable of giving, not by imposing my own preconceived notions, no matter how well-intentioned they might be."

Notice that Hampl gives her early drafts the power of revealing themselves to her. By returning to a piece in process and "paying attention," we can approach it with an attitude of curiosity, with a desire for "revelation." This is a very different stance than one of imposing meaning on a narrative and it requires a delicate balance between writer and story. It is, however, an essential relationship that you will want to cultivate with your work. Stories grow out of an evolving process and that process ranges across raw feeling and memory, an observant eye, a shade of meaning here or there, a burst of vivid detail, then back to poking around patiently—getting it down, going back and forth—shaping, tinkering, and exploring the byways. And, we are never sure all this will lead us anywhere, at least not in the moment of writing. That is why stories also grow out of courage—the courage it takes to try out detours, reversing out of dead-ends until a story begins to take us where *it* wants *us* to go. Only then will we have a destination—one that is simultaneously new and familiar.

This respect for the story, this willingness to look to the story for guidance and to work cooperatively with it, requires that we try not to impose foregone conclusions on it. It is important to remember that the story is not the experience. If we want to hold onto our memories as they are, as Annie Dillard advises in "To Fashion a Text," then by all means avoid writing about them. After we've written about any experience, our original memories—those elusive, fragmentary patches of color and feeling—will be gone—replaced by the work. "The work is a sort of changeling on the doorstep—not your baby but someone else's baby rather like it, different in some way that you can't pinpoint," she warns, "and yours has vanished."

In other words, we know our story intimately, yet by the final draft it has become something else altogether. Perhaps it is time to send it out into the world acknowledging its new existence as *artifact*, bearing an interpretive life all its own.

Readings

Writers on Writing

"*Memory and Imagination*," Patricia Hampl

Memoir

"*Serviam*," Madeleine Blais

Literary Journalism

"*The Khan Men of Agra*," Pamela Michael

Short

"*The Deck*," Yusef Komunyakaa

Prose Poem

"*The Quality of Mercy*," Jane Brox

Memory and Imagination
Patricia Hampl

When I was seven, my father, who played the violin on Sundays with a nicely tortured flair which we considered artistic, led me by the hand down a long, unlit corridor in St. Luke's School basement, a sort of tunnel that ended in a room full of pianos. There, many little girls and a single sad boy were playing truly tortured scales and arpeggios in a mash of troubled sound. My father gave me over to Sister Olive Marie, who did look remarkably like an olive.

Her oily face gleamed as if it had just been rolled out of a can and laid on the white plate of her broad, spotless wimple. She was a small, plump woman; her body and the small window of her face seemed to interpret the entire alphabet of olive: Her face was a sallow green olive placed upon the jumbo ripe olive of her habit. I trusted her instantly and smiled, glad to have my hand placed in the hand of a woman who made sense, who provided the satisfaction of being what she was: an Olive who looked like an olive.

My father left me to discover the piano with Sister Olive Marie so that one day I would join him in mutually tortured piano-violin duets for the edification of my mother and brother who sat at the table spooning in the last of their pineapple sherbet until their part was called for: They put down their spoons and clapped while we bowed, while the sweet ice in their bowls melted, while the music melted, and we all melted a little into one another for a moment.

But first Sister Olive must do her work. I was shown middle C, which Sister seemed to think terribly important. I stared at middle C, and then glanced away for a second. When my eye returned, middle C was gone, its slim finger lost in the complicated grasp of the keyboard. Sister Olive struck it again, finding it with laughable ease. She emphasized the importance of middle C, its central position, a sort of North Star of sound. I remember thinking, Middle C is the belly button of the piano, an insight whose originality and accuracy stunned me with pride. For the first time in my life I was astonished by metaphor. I hesitated to tell the kindly Olive for some reason; apparently I understood a true metaphor is a risky business, revealing of the self. In fact, I have never, until this moment of writing it down, told my first metaphor to anyone.

Sunlight flooded the room; the pianos, all black, gleamed. Sister Olive, dressed in the colors of the keyboard, gleamed; middle C shimmered with meaning and I resolved never—never—to forget its location: It was the center of the world.

Then Sister Olive, who had had to show me middle C twice but who seemed to have drawn no bad conclusions about me anyway, got up and went to the windows on the opposite wall. She pulled the shades down, one after the other. The sun was too bright, she said. She sneezed as she stood at the windows with the sun shedding its glare over her. She sneezed and sneezed, crazy little convulsive sneezes, one after another, as helpless as if she had the hiccups.

"The sun makes me sneeze," she said when the fit was over and she was back at the piano. This was odd, too odd to grasp in the mind. I associated sneezing with colds, and colds with rain, fog, snow, and bad weather. The sun, however, had caused Sister Olive to sneeze in this wild way, Sister Olive who gleamed benignly and who was so certain of the location of the center of the world. The universe wobbled a bit and became unreliable. Things were not, after all, necessarily what they seemed. Appearance deceived: Here was the sun acting totally out of character, hurling this woman into sneezes, a woman so mild that she was named, so it seemed, for a bland object on a relish tray.

I was given a red book, the first Thompson book, and told to play the first piece over and over at one of the black pianos where the other children were crashing away. This, I was told, was called practicing. It sounded alluringly adult, practicing. The piece itself consisted mainly of middle C, and I excelled, thrilled by my savvy at being able to locate that central note amidst the cunning camouflage of all the other white keys before me. Thrilled too by the shiny red book that gleamed, as the pianos did, as Sister Olive did, as my eager eyes probably did. I sat at the formidable machine of the piano and got to know middle C intimately, preparing to be as tortured as I could manage one day soon with my father's violin at my side.

But at the moment Mary Katherine Reilly was at my side, playing something at least two or three lessons more sophisticated than my piece. I believe she even struck a chord. I glanced at her from the peasantry of single notes, shy, ready to pay homage. She turned toward me, stopped playing, and sized me up.

Sized me up and found a person ready to be dominated. Without introduction she said, "My grandfather invented the collapsible opera hat."

I nodded, I acquiesced, I was hers. With that little stroke it was decided between us—that she should be the leader and I the sidekick. My job was admiration. Even when she added, "But he didn't make a penny from it. He didn't have a patent"—even then, I knew and she knew that this was not an admission of powerlessness, but the easy candor of a master, of one who can afford a weakness or two. With the clairvoyance of all fated relationships based on dominance and submission, it was decided in advance: That when the time came for us to play duets, I should always play second piano, that I should spend my allowance to buy her the Twinkies she craved but was not allowed to have, that finally, I should let her copy from my test paper, and when confronted by our teacher, confess with convincing hysteria that it was I, I who had cheated, who had reached above myself to steal what clearly belonged to the rightful heir of the inventor of the collapsible opera hat. . . .

There must be a reason I remember that little story about my first piano lesson. In fact, it isn't a story, just a moment, the beginning of what could perhaps become a story. For the memoirist, more than for the fiction writer, the story seems already *there*, already accomplished and fully achieved in history ("in reality," as we naively say). For the memoirist, the writing of the story is a matter of transcription.

That, anyway, is the myth. But no memoirist writes for long without experiencing an unsettling disbelief about the reliability of memory, a hunch that memory is not, after all, *just* memory. I don't know why I remembered this fragment about my first piano lesson. I don't, for instance, have a single recollection of my first arithmetic lesson, the first time I studied Latin, the first time my grandmother tried to teach me to knit. Yet these things occurred too and must have their stories.

It is the piano lesson that has trudged forward, clearing the haze of forgetfulness, showing itself bright with detail decades after the event. I did not choose to remember the piano lesson. The experience was simply there, like a book that has always been on the shelf, whether I ever read it or not, the binding and title showing as I skim across the contents of my life. On the day I wrote this fragment I happened to take that memory, not some other, from the shelf and paged through it. I found more detail, more event, perhaps a little more entertainment than I had expected, but the memory itself was there from the start. Waiting for me.

Wasn't it? When I reread the piano lesson vignette just after I finished it, I realized that I had told a number of lies. I *think* it was my father who took me the first time for my piano lesson, but maybe he only took me to meet my teacher and there was no actual lesson that day. And did I even know then that he played the violin—didn't he take up his violin again much later as a result of my piano playing and not the reverse? And is it even remotely accurate to describe as "tortured" the musicianship of a man who began every day by belting out "Oh What a Beautiful Morning" as he shaved? More: Sister Olive Marie did sneeze in the sun, but was her name Olive? As for her skin tone—I would have sworn it was olivelike. I would have been willing to spend the better part of a morning trying to write the exact description of an imported Italian or Greek olive her face suggested: I wanted to get it right.

But now, were I to write that passage over, it is her intense black eyebrows I would see, for suddenly they seem the central fact of that face, some indicative mark of her serious and patient nature. But the truth is, I don't remember the woman at all. She's a sneeze in the sun and a finger touching middle C.

Worse: I didn't have the Thompson book as my piano text. I'm sure of that because I remember envying children who did have this wonderful book with its pictures of children and animals printed on the pages for music.

As for Mary Katherine Reilly. She didn't even go to grade school with me (and her name isn't Mary Katherine Reilly—but I made that change on purpose). I met her in Girl Scouts and only went to school with her later, in high school. Our relationship was not really one of leader and follower; I played first piano most of the time in duets. She certainly never copied anything from a test paper of mine: She was a better student, and cheating just wasn't a possibility for her. Though her grandfather (or someone in her family) did invent the collapsible opera hat and I remember that she was proud of this fact, she didn't tell me this news as a deft move in a childish power play.

So, what was I doing in this brief memoir? Is it simply an example of the curious relation a fiction writer has to the material of her own life? Maybe. But to tell the truth (if anyone still believes me capable of the truth), I wasn't writing fiction. I was writing memoir—or was trying to. My desire was to be accurate. I wished to embody the myth of memoir: to write as an act of dutiful transcription.

Yet clearly the work of writing a personal narrative caused me to do something very different from transcription. I am forced to admit that memory is not a warehouse of finished stories, not a gallery of framed pictures. I must admit that I invented. But why?

Two whys: Why did I invent and, then, if memory inevitably leads to invention, why do I—why should anybody—write memoir at all?

I must respond to these impertinent questions because they, like the bumper sticker I saw the other day commanding all who read it to QUESTION AUTHORITY, challenge my authority as a memoirist and as a witness.

It still comes as a shock to realize that I don't write about what I know, but in order to find out what I know. Is it possible to convey the enormous degree of blankness, confusion, hunch, and uncertainty lurking in the act of writing? When I am the reader, not the writer, I too fall into the lovely illusion that the words before me which read so inevitably, must also have been written exactly as they appear, rhythm and cadence, language and syntax, the powerful waves of the sentences laying themselves on the smooth beach of the page one after another faultlessly.

But here I sit before a yellow legal pad, and the long page of the preceding two paragraphs is a jumble of crossed-out lines, false starts, confused order. A mess. The mess of my mind trying to find out what it wants to say. This is a writer's frantic, grabby mind, not the poised mind of a reader waiting to be edified or entertained.

I think of the reader as a cat, endlessly fastidious, capable by turns of mordant indifference and riveted attention, luxurious, recumbent, ever poised. Whereas the writer is absolutely a dog, panting and moping, too eager for an affectionate scratch behind the ears, lunging frantically after any old stick thrown in the distance.

The blankness of a new page never fails to intrigue and terrify me. Sometimes, in fact, I think my habit of writing on long yellow sheets comes from an atavistic fear of the writer's stereotypic "blank white page." At least when I begin writing, my page has a wash of color on it, even if the absence of words must finally be faced on a yellow sheet as much as on a blank white one. We all have our ways of whistling in the dark.

If I approach writing from memory with the assumption that I know what I wish to say, I assume that intentionality is running the show. Things are not that simple. Or perhaps writing is even more profoundly simple, more telegraphic and immediate in its choices than the grating wheels and chugging engine of logic and rational intention suppose. The heart, the guardian of intuition with its secret, often fearful intentions, is the boss. Its commands are what a writer obeys—often without knowing it.

This is the beauty of the first draft. And why it's worth pausing a moment to consider what a first draft really is. By my lights, the piano lesson memoir is a first draft. That doesn't mean it exists here exactly as I first wrote it. I like to think I've cleaned it up from the first time I put it down on paper. I've cut some adjectives here, toned down the hyperbole there (though not enough), smoothed a transition, cut a repetition—that sort of housekeeperly tidying up.

But the piece remains a first draft because I haven't yet gotten to know it, haven't given it a chance to tell me anything. For me, writing a first draft is a little like meeting someone for the first time. I come away with a wary acquaintanceship, but the real friendship (if any) is down the road. Intimacy with a piece of writing, as with a person, comes from paying attention to the revelations it is capable of giving, not by imposing my own notions and agenda, no matter how well intentioned they might be.

I try to let pretty much anything happen in a first draft. A careful first draft is a failed first draft. That may be why there are so many inaccuracies in the piano lesson memoir: I didn't censor, I didn't judge. I just kept moving. But I would not publish this piece as a memoir on its own in its present state. It isn't the "lies" in the piece that give me pause, though a reader has a right to expect a memoir to be as accurate as the writer's memory can make it.

The real trouble: The piece hasn't yet found its subject; it isn't yet about what it wants to be about. Note: What *it* wants, not what I want. The difference has to do with the relation a memoirist—any writer—has to unconscious or half-known intentions and impulses in composition.

Now that I have the fragment down on paper, I can read this little piece as a mystery which drops clues to the riddle of my feelings, like a culprit who wishes to be apprehended. My narrative self (the culprit who invented) wishes to be discovered by my reflective self, the self who wants to understand and make sense of a half-remembered moment about a nun sneezing in the sun.

We store in memory only images of value. The value may be lost over the passage of time (I was baffled about why I remembered my sneezing nun), but that's the implacable judgment of feeling: *This*, we say somewhere within us, is something I'm hanging on to. And, of course, often we cleave to things because they possess heavy negative charges. Pain has strong arms.

Over time, the value (the feeling) and the stored memory (the image) may become estranged. Memoir seeks a permanent home for feeling and image, a habitation where they can live together. Naturally, I've had a lot of experiences since I packed away that one from the basement of St. Luke's School; that piano lesson has been effaced by waves of feeling for other moments and episodes. I persist in believing the event has value—after all, I remember it—but in writing the memoir I did not simply relive the experience. Rather, I explored the mysterious relationship between all the images I could round up and the even more impacted feelings that caused me to store the images safely away in memory. Stalking the relationship, seeking the congruence between stored image and hidden emotion—that's the real job of memoir.

By writing about that first piano lesson, I've come to know things I could not know otherwise. But I only know these things as a result of reading this first draft. While I was writing, I was following the images, letting the details fill the room of the page and use the furniture as they wished. I was their dutiful servant—or thought I was. In fact, I was the faithful retainer of my hidden feelings which were giving the commands.

I really did feel, for instance, that Mary Katherine Reilly was far superior to me. She was smarter, funnier, more wonderful in every way—that's how I saw it. Our friendship (or she herself) did not require that I become her vassal, yet perhaps in my heart that was something I sought. I wanted a way to express my admiration. I suppose I waited until this memoir to begin to find the way.

Just as, in the memoir, I finally possess that red Thompson book with the barking dogs and bleating lambs and winsome children. I couldn't (and still can't) remember what my own music book was, so I grabbed the name and image of the one book I could remember. It was only in reviewing the piece after writing it that I saw my inaccuracy. In pondering this "lie," I came to see what I was up to: I was getting what I wanted. Finally.

The truth of many circumstances and episodes in the past emerges for the memoirist through details (the red music book, the fascination with a nun's name and gleaming face), but these details are not merely information, not flat facts. Such details are not allowed to lounge. They must work. Their labor is the creation of symbol. But it's more accurate to call it the *recognition* of symbol. For meaning is not "attached" to the detail by the memoirist; meaning is revealed. That's why a first draft is important. Just as the first meeting (good or bad) with someone who later becomes the beloved is important and is often reviewed for signals, meanings, omens, and indications.

Now I can look at that music book and see it not only as "a detail" but for what it is, how it acts. See it as the small red door leading straight into the dark room of my childhood longing and disappointment. That red book *becomes* the palpable evidence of that longing. In other words, it becomes symbol. There is no symbol, no life-of-the-spirit in the general or the abstract. Yet a writer wishes—certainly we all wish—to speak about profound matters that are, like it or not, general and abstract. We wish to talk to each other about life and death, about love, despair, loss, and innocence. We sense that in order to live together we must learn to speak of peace, of history, of meaning and values. The big words.

We seek a means of exchange, a language which will renew these ancient concerns and make them wholly, pulsingly ours. Instinctively, we go to our store of private associations for our authority to speak of these weighty issues. We find, in our details and broken, obscured images, the language of symbol. Here memory impulsively reaches out and embraces imagination. That is the resort to invention. It isn't a lie, but an act of necessity, as the innate urge to locate truth always is.

All right. Invention is inevitable. But why write memoir? Why not call it fiction and be done with it? And if memoir seeks to talk about "the big issues," of history and peace, death and love—why not leave these reflections to those with expert or scholarly knowledge? Why let the common or garden variety memoirist into the club? I'm thinking again of that bumper sticker: Question Authority. Why?

My answer, naturally, is a memoirist's answer. Memoir must be written because each of us must possess a created version of the past. Created: that is, real in the sense of tangible, made of the stuff of a life lived in place and in history. And the downside of any created thing as well: We must live with a version that attaches us to our limitations, to the inevitable subjectivity of our points of view. We must acquiesce to our experience and our gift to transform experience into meaning. You tell me your story, I'll tell you mine.

If we refuse to do the work of creating this personal version of the past, someone else will do it for us. That is the scary political fact. "The struggle of man against power," Milan Kundera's hero in *The Book of Laughter and Forgetting* says, "is the struggle of memory against forgetting." He refers to willful political forgetting, the habit of nations and those in power (Question Authority!) to deny the truth of memory in order to disarm moral and ethical power.

It is an efficient way of controlling masses of people. It doesn't even require much bloodshed, as long as people are entirely willing to give over their personal memories. Whole histories can be rewritten. The books which now seek to deny the existence of the Nazi death camps now fill a room.

What is remembered is what becomes reality. If we "forget" Auschwitz, if we "forget" My Lai, what then do we remember? And what is the purpose of our remembering? If we think of memory naively, as a simple story, logged like a documentary in the archive of the mind, we miss its beauty but also its function.

The beauty of memory rests in its talent for rendering detail, for paying homage to the senses, its capacity to love the particles of life, the richness and idiosyncrasy of our existence. The function of memory, while experienced as intensely personal, is surprisingly political.

Our capacity to move forward as developing beings rests on a healthy relation with the past. Psychotherapy, that widespread method for promoting mental health, relies heavily on memory and on the ability to retrieve and organize images and events from the personal past. We carry our wounds and perhaps even worse, our capacity to wound, forward with us. If we learn not only to tell our stories but to listen to what our stories tell us—to write the first draft and then return for the second draft—we are doing the work of memory.

Memoir is the intersection of narration and reflection, of storytelling and essay writing. It can present its story *and* consider the meaning of the story. The first commandment of fiction—Show, Don't Tell—is not part of the memoirist's faith. Memoirists must show *and* tell. Memoir is a peculiarly open form, inviting broken and incomplete images, half-recollected fragments, all the mass (and mess) of detail. It offers to shape this confusion—and, in shaping, of course, it necessarily creates a work of art, not a legal document. But then, even legal documents are only valiant attempts to consign the truth, the whole truth, and nothing but the truth to paper. Even they remain versions.

Locating touchstones—the red music book, the olive Olive, my father's violin playing—is satisfying. Who knows why? Perhaps we all sense that we can't grasp the whole truth and nothing but the truth of our experience. Just can't be done.

What can be achieved, however, is a version of its swirling, changing whole-ness. A memoirist must acquiesce to selectivity, like any artist. The version we dare to write is the only truth, the only relationship we can have with the past. Refuse to write your life and you have no life. That is the stern view of the memoirist.

Personal history, logged in memory, is a sort of slide projector flashing im-ages on the wall of the mind. And there's precious little order to the slides in the rotating carousel. Beyond that confusion, who knows who is running the projec-tor? A memoirist steps into this darkened room of flashing, unorganized images and stands blinking for a while. Maybe for a long while. But eventually, as with any attempt to tell a story, it is necessary to put something first, then something else. And so on, to the end. That's a first draft. Not necessarily the truth, not even *a* truth sometimes, but the first attempt to create a shape.

The first thing I usually notice at this stage of composition is the appalling inaccuracy of the piece. Witness my first piano lesson draft. Invention is scream-ingly evident in what I intended to be transcription. But here's the further truth: I feel no shame. In fact, it's only now that my interest in the piece quickens. For I can see what isn't there, what is shyly hugging the walls, hoping not to be seen. I see the filmy shape of the next draft. I see a more acute version of the episode or—this is more likely—an entirely new piece rising from the ashes of the first attempt.

The next draft of the piece would have to be true re-vision, a new seeing of the materials of the first draft. Nothing merely cosmetic will do—no rouge buff-ing up the opening sentence, no glossy adjective to lift a sagging line, nothing to attempt covering a patch of gray writing.

I can't say for sure, but my hunch is the revision would lead me to more writing about my father (Why was I so impressed by that ancestral inventor of the collapsible opera hat? Did I feel I had nothing as remarkable in my own background?). I begin to think perhaps Sister Olive is less central to this busi-ness than she appears to be. She is meant to be a moment, not a character. I'm probably wasting my time on her, writing and writing around her in tight de-scriptive circles, waiting for the real subject to reveal itself. My father!

So I might proceed, if I were to undertake a new draft of the memoir. I be-gin to feel a relationship developing between a former self and me.

And even more important, a relationship between an old world and me. Some people think of autobiographical writing as the precious occupation of the unusually self-absorbed. Couldn't the same accusation be hurled at a lyric poet, at a novelist—at anyone with the audacity to present a personal point of view? True memoir is written, like all literature, in an attempt to find not only a self but a world.

The self-absorption that seems to be the impetus and embarrassment of au-tobiography turns into (or perhaps always was) a hunger for the world. Actually, it begins as hunger for *a* world, one gone or lost, effaced by time or a more sud-den brutality. But in the act of remembering, the personal environment expands, resonates beyond itself, beyond its "subject," into the endless and tragic recol-lection that is history. We look at old family photographs in which we stand next to black, boxy Fords, and are wearing period costumes, and we do not gaze fascinated because there we are young again, or there we are standing, as we never will again in life, next to our mother. We stare and drift because there we are historical. It is the dress, the black car that dazzle us now and draw us beyond our mother's bright arms which once caught us. We reach into the attractive impersonality of something more significant than ourselves. We write memoir, in other words. We accept the humble position of writing a version, the consolation prize for our acknowledgment we cannot win "the whole truth and nothing but."

I suppose I write memoir because of the radiance of the past—it draws me back and back to it. Not that the past is beautiful. In our communal memoir, in history, the darkness we sense is not only the dark of forgetfulness. The darkness is history's tunnel of horrors with its tableaux vivants of devastation. The blasted villages, the hunted innocents, the casual acquiescence to the death camps and tiger cages are back there in the fetid holes of history.

But still, the past is radiant. It sheds the light of lived life. One who writes memoir wishes to step into that light, not to see one's own face—that is not possible—but to feel the length of shadow cast by the light. No one owns the past, though typically the first act of new political regimes, whether of the left or the right, is an attempt to rewrite history, to grab the past and make it over so the end comes out right. So their power looks inevitable.

No one owns the past, but it is a grave error (another age would have said a grave sin) not to inhabit memory. Sometimes I think it is all we really have. But that may be melodrama, the bad habit of the memoirist, coming out. At any rate, memory possesses authority for the fearful self in a world where it is necessary to claim authority in order to Question Authority.

There may be no more pressing intellectual need in our culture than for people to become sophisticated about the function of memory. The political implications of the loss of memory are obvious. The authority of memory is a personal confirmation of selfhood, and therefore the first step toward ethical development. To write one's life is to live it twice, and the second living is both spiritual and historical, for a memoir reaches deep within the personality as it seeks its narrative form and it also grasps the life-of-the-times as no political analysis can.

Our most ancient metaphor says life is a journey. Memoir is travel writing, then, notes taken along the way, telling how things looked and what thoughts occurred. Show *and* tell. But I cannot think of the memoirist as a tourist. The memoir is no guide book. This traveler lives the journey idiosyncratically, taking on mountains, enduring deserts, marveling at the lush green places. Moving through it all faithfully, not so much a survivor with a harrowing tale to tell as that older sort of traveler, the pilgrim, seeking, wondering.

Serviam

Madeleine Blais

*W*e were, in a way, saved by the nuns.

My mother had driven me to Ursuline for Mission Day, a chaste little carnival that had in my opinion only two advantages: classes were canceled, and we could wear normal civilian clothes. Throughout the day a girl in a white dress, wearing a crown, circulated the gym, dispensing robotic hellos. She was our Mission Day Queen, elected solely on the basis of her goodness, which meant she had, during private consultations about her spiritual future, let it be known that a religious vocation was not entirely out of the question and, also, that her favorite color was blue, the same as the Blessed Mother's. A car was raffled. Elaborate exhibits showed foreign children in uniforms studying at Catholic schools supported by events like our fair. There would be scads of offspring, barefoot and brown, standing in front of smiling parents with downcast eyes. The parents were forever being quoted as saying that as long as you had faith, food didn't matter. You could purchase pictures of saints and pricey rosaries and little pins with the school motto, which was the same as that of the Jesuit school attended by Stephen Dedalus in *A Portrait of the Artist as a Young Man,* "Serviam," Latin for "I shall serve."

Mother Francis and our mother discussed literature that day. Not much later, a phone call came.

Ursuline was expanding; lay teachers were needed to complete the staff, especially at the coed elementary school level. My mother's salary of $270 a month would be sweetened with free tuition for all four girls. At the time, the starting salary for stewardesses at United Air Lines was $325 per month with the potential of a $90 monthly bonus. This would solve my commuting problem: she would be our chauffeur. And now all the Blais girls were guaranteed that Ursuline gloss.

On the surface the biggest differences between Ursuline and public school were the absence of boys and the uniforms: those ugly gray blazers, box-pleated green gabardine skirts, loafers, and nylons. But more than that, the nuns had a way of micromanaging our social interactions, ensuring that even the sorriest girls had some kind of circle. Someone who in a different school would have been ripe for hazing, given her assorted social handicaps—such as never shaving her legs, never closing her mouth, or possessing a retarded aunt—even she had friends. The nuns made a point of informing us that the more humble and penitential our behavior in this life, the more days we could lop off purgatory in the next through a complicated system of plenary and supplementary indulgences. Their main disciplinary strategy was to treat misdemeanors as if they were felonies. You earned demerits if your nylons sagged or had runs: a messy outer life announced an equally sloppy inner one. In between classes we walked in silence in single file. Lunch consisted of a bleak sandwich composed of a lonely piece of see-through meat. Most of us were so hungry we kept secret bags of chips and candy in our blazer pockets, which we learned to extract piece by piece during class and consume noiselessly without ever being caught.

One time, some girls got suspended for playing Spin the Bible with some elementary school boys on the bus. Their faces were stricken and frightened when they were summoned one by one from their classrooms to explain themselves to the principal.

Encouraging kissing games was bad.

Using the Bible for twisted purposes was worse.

The combination of the two?

Unspeakable.

At each report card, the students who were well behaved got a blue ribbon to wear on the sleeve of their blazers. Girls who were good, and bright to boot, got blue and gold ribbons, and once in a while a brilliant sinner merely got the gold, a cold secular trophy revealing a weak nature and an underdeveloped conscience. Our grades were arrived at with pinpoint precision: Math 86.7%. When I flunked a major chemistry final during my senior year, the grade was written on my report card in red ink: "67%." I asked Jacqueline, "Do you think Mom will be mad?"

"Try her," said Jacqueline.

She wasn't mad at all. "Don't worry about it. You won't need science. I never did."

At Ursuline, we were, most of us, the children and grandchildren of immigrants. The Cuban girls were the only genuine newcomers. They showed up overnight, mysteriously, shortly after the Bay of Pigs, their only baggage their colorful pasts, musical accents, and pierced ears. The principal, the daughter of a Bronx cop, used to brag, "This is a dictatorship, not a democracy," which must have been especially disappointing to them. When we prayed, we listed our intentions, and after Conchita and Mercedes arrived, we added our hope that someday they would get good enough in English to dream in it.

Our last names were Marinello and Giamalvo, Cosgriff and Glynn, and Conway and McCarthy. Although in 1960 a Catholic was elected president, we still imagined we were living on America's margins, fearful of quotas and closed doors.

It was also a tricky business, back then, the education of girls. No one worried about our sabotaging ourselves with bouts of low self-esteem; society had ensured that that would be redundant. We knew our education had a hot-house ornamental quality. After disappearing into our grown-up fates, all that Latin and all that business with Bunsen burners would be useless. We were to marry: Jesus, a man, or Service to Others in the form of spinsterish devotion to jobs at, say, the soul-eroding Registry of Motor Vehicles or in mournful classrooms filled with interchangeable unruly pupils year after year. If we didn't watch out, our intellects would be like all those Christmas trees on curbsides in January, denuded, discarded, and the impulse to duty and good deeds would be all we had left. We prayed in Latin, English, and French. Amen with a toga, amen with a baseball cap, amen with a beret.

Very few of our mothers worked outside the house. The fathers had Chevrolet dealerships or they practiced medicine or they did legal work for the diocese. Tiny, freckled, with a high, happy voice, a girl named Connie Breck, about whom everyone said *She has good hair, thank God*, was our only celebrity. Her father was a shampoo and hair conditioner magnate. This was the golden era of the famed Breck ads, with their idealized girls with gleaming hair and glowing complexions, fixtures in every reputable magazine with a female clientele. "Who is the girl in the Breck portrait?" the ad would ask itself. "She's a teenager in Tucson, a homemaker in Fargo, a career girl in New York. She's like you in many ways. Loves the things you love . . . home, family, children. Most of all she loves to be loved."

It really said that: *Most of all she loves to be loved.*

We asked Connie how it was that each Breck girl possessed the exact same degree of prettiness as the next. At first she wouldn't tell us, holding us at bay until finally, clearly against her better instincts, she relented and whispered, in strictest confidence, of course, what we took to be a well-guarded company secret: "It's all in the lighting."

The nuns gave us lessons in graciousness. Now that a Catholic president was in the White House, our horizons as young women had suddenly expanded. They saw us all as future Jacqueline Kennedys, an amazing leap when you consider that we all had Frito breath. But still they persisted in seeing us in the most hopeful light, the way the Irish describe vicious downpours as nothing more than an overactive mist. Maybe we too would marry a world leader, in which case we had to know where to stand in a reception line, how to curtsey before a monarch, and what to say during conversations with men of substance at a state dinner. "What would you do," we were asked, "if by chance you were seated next to a nuclear physicist? What would you say to him?"

Our blank faces must have been frustrating.

The nuns provided the answer. "Talk to him about himself and his work, of course. Find out where he's from. Ask: What's nuclear? What's physics?"

"Girls, here's something to ponder," said the priest who was leading our weekend retreat. "What age would you be if you could be any age at all?"

We were all fifteen. Our answers did not vary much. Sixteen, seventeen, maybe twenty-one.

"Does anyone want to be younger?"

No one did.

"An infant, perhaps?"

Again, no takers.

His face lit up: bull's-eye. "No one would ever choose to go back to being a baby, yet that is exactly what Jesus Christ our Lord and Saviour was willing to do when He came down to earth in order to die for our sins. That's just one more example of the kind of sacrifice He made so willingly, and look at you, not one of you willing to be even one day younger. How many of you have heard the song that goes, 'To know, know, know him is to love, love, love him'?"

We all knew and liked the song, by a group called the Teddy Bears.

We all guessed, correctly, that he was about to ruin it.

"What does it mean? Does it mean that the more you get to know a boy, the more you like him?"

We exchanged glances: this guy was a real genius.

He moved in for the kill. "The same is true for our Lord, you know.

"Some of you, I know, are wondering about the ways in which you can honor the Lord. Every day, He gives us the opportunity to honor Him in large ways and in small ones. Let's look at one of the small ones: lipstick. Many of your parents have asked that you wait until you are older before you start wearing lipstick. Why? Because you are vessels of the Lord, you are His handmaidens, and the wearing of excess color can be an invitation to lust. A modest amount can be an enhancement in a much older woman, but you girls are still very young and surely nature at this stage requires no enhancement. It will ergo be considered a violation of your uniform if you paint your face in an excessive manner. We must constantly remind ourselves that we have been conceived in original sin, and we are born into a state of darkness, from which the Lord in His infinite mercy has seen fit to rescue us through the Blessed Sacraments of Baptism and Holy Communion. For these blessings we must offer constant thanks and daily witness, through prayer and in our actions. Our lives must be conducted in a meritorious fashion so that eventually we can enter the Heavenly Kingdom ruled by the almighty risen Lord and we can achieve the highest goal of mankind: we can bask in the Beatific Vision, the dazzling light of His goodness.

"The eating of meat on Friday.

"The missing of church on Sunday or on Holy Days of obligation.

"The failure to perform one's Easter duty.

"The tragedy of marrying outside the faith.

"These are the large transgressions with which we are all familiar. But sometimes I fear that in our enthusiasm to avoid these sins we relax our vigilance against Satan's less dramatic beckonings, the small moments that are also sinful but perhaps not as public in their depravity. I am talking about some of the thoughts that might occur to you as you bathe. I am referring to the sin of self-pollution. I am referring to the all too popular custom of close dancing, to driving around in cars sitting on the laps of boys, to the lure of liquor in all its cheap perdition. Convertible automobiles, racing toward pleasure: a prime example of the insidious nature of Temptation, arriving as it does in the finest of outward apparel, masking its rotten core. The serpent did not appear in a swamp; he came to Adam and Eve in a garden. Let us now pray to our Blessed Mother for divine guidance to recognize Satan in all his guises, great and small. Mother, most holy, tower of strength."

Every first Friday of the month as well as on Holy Days of obligation, we celebrated the mass. Because the altar boys were at their own schools celebrating their own masses, we females were allowed as an assembly to give the response to the priest, and to this day when some middle-aged man is discovered to be an altar boy of that vintage, I will challenge him to see who can remember the most liturgical responses, a contest I sometimes win, my one shiny nickel, the verbal equivalent of a three-point shot.

Once and only once, as I recall, a priest was brought in to hear everyone's confession: I've wondered since then if he didn't have a secret task of ferreting out a rumored pregnancy.

We filed into the makeshift confessional, reciting the boilerplate offenses for girls our age:

Bless us, Father, oh how we have sinned: We listened to the radio after lights out, we snuck a cigarette from our mother's purse, we sipped some beer at Polly's New Year's Eve party, we stopped at Friendly's when we said we were coming straight home. And then pausing, our voices becoming softer and more serious: we touched ourselves, we allowed ourselves to be touched. More details: the edge of someone's underpants had been stroked by a boy on the dock outside Doreen's beachhouse in Old Lyme one summer night, a bra had been loosened from its mooring after dark in some boy's car. The vision of all of us in our turn confiding to a dark, shapeless creature, dressed in robes, seated inside a box, has a lingering air of the absurd and frightening and the kinky: Samuel Beckett meets the Inquisition meets *Penthouse* magazine.

For people who had taken a vow of chastity, the nuns certainly enjoyed talking about sex a lot, only they called it fancy names like "concupiscence" and "the marital debt." Out-of-wedlock babies were a major obsession, and the nuns all had well-thumbed pamphlets, supposedly actually authored by a fetus before it died in an abortion. They would reach inside the billowing black folds of their habits, extract the pamphlet, and read details about each of the fetus's developmental triumphs, such as its first little kick or faint heartbeat, leading up to Month Three and the startling revelation "Today my mother killed me."

The nuns believed in something called moral hygiene, a loophole that meant that even if you were inclined toward wrongdoing, you could cleanse your soul with really good deeds. Every now and then we got to go on class trips, but it wasn't like at the public school, where the kids took big yellow buses to Mountain Park or Riverside and got to ride on the Cyclone all day and gorge on cotton candy. We drove around in kids' mothers' station wagons, and our excursions were designed to result in a corporal or spiritual work of mercy. And we didn't sing fun songs like "99 Bottles of Beer on the Wall," either. We sang songs like:

An army of youth
Flying the banner of truth
We're fighting for Christ the Lord
Heads lifted high
Catholic action our cry
And the cross our only sword

One time we brought brownies and root beer to an orphanage, where a little boy who kept scratching his head tried to sell me a slingshot. Another time we gave homemade sock puppets to some people at a hospital who drooled and made noises you couldn't understand, but which the nuns said meant thank you. Then it was off to a home for veterans. During "Jingle Bells," an old man reached into his pants and started singing along, the same words but totally off key. Later, he asked one of the prettiest girls if she liked sarsaparilla, which he said would put hair on your chest, and then collapsed into a smoker's hacking laughter at the word "chest." On the way back it was decided that we made a mistake when we sang secular songs about reindeer and white Christmases and we should have stuck with the holy ones with their calming emphasis on sleeping infants. The orphans and the sock puppet recipients and the old soldiers were united by one redeeming characteristic: they were all Catholic.

One nun stood out as possessing a gypsy streak, our mother's benefactor, the French teacher, Mother Francis Regis, or Franny, as we called her behind her back. Franny was by far the most temperamental and, as a result, the most invigorating of our teachers. Her favorite dictum was, *"Pensez-y and profitez-en."* Think about it and profit from it. She was Miss Universe for *le mot juste*. She had those frequent displays of impatience that often characterize teachers of foreign languages, and her way of showing it was to recruit some sorry specimen to stand in front of the room and be the object lesson for the words that embodied our failings:

Mademoiselle is messy.

Mademoiselle has holes in her clothes.

Mademoiselle has scuffs on her shoes.

Franny reserved the worse circle of hell for mumblers. "How can it be," she would rail at some girl whose natural-born shyness caused her chin to be devoured by her neck, "that despite all my best efforts I have failed so totally to turn you into an exhibitionist!"

Franny was also the drama coach, a title she welcomed because it gave her the chance to travel from Stockbridge to Boston, to cut loose and indulge certain flesh-driven cravings. It was well known that she never refused an offer to stop along the pike at Howard Johnson's for the all-you-can-eat fried clam special.

When she wasn't goading us to do better, she would invite us into her special club involving male-female intrigue. She was the driving force behind our tea dances, awkward daylight events in which the partners were often students' brothers and cousins, with the exception of the occasional paper boy innocently delivering the *Union*, only to be collared by a large nun and ordered onto the dance floor. While inside the school we were shuffling our feet to the music, Franny would be standing at the door, scanning the horizon for more male recruits. These dances were always held in the winter, and she would pretend to be drawn to a snowfall. "Ah," she would say, quoting, I believe, James Joyce, "the filigree petals, falling so purely, so fragilely surely," clasping her rosary against her bosom, secretly praying, "Dear St. Ann, send a man."

Although not in the world in the least, she was clearly drawn to it. She told a story that was both confused and sorrowful about how as part of her religious training she was cloistered for a year in the early 1940s, cut off from all communication. During the war, while transferring from one convent to another by train, she entered a car filled with soldiers close to her in age.

"Pray for us, sister," they said.

"Of course I'll pray for you. Is there any special reason?"

"You know the reason, sister. We're going to war."

She gazed at them and did not dare ask, "What war? With whom?"

She hid *Life* magazines under her mattress because in the convent they amounted to contraband, filled with shocking information about parties and the Pill and movie stars of dubious virtue. She would sneak them into class, drawing them forth from the folds of her habit, and whisper, "Look here, girls."

"Brigitte Bardot," she would tell us, "is a famous French actress. Let's hear you say it right."

Bridge Eat Bar Dough, we would reply.

"What's the terrible thing that happened to Clark Gable shortly after he filmed *The Misfits* with Marilyn Monroe?"

"He died of a heart attack."

"*En français, s'il vous plait.*"

"*Monsieur Gable est mort d'une attaque du coeur.*"

"What kind of woman is Marilyn Monroe? *En français, s'il vous plait.*"

"*Une femme fatale.*"

We followed Franny, those of us who also wanted to break loose, to various contests in which we intoned passages from *The Hunchback of Notre Dame* ("Sanctuary, sanctuary") and invoked the oratory that preceded the death by hanging of Irish Freedom Fighters, as well as reciting the more maudlin poetry of William Butler Yeats, including "The Ballad of Moll Magee." This doomed soul, Moll Magee, had the horrible misfortune of lying on top of her infant baby and suffocating him after a long day of work at the salting shed.

So now, ye little children,
Ye won't fling stones at me;
But gather with your shinin' looks
and pity Moll Magee.

Franny was the coach when I entered the Voice of Democracy speech contest and helped me write a tribute to Herbert Hoover, that often overlooked statesman, who as a child helped support his widowed mother with a paper route, working his way slowly but surely to the top, becoming president of the United States, then through his actions helping to create a depression, thus affording millions of other youngsters the chance to follow his lead and raise themselves up by their bootstraps.

The dramatic selections for the girls of Ursuline were always safe, laudable, and above all clean. Other students from other schools performed the more daring works of Edward Albee and Tennessee Williams, who would have been considered too modern and transitory and crass for us to study formally. Albee's Everyman on the bench in *The Zoo Story*, who felt that sometimes you had to go a long way out of your way to come back a short way correctly, and Williams's flighty character in *A Streetcar Named Desire*, Blanche Dubois, the one who depended on the kindness of strangers. Who needs their shabby posturing? There was something suspect about them. If you saw them walking toward you, you'd think: Iffy, iffy.

To the Blais family, the Kennedy White House was proof that we had arrived. If, as it so often seemed in our world, the highest status accrued to families with a priest in their ranks, because then you had your own special pipeline to the divine, having an Irish Catholic in the White House had the same feeling of privilege and intimacy. The whole nation had been shrunk to something smaller and more manageable, to parish. One of ours was at the helm.

We followed the entire presidency, of course, but we were most enamored of Jacqueline Kennedy's televised tour of the White House. She had grace and class; what's more, she wasn't afraid to express her opinions, telling the audience: "When General Grant became President Grant, he put false, elaborate timbers across the ceiling and furnished the room in a style crossing ancient Greece with what someone called 'Mississippi River Boat.'" In that famously breathy voice she praised Gilbert Stuart's portrait of Washington but also complained, "So many pictures of later presidents are by really inferior artists. . . . I just think everything in the White House should be the best." Of course, we concurred.

At home, we played a game based on the Kennedy women. Our mother wanted to know which one she most closely resembled.

We were honest.

"Not Joan," we said. Too young and too fluffy.

She seemed to agree.

"Not Ethel, either." Ethel was too toothy and too tennis, anyone?

Again, no argument.

We paused when we came to President Kennedy's wife.

Maureen Shea Blais looked up, hope flashing.

We knew we would hurt our mother's feelings, but we all need to face facts. "Not Jackie, either." No, not Jackie with her perfect hair, perfect pearls, and perfect life.

There was one right answer: "Rose," we said with a flourish, yes, yes, yes, Rose, with her hats and her head held high, her daily mass and her constant campaign teas for her baby, Ted.

The static-swaddled crackle of the voice of the principal came over the intercom: Mother Mary Austin, announcing the news that the president had been shot.

"There has been terrible news about President Kennedy. The president has been shot."

Stunned, silent, without being told, we knew we should fall to our knees onto the hard linoleum, a torture we gladly endured because after all Christ had allowed Himself to be crucified for our sins and you had to ask yourself, which was worse, and we began to pray for his recovery. The prayers of course did no good: Kennedy died soon after we heard he had been shot, but still we remained kneeling, shifting gears, praying now for the repose of his soul, as if there could be any doubt that someone as handsome as he was, from our own home state no less, a devoted father and family man, a believer in the one true holy apostolic faith, would have any trouble whatsoever getting into heaven. "Think about it," said one of my classmates, like all of us a sudden expert on the subject of eternal salvation. "If anyone deserves to bask in the Beatific Vision, surely it is President Kennedy. We are talking State of Grace to the nth degree."

At home, we spent the weekend watching scenes of the first lady climbing on top of the car, ruining her suit with blood, wearing, if truth be told, that unflattering little hat. Later, we witnessed the commotion at the jail when Oswald suddenly slumped over and Jack Ruby was arrested for his murder. We watched the funeral cortege—a new big word—with the riderless horse clomping down some big wide street in Washington. The horror and the spectacle were a leavening force, humbling evidence that everyone could have it tough, even the high and mighty.

Clichés are the most self-respecting of phrases; you don't get to become one unless you embody an extreme and unassailable truth. The more I thought about the randomness at the heart of human existence and the more I contemplated the bullet that killed Kennedy, shot from the textbook depository, the more anxious I became. I said three Hail Marys to myself at the drop of a hat, and I made the sign of the cross all the time, unremarked, in the palm of my hand. I knew a girl at Ursuline who liked to invent forms of penance. She put rice on the stairs and walked up them on her knees; at school she would offer to sharpen everyone's pencils. I thought if I wanted to enter a similar black hole of pain and frustration, I could always try to match all the socks in our house.

In Franny's class, for weeks on end, the formal study of French was suspended. Instead, she read the accounts of the funeral out loud:

The terrible ordeal of Mrs. Jacqueline Kennedy reached its final phase today.

The widow of the dead President, still bearing up proudly three days after her husband's murder, chose to walk instead of ride behind the caisson bearing her husband's body to the funeral mass.

Before that, the 34-year-old Mrs. Kennedy, who marked her 10th wedding anniversary in September, made her third sorrowful trip to the Capitol in less than 20 hours this morning. This time it was to accompany the body to St. Matthew's Cathedral for a low Pontifical Mass.

Mrs. Kennedy left the White House shortly before 10:30 a.m. EST, to go to the Capitol. There she stood on the steps as the flag-draped casket was slowly brought from the Rotunda and placed on the horse-drawn caisson. A dirge sounded in the background.

She visited the casket in the Rotunda three times and kissed it twice.

"Girls," said Franny, smuggling forth yet one more piece of paper from her capacious sleeve, "I have here a quote from the *London Evening Standard* that says it all: 'Jacqueline Kennedy has given the American people from this day on the one thing they have always lacked—majesty.' Repeat after me."

And we did, our voices lingering on the word "majesty" as if it were a crown in and of itself.

My sisters and I did what insecure people so often do in the face of overwhelming external events that have no clear link to their lives: we found a connection. As fatherless children, John-John and Caroline were now, on some level, like us, a blood brother and a blood sister. Our feelings were mixed. While it was heady to be considered in their category, it also made us less singular. They would know, as we did, death's great contradiction: the profound presence of those who are forever absent.

The Khan Men of Agra
Pamela Michael

One good thing about monsoons: they sure keep the dust down, I thought to myself, peering out the milky window of the Taj Express. I surveyed the approaching station from my uncertain perch between two lurching cars, ready to grab my bag and disembark purposefully. Despite the early hour, the platform slowly scrolling past me was packed with people.

Of the dozen or so bony hands struggling to wrench my suitcase from my grip as I stepped off the train at Agra, perhaps two were porters, four or five were rickshaw drivers, three or four were taxi drivers, and maybe a couple were thieves. The sudden rush of mostly barefoot men in states of undress ranging from rags to britches brought me face to face with the difficulty of "reading" a person's demeanor or intentions in an unfamiliar culture. What to do?

I already knew from my few days in New Delhi that I would have to choose one of these men—not because I didn't want to carry my own bag, but because I would be hounded mercilessly until I paid someone to do it for me. It's a defensive necessity, and an effective hedge for women traveling alone who must rely on their own wits and the unreliable kindness of strangers—the taxi-*wallah* as protector and guide. In Delhi, though, the competitive tourist market is based more on ingenuity and charm than intimidation. Many of the drivers had developed very engaging come-ons, my favorite being the rickshaw driver who purred, "And which part of the world is suffering in your absence, Madam?"

My reluctance to hire anyone apparently was being interpreted as a bargaining ploy. Several men had begun to yell at each other and gesture toward me, ired by the low rates to which their competitors were sinking for the privilege of snagging a greenhorn tourist fresh off the train. Not wanting to see the end result of such a bidding war, I handed over my bag to the oldest, most decrepit-looking of the bunch, deciding I might be able to outrun (or overtake?) him if I had to and also because he had an engaging (if toothless) smile.

Triumphant, he hoisted my bag on top of his turban and beckoned me to follow as he set out across the tracks. For the first few minutes the old man had to fend off a persistent few rival drivers who thought they could convince me to change my mind by casting aspersions on the character, safety record, and vehicle of the man I had chosen, whose name, he told me, was Khan, Kallu Khan.

Halfway through the station, in a particularly crowded spot, Kallu handed my bag to another (much younger and, I theorized, more fleet-footed) man.

"Hey, wait a minute!" I protested.

"My cousin Iki," Kallu assured me.

"So, what's he doing with my bag?" I asked.

"Helper," I was told.

I went into red alert and quickened my pace to keep up with Iki and my luggage. As we reached the street it began to rain again, part of the deluge/blue sky monsoon cycle to which I had become accustomed. Over my objections, Iki put my bag in the trunk of their car, a battered Hindustan Ambassador that was unmarked except by mind, no reassuring "Agra Taxi Company" emblazoned on the door.

"Thief might steal suitcase in backseat, Madam," Kallu explained. I acquiesced—the dry shelter of the "taxi" looked inviting and I was worn down by the ceaseless demands on my ability to communicate, decipher, make decisions, find, respond, protect, etc., that travel entails, even in a four-star situation, which the Agra train station was decidedly not.

Once under way, my relief at having escaped the crowd and rain was somewhat dampened by my realization that I was on a rather deserted road with two men who were probably making the same kind of un- and misinformed assumptions about me that I was making about them. I peered out the rain-streaked window to my right to get my bearings and to take in some of the sights I had come to India to see. I was also tentatively toying with escape options. All I could see was a blur of red, towering overhead and as far into the distance as I could make out. The Red Fort, of course, I had done my homework, so I knew the walls were seventy feet high, surrounded by a moat. On my left was a long stretch of sparse forest, separated from the roadway by a crumbling low iron fence.

Suddenly, Iki pulled the car over on the left and stopped alongside a broken place in the fence. Kallu got out of the passenger side and opened my door, saying, "Now I show you something no tourist ever see, Madam."

"That's all right," I said, "let's just get to the hotel. Tomorrow is better," I demurred.

"Please, Madam," he insisted, and, sensing my concern about my suitcase, he added, "Don't worry, Iki stay here with your bag."

I was already chastising myself for being so naive and trying to decide how much real danger I was in when I looked—really looked—into Kallu's eyes for the first time. They were kind; kind and bloodshot, but kind. In an instant I made the sort of decision that every traveler has to make from time to time: you decide to take a risk, trust a stranger, enter a cave, explore a trail, act on intuition, and experience something new. It is this giving oneself over to a strange culture or environment that often reaps the most reward, that makes travel so worthwhile and exhilarating.

As if to affirm my decision, the rain stopped. "OK, Mr. Khan, you show me," I said. We walked down a muddy path through a stand of stilted trees, leaving Iki behind, smoking a *bidi*. My courage faltered a couple of times, when I caught a glimpse of a spectral, loinclothed man through the leaves, but I said nothing and slogged on, hoping for the best.

It came quickly and totally unexpectedly: an enormous mauve river, its banks aflutter with river-washed tattered clothes hanging from piles and vines—work in progress of dhobi-*wallahs*, the laundrymen. Directly across the river, luminescent in a moisture-laden haze, was the Taj Mahal, seen from an angle that, to be sure, few tourists ever see and shared with affection by a man who clearly derived great pride from its grandeur. The monument's splendor was all the more striking, its manifest extravagance even more flamboyant in contrast to the faded homespun garments flapping rhythmically in the humid monsoon breeze. We could only stand there and beam at each other on the shores of the mighty Yamuna, the Khan man and I. I like to think it was a sweet kind of victory for us both.

The Deck

Yusef Komunyakaa

I have almost nailed my left thumb to the 2 × 4 brace that holds the deck together. This Saturday morning in June, I have sawed 2 × 6s, T-squared and leveled everything with three bubbles sealed in green glass, and now the sweat on my tongue tastes like what I am. I know I'm alone, using leverage to swing the long boards into place, but at times it seems as if there are two of us working side by side like old lovers guessing each other's moves.

This hammer is the only thing I own of yours, and it makes me feel I have carpentered for years. Even the crooked nails are going in straight. The handsaw glides through grease. The toenailed stubs hold. The deck has risen up around me, and now it's strong enough to support my weight, to not sway with this old, silly, wrong-footed dance I'm about to throw my whole body into.

Plumbed from sky to ground, this morning's work can take nearly anything! With so much uproar and punishment, footwork and euphoria, I'm almost happy this Saturday.

I walk back inside and here you are. Plain and simple as the sunlight on the tools outside. Daddy, if you'd come back a week ago, or day before yesterday, I would have been ready to sit down and have a long talk with you. There were things I wanted to say. So many questions I wanted to ask, but now they've been answered with as much salt and truth as we can expect from the living.

The Quality of Mercy
Jane Brox

*A*fter syntax is gone, and the liturgy, the maxims, the songs, even after no one can read anything of the old alphabet, and the names of things that remain are recognizable only to the few—after all, ragged bits of story still come down from the old country and are told in a new tongue: dry, sturdy, thin as the last weeds to be covered by a January snow. Sometimes those stories feel like tests when they're told. *Don't you remember . . . Haven't you heard . . .* how she was smuggled into this country under her mother's skirts, how they had to get him out after he'd killed that man in a fistfight, how they wanted to send her back because of the weeping in her eye . . .

Research and Practice Strategies

1. In "Memory and Imagination," Patricia Hampl plumbs her memory to come to some understanding of why she remembers her first piano lesson and not, for example, her first arithmetic lesson, or her introduction to Latin, or the first time her grandmother tried to teach her to knit. Why does the piano lesson show itself "bright with detail more than thirty years after the event"? What are some of your earliest memories? Focus especially on those that represent "firsts." You might recall the first day of school, or the first time you rode a bicycle, or the first time . . . you fill it in. Just start out with a cluster of firsts. You might jot down "the first time I . . ." and take it from there. If you find yourself getting stuck, just go back to the refrain "the first time" and see where it takes you. Some of these associations may be vivid; some will be vague. That's okay. You'll explore them later in a freewrite. For now, just get them down onto paper.

2. Once you've concretely captured some of your earliest memories, consider their emotional tenor. What feelings do you associate with them? Excitement? Fear? Sadness? Anger? Invigoration? Helplessness? Select one of the memories you explored in the previous exercise and write down every emotion that you associate with it. This can be done as a cluster initially, where you jot down words and phrases as you allow yourself to leap among emotional associations while reflecting on the memories.

3. Now that you've tied emotions to a specific memory, try to put the memory into a larger context: how old were you—five years old and

just beginning kindergarten? Where did you live—a suburb with a big backyard? A small house in the country? An urban apartment? What was your bedroom like at the time of the memory? Did you share it with a sibling? Could you hear the plumbing in the walls? And your kitchen?—was it the hub of family life, always occupied and chaotic? Or a quiet haven where you did your homework? Do you remember your backyard? What games did you play there? Did you have a swingset? Who were the significant people in your life? Did you have a younger brother or sister? Older siblings? Pets? Did you play outdoors? Who were your friends? What about times you spent playing in solitude; what were they like?

4. Once you've clustered, mapped, and completed a few freewriting sessions with the above material, consider how you might best structure the story you are about to tell. Do you want to move back and forth between your interior imaginative world and the external world that surrounded you in childhood? Would you prefer to write it with your present understanding woven in as adult narrative? Will you write it as a present reflection on the past or would you like to re-enter the child's mind and work from inside the scene to achieve more current understanding of the scene? In any case, consider these concerns as you get a first draft going and we will return to it as we move into Part 2 and more specifically address matters of craft.

5. Annie Dillard distinguishes between the world and the art of the story. To work with a piece that sets out not only to convey the world, but also be regarded as art, you could choose from some of your pieces you've begun to work with from previous exercises. See how you might juxtapose and connect them. What do you need to do to make them come together? A first-person narrative? Subheadings? Transitional scenes? Summary and reflection? Bits of poetry? Journal jottings? Song lyrics? Excerpts from news stories? If this approach doesn't work out well for you, try cutting up an earlier essay, or essays, into several parts and begin to play with structural possibilities by moving them around like puzzle pieces. See if you can make the piece become something entirely new. If you need to write new parts to add to what you already have, that's fine; you will always have the original version, as well.

6. Once you've got a decent first draft of your pieced-together work, consider Patricia Hampl's discussion of how her essay evolved from an exploration of the mechanisms of memory. This becomes the focal point of the essay and must have been a bit disconcerting at first as she decided whether or not to incorporate her realizations about how her

memory had tricked her. Should this be kept outside a tidy process that insisted on staying with the initial sketch of her first piano lesson? By being willing to head into dangerous territory—questioning even the veracity of her memory of the event about which she is writing—Hampl comes to a much larger idea whose theme resonates with more questions than answers. That's fine with Hampl for she views the essay as a medium for exploration, where thought is represented as the fluid process that it is and not a site for absolutes.

7. As you begin to workshop your writing in class, you'll need to learn how to provide helpful feedback. Here's how you might practice that. Read Pamela Michael's "The Khan Men of Agra" included in this chapter. Draw a line down the middle of a piece of notebook paper. On the left side, write a quick list of the trajectory of the scenes in this short nonfiction piece, from beginning to end. That is, from the top of your piece of paper to the bottom, on the left side, jot down the main and actual movements Michael makes, from arriving in Agra, to standing across the river from the Taj Mahal, and her movements in between. Use general words to describe where she is and a word or two to describe what is happening. After creating this list of "movement of scenes," make another list on the right side of the paper, beside those scenes on the left, jotting down your emotional reaction to each of her scenes. In other words, what were you feeling as you read each scene? Now cover up the left side with a piece of paper and study the right side. From that, write a brief summary as if you are offering Michael reader feedback, using the "prompts" for constructive peer critiques discussed in this chapter. Think about what worked for you and what didn't, and how you might apply some of what you've just learned to your own writing.

PART II

Craft Matters:
Techniques for Practice

CHAPTER 5

Writing in Scenes— Painting Word Pictures

If you are one who responds to the moment you can never really explain it, you can only describe what it felt like.

—VIVIAN GORNICK

Scene and Summary

At the heart of narrative writing is the scene. Story evolves out of scene; summary revolves around it, making connections, providing back story, filling the reader in on the larger context, explaining here and there, while reflection takes us into the soul of the story. Although a scene reconstructs a situation, it is not a static snapshot; rather, it represents the dynamic action and interactions within a moment in time. Scenes shape the arc of a story—its direction, its movement, its intention. Scenes draw on sensory detail to *show* the reader what is happening. Scenes are the camera lens on zoom, capturing the minute details of a moment in time. Summary, on the other hand, pulls back, takes a wide-angle view of the situation and *tells* the reader about what has happened over a span of time. Summary may provide background, it may foreshadow, or it may provide insight into and analysis of a situation at hand. Sensory impression (showing), combined with idea (telling), creates vivid prose that is more emotionally and intellectually satisfying than merely telling the reader what it is we want them to know. There is no substitute for the intimacy of taking our reader with us into the moment, the memory, the mind.

Imagery and the Senses

An image is a word picture charged with feeling, which has freshness of vision, intensity, evocative power—freshness to reveal what we had forgotten to see; intensity to concentrate the most significance into a small space; evocative power to elicit emotional response.

—GABRIELE RICO, WRITING THE NATURAL WAY

119

Like scenes, images appeal to the senses and emotions. When used effectively, imagery heightens a scene's immediacy and enlarges its meaning. Journalist, essayist, and poet Diane Ackerman describes an image as "a kind of tripwire for the emotions."

Consider the two sentences below that open "Whistling Swan" from Terry Tempest Williams's *Refuge*, a work that weaves Williams's interests as a naturalist, her sense of being at home in the landscape of the Utah desert, and her autobiographical experience.

The snow continues to fall. Red apples cling to bare branches.

What do we learn from these two seemingly simple declarations? First, we learn that it's snowing and has been for some time. It appears to be early winter. The branches are bare, yet apples still hang on the trees. Perhaps it's still fall. The vivid contrast of the image strikes me first: red apples against white snow. But the image is also jarring. Apples usually aren't hanging on trees during winter snowstorms. Added to that thought is the verb cling, which Williams so adeptly uses to enhance the already vivid image. Strong, active *verbs* serve as images, too, in that we *see* them. The verb, "cling," takes us beyond the visual image of red apples against white snow, suggesting an emotional component. Finally, it is the cumulative effect that is at work here: snow, red apples, cling, bare branches. What kind of emotional feeling do we associate with this scene?

Scenes and the Senses

As creative writers we hear a great deal about the importance of drawing on the five senses, but rarely are we told how to get in touch with them. Instead, too often we rely on sensory detail as a means to an end—the end being descriptiveness because it is required, not because we can actually sense it. Unless we are authentically engaged with our senses—all five of them—our descriptive endeavors are likely to be mechanical and lifeless. They will lay flat on the page, lacking the emotional resonance of genuine understanding. If you find yourself having difficulty recapturing a particular scene, you should revisit Chapter 3's discussion of prewriting techniques. This will help you to move more fully back into the scene you are attempting to reconstruct.

Because scenes are cinematic they incorporate dramatic action, characterization, dialogue, and/or internal monologue. Drawing on sensory impressions, scenes rely on sight, sound, smell, taste, and touch, carrying an immediacy of effect that talking *about* an event seldom achieves. Telling explains. Showing evokes. Telling tends to stimulate the intellect, while showing is more likely to directly affect the emotions. You may find it helpful to think of the scene as being recreated on stage or in a film. Playwrights and screenwriters have the advantage here since their media require that they reveal their intended meaning through action and interaction, dialogue and monologue, movement and gesture, diction and tone of voice.

The well-intentioned advice—"show, don't tell"—is given to encourage strong scenes with descriptive detail, concrete imagery, and dramatic action. In creative nonfiction, however, the narrator often has a strong presence in the narrative—be it memoir, essay, or literary journalism—and showing *and* telling tend to shuttle back and forth between what is happening and what the narrator thinks about what is happening. Showing may be considered to be stronger than telling, but bringing *both* into your work will provide more texture. Take a look at the following examples and see which you find most evocative.

Show and Tell

Telling

Janet looked tired.

Showing

Janet trudged into class, dropped her bag on the floor next to her desk, and plopped into her seat.

Showing and Telling

Janet trudged into class, dropped her bag on the floor next to her desk, and plopped into her seat. She was clearly exhausted from having trained for the marathon over the weekend.

Telling

The old man enjoyed eating sunflower seeds out of a paper bag.

Showing

Hunched over a paper bag crushed between his hands, the old man spit empty sunflower shells at a great flock of pigeons, which swooped down each time in hopes of getting the next morsel.

Showing and Telling

Hunched over a paper bag crushed between his hands, the old man spit empty sunflower shells at a great flock of pigeons, which swooped down each time in hopes of getting the next morsel. Offended, they strutted away, only to be fooled the next time he spit. You'd think he could spit an occasional sunflower heart their way every now and then, but he seemed to enjoy their disappointment.

When you show, you want to be as specific as possible. Although novice writers defend generalized descriptions, arguing that the generalization will make their work more "universal," this seldom, if ever, is the case. One of the paradoxes of creative writing is that the more specific you are, the greater the universal appeal. Here are some examples of general and specific descriptions.

General Descriptions

General descriptions are at the top of a given group: forest, city, automobile, people.

Specific Descriptions

Specific descriptions move into the category and name a part of it: oaks and elms, Boston, Toyota, Susan and Jake, or the old woman wearing the floppy red hat.

Describing a scene for a reader calls on similar storytelling skills. You bring the memory to your audience—not just the scene, but its context, its feeling, ultimately its meaning. You take them there.

Notice how the following scene, which opens the title story (included in this chapter) in Joan Nestle's memoir, *A Restricted Country*, takes us into the moment—concrete, specific, and dramatic.

When the plane landed on the blazing tar strip, I knew Arizona was a new world. My mother and brother stared with me out at the mountain-fringed field of blue. The Nestles three on their first vacation together had crossed the Mississippi and entered the shining new land of the American West. The desert air hit us with its startling clarity: this was not the intimate heat of New York, the heat that penetrated flesh and transformed itself into our sweat and earned our curses. We walked through it, like the others, and stood waiting for the station wagon to pick us up.

In this scene, Nestle takes us not just to the American West, she puts us onto the Arizona airport's tarmac. A strong visual image brings the larger setting into view: "My mother and brother stared with me out at the mountain-fringed field of blue." The detail here is specific rather than generalized, not mountains in the distance, but "the mountain-fringed field of blue." And Nestle doesn't just say it's hot; she lets us feel the desert heat. "The desert air hit us with its startling clarity." It doesn't just "hit us," it hits us "with its startling clarity." Notice the strong verbs that strengthen the action of the scene: *stared, hit, penetrated, transformed.*

Notice, too, that the scene achieves more than concrete description. Woven into the description are a number of details that begin laying the groundwork for story. The key characters are introduced. Context is provided as the reader learns that Nestle and her mother and brother are on their first vacation together, that never before have they been west of the Mississippi. Another, more subtle, dimension is at work in this scene, **connoting** meaning beyond the specific scene itself. In describing Arizona as a "new world," the American West as a "shining new land," Nestle moves beyond the personal to suggest historical and cultural implications. A sense of hope and possibility resides in the description. The Nestles' world is opening up in a way that suggests new horizons, discoveries, and potential. In another excerpt, Nestle wastes no time introducing complication. "I should have known from the skeptical look on my mother's face that we were in for trouble, but I chalked it up to the fact that she had never traveled further west than New Jersey."

The reader sits up and takes notice of "I should have known . . ." And when the narrator sees the skeptical look on Nestle's mother's face, she feels a sense of foreboding. **Dramatic tension** is set up and the reader wants to know what is going to happen. We are drawn into the story to find out.

Having introduced a **complication**, Nestle summarizes the **situation** for the reader. Her brother's new employer, American Airlines, compensated employees for low wages by offering discount vacation packages, among them the package that includes the guest ranch. Many of his fellow workers recommended this particular ranch as the "best bargain."

When writers describe simply for the sake of describing, because they are taught this is a better way of writing, a story stands still. When a story stands still readers get restless and restless readers will usually give up on a story unless it pulls them back in. Descriptive narrative should bring the reader into the immediacy of the scene, while simultaneously moving the story along by advancing **action** and **meaning**.

For example, having given us a basic summary of how the family came to be at the guest ranch, narrative point of view shifts to Nestle's childhood. Clearly, this vacation is a rare and special event, one that the young Nestle "could not believe . . . was really going to happen." She had "dreamed" of horses for all of her 16 years (notice how she slips in her age), "played wild stallion in the Bronx vacant lots that were [her] childhood fields. . . read every book about wild horses, mustangs, rangy colts that I could find, and through all the splintering agonies of my family I galloped on plains that were smooth and never-ending." Notice the significant detail that is given to the reader in one descriptive sentence: the narrator was sixteen at the time of this trip, had been an avid reader as a youngster, loved reading about horses, used reading to escape an unhappy family life (perhaps even tragedy), and in her imagination, at least, remained innocent and hopeful. Nestle's facility with **metaphor** and **imagery** is strong. The vacant lots of the Bronx may have been her "childhood fields," but she "galloped on plains that were smooth and never-ending" in her imagination. If Nestle had told us that the break-up of her family in childhood had been very painful, as was living in urban poverty, we would not have been nearly as moved as we are by her chosen descriptions. The distinction lies between telling and showing: nonfiction as explanation—**telling**; and creative nonfiction is evocation—**showing**.

As a narrative builds, meaning accumulates. Flat writing—writing that doesn't enlarge meaning beyond the concrete event being described—leaves a reader feeling cheated. Readers tune out, realizing that the writer hasn't even begun to wrestle with what the experience really means. How then, could the author possibly convey the story's meaning to us? Students in my writing workshops frequently worry that readers will not want to read about their personal lives. While this is a real concern, the important point to understand is that, yes, this is about the writer's personal life; it's about his personal point of view; it's about those things that matter to him. He is, after all, the one writing the story. But it is never merely about the writer. As writers engage with the task of shaping nonfiction narrative creatively, the task is to learn how to lift the story up out of ourselves, and by enlarging the personal, the very minutia of our lives becomes relevant to others.

When we invite readers to come into our world we want to make it worth their time. One way to do this is to continually remind ourselves that personal experience, *as represented* in creative nonfiction, is capable of resonating with the larger life themes of humanity and to strive toward having our narrative do this. For example, when Nestle's family is told that the guest ranch is "restricted to members of the Gentile faith only," Nestle doesn't limit her realizations and reactions to what her Jewish identity means to the people at the ranch; instead she moves into a moment of deep insight in which she finds herself a part of a much larger historical context.

> *For one moment it wasn't 1956 but another time, a time of flaming torches and forced marches. It wasn't just my Jewishness that I learned at that moment: it was also the stunning reality of exclusion unto death. It was the history lesson of those judged not to be human, and I knew our number was legion and so were our dyings.*

"A Restricted Country" explores and dramatizes a number of themes—socioeconomic class, coming of age, loss of innocence, cultural exclusion, and ethnic identity. As we read actively—*as a writer*—we become capable of discussing, not simply *what* the narrative means, but *how* it achieves its meaning.

Imagery, Metaphor, and Theme

Pleasure or pain, excitement or anxiety, love or hate, it's difficult to convey an emotion in narrative without finding what T. S. Eliot described as an "objective correlative"—an image, situation, scene, or sensory detail that becomes the carrier of the feeling. After all, words are metaphorical, they are not the *thing*, itself, but represent the idea, experience, or thing being represented. Some words, however, carry their meaning in a fairly direct way—**denoting** meaning. Other words suggest meaning in a figurative way—**connoting** meaning, leaving more room for the reader to interpret the words' implications. When images *connote* meaning, they have greater potential for ambiguity, for example, for evoking physical and emotional sensations that connect us with our own lives and experiences. Connotative words take on nuances of meaning, extending beyond the concrete. Like narrative patterns, they ripple out and become suggestively rich with thematic possibilities.

Denoting

> *She put the purple and yellow pansies in a glass vase and set them in the window. They practically glowed against the white snow.*

Connoting

> *He sent a dozen crimson roses for Valentines Day. She took one look and threw them in the trash, not bothering to read the card.*

The working of imagery as metaphor is an organic process and it happens at all stages of writing. It usually happens unconsciously in prewriting, but once you begin composing you become more conscious of how the images you select are working in your story, even as the story takes shape. As you read back over a draft to discover what you have written, you will discover that some images are key and you will want to extend their effect so they take on greater significance, perhaps becoming metaphorical. **Metaphor** takes something that is abstract and helps the reader understand it in a concrete manifestation.

Making Metaphor

"I touched her hand. It was marble, it was brick."

Wonderful examples of metaphorical imagery are found in "Hypertext," taken from Dorothy Allison's memoir, *Two or Three Things I Know for Sure* (included in this chapter). Allison draws on the image of a brick wall, each brick representing an image or a scene from her life. When touched, the brick falls away, opening onto that scene like a link on the internet:

> *My story was on this wall.*
> *I stood in front of my wall. I put my hand on it. Words were peeling across the wall, and every word was a brick. I touched one.*
> *"Bastard."*

The brick fell away and a window opened. My mother was standing in front of me. She was saying, "I'm not sick. I would tell you if I was sick, girl. I would tell you."

I touched her face and the window opened.

She was behind it, flesh cooling, still warm. Hair gone, shadows under her eyes. I was crying. I touched her hand. It was marble, it was brick. It fell away. She was seventeen and she was standing on the porch. He was sitting on the steps. She was smiling at him. She was saying, "You won't treat me bad, will you? You'll love my girls, won't you?"

I touched the brick. It fell away.

After reading "Hypertext," consider how Allison uses images to represent the larger meaning of these key scenes from her life. Notice how just an image or two brings the reader into the emotional atmosphere of her experience.

Imagery and Memory

Personal imagery, especially those imprinted by childhood experiences, often rise spontaneously in the course of writing, bringing with them shades of meaning. Such imagery infuses subtle and suggestive layers of meaning into a narrative and can be a rich resource for exploration.

By the time we are adults we carry inside us a community made up of thousands, perhaps even millions, of previous impressions. Some are conscious; most are unconscious. Like an iceberg, those that are conscious make up only a tiny tip at the top; the rest are submerged beneath the passage of time and come to the surface only when something happens that nudges (or blasts) them from their resting place. It is not only novice writers, new to the process of developing a sustainable writing practice, who appreciate fresh ideas, prompts, and strategies to spark creative inspiration. Professional writers seek suggestions for bringing forth impressions from beneath the layers of ordinary consciousness. The practice strategies in this book are offered in that spirit, intended to direct writers toward meaningful memories and story ideas, toward raw material that has the potential to sustain interest throughout the various stages of writing—not just the prewriting stage, but also the longer compositional, developmental, revision-oriented stages.

A family photo, for example, in front of a childhood home, may have the power to bring back an entire era, evoke the tenor of our lives lived in that particular house. We aren't held to the photograph, but move inside, and as time melts away the mind's eye takes us back to those childhood years with full emotional force. The kitchen where we had breakfast before school each morning, our childhood bedroom in all its familiar detail, the dinner hour. These all carry emotional content.

If we show the same photo to friends, they will not have the same associations, but will need to be told why this photo is so meaningful, what it calls forth for us, why we are sharing it. More than likely, we will not show them the photo and say, "This was a happy time in my life," but rather, "We lived here when I got my first bicycle—the blue one with the silver stripes. I rode it all the way to Jimmy's house that summer and that was the farthest I had ever gone by myself."

Sometimes such moments come as poignant images, at other times an entire scene will play out in our minds. Memories tend to come in bursts. Some sensory stimulus in our environment—something we see or hear, touch, taste, or smell—and we find ourselves tuned to a moment from the past.

> A scent throws open a window onto a joyful scene of a sunny spring afternoon of childhood when . . .
>
> A song comes on the radio and we are transported to that first heartbreaking love. We are out for a drive with the windows rolled down, the wind full on our face and . . .
>
> We walk into a friend's dining room and there in the window, exquisite against the framed image of the snowy outdoor landscape, is a yellow orchid, just like the one Grandma always fussed over. We remember her presence, her care, the meal she would have prepared upon our arrival.

Sometimes our feelings are accompanied by vivid remembrance like those above, sometimes by a vague, nonverbal feeling deep within. Whether such emotional surges are subtle or strong, when working with memory, the creative writer is delving into the past, bringing forth and holding up to the light of day, images and scenes hidden beneath layers of time. Once the past is culled from memory, the task is to find a way to break open the truth it has to offer. In this sense, writing is not an escape from the world, but a means of encounter that helps us more fully understand that world, as well as our place in it. For the creative nonfiction writer, the world isn't always *out there*, sometimes it's *in here*, within the depths of our own psyche. In "The Whole Truth" (included in Chapter 7), Peter Ives writes, "If in your writer's soul you remember the smell of wool mittens more than you remember climbing Everest with your father, you may have to write the wool mittens."

An odd phenomenon—memory—capable of bringing the past into the present with startling clarity. In *This is My Life* Barry Lopez writes that it is those images that are laden with meaning that are "still vivid as a bowl of oranges on a summer windowsill." Sometimes, though, we seem to be peering in at the memory from the other side of a foggy window and it needs to be coaxed forth from the outer edges of consciousness. Like dreams, memories often exist in bits and pieces, a kind of mosaic of our lives. For example, think about the third grade. Where did you attend school? Who was your teacher? What memories do you carry from that year? You probably remember a few, perhaps several meaningful events. But, no one can remember every day, beginning with the first day of classes right through until summer break. Memory doesn't work that way. When we recall an image from third grade, we find ourselves moving into memory's reservoir and then up pop a few select moments from that era, seemingly of their own volition. Try doing it as a cluster exercise in your journal. Here is mine:

A Cluster

penmanship

stay in

recess

rewrite

pregnant

changing schools

Mrs. Crane

no friends

prosper

new place

Third Grade

strict

cursive

Veronica

begin

slinky

best friend

puppies

Living on the hill

rainbow

dress

Helen

class photo

dead

What was her name?

wheelchair

down hill

fast

polio

In "Memory and Imagination" (included in Chapter 4) Patricia Hampl notes that "the truth of many circumstances and episodes in the past emerges for the memoirist through details."

How true this is. The blue, magenta, and yellow dress from my third grade class photo brings to mind an image of me pushing a neighbor girl in her wheelchair down a hill in front of our houses, picking up speed, until ultimately I was trying to keep up with the chair. I remember feeling her pleasure in the speed, something she could not achieve on her own safely, the sense of abandonment our laughter conveyed. But that image leaps immediately into a litter of puppies our Weimaraner had while we lived in the same house and what was a tragic experience for me as a child—the death of all of the puppies as they were smothered, one by one, by the large, heavy, inexperienced mother whose name I cannot recall. I spent a great deal of time peering out onto the back porch to make sure they were okay, but inevitably the next morning a new pup would be dead. Why does one image of abandonment and freedom dip immediately into the sense of loss and dread I felt over the gradual demise of that litter? This is what is beneath the tip of the iceberg that I would have to explore if I were to move this prewriting and brief reflection into a narrative, learning as much from the process as my reader might.

Imagery and the Observing Eye

You have got to learn to paint with words.

—FLANNERY O'CONNOR

Visual artists spend years learning how to *see* in order to recreate a realistic image on the canvas. As writers we must do the same. The world around us exists as an array of images, but in a modern, fast-paced world we are often on such sensory overload that we do not "see" what is right in front of us. To begin to develop the subtle eye of a writer, we have to find ways to slow down our daily pace and take in our surroundings for reasons other than functionality, productivity, and efficiency. Children and poets may be our best teachers here. Children come by it naturally and poets cultivate it, given that their artistic medium is largely imagistic. Because images suggest more than pure fact, poets use imagery to describe inner states of mind to convey the relationship between outer and inner worlds and to embody what John Crowe Ransom describes in *Poems and Essays* as "a primordial freshness, which idea can never claim." Children use images because they have to. They haven't yet mastered the ability to abstract meaning from the concrete. In their excitement and wonder in discovery, children spend their days in contact with the world around them; they touch, taste, smell, sing, squeal, shriek, play pretend games—exercising their sensory perception and expressing themselves with creative abandon until we gradually civilize them into what we consider to be "appropriate" behavior.

Of course, appropriate behavior has its place; we wouldn't like it if everyone sat around with their feet on the dining room table or plunged into the chocolate mousse with both hands like it was a mud-pie. Still . . . something happens when we begin school and are taught in a systematic way that there are right and wrong ways to express ourselves. Learning the necessary conventions of written expression can be both helpful and harmful to our creative endeavors. The codification of the world into categories is a necessary step in establishing coherence as we make sense of things we do not understand. On the other hand, there is a tendency to develop a conventional way of looking at the world, and as we lose our ability to play and imagine, to find pleasure in the moment, the world loses its ability to make us wonder.

Creative writers find any number of ways to generate a playful, imaginative quality in their writing process (remember Diane Ackerman's "Courting the Muse," in Chapter 3?) and the prewriting journal is a great place for this. You shouldn't forget to devote some of your writing time each week to cultivating the powers of observation. You must take yourself to new places, view familiar places through a stranger's eyes, take a moment each day to inhale the plethora of imagery and texture and color all around you, even as you go about your daily life. Writers do this.

Setting Is Part of the Story

Often interwoven with scene, setting may have to do with the story arc; or it may simply be where the action takes place. Stories rarely take shape, however, without a strong sense of place.

In most situations setting is an essential part of scene. In such instances setting may include sights and sounds, weather and mood, the season, the smells of an annual holiday meal, the familiarity of a childhood room. Setting may be fifth-grade recess, the nursing home where our grandmother resided, the emergency room where we went as a kid with a broken arm, or our grandfather's worn and faded, but favorite chair.

The important thing is that setting isn't simply a backdrop against which we write our story; it is part of the story. In narrative nonfiction embued with themes of nature or travel or place, setting takes on an even greater significance and may be treated as a character in its own right. Consider the following excerpt from a lyric essay included in this chapter by Marjorie Agosín entitled "A Map of My Face."

> For me traveling was that sensation of awaking alone in a hotel, then facing the window in expectation of a new day. . . . I approached a fountain in the middle of a plaza and felt precisely that, the other life, the lives of others, and now my own existence brushing up against my gaze. The pleasure of being in another place intensified; nothing reminded me of what I was or had been. . . . The pleasure of a journey lies in knowing one is guided only by uncertainty and that no mirror will reflect yesterday's face.

The scene and the narrative reflections are woven in such a way that they accomplish much in the way of story. The passage is at once descriptive and revelatory. It describes setting as well as its effect on the narrator. In this way the passage becomes not simply setting, but also scene. The techniques of setting, like those of scene, include the use of concrete description to emphasize those aspects of place that not only advance the narrative's trajectory, but also the revelation of theme.

Setting Reveals Character

Make a list of everything you learn about Jane Brox's grandmother in the following short passage from her memoir "The Quality of Mercy." Notice how all that we know about her is given to us as setting. Notice too how the setting is not a pause for an aside about the landscape, but already an element in the story, moving it along.

> *My grandmother, not yet eighteen, traveled with her goods along the roads surrounding Olean, New York, and, as she exchanged lace and thread and her own handiwork for pennies, she glimpsed through each opened farmhouse door another life in the offing—the rush of warmth from the stove heat, the smell of hard soap, of johnnycake and drying apples.*

We each have a profoundly personal relationship to place. Our sense of identity, both personal and cultural, is inextricably woven into the place and period of our legacy. Whether we grew up on the coast—the east coast is very different from the west—or in the middle of the continent; whether we lived in an urban or suburban environment, traveled extensively or remained close to home; whether we or our parents or grandparents were born in another country; this affects how we view personal, familial, and cultural identity. A sense of place has shaped us and will shape our stories, even when they aren't explicitly about us or our origins.

Here is Dorothy Allison describing setting in her memoir, *Two or Three Things I Know for Sure*, from which the excerpt, "Hypertext" (included in this chapter), is taken.

> *Where I was born—Greenville, South Carolina—smelled like nowhere else I've ever been. Cut wet grass, split green apples, baby shit and beer bottles, cheap makeup and motor oil. Everything was ripe, everything was rotting. . . . That country was beautiful, I swear to you, the most beautiful place I've ever been. Beautiful and terrible.*

For Allison the setting of her birthplace and childhood recalls far more than mere location; it is about sensory perception: smells, sounds, sights, physicality. The setting she now carries inside herself is imbued with emotional depth and meaning, both "beautiful and terrible." Setting is an inextricable part of the identity of the writer, and, in Allison's case, it foreshadows deeper and more complicated truths.

Setting and Symbol

The unfortunate mistake novice writers sometimes make is in bringing in the thunderstorm to darken the mood. Springtime is happy and alive with flowers, fall is old age and decay; winter is death. Anyone who has studied the British Romantics can appreciate these tropes; however, symbols aren't waiting in a drawer ready to be applied to the appropriate situation, and when they are, too often they are tired clichés. What is symbolic of fear for one may be very different for another. Likewise with the concept of, say, pleasure. If we stay with our writing practice and do our prewriting from that state Virginia Woolf described as an "active receptivity," we will begin to discover in a deeply satisfying way that we have a personal symbolic system that is as particular to us as a fingerprint, or DNA. It's simply an aspect of who we are, and like syntax and diction, the images and symbols that speak to us will be woven organically into the themes of our work. They will not be decoration.

Playing with Cliché

Try writing down as many clichés as you can come up with in three to five minutes. Be sure to include clichés you tend to use without thinking. These you will want to weed from your writing when you revise and edit your work. Don't worry about them in early drafts, however, or you will slow down your creative process. Here are a few:

- over the hill
- beauty is only skin deep
- dry as a bone
- like father like son
- bone-chilling cold
- nose to the grindstone
- an axe to grind

Readings

Writers on Writing

"The Five Rs of Creative Nonfiction," Lee Gutkind

Memoir

"A Restricted Country," Joan Nestle

Lyric Essay

"A Map of My Face," Marjorie Agosín

The Short

"Hypertext," Dorothy Allison

Prose Poem

"What We Remember and What We Forget," Karen Salyer McElmurray, from
    Surrendered Child

The Five Rs of Creative Nonfiction
Lee Gutkind

*I*t is three a.m. and I am standing on a stool in the operating room at the University of Pittsburgh Medical Center in scrubs, mask, cap, and paper booties, peering over the hunched shoulders of four surgeons and a scrub nurse as a dying woman's heart and lungs are being removed from her chest. This is a scene I have observed frequently since starting my work on a book about the world of organ transplantation, but it never fails to amaze and startle me: to look down into a gaping hole in a human being's chest, which has been cracked open and emptied of all of its contents, watch the monitor and listen to the rhythmic sighing sounds of the ventilator, and know that this woman is on the fragile cusp of life and death and that I am observing what might well be the final moments of her life.

Now the telephone rings; a nurse answers, listens for a moment and then hangs up. "On the roof," she announces, meaning that the helicopter has set down on the hospital helipad and that a healthy set of organs, a heart, and two lungs, en bloc, will soon be available to implant into this woman, whose immediate fate will be decided within the next few hours.

With a brisk nod, the lead surgeon, Bartley Griffith, a young man who pioneered heart-lung transplantation and who at this point has lost more patients with the procedure than he has saved, looks up, glances around and finally rests his eyes on me: "Lee," he says, "would you do me a great favor?"

I was surprised. Over the past three years I had observed Bart Griffith in the operating room a number of times, and although a great deal of conversation takes place between doctors and nurses during the long and intense surgical ordeal, he had only infrequently addressed me in such a direct and spontaneous manner.

Our personal distance is a by-product of my own technique as an immersion journalist—my fly-on-the-wall or living-room-sofa concept of immersion: Writers should be regular and silent observers, so much so that they are virtually unnoticed. Like walking through your living room dozens of times, but paying attention to the sofa only when suddenly you realize that it is missing. Researching a book about transplantation, *Many Sleepless Nights* (W.W. Norton), I had been accorded great access to the OR, the transplant wards, ethics debates, and the most intimate conversations between patients, family members, and medical staff. I had jetted through the night on organ donor runs. I had witnessed great drama—at a personal distance.

But on that important early morning, Bartley Griffith took note of my presence and requested that I perform a service for him. He explained that this was going to be a crucial time in the heart-lung procedure, which had been going on for about five hours, but that he felt obligated to make contact with this woman's husband who had traveled here from Kansas City, Missouri. "I can't take the time to talk to the man myself, but I am wondering if you would brief him as to what has happened so far. Tell him that the organs have arrived, but that even if all goes well, the procedure will take at least another five hours and maybe longer." Griffith didn't need to mention that the most challenging aspect of the surgery—the implantation—was upcoming; the danger to the woman was at a heightened state.

A few minutes later, on my way to the ICU waiting area where I would find Dave Fulk, the woman's husband, I stopped in the surgeon's lounge for a quick cup of coffee and a moment to think about how I might approach this man, undoubtedly nervous—perhaps even hysterical—waiting for news of his wife. I also felt kind of relieved, truthfully, to be out of the OR, where the atmosphere was so intense.

Although I had been totally caught-up in the drama of organ transplantation during my research, I had recently been losing my passion and curiosity; I was slipping into a life-and-death overload in which all of the sad stories from people all across the world seemed to be congealing into the same muddled dream. I recognized this feeling from experience—a clear signal that it was time to abandon the research phase of this book and sit down and start to write. Yet, as a writer, I was confronting a serious and frightening problem: Overwhelmed with facts and statistics, tragic and triumphant stories, I felt confused. I knew, basically, what I wanted to say about what I learned, but I didn't know how to structure my message or where to begin.

And so, instead of walking away from this research experience and sitting down and starting to write my book, I continued to return to the scene of my transplant adventures waiting for lightning to strike…inspiration for when the very special way to start my book would make itself known. In retrospect, I believe that Bart Griffith's rare request triggered that magic moment of clarity I had long been awaiting.

Defining the Discussion

Before I tell you what happened, however, let me explain what kind of work I do as an immersion journalist/creative nonfiction writer and define what I am doing, from a writer's point of view, in this essay.

But first some definitions: Immersion journalists immerse or involve themselves in the lives of the people about whom they are writing in ways that will provide readers with a rare and special intimacy.

The other phrase to define, a much broader term, creative nonfiction is a concept that offers great flexibility and freedom, while adhering to the basic tenets of nonfiction writing and/or reporting. In creative nonfiction, writers can be poetic and journalistic simultaneously. Creative nonfiction writers are encouraged to utilize fictional (literary) techniques in their prose—from scene to dialogue to description to point of view—and be cinematic at the same time. Creative nonfiction writers write about themselves and/or capture real people and real life in ways that can and have changed the world. What is most important and enjoyable about creative nonfiction is that it not only allows but encourages the writer to become a part of the story or essay being written. The personal involvement creates a special magic that alleviates the suffering and anxiety of the writing experience; it provides many outlets for satisfaction and self-discovery, flexibility, and freedom.

When I refer to creative nonfiction, I include memoir (autobiography), and documentary drama, a term more often used in relation to film, as in *Hoop Dreams*, which captures the lives of two inner-city high school basketball players over a six-year period. Much of what is generically referred to as literary journalism or, in the past, "new journalism," can be classified as creative nonfiction. Although it is the current vogue in the world of writing today, the combination of creative nonfiction as a form of writing and immersion as a method of research has a long history. George Orwell's famous essay, "Shooting an Elephant" combines personal experience and high quality literary writing techniques. The Daniel DeFoe classic, *Robinson Crusoe*, is based upon a true story of a physician who was marooned on a desert island. Ernest Hemingway's paean to bullfighting, *Death in the Afternoon*, comes under the creative nonfiction umbrella, as does Tom Wolfe's, *The Right Stuff*, which was made into an award-winning film.

Currently, many of our best magazines—*The New Yorker, Harper's, Vanity Fair, Esquire*—publish more creative nonfiction than fiction and poetry combined. Universities offer Master of Fine Arts degrees in creative nonfiction. Newspapers are publishing an increasing amount of creative nonfiction, not only as features, but in the news and op-ed pages as well. Most important, from my personal point of view, a literary journal—the triquarterly I edit called (quite appropriately) *Creative Nonfiction*—is devoted entirely to original new work of dramatic nonfiction prose.

The Five Rs

Reading, 'Riting, 'Rithmitic—the three Rs—was the way in which basic public school education was once described. The "five Rs" is an easy way to remember the basic tenets of creative nonfiction/immersion journalism.

The first "R" has already been explained and discussed: the immersion or *real life* aspect of the writing experience. As a writing teacher, I design assignments that force my students out into their communities for an hour, a day, or even a week so that they see and understand that the foundation of good writing emerges from personal experience. Some writers (and students) may utilize their own personal experience rather than immersing themselves in the experiences of others. In a recent introductory class I taught, one young man working his way through school as a sales person wrote about selling shoes, while another student, who served as a volunteer in a hospice, captured a dramatic moment of death, grief, and family relief. I've sent my students to police stations, bagel shops, golf courses; together, my classes have gone on excursions and participated in public service projects—all in an attempt to re-create from personal experience real life.

In contrast to the term *reportage*, the word *essay* usually connotes a more personal message from writer to reader. "An essay is when I write what I think about something," students will often say to me. Which is true, to a certain extent—and also the source of the meaning of the second R for *reflection*. A writer's feelings and responses about a subject are permitted and encouraged, as long as what they think is written to embrace the reader in a variety of ways.

As editor of *Creative Nonfiction*, I receive approximately one hundred fifty unsolicited essays, book excerpts and profiles a month for possible publication. Of the many reasons the vast majority of these submissions are rejected, two are most prevalent, the first being an overwhelming egocentrism; in other words, writers write too much about themselves without seeking a universal focus or umbrella so that readers are properly and firmly engaged. Essays that are so personal that they omit the reader are essays that will never see the light of print. The overall objective of the personal essayist is to make the reader tune in—not out.

The second reason *Creative Nonfiction* and most other journals and magazines reject essays is a lack of attention to the mission of the genre, which is to gather and present information, to teach readers about a person, place, idea, or situation combining the creativity of the artistic experience with the essential third R in the formula: *Research*.

Even the most personal essay is usually full of substantive detail about a subject that affects or concerns a writer and the people about whom he or she is writing. Read the books and essays of the most renowned nonfiction writers in this century and you will read about a writer engaged in a quest for information and discovery. From George Orwell to Ernest Hemingway to John McPhee, books and essays written by these writers are invariably about a subject other than themselves, although the narrator will be intimately included in the story. Personal experience and spontaneous intellectual discourse—an airing and exploration of ideas—are equally vital. In her first book, *Pilgrim at Tinker Creek*, which won the Pulitzer Prize, and in her other books and essays, Annie Dillard repeatedly overwhelms her readers with factual information, minutely detailed descriptions of insects, botany and biology, history, anthropology, blended with her own feelings about life.

One of my favorite Dillard essays, "Schedules," which appears in this collection, focuses on the importance of writers working on a regular schedule rather than writing only intermittently. In "Schedules," she discusses, among many other subjects, Hasidism, chess, baseball, warblers, pine trees, june bugs, writers' studios, and potted plants—not to mention her own schedule and writing habits and that of Wallace Stevens and Jack London.

What I am saying is that the genre of creative nonfiction, although anchored in factual information, is open to anyone with a curious mind and a sense of self. The research phase actually launches and anchors the creative effort. Whether it is a book or essay I am planning, I always begin my quest in the library—for three reasons. First, I need to familiarize myself with the subject. If it is something about which I do not know, I want to make myself knowledgeable enough to ask intelligent questions. If I can't display at least a minimal understanding of the subject about which I am writing, I will lose the confidence and the support of the people who must provide access to the experience.

Secondly, I will want to assess my competition. What other essays, books, and articles have been written about this subject? Who are the experts, the pioneers, the most controversial figures? I want to find a new angle, not write a story similar to one that has already been written. And finally, how can I reflect and evaluate a person, subject, or place unless I know all of the contrasting points of view? Reflection may permit a certain amount of speculation, but only when based upon a solid foundation of knowledge.

So far in this essay I have named a number of well-respected creative nonfiction writers and discussed their work, which means I have satisfied the fourth R in our *five*-R formula: *Reading*. Not only must writers read the research material unearthed in the library, but they also must read the work of the masters of their profession. I have heard some very fine writers claim that they don't read too much anymore—or that they don't read for long periods, especially during the time they are laboring on a lengthy writing project. But almost all writers have read the best writers in their field and are able to converse in great detail about their stylistic approach and intellectual content. An artist who has never studied Picasso, Van Gogh, Michelangelo, even Warhol, is an artist who will quite possibly never succeed.

To this point, we have mostly discussed the nonfiction or journalistic aspects of the immersion journalism/creative nonfiction genre. The fifth R the *riting* part is the most artistic and romantic aspect of the total experience. After all of the preparatory (nonfiction) work is complete, writers will often create in two phases. Usually, there is an inspirational explosion, a time when writers allow instinct and feeling to guide their fingers as they create paragraphs, pages, and even entire chapters of books or complete essays. This is what art of any form is all about—the passion of the moment and the magic of the muse. I am not saying that this always happens; it doesn't. Writing is a difficult labor, in which a regular schedule, a daily grind of struggle, is inevitable. But this first part of the experience for most writers is rather loose and spontaneous and therefore more creative and fun. The second part of the writing experience—the craft part, which comes into play after a basic essay is written—is equally important—and a hundred times more difficult.

Writing in Scenes

Vignettes, episodes, slices of reality are the building blocks of creative nonfiction—the primary distinguishing factor between traditional reportage/journalism and literary and/or creative nonfiction and between good, evocative writing and ordinary prose. The uninspired writer will tell the reader about a subject, place, or personality, but the creative nonfiction writer will show that subject, place, or personality in action. Before we discuss the actual content or construction of a scene, let me suggest that you perform what I like to call the "yellow test."

Take a yellow Hi-Liter or Magic Marker and leaf through a favorite magazine—*Vanity Fair, Esquire, The New Yorker*, or *Creative Nonfiction*. Or return to favorite chapters in books by Dillard, Ackerman, etc. Yellow-in the scenes, just the scenes, large and small. Then return to the beginning and review your handiwork. Chances are, anywhere from 50 to 80 percent of each essay, short story, novel selected will be yellow. Plays are obviously constructed with scenes, as are films. Most poems are very scenic.

Jeanne Marie Laskas, the talented columnist for the *Washington Post Magazine*, once told me: "I only have one rule from start to finish. I write in scenes. It doesn't matter to me in which order the scenes are written; I write whichever scene inspires me at any given time, and I worry about the plot or frame or narrative later. The scene—a scene—any scene—is always first."

The Elements of a Scene

First and foremost, a scene contains action. Something happens. I jump on my motorcycle and go helter-skelter around the country; suddenly, in the middle of July in Yellowstone National Park I am confronted with twenty inches of snow. Action needn't be wild, sexy, and death-defying, however. There's also action in the classroom. A student asks a question, that requires an answer, that necessitates a dialogue, that is a marvelously effective tool to trigger or record action. Dialogue represents people saying things to one another, expressing themselves. It is a valuable scenic building block. Discovering dialogue is one of the reasons to immerse ourselves at a police station, bagel shop, or at a zoo. To discover what people have to say spontaneously—and not in response to a reporter's prepared questions.

Another vehicle or technique of the creative nonfiction experience may be described as intimate and specific detail. Through use of intimate detail, we can hear and see how the people about whom we are writing say what is on their minds; we may note the inflections in their voices, their elaborate hand movements and any other eccentricities. "Intimate" is a key distinction in the use of detail when crafting good scenes. Intimate means recording and noting detail that the reader might not know or even imagine without your particular inside insight. Sometimes intimate detail can be so specific and special that it becomes unforgettable in the readers mind. A very famous intimate detail appears in a classic creative nonfiction profile, "Frank Sinatra Has a Cold," written by Gay Talese in 1962 and published in *Esquire Magazine*.

In this profile, Talese leads readers on a whirlwind cross-country tour, revealing Sinatra and his entourage interacting with one another and with the rest of the world and demonstrating how the Sinatra world and the world inhabited by everyone else will often collide. These scenes are action-oriented; they contain dialogue and evocative description with great specificity and intimacy such as the gray-haired lady spotted in the shadows of the Sinatra entourage—the guardian of Sinatra's collection of toupées. This tiny detail—Sinatra's wig lady—loomed so large in my mind when I first read the essay that even now, thirty-five years later, anytime I see Sinatra on TV or spot his photo in a magazine, I find myself unconsciously searching the background for the gray-haired lady with the hatbox.

The Narrative, or Frame

The frame represents a way of ordering or controlling a writer's narrative so that the elements of his book, article, or essay are presented in an interesting and orderly fashion with an interlaced integrity from beginning to end.

Some frames are very complicated, as in the movie, *Pulp Fiction*; Quentin Tarantino skillfully tangles and manipulates time. But the most basic frame is a simple beginning-to-end chronology. The dramatic documentary (which is also classic creative nonfiction) *Hoop Dreams*, for example, begins with two African-American teenage basketball stars living in a ghetto and sharing a dream of stardom in the NBA and dramatically tracks both of their careers over the next six years.

As demonstrated in *Pulp Fiction*, writers don't always frame in a strictly chronological sequence. My book, *One Children's Place*, begins in the operating room at a children's hospital. It introduces a surgeon, whose name is Marc Rowe, his severely handicapped patient, Danielle, and her mother, Debbie, who has dedicated her every waking moment to Danielle. Two years of her life have been spent inside the walls of this building with parents and children from all across the world whose lives are too endangered to leave the confines of the hospital. As Danielle's surgery goes forward, the reader tours the hospital in a very intimate way, observing in the emergency room; participating in helicopter rescue missions as part of the emergency trauma team; attending ethics meetings, well-baby clinics, child abuse examinations—every conceivable activity at a typical high-acuity children's hospital so that readers will learn from the inside out how such an institution and the people it services and supports function on an hour-by-hour basis. We even learn about Marc Rowe's guilty conscience about how he has slighted his own wife and children over the years so that he can care for other families.

The book ends when Danielle is released from the hospital. It took two years to research and write this book, returning day and night to the hospital in order to understand the hospital and the people who made it special, but the story in which it is framed begins and ends in a few months.

Back to the Beginning—That Rare and Wonderful Moment of Clarity

Now let's think about this essay as a piece of creative nonfiction writing, especially in relation to the concept of framing. It begins with a scene. We are in an operating room at the University of Pittsburgh, the world's largest organ transplant center, in the middle of a rare and delicate surgery that will decide a dying woman's fate. Her heart and both lungs have been emptied out of her chest and she is maintained on a heart-bypass system. The telephone alerts the surgical team that a fresh and potentially lifesaving set of organs has arrived at the hospital via helicopter. Suddenly the lead surgeon looks up and asks an observer (me) to make contact with the woman's husband. I agree, leave the operating room and then stop for a coffee in the surgeon's lounge.

Then, instead of moving the story forward, fulfilling my promise to Dr. Griffith and resolving my own writing dilemma, I change directions, move backwards (flashback) in time and sequence and begin to discuss this genre: immersion journalism/creative nonfiction. I provide a mountain of information—definitions, descriptions, examples, explanations. Basically, I am attempting to satisfy the nonfiction part of my responsibility to my readers and my editors while hoping that the suspense created in the first few pages will provide an added inducement for readers to remain focused and interested in this Introduction from the beginning to the end where, (the reader assumes) the two stories introduced in the first few pages will be completed.

In fact, my meeting with Dave Fulk in the ICU waiting room that dark morning was exactly the experience I had been waiting for, leading to that precious and magic moment of clarity for which I was searching and hoping. When I arrived, Mr. Fulk was talking with an elderly man and woman from Sacramento, California, who happened to be the parents of a twenty-one-year-old US Army private named Rebecca Treat who, I soon discovered, was the recipient of the liver from the same donor who gave Dave's wife (Winkle Fulk) a heart and lungs. Rebecca Treat, life-flighted to Pittsburgh from California, had been in a coma for ten days by the time she arrived in Pittsburgh; the transplanted liver was her only hope of ever emerging from that coma and seeing the light of day.

Over the next half hour of conversation, I learned that Winkle Fulk had been slowly dying for four years, had been bedridden for three of those years, as Dave and their children watched her life dwindle away, as fluid filled her lungs and began to destroy her heart. Rebecca's fate had been much more sudden; having contracted hepatitis in the army, she crashed almost immediately. To make matters worse, Rebecca and her new husband had separated. As I sat in the darkened waiting area with Dave Fulk and Rebecca's parents, I suddenly realized what it was I was looking for, what my frame or narrative element could be. I wanted to tell about the organ transplant experience—and what organ transplantation can mean from a universal perspective—medically, scientifically, personally for patients, families, and surgeons. Rebecca's parents and the Fulk family, once strangers, would now be permanently and intimately connected by still another stranger—the donor—the person whose tragic death provided hope and perhaps salvation to two dying people. In fact, my last quest in the research phase of the transplant book experience was to discover the identity of this mysterious donor and literally connect the principal characters. In so doing, the frame or narrative drive of the story emerged.

Many Sleepless Nights begins when fifteen-year-old Richie Becker, a healthy and handsome teenager from Charlotte, North Carolina, discovers that his father is going to sell the sports car that he had hoped would one day be his. In a spontaneous and thoughtless gesture of defiance, Richie, who had never been behind the wheel, secretly takes his father's sports car on a joy ride. Three blocks from his home, he wraps the car around a tree and is subsequently declared brain dead at the local hospital. Devastated by the experience, but hoping for some positive outcome to such a senseless tragedy, Richie's father, Dick, donates his son's organs for transplantation.

Then the story flashes back a half century, detailing surgeons' first attempts at transplantation and all of the experimentation and controversy leading up to the development and acceptance of transplant techniques. I introduce Winkle Fulk and Private Rebecca Treat. Richie Becker's liver is transplanted into Rebecca, while his heart and lungs are sewn into Mrs. Fulk by Dr. Bartley Griffith. The last scene of the book three hundred seventy pages later is dramatic and telling and finishes the frame three years later when Winkle Fulk travels to Charlotte, North Carolina, a reunion I arranged to allow the folks to personally thank Richie's father for his son's gift of life.

> At the end of the evening, just as we were about to say goodbye and return to the motel, Dick Becker stood up in the center of the living room of his house, paused, and then walked slowly and hesitantly over toward Winkle Fulk, who had once stood alone at the precipice of death. He eased himself down on his knees, took Winkle Fulk by the shoulder and simultaneously drew her closer, as he leaned forward and placed his ear gently but firmly between her breasts and then at her back.
>
> Everyone in that room was suddenly and silently breathless, watching as Dick Becker listened for the last time to the absolutely astounding miracle of organ transplantation: the heart and the lungs of his dead son Richie, beating faithfully and unceasingly inside this stranger's warm and loving chest.

A Restricted Country

Joan Nestle

1

When the plane landed on the blazing tar strip, I knew Arizona was a new world. My mother and brother stared with me out at the mountain-fringed field of blue. The Nestles three on their first vacation together had crossed the Mississippi and entered the shining new land of the American West. The desert air hit us with its startling clarity: this was not the intimate heat of New York, the heat that penetrated flesh and transformed itself into our sweat and earned our curses. We walked through it, like the others, and stood waiting for the station wagon to pick us up.

I should have known from the skeptical look on my mother's face that we were in for trouble, but I chalked it up to the fact that she had never traveled further west than New Jersey. My brother's new job at American Airlines had made this trip possible: the company compensated for low wages by offering its employees special cut-rate vacation packages, and many of his fellow workers had recommended this one-week stay at Shining Star Guest Ranch as the best bargain. From the moment he had told us of the possibility, to the time we were standing in front of the Tucson Airport, I could not believe the trip was really going to happen. I had dreamed horses all my sixteen years, played wild stallion in the Bronx vacant lots that were my childhood fields, had read every book about wild horses, mustangs, rangy colts that I could find, and through all the splintering agonies of my family I galloped on plains that were smooth and never-ending. For my brother, who had seldom been with my mother and me, this trip was both a reunion and an offering. After years of turmoil, mistakes, and rage, he was giving us the spoils of his manhood. He lay this vacation at the feet of our fatherless family as if it were a long-awaited homecoming gift. For my mother, it was a simple thing: her week's vacation from the office, her first trip in over twenty years.

We finally spotted the deep-purple station wagon that bore the ranch's name and hurried to it. A large man in a cowboy hat asked if we were the Nestle family, looked at us intently, and then fell silent as he loaded our suitcases into the wagon. We rode though the outskirts of Tucson and continued into the desert. The man never said another word to us, and feeling the strangeness of the desert, we too fell silent. Cacti rose around us, twisted strong creatures that, like the untouching heat, seemed only to tolerate the temporary intrusion of roads into their world. I felt the desert clumps of tufted grass under my feet. I was already moving my horse's haunches, for now it was only a sheet of glass that separated me from Annie Oakley. Dusk came suddenly and the heat fled.

We pulled into the ranch, and another man poked his head into the front window and stared at the three of us. "Do you want fish or meat for dinner?" were his only words. My mother answered that it made no difference, meat would be fine. Everything was still in the blue-black night as we were shown our rooms and then led to the dining room. The room was long, low-roofed with heavy beams; a fireplace glowed at one end. All the other guests were seated at the same table, ladling out huge portions of food from communal platters. We were seated at the long last table, a far distance from the rest, near the large stone fireplace. As our places were being set, the waitress placed a small white card near each of our plates. I picked up mine and read. *Because this guest ranch is run like a family, we are restricted to members of the Gentile faith only.* I could now envision the chain of events that our arrival had set in motion. The man who peered in at us must have realized we were Jewish, rushed in to tell his boss, who pulled out the appropriate cards to be served with our dinner. My brother and I sat stunned; my mother said we would talk to the manager after dinner.

As I tried to eat, the voices of the other guests caught in my throat. I had grown up with the language of New York's garment district. I knew the word *goy*, but this was my introduction to *Gentiles*. We can't stay here, my mother said. My brother kept saying he was sorry, he didn't know. How could his coworkers recommend this place? How could American Airlines have a working agreement with such a place? When we finished eating, my mother asked to speak to the manager. She and my brother were led to his office. I stayed outside in what seemed to be a reading room. I paced the room, looking at the books lining the wall. Finally, I found what I knew had to be there: a finely bound volume of *Mein Kampf*. For one moment it wasn't 1956 but another time, a time of flaming torches and forced marches. It wasn't just my Jewishness that I learned at that moment: it was also the stunning reality of exclusion unto death. It was the history lesson of those judged not to be human, and I knew our number was legion and so were our dyings.

Huddled in the privacy of our room, my mother and brother told me what the manager had said. Since it was off-season, he was willing to compromise. If we told no one that we were Jewish, if we left and entered through the back door, and if we ate our meals by ourselves, we could stay. We looked at each other. Here was an offer to the Nestles to pass as Gentiles. To eat and walk in shame.

We waited until the morning to tell the manager our decision. I stayed in our room while my mother and brother went in for breakfast. In a strange twist of feeling, my anger had turned to shyness. I thought of the priest I had noticed sitting at the table the night before, and I could not bear the thought of making him see we were human. I could not bear the challenge to his geniality that we would represent. After breakfast, the three of us entered the manager's office to tell him we would not stay under his conditions.

I stared at the man as my mother spoke for us, looking for his embarrassment, waiting for the moment when he would say this was all a joke. His answer was that he was sure we would not want to stay some place we were not wanted, but there was a Jewish dude ranch several miles away. Perhaps the owners would consider allowing us to stay there for the same price. He made the call for us, saying, "By mistake some of your people came here." The voice on the other end agreed to take us. Once again we were ushered into the station wagon and driven to a parking lot in downtown Tucson. We sat on the curb waiting for the new station wagon to pick us up. The men walking by wore big brown belts with turquoise stones embedded in the leather, pointed boots, and wide-brimmed hats. The sun shone with that same impersonal heat, and the shimmering mountains were still waiting for us in the distance.

2

When the station wagon pulled into our new destination, we were greeted by a small circle of elderly guests who welcomed us with hugs and low-voiced comments to my mother about "the *kinder*." After the novelty of our sad mistake wore off, the three of us were left to our own devices. As the youngest person at the ranch, I was indulged in my unladylike ways. Riding clothes were lent to me, and my desire to smell as much like a horse as possible was humorously accepted. My brother spent his time playing tennis and dating a young woman who cleaned the rooms. As soon as it grew dark, they would take off for the nearest town. My mother, however, had a harder time in our Jewish haven. All the other guests were retired, wealthy married couples who moved with ease in this sunlit world. While they were sympathetic to my mother, a woman alone raising two kids, they were also embarrassed by her. She dressed wrong and did not know how to enjoy herself.

My mother was a dedicated gin and poker player. Shortly after our arrival she tried to join the nightly card game, but here, under the Arizona sun, the stakes had multiplied beyond her resources. I watched her as she approached the table of cigar-smoking men. She sat for one round, growing smaller in her seat while the pile of chips grew bigger and bigger in the center of the table. She was a working-class gambler who played with her week's salary while these men played with their retired riches. Her Seventh Avenue bravado could not cover her cards. For the first time in my life, I saw my mother defeated by the people she said she despised. She could not fight the combination of a strange country, high fashion, pity, money, and physical pride.

One afternoon I noticed a crowd of guests gesturing and laughing at something in the center of the riding ring. I pushed through and saw it was my mother. Dressed in her checked polyester suit, she sat on top of a large brown gelding attempting to move it. She rocked back and forth in the saddle as if she were on a rocking horse, or making love, while voices cried out to her, "Come on, Regina, kick him. You can do it." The intimate spectacle of my mother's awkwardness, the one-sided laughter, and the desperate look on her face pushed me back from the railing. These people were my people: they had been kind to me. But something terrible was going on here. We were Jewish, but we were different.

Toward evening, at the end of our stay, I went in search of my mother. I looked by the pool, in the lounge, and everywhere else the other guests habitually gathered, but I could not find her. I wandered to the far end of the ranch and saw her in the distance. She was sitting on a child's swing, trailing one leg in the dust. A small round woman whose belly bulged in her too-tight, too-cheap pants. Her head was lowered, and the air shimmered around her as if loneliness had turned to heat. Where was Seventh Avenue, the coffee shops, the crowded subways, the city which covered her aloneness because she had work to do there. Arizona was not for Regina Nestle, not this resort with its well-married ladies. While I scrambled over this new brown earth, my mother sat in the desert, a silent exile.

3

Bill, the tired, aging cowboy who ran the corral, was my date for the evening. Elliot was with Mary, a woman in her twenties who worked at the ranch. We had been to see a movie and were now parked behind the ranch house. Bill kissed me as we twisted around in the front seat. His bony hand pushed into my crotch while his tongue opened my mouth. I pushed his hand away, sure of what I wanted and of what I did not. I did not want his fingers in me, but I did want to see his cheek against my breast. My brother and Mary gave up their squirming in the back seat and left the two of us alone. Bill was respectful. One word from me was enough to get him to stop his attempts at penetration. "Lay in my arms," I told him. He slipped his long legs through the open window at one end of the front seat and leaned back into my arms. His lips pulled at my nipples. We sat that way for a long time as the Arizona sky grew darker and darker. Right before he fell asleep, he said, "Best thing that's happened to me in twenty years." I knew this did not have very much to do with me, but a lot to do with my sixteen-year-old breasts. I sat there holding him for what seemed like hours, afraid to move because I did not want to wake him, when suddenly he jerked in his sleep and knocked into the steering wheel, setting off the horn. The desert stillness was split by its harsh alarm, and I knew my idyll was coming to an end.

One by one, the lights came on in the guest cottages. My brother was the first to reach the car, his pajamas shining white in the moonlight. "I'm alright, I'm alright," I whispered, as I maneuvered my body away from Bill's. I wanted to escape before the other guests came pouring out, to save Bill from having to explain what we were doing. He would be held responsible for breaking the boundaries between guests and workers, between young girls and old men, and I would never be able to convince them that I knew exactly what I was doing, that tenderness was my joy that night, that I danced in the moonlight knowing my body could be a home in the freezing desert air.

<h1 style="text-align:center">4</h1>

I spent most of my time around the horses, following Bill on his daily chores. He eventually gave me his chaps to wear because I was constantly riding into the cholla plants and ending up with their needles sticking into my thighs. My horse for the week was not the sleek stallion I had dreamed of, but a fat wide-backed white mare that was safe. Ruby and I were always on the tail end of the rides, but I did not care: the Bronx streets had disappeared, and I could bend over and talk to my steed while I stroked her powerful neck.

Each day we rode up into the mountains, the same mountains that had looked so distant from the airport. Our party was usually Elliot and myself, and Bill and Elizabeth. Elizabeth was a small muscular woman in her fifties whose husband was dying of Parkinson's disease. She had made my riding possible by lending me a pair of boots. Each morning her husband, a large burly man who walked in tiny trembling steps, would stand in the doorway of their cottage and slowly raise his hand to wave good-bye. Elizabeth loved him deeply, and each morning I saw the grief on her face. She would ride her horse like a demon far up into the mountains, leaving the rest of us behind. As the week passed, I slowly realized that she and Bill were lovers. I saw the tenderness between them as if it were an invisible rope that kept them both from falling off the rocky hills. Like two aging warriors, both grey and lean, they fought off sadness with sharp, quick actions. We would ride up into the mountain clefts, find a grassy spot to stretch out on in the afternoon sun, and silently be glad for each other's company. I never spoke or intruded on their moments together. I just watched and learned from their sad, tough, erotic connection all I could bear about illness and love and sexuality. On the way home, stumbling down the stony trails, I would ride as close as I could to these two silent adults.

Then it was our last ride together. We had come down from the mountains on a different path. We found a dirt road, smooth enough for cars, and I started to see real estate signs announcing that this area was the most restricted country in Arizona. I pushed my horse closer to Elizabeth and Bill and asked, "What does *restricted* mean?"

"No Jews allowed," Elizabeth answered. I looked around again in wonder at this land we were moving through. The distant hills had become known, and I loved this earth so different from my own. I silently rode beside my two older friends, wanting to be protected by their gentle toughness and not understanding how the beauty of the land could be owned by ugliness.

A Map of My Face

Marjorie Agosín

Creating a Map

I navigated without maps or precise schedules. I intuited that genuine cartography is hidden, invisible to hours and routes. I allowed myself to be swept along as if my body were blank. I eschewed directions and travel times. I understood that no one awaits a true traveler; that I was alone. Day and night were contained within me. I looked at my hands and understood heredity. I understood how the rhythm of a heart devoid of armor creates a map, imprecise yet full of remembrance and discoveries, like entering a secret.

The Murmur of the Road

And I know that I will find neither offerings nor promises. All that matters is listening to the murmur of the road, following the route, ignoring other tracks, traveling as if only one possible path existed: the present.

Promises

And I travel by choice and by chance in order to recover a fragrance or perhaps to honor the memory of someone who asks me to visit a certain place, this island or that cemetery wrapped in mist. And the places call upon me to fulfill promises, and my feet, free of reason's watchful eye, dance upon the earth, invited by the splendor of all journeys and the marvels of every trail.

A Compass and a Purple Sailboat

I surrounded myself with tiny objects that reminded me of certain cities: a purple sailboat, an erratic compass, an imaginary talisman, and a heart left in the shadows.

The City of Memory

In order to draw near to the City of Memory, I must exercise caution and accept both the ambiguity and the clear texture of the place. I must let the city rest peacefully, undisturbed by the resurgence of haste. Memory does not betray, and no matter how often denied, it suddenly appears like a veiled woman, cloud-like and solitary, searching for a word that will name her and find her. In the cities of memory, I must choose unhurried time, the seasons of light, and allow myself to be swept away by origins.

I searched in vain. At the end of the day, and despite all my efforts, I failed to return to the blue house or the patio where I took my first steps. No remnant of the house remained standing, only the cobwebs besieged by a ribbon of smoke. I wanted to find the ship that had taken me to the other side and the wise old women who blessed my crossing before it began. I found only the defoliated skin of death. I understood there would be no way to return to my country. I belonged to a population condemned to vagrancy, to exile, and to homecomings that take place only in dreams.

The City of Books

I entered the City of Books, dark jewels hoarded in temples and cathedrals. In this city I found buried candelabra and stories waiting to be read during nights of sea and moon. I loved the City of Books where lost gazelles wandered in search of signs. Like a cabalist, I searched for signs in order to invent myself through memory. And I read, insensible to my lips, surrounded by dolls, my hands placed passionately upon the letters, my voice like a river. That's how I reached the City of Books. By caressing their spines and edges, I reclaimed the beauty of their hard covers. Each letter emanated a story, each story was a secret and clairvoyant letter.

The City of Love

Last night I wanted to make of your body a city. I was not cautious. I lost myself in the fire of your face that in my hands became clear like a sacred flame. In the deepest recesses and at the moment of joy, when your mouth was a harbor or a never distant beacon. I told myself that the City of Love is like a body awaiting surrender, a body yearning for another without haste, exhaling day and night, light and darkness. Two people making love, the astonishment released by entwined arms, a tongue suspended like a drawbridge above another. Then I told myself that I had arrived at the City of Love, walking slowly with the gentle beating of beloved objects that appear on the riverbanks of dreams.

A Map of My Face

Little by little I discovered that my face was a fragile, dangerous, and enigmatic map. Each wrinkle pointed toward a clear and dark destiny. I learned to count the crevices in my skin as a person tallies loves, those required and not. I paused to consider each one, some like expanding cypresses, others like small boats adrift on the sea. Wise men will tell you that the face is a map of the soul. Such ancient men believe that growing old is the greatest possible honor, as only from the depths of one's soul can a heart take shape, like a pitcher of water, a magic vessel in which promises are kept.

My face and I traversed all the cracks and crevices that underscored the fragility, fear, and everyday apprehension yet pointed above all towards happiness.

The Traveler and the Mapmaker

I feared travel and uncertain arrivals at cities with ports. I feared hearing strangers. That is why I preferred to sit on the edge of the road and listen to the stories, songs, and fables of others. That is how I came to know unimagined rivers, pyramids, and minarets, until one day I decided to create my own world. I studied the secrets of cartography and palmistry, drew maps and imagined compasses to help me reach longed-for grottoes. I did not worry about losing my way as I traversed labyrinths. I felt certain I would find what I sought and that I would come to know the night, a desired caress along my arched skin. The map indicated certain possibilities: it made me see the beauty of cities and forests. The world fit in my hands, the ones I myself had drawn. I finally felt lovely, and I navigated freely with a crystal compass, a violet pen, and the wind in my hair as protective guides. I lost my fear of uncertainty and knew that I would always find what I had imagined at the root of my dreams, with God's light illuminating things like a brilliant lamp.

Cities of Water

I loved the cities of water—Alexandria, Beirut, Recife, and Vina del Mar—but I did not linger in their ports or bays. Instead I imagined the sea, the water, or a path headed to the shore across all distances.

Beyond a change in fortune, beyond returning home, it was the illusion of an arrival, the journey across fields and small hills, like delicate caresses thrilling my body. Then I would enter the cities like someone leaving the concave arc of sleep.

Traveling

For me traveling was that sensation of awaking alone in a hotel, then facing the window in expectation of a new day. In the silence of the room, I imagined my movements: small steps, the moist tiles caressing my feet, and the recognition of noises from outside my own being. I approached a fountain in the middle of a plaza and felt precisely that, the other life, the lives of others, and now my own existence brushing up against my gaze. The pleasure of being in another place intensified: nothing reminded me of what I was or had been. Traveling is a present, a walk along the abyss of dreams. It replaces past memories with new adventures. The pleasure of a journey lies in knowing one is guided only by uncertainty and that no mirror will reflect yesterday's face. Instead every mirror points towards doubt and paths strewn with brambles, labyrinths, and pyramids of fire.

I knew that traveling was like making love, the confidence of a body always unknown, adding other landscapes to the soul, allowing life to be an impulse, a flow of dreams. Traveling meant not desiring the quotidian. It was an obsession with astonishment, the wished-for tracks that lead into forbidden enclosures, the discovery of a waterfall, a breath of light and freshness.

The Treasures of Arrival

And as I traveled I became smaller and smaller. More than progress I treasured arrivals so that I could begin to narrate my increasingly uncertain and distant journeys.

Hypertext
Dorothy Allison

*O*ther night I went over to Providence to read in a line, a marathon of poets and fiction writers.

Afterwards, as I was sipping a Coke, a young man came up to me, fierce and tall and skinny, his wrists sticking out of his sleeves.

He said, "Hypertext. I've been wanting to tell you about it."

"Hypertext?"

"Your work. I've read everything you've ever published three or four times—at least. I know your work. I could put you in hypertext."

There was a girl behind him. She reached past his sleeve, put her hand on mine, said, "Oh yes, we could do it. We could put you in hypertext." She spoke the word with conviction, passion, almost love.

"Hypertext?" I spoke it through a blur of bewilderment.

"CD-ROM, computers, disks or files, it doesn't matter," the boy said in a rush of intensity. "It's the latest thing. We take one of your stories, and we put you in. I know just the story. It goes all the way through from beginning to end. But all the way through, people can reach in and touch a word. Mouse or keyboard or a touchable screen. Every time you touch a word, a window opens. Behind that word is another story. You touch the word and the story opens. We put one of your stories behind that story. And then maybe, maybe you could write some more and we could put in other things. Every word the reader touches, it opens again."

The girl tugged my arm urgently. "It's so beautiful," she said. "After a while it's like a skin of oil on the water. If you look at it from above it's just one thing, water and oil in a spreading shape. But if you looked at it from the side, it would go down and down, layers and layers. All the stories you've ever told. All the pictures you've ever seen. We can put in everything. Hypertext."

The boy nodded.

I reached for a glass of wine. I took a long drink, rubbed my aching back, said, "Yeah, right, I'll think about it."

That night I had a dream.

I was walking in a museum, and I was old. I was on that cane I had to use the whole length of 1987. My right eye had finally gone completely blind. My left eye was tearing steadily. I saw everything through a scrim of water, oily water. Way way down three or four corridors, around a turn, I hit a wall.

My story was on this wall.

I stood in front of my wall. I put my hand on it. Words were peeling across the wall, and every word was a brick. I touched one.

"Bastard."

The brick fell away and a window opened. My mother was standing in front of me. She was saying, "I'm not sick. I would tell you if I was sick, girl. I would tell you."

I touched her face and the window opened.

She was behind it, flesh cooling, still warm. Hair gone, shadows under her eyes. I was crying. I touched her hand. It was marble, it was brick. It fell away. She was seventeen and she was standing on the porch. He was sitting on the steps. She was smiling at him. She was saying, "You won't treat me bad, will you? You'll love my girls, won't you?"

I touched the brick. It fell away.

He was standing there. I was holding my arm. The doctor was saying, "What in God's name happened to this child?"

I touched the wall and the brick fell away.

My mama had her hand on my neck. She was handing me pictures. She was saying, "I didn't want to know who they were. I don't know what happened. I never wanted to tell you what happened. You make it up for yourself."

I put my hand on the photograph and the window opened onto a movie. I was eight years old. Cousins and aunts and strangers were moving across the yard. I was clinging to my mother's neck. I was saying "Mama" in that long, low plea a frightened child makes.

She reached for me, put her arms around me. I fell away. She was holding onto her mama's neck, saying the same thing, saying "Mama" in that same cry. My hands met the brick of her flesh. She fell away.

My son was climbing up my lap into my arms, putting his arms around my neck.

He said, "Mama."

The last brick fell down. I was standing there looking up through tears. I was standing by myself in the rubble of my life, at the bottom of every story I had ever needed to know. I was gripping my ribs like a climber holding on to rock. I was whispering the word over and over, and it was holding me up like a loved hand.

I can tell you anything. All you have to believe is the truth.

What We Remember and What We Forget from *Surrendered Child*
Karen Salyer McElmurray

*M*y memories of 1973 are sharp as cutlery stolen from a Washington hotel, and those memories are a tape I replay in my head for years. *Tell me*, I demand. *Tell me the truth.* There is no proof my son ever existed. No baby shoes in bronze, no lock of hair and a satin ribbon and a little paper book that says, *Welcome him, our boy.* My womb, after 1973, was clean and pure. Clean and free, I told myself, of indiscretions, of the manifestations of wayward desire. And yet for years to come, for all my life, I will be able to close my eyes and remember. I will cup my hands over my heart and I will listen and I will be able to follow the sounds inside me down to the way my womb once moved, echoing with the unalterable truth of my son.

I'm twenty and I speak with my father about the vicissitudes of responsibility, about the reasons time hurts and love is lost. It's 1973 and I'm sixteen and I birth a boy I will never see, the son I put up for adoption. *Put up*, like green beans or beets in jar. I'm fourteen and my mother leaves our home at gunpoint, or so she later says.

I was eight when I spent two weeks with my father's mother in eastern Kentucky. It was summer, so hot some afternoons I went behind the main house to the root cellar for the cool. I loved its smell of potatoes and the slick, wet walls lined with canning jars. In one corner was a boarded-over spring that cooled this cellar, which we called the warm house. One afternoon, I knelt and pried up the cover and bent over the spring, close enough to let my lips and forehead touch my own shadow. The surface of the water rose and I held still, not letting my reflection break. The blackness made me think of locusts and tree frogs and of how I wished my mother were one to tell me stories about the look of trees at night when there is no moon. But my mother was odd-turned, as they said, and when she tucked me in at bedtime, she wore white gloves and her hands were not kind.

Cohesion and adhesion, my father once told me, are properties of the same logical truth. Molecular attraction by which the particles of a body are united. My father told me water doesn't spill at all. It trails after itself, a single, silvery mass, molecule upon molecule, fluid as time. I touched the spring water again and again with my lips and my palms, feeling my reflection approach and recede.

Time is present, past, future. I am in search of that one place, an unreachable moment, a truth my father calls *the quintessential now* or *nothing at all*. Time is a carnival ride going fast enough to whirl up into the unfathomable sky. Time is a vortex in which I am spinning and spinning, fast enough for the world to vanish, leaving no sign of myself. I reach out and I want to hold on, to hold on and never let go. I want to find it, that one point, that one essential moment called forgiveness.

Research and Practice Strategies

1. Find a central image in an earlier piece you have written and consider whether there may be ways you can enhance the image's effectiveness in terms of its relationship to the rest of the piece. Revise the piece with this resonating relationship in mind.

2. Recall some significant places from your life. This may be of a street corner, a backyard, a place in nature, a room in your home, or a family vacation. Re-enter these settings, drawing on sensory perceptions and strong, specific details. See what kinds of associations your descriptions bring forth. There may be a story here.

3. Put yourself in a familiar setting; it may be a coffee shop or an airport, a subway stop or the beach. Don't write where you are or what time of day or night you are there. Let the reader find out about the setting while he is also becoming engrossed in your story; let your descriptions of the space you are in—sights, sounds, food or drink, your own actions and thoughts—drive your story. That is, try not to describe anything merely for the sake of description. Do your descriptions suggest mood? Do they suggest leisure activity or work? Anxiety or pleasure? Are you on vacation? On a date? Waiting for someone? Trying to accomplish something by a deadline? Your descriptions should suggest answers to these kinds of questions.

4. Recall a time when you were in a place and situation that made you feel a sense of pride. Try one in which you felt lucky. Now write a sketch of a time and place where you felt isolated. Are there other emotional moments you can represent through scene?

5. Write two or three paragraphs that describe a scene or setting with such precision that the reader can see, smell, hear its details. This can

be a room or a yard, or an historical moment other than your own. It could be written in the time of an ancestor, for example. It doesn't matter. What does matter is that you know it intimately and that you bring an emotional hue to your description. Enlarge the meaning while relying on the description of specific qualities inherent in the place and period you are describing.

6. Using Allison's "Hyptertext" as a guide, choose one (or a few) object(s) or image(s) from an earlier cluster (or develop a cluster based on images and objects that suggest moments from your life, especially within the context of family life) and use them as metaphors to write about yourself.

7. This exercise is divided into three parts: (a) Drawing on memory take a moment that had a strong impact on you, perhaps drawing on some of your previous clusters. Write a short, detailed scene, beginning with the phrase "I remember." Write the piece in retrospect, providing adult insight on the experience. (b) Now, write about the same moment from the age and perspective of the actual experience. Move back into the experience and recreate it as though you were actually in the moment, drawing on age-appropriate language and understanding. (c) When you have finished with both versions, read them aloud. Write a one-page reflection on the differences and similarities you find between them. Are you drawn to one more than another and if so, why? Do you see potential for integrating the two versions, perhaps developing one aspect more than another? If so, do this. If not, develop the version you are most drawn to.

Pointers and Potential Pitfalls

- One of the challenges when setting is central to a narrative is keeping the pace of the story moving, rather than having it halt while you describe. Descriptions aren't pauses, nor are they asides; they are part of the story. In Allison's "Hypertext," for example, descriptions of the brick wall are metaphorical, but the image is woven into the action of the narrative, even as it provides thematic dimension to the piece.
- The forced image or metaphor is the one you insert because you think you should. It didn't arise organically from your writing and thinking, but became a mechanical addition for the sake of metaphor. These are almost always overly obvious and ineffective.
- Be wary of the easy description; it's often a cliché—a tired, overused phrase that doesn't surprise or interest us anymore.

- Don't underestimate the power of the unstated. An image is made comprehensible to us by what isn't there—what artists and photographers refer to as negative space—as surely as by what is. Similarly, we respond to narrative by inference from what is and is not presented to us as readers. A common mistake I see in students' writing is a lack of trust that what they have shown the reader will be properly interpreted. So, they proceed to tell the reader what the previous scene actually meant. This kind of double effort not only distrusts the reader's abilities, it actually encourages passive reading. After all, if the writer is going to do all the work for the reader, why should the reader work at bringing her own associations and interpretations to the text? This is especially a problem when concluding an essay or memoir piece. Here the distrustful writer wraps it all up in a tidy package and ties a nice bow on the top that says: finished!

- Yes, there is always the possibility that a reader will misinterpret your writing, but if you carefully hone your work you should be able to trust that you've provided sufficient touchstones along the way; after all, readers and viewers are really co-creators of any art form. Their experience counts, too. My students are often happily surprised at some of their peers' "readings" of their work. They sometimes say that it hadn't occurred to them that a scene or image would suggest that particular meaning, but that they like the possibilities. Sometimes such responses will lead a writer in a new direction with a piece that is still in progress. We'll talk more about responding to peer readings and workshopping your work in a later chapter on revision.

CHAPTER 6

When Characters Are
Real People

*All writing is communication; creative writing is communication through
revelation—it is the Self escaping into the open.*

— E. B. WHITE

Creating Real People on the Page

Although writers refer to people who are represented in narrative nonfiction as
characters, it is important to remember that they are *real people*—you aren't
making them up and they aren't here to do your bidding. In that sense your
contract with your reader is to tell the truth, but your obligation to the characters in your work is to make them real—not stick figures. Sometimes this will
require figuring out why you want to write the story in the first place. At other
times, it will have to do with point of view. Often, it will mean that you will have
to get involved in the lives of those whose stories you are telling. As Natalia
Rachel Singer shares in "Nonfiction in First Person, Without Apology" (included in this chapter), if we don't approach writing about others with empathy
and care, we may find ourselves, like her, winning journalism prizes, but losing
friends.

Characterization is an element of story that unfolds organically out of the
exploration of experience—decisions, choices, actions, consequential reactions,
but also discernment, perception, sensibility. Just as situation is inherent in any
story, so complication is inextricable from characterization.

Character and Complication

As you write about people in nonfiction, you will be writing about them within
the context of specific situations. In working with situation, **character** and
complication become intertwined, creating the kind of **tension** that pulls readers into a story and makes them want to know what is going to happen next and
how things are going to turn out for a character they care about. What kinds of
decisions will the character make? Will she change? How will he choose among

the options available to him? Why does she move in this direction and not that? What was he thinking when he said that? Such questions address complication.

In the excerpt from Sonia Nazario's Pulitzer Prize-winning feature story, "Enrique's Journey" (included in this chapter), the author moves immediately into the character and consciousness of both Enrique and Lourdes, his mother. Nazario does this by reconstructing the scene of their parting, a scene that represents the last time Enrique will see his mother for more than 11 years, and it is those years that will be the shaping forces of Enrique's character. Read the following opening to "Enrique's Journey." Consider how character and complication are set up simultaneously.

> *The boy does not understand.*
>
> *His mother is not talking to him. She will not even look at him. Enrique has no hint of what she is going to do.*
>
> *Lourdes knows. She understands, as only a mother can, the terror she is about to inflict, the ache Enrique will feel and finally the emptiness.*
>
> *What will become of him? Already he will not let anyone else feed or bathe him. He loves her deeply, as only a son can. With Lourdes, he is a chatterbox. "Mira, Mami." Look, Mom, he says softly, asking her questions about everything he sees. Without her, he is so shy it is crushing.*

Following this poignant opening, Nazario retraces the Honduran boy's childhood and his 12,000-mile journey to the United States in search of his mother. It is through a description of the challenges he faces on this harrowing journey that she reveals his character and the strength of his desire as he risks everything to reunite with the mother he remembers from childhood.

Nazario takes a risk in moving into the thoughts and emotions of Enrique and Lourdes in this piece. This kind of creative license must be sure of its interpretive leap and the research must back it up. We will discuss this more fully as we explore narrative point of view in Chapter 7.

Characterization and Description

Read "Bricklayer's Boy" (included in this chapter) and pay close attention to how Alfred Lubrano, a journalist, uses observation and descriptive detail to underscore the distinction between his own developing white-collar identity and the working-class world of his father. Here is a brief scene that demonstrates the journalist's sharp eye for detail as Lubrano shows his father preparing for an exam that will provide for a foreman's job.

> *It was so hard for my dad. He had to take a Stanley Kaplan-like prep course in a junior high school three nights a week after work for six weeks. At class time, the outside men would come in, twenty-five construction workers squeezing themselves into little desks. Tough blue-collar guys*

*armed with No. 2 pencils leaning over and scratching out their practice
essays, cement in their hair, tar on their pants, their work boots too big
and clumsy to fit under the desks.*

We don't know if Lubrano ever actually went to one of his father's classes
or if his father described it to him. What we do know is that Lubrano has aptly
portrayed the contrast in size and presence between the construction worker
and the junior high school desk. His use of adjectives such as little, tough, big,
and clumsy serve this purpose. As an experienced writer, Lubrano creates his
scenes and characters with sufficient descriptive detail to get across the message he intends and at the same time, writes with economy. A less capable
writer might have been tempted to use too many adjectives—a mistake that
leads to readers' distrust. Had Lubrano written "twenty-five burly, sunburned
construction workers" instead of simply "twenty-five construction workers" it
might have appeared as though he were attempting to sell us too hard on the
scene, thus rendering it suspect. As he wrote it, with simplicity and eloquence,
we understand that these men are the working-class "outsiders," and we need
no further elaboration.

The following scene from "Bricklayer's Boy" dramatizes a situation that sets
up the central conflict between Lubrano and his father—the memoir's two main
characters. In so doing Lubrano reveals character by focusing on a specific scene
and a specific interaction. The larger complication of the story centers on this
conflict. The immediate conflict is about the kind of job Lubrano wants to take
and his father's reaction. But the larger complication of the story is about a cultural clash between classes—Lubrano's movement into a white-collar career and
what Lubrano calls his father's blue-collar values.

*In 1980, after college and graduate school, I was offered my first job, on a
now-dead daily paper in Columbus, Ohio. I broke the news in the kitchen,
where all the family business is discussed. My mother wept as if it were
Vietnam. My father had a few questions: "Ohio? Where the hell is Ohio?"*

*I said it's somewhere west of New York City, that it was like
Pennsylvania, only more so. I told him I wanted to write, and these were
the only people who'd take me.*

*"Why can't you get a good job that pays something, like in advertis-
ing in the city, and write on the side?"*

*"Advertising is lying," I said, smug and sanctimonious, ever the
unctuous undergraduate. "I wanna tell the truth."*

*"The truth?" the old man exploded, his face reddening as it does
when he's up twenty stories in high wind. "What's truth?" I said it's
real life, and writing about it would make me happy. "You're happy
with your family," my father said, spilling blue-collar rule No. 2.
"That's what makes you happy. After that, it all comes down to dollars
and cents. What gives you comfort besides your family? Money,
only money."*

Character revelation can be achieved in a number of ways, but the one that involves the reader most is situational. While you may *tell* your readers everything you want them to know about yourself or a character, you will provide readers with a great deal more pleasure if you *reveal*, through the immediacy of description and dramatic action, aspects of character, letting your readers interpret those actions. While you're doing this, you will begin to notice that you aren't simply describing your characters; you're setting up the terms and trajectory of the unfolding story. What meaning would have been sacrificed had Lubrano left out the fact that this interaction was taking place in the kitchen "where all the family business is discussed?" What would we have missed if he had not characterized himself as the "unctuous undergraduate" or if he had not revealed the "spilling" of "blue-collar rule No. 2?" We would have missed cultural components key to this piece. We would have been excluded from the intimate conflict taking place inside this family's home. Although we would have seen and heard the father-son conversation, had Lubrano left out these details, we would not have understood so fully who these two men really are—their understandings and misunderstandings. This is the beauty of writing *through situation* to get at *character.*

You will rarely rely primarily on description to do all the work, as it is typically far more effective to have "showing" and "telling" commingle in nonfiction narrative. Having said that, however, the following Short, "Around the Corner," by Sharon Bryan (also included at the end of the chapter), is a fine example of how "telling" can also be a kind of "showing." Bryan describes in detail specific objects she finds that belong to her mother, and by describing them and her mother's reactions, as well as her own, we come to understand a deeper meaning embedded within the objects. Consider what those deeper meanings suggest about both Bryan and her mother's character.

> *When I was small, maybe seven or eight, I noticed some crinkled leather boots in my mother's closet, some I knew I had never seen her wear. She told me they were for horseback riding and showed me some funny-shaped pants. "They're called jodhpurs," she said, and spelled it for me. She said she'd ridden when she was in college. She had taken archery, too. She had planned to major in journalism so she could meet with world leaders, and she had interviewed the university president for the student newspaper. She had taken Spanish, and sometimes spoke phrases of it around the house: "You're loco in la cabeza," she would say to my father, and she had taught me to count from uno to diez. She also knew another language: shorthand. Her mother had made her take it because it was practical, and my mother had used it when she worked as a secretary at the truckline. She wrote her Christmas lists in shorthand—and anything else she didn't want me or my father to read, like her diary. It was a little red leather book with gilt-edged pages, and I was most intrigued by its little gold lock. As I remember it, my mother showed it to me, and maybe even read some passages to me. Looking*

over her shoulder I could see that some parts were in shorthand. When I asked what they said she just laughed and turned the page.

My mother seemed to treat the diary—and the boots and jodhpurs, the glamorous pictures of herself that she had sent to my father overseas, her dreams of becoming a famous journalist—as relics of a distant past that no longer had much to do with her. She had left them all behind for life with my father, and me, and eventually my two brothers. I loved my mother, and thought she was beautiful. I was grateful for the sort of mother she was—she had milk and cookies waiting when I came home from school, packed my lunch box each morning. Every holiday was full of treats and surprises: a present by my plate on Valentine's Day, eggs hidden all over the house on Easter morning, Kool-Aid in my thermos on my birthday. Yet at the same time that I basked in the attention my mother lavished on me, I was haunted by the image of the person who seemed to have disappeared around the corner just before I arrived.

Characters who experience no emotional tension within the story being told—conflict, desire, or realization—are flat characters. Usually they are **minor characters** who are marginal to the story. Similarly, if the narrator resides within the narrative as a flat character he too will be marginal and the reader will either be disinterested in the story or feel distrust of the writer. **Flat characters** and narrators make no discoveries, achieve no insights, experience no revelations, and when they do, their discoveries appear premeditated and mechanical. If there is no sense of discovery on the part of a character or narrator there will be no sense of discovery for the reader. It is the dynamic, complex characters undergoing life's inevitable challenges, such as Bryan's mother, with which readers identify. Such challenges do not have to be earth shattering; even subtle realizations create dimension in a character and are worthy of story.

Revealing Character Through Dialogue

As you bring your characters to life on the page, you want to reflect on the kind of voice they have and consider how you might best represent an individual's unique voice. For example, consider the individual's diction, syntax, and inflection. Is colloquial language used? Formal grammar? Does he speak in a soft voice? Does she shout? All of these elements of voice lend themselves to revealing character.

Listen to how Lubrano's father, described by his son as "a blue-collar man," speaks in the following passage:

When I broke the news about what the paper was paying me, my father suggested I get a part-time job to augment the income. "Maybe you could drive a cab." Once, after I was chewed out by the city editor for something trivial, I made the mistake of telling my father during a visit home. "They pay you nothin', and they push you around too much in

that business," he told me, the rage building. "Next time, you gotta grab
the guy by the throat and tell him he's a big jerk."
    "Dad, I can't talk to the boss like that."
    "Tell him. You get results that way. Never take any shit."

This scene not only sets up the story's complication, which is ostensibly
about money, but its theme, which is really about class differences and their
effect on the relationship between Lubrano and his father. The most obvious
decision Lubrano made in this passage was to use dialogue in the first place.
He could have simply stated that his father suggested he get a part-time job,
leaving out "maybe you could drive a cab." Instead, he lets his father speak
using his own words. Notice how Lubrano uses spelling to convey his father's
use of language: nothin', gotta. Notice, too, how Lubrano describes his father
reacting to his situation: "Next time, you gotta grab the guy by the throat and
tell him he's a big jerk." While Lubrano's father speaks to him, Lubrano limits
his own dialogue in this passage to one line. He relies instead on being the
narrator of the scene, speaking to his reader instead of to his father. In his
narration to the reader, it is important that Lubrano lets the reader know that
he "made the mistake" of telling his father about the incident with his editor.
This accentuates the growing difference in perspective between father and
son and begins to convey the narrator's point of view, something we talk more
about in Chapter 7.

Character and Voice

In the prologue to her auto/biography, *In My Mother's House* (an excerpt
from which is included in Chapter 8), Kim Chernin discusses some of the
challenges she faced in writing her mother's story. After repeated requests,
Chernin had become the reluctant biographer of her mother's life and career
as a labor organizer during the McCarthy era. Attempting to capture her
mother's considerable ability to captivate an audience with a good story, especially since she, too, had been one of those enraptured listeners, Chernin was
disconcerted to find that some elusive quality in her mother's voice and character simply did not come through in the written word. Yet it was this very
quality that, as a writer, she had to bring to life on the page. Here is Chernin
discussing her mother's character and its relationship to voice.

At that time in her life my mother had no sense of humor. Her modes
were tragedy and fighting back against fate. I knew she secretly pre-
ferred the tragic but thought she should tell me the stories about fight-
ing against fate. She also had several voices. The dark voice was the
best; it was made in her chest, it was rich and heavy, if I leaned up
against her I could hear it breathing. There was a dry voice, for bitter

tales, a voice like rain falling when she talked about her mother, but mostly I heard the voice of someone telling stories for the purpose of fighting. What she was fighting was never named.

It was the unnamed from which In My Mother's House *one day emerged.*

The challenge Chernin faced as biographer was capturing her mother's complexity of character. And the simple transcription of her mother's words, once beached on the page, didn't do it. Voice, then, is more than words, just as character is more than action. Chernin remembers her childhood sense of her mother's strong presence.

When I was a girl my mother used to smell of lemons and rosewater. Her voice included that. It carried her gravity, the melancholy made over into outrage, a characteristic gesture, flinging her arm wide, staring over my head, looking at me but not seeing, in a rapture of remembering, deft fingers braiding my hair.

When I first began to work on In My Mother's House *I recorded my mother telling her stories, then transcribed the tapes. The words missed her, they suffered from her absence. It was hard to believe they were the same words. That made me aware how many things, when spoken, words are beside words. The silence that strings them together, the excited rush that carries them out, the brightness of their delivery, the slower measure by which they pause, falter, hesitate, almost stop, suddenly veer off to get going again, with a sharp exhalation of breath, a small, dark hand waving the specter away. Spoken words carry, and make use of, the incidental. The way my mother could commandeer a coffee cup, sip, tap, stir, as part of her story. To get my mother to sound like my mother on a page, I had to find a voice that was as richly textured as her presence, a voice that could, being a paper voice, rely entirely on itself, having been forced to dispense with lemon, teacups, apples, living breath. It had to sound like my mother, but not the way my mother literally sounded; it had to have something of her in it but something of me as well, of the way I had listened to her voice as, throughout our life together, it had told her story to me.*

While reading "Oy, My Enlightenment" (included in Chapter 8), we can consider how Chernin resolved the problem of character revelation and voice—as spoken, as written—and think about how we might best do this with an individual whose gestures, tone, and inflections are as essential a part of how she expresses herself as her words, an individual whose words simply do not do them justice when separated from their actions. As explored more fully in Chapter 8, "Finding Story in Situation: Resonance and Theme," an effective approach is to find specific situations through which those individuals we are writing about might most effectively be revealed.

Revealing Character Through Action

When you represent people in creative nonfiction, exploring how they act and interact within particular situations—called **dramatic action**—you are well on your way to the development of character. As readers we don't know what the mother of Kelly Cunnane's prose poem, "Clip from A Winter Diary," or her young children look like, but we do have a strong sense of her daily life and we get to see her in action in this vividly described winter scene (also included at the end of the chapter).

> *In the middle of the morning, she makes slices of herb bread with melted cheese. When they fuss, all day she cuts small squares and hands them to the complaining mouths. Later, she finds black cheese stuck in the rug, on the couch, but she has given, and that is all they want, although she knows it is not food they desire. Sometimes she gives out a story, and they huddle next to her and put her arm around them and fight about who has the most of her body next to them. The four of them are a corral, a fence within which she moves. She may run, but not too far or fast. She may do whatever she wishes but inside the fence of them. The movement of them and the way they appear draws her toward them. She offers hot chocolate, a bubble bath, and they bound at her, squeeze her, and she turns on the TV and they disappear into its living color.*
>
> *With snow on the ground, there is hope, and she bundles them and goes out into the pinched whiteness, its scrunch, scrunch. The noise of them dissipates and falls powdery off the branches of evergreens. She tucks the baby in a box with a blanket, so that only his round eyes show, and tugs him around and around and around the yard. Her back hot and her cheeks burning. Anything that requires her mind can only occur in small, indecent intervals. Her body carries on with sweeping, crying, bursting out in laughter, and bends 100 times a day toward a toy, a child, mechanically, rhythmically. The computer, house building plans, articles to write, lie untended, five minutes here, twenty there. The snow and the sleigh bring her to life, and the moon comes up over the trees and when she lifts the baby from the box, he is still warm.*

There is no dialogue in this piece and the adjectives are so few they can be counted on one and a half hands, and in fact are not used to describe the characters at all. While we do not know if the mother is short, has brown hair falling around her neck, if the children are boys or girls, if they have curls or dimples, we do know the mother is loving, attentive, the children wanting her love, busy with the moments of life the way small children are. We see, through action, through the verbs fuss, gives, huddles, offers, bundles, lifts, and many revealing others, that these characters of mother and four children are as real as they would have been had they been represented as wearing red snow boots or speaking with their child voice.

Readings

Writers on Writing

"Nonfiction in First Person, Without Apology," Natalia Rachel Singer

Memoir and Auto/Biography

"Bricklayer's Boy," Alfred Lubrano

Literary Journalism

from "Enrique's Journey," Sonia Nazario

Short

"Around the Corner," Sharon Bryan

Prose Poem

"Clip from a Winter Diary," Kelly Cunnane

Nonfiction in First Person, Without Apology
Natalia Rachel Singer

*I*n his introduction to the 1989 *The Best American Essays*, Geoffrey Wolff tells a story about how, in writing an essay on "King Lear" as a young boarding school boy, he could not help but narrate some of his own misunderstandings with his Duke of Deception father to illustrate his sympathy with Cordelia. Wolff's teacher wrote the customary "Who cares?" in red ink on his essay, insisting, as we were all taught, that when one writes nonfiction, it is necessary to "take facts in, quietly manipulate them behind an opaque scrim, and display them as though the arranger never arranged." Reading Wolff's story made me think of my childhood in Cleveland, and my decision, at the ripe age of five, to devote my life to becoming a writer. I remember thinking, as I watched my parents' marriage dissolve, and I stayed up late staring out the window at the oak tree in the yard and listening to the cranes at the city dump two blocks away scoop up crushed aluminum, that if I could record *this*: parents fighting, squirrels crunching acorns, garbage sorted like bad memories—that if I could find words to make sense of my own life—I could write anything. But in the neighborhood I grew up in, to be a writer meant to be a dead English novelist, like Charles Dickens. It simply wasn't done. Some people had heard of Ernest Hemingway, but you had to know something about fishing and bullfighting. Women writers usually went mad or changed their names to George. I wanted to continue to be a female person, and I wanted to tell "the truth." I wanted to explore "real life." Mine, at least for starters. I would have liked to have written my memoirs, but only famous people wrote their memoirs. To my teachers, writing about "real life" meant only one thing, and I was tracked early on to write for newspapers.

By the time I got to high school I was writing most of the feature stories on our school paper. I was often asked to go after "difficult and sensitive" subjects which required intimate self-disclosures from the interviewees. My portfolio is filled with family tales of woe and grief. Picture me at fifteen, asking a laid-off worker from the Acorn Chemical Corporation plant, the father of eight, what it feels like now that his house has just burned down and all of his family's possessions have been destroyed. Imagine me interviewing the pastor's wife after her son, who was in my homeroom on the rare days he showed up, has just fatally overdosed on window-pane. It is no wonder that I was soon nicknamed "The Sob Story Queen."

I did not know that I would someday decide I had exploited the people I wrote about. It never occurred to me to question why these stories did not satisfy my burning desire to write, or why, after writing them quickly and easily, I would hop on the back of Gary Pritchik's big black motorcycle and ride to the river where we tried again and again, beneath the blinking yellow factory lights, to set the Cuyahoga on fire. As a highschooler, I did not aim to achieve High Art; I wanted to pile up enough extra-curricular activities on my record to get into a decent college as far away from Cleveland as possible.

When I was asked to write a feature story on a friend of mine named Sharon who was suffering from Lupus, I realized that I was getting uncomfortable with this form of writing. I did it anyway, and the story won me a major journalism prize in Ohio, plus a scholarship to the Medill School of Journalism at Northwestern University, but it cost me a friend. After I wrote the story, Sharon and I simply never felt comfortable with one another again. It was as though, as Native Americans once said about their photographers, that I had stolen her soul. What interests me now about this incident is that out of all the people who might have written the article, I was truly the most familiar with Sharon's "before-and-after story," because I knew her body like I knew my own. Sharon and I had gone on our first diet together back in eighth grade. We had taken each other's measurements week after week and finally, one spring morning, had pronounced each other beautiful. We had coached each other on what to expect from boys. None of that was in the story because my hard-nosed editor would have written "Who cares?" across the front with his favorite grease pencil. Sharon remained other and her situation was simply tragic. Stripped of the noisy, meddling, "I," the writer whose observations affect and interact with and ultimately bring life to the observed, Sharon as subject was now reduced to an object; she was not that living, wisecracking teen-age girl with whom I'd once compared bellies and thighs.

Our first year in journalism school we had to take a course called Basic Writing: 50 percent of our grade was based on our final feature story which would be read in front of the class. I had not written a feature since the one I wrote on Sharon, and I was gun-shy. I searched the campus desperately for story ideas until one day, in the middle of Sex Role Socialization Class, my professor told us about a fascinating woman she'd met at a party the night before who was a preschool teacher by day, and madam for the most elite massage parlor in Chicago by night. This was before the time when we began to have suspicions about some of our preschool teachers. The madam—whose name I've since forgotten but it was something very unexotic, like Doris—would be coming to the next class, and was eager to talk to any of us in private.

The next Saturday the madam drove out to Evanston in her beat-up orange Opal and sat across from me in my dorm room beneath my Arthur Rackham poster of Alice in Wonderland, eating the cookies and milk I'd bought at the campus snack shop. She reminded me of Mama Cass turned bombshell in her flowing Indian skirts and her low-cut blouse with the shiny red heart she'd lipsticked onto her considerable cleavage. When she laughed her whole body shook, and the heart bobbed up and down like a fish. Outside the window there were kids playing Frisbee while she told me everything I wanted to know, and more. Finally, after we'd talked for hours, she picked up my stuffed koala bear with its N.U. garter belt looped around its waist like a goofy satin hoola hoop, and she set it down again on top of the tape recorder. "You aren't going to get the real story inside your sweet little ivory tower over here," she said. "If you really want to know your material, you have to spend a day at 'the house.'"

"The house" was not as seedy as I'd imagined. The "waiting area" was furnished discreetly with beige couches and chairs, Impressionist prints, potted plants, and a stereo that was playing the Brandenburg Concertos. I would have thought I was in an upscale dentist's office if not for the two women posing at the window in fancy lingerie. One of these women told me that before she'd started hooking six months before she'd only slept with one man in her life, her abusive ex-husband. She was twenty-seven. She looked at me with anger, imagining condemnation in my eyes. The other woman was eighteen, just my age, and I took to her immediately. Both were black, although the madam assured me that the massage parlor was a veritable melting pot of colors and Chicago neighborhoods, and that white girls who looked like junior varsity cheerleaders were in high demand.

As the madam had promised, the house catered to men's fantasies, and women were hired on the basis of whether or not they fit a "type." There was also a room full of costumes and make-up which could have serviced a theatre's full repertory season, from "MacBeth" to "A Streetcar Named Desire." My new friend, the eighteen-year-old, was six feet tall, and she'd been hired to deal specifically with men who needed women to be big. Her most frequent client was a prosecuting attorney who happened to be nearly seven feet tall. When he appeared socially with his wife, who was not quite five feet, people called them Mutt and Jeff. When the prosecutor visited the house, his lady for hire donned boxing gloves, duked it out with him in their imaginary ring, and knocked him down. Afterwards he would leap up unharmed, take off his gloves and hers, measure all seventy-two inches of her against the bedroom door with a yardstick, and then promptly carry her to bed, a redeemed slugger.

Then there was the pediatric prof at the medical school who wrote medical books by day and kinky fairy tales at night. The management required its women to be eighteen-and-over but they had no trouble finding voting-age gals who looked undeveloped, ponytailed, and girly-girlish enough to play Little Red Riding Hood to his Big Bad Wolf in those alliterative scripts he brought with him. And then there was the tax accountant necrophiliac.

The only client I talked to was the priest, who went there every Sunday after church and stayed all day. He loved to bake for his women and today he brought a loaf of bread which we all broke together and washed down with Diet Pepsi instead of wine. He was a lonely, inarticulate man with a voice that sighed instead of sang, and I could not imagine him inspiring fervor and faith from behind his pulpit. Nor, for that matter, could I—or did I want to—picture him naked and panting with one of these women, but that's exactly what I ultimately saw. Just as I was getting ready to leave, the twenty-seven-year-old insisted that if I were a true journalist and not a princess from the suburbs that I'd complete my research from behind the bedroom door. Before I could think about it I was in the same room with them, watching, notebook in hand, while they oiled, massaged, and stroked the priest to transcendence, all "on the house."

That night, tucked safely inside my dorm room, I began to wade through all this rich material. Immediately I was pressed with many writerly problems. How was I to deal with point of view? Whose story was it? The working women's? The clients'? My original goal had been to profile the madam, but she was swiftly being eclipsed by the prosecutor, the pediatrician, the necrophiliac, and the priest, who were all far stranger than she was. How much of the dirt should I put in? What should I leave to the imagination? What about what I'd seen with my own eyes inside that room?

I finally chose to make the place and its strange characters the subject of my article, and to do this I took myself entirely out of the story. I wrote it as though I were a bug on the wall watching a typical day in the house, but I tried to use the voice of the madam as much as I could.

As it turned out, the teaching assistant took me aside later and told me he thought I could publish it in *The Chicago Reader*. Other students in the class had interviewed the Chicago journalists they hoped to line up internships with for the summer and he and the prof were thankful that I'd gone for something with "grit." There was only one problem, he said, and that was the style. It was simply too literary. If I cut out all the adjectives, he said, I would be on my way to becoming a journalist.

I turned down his generous offer, as flattered as I was, because I'd promised the women I wouldn't publish the piece. Now that I look back, it seems that there were other reasons why I didn't want to sell this story to the *Reader*. One was that I wasn't interested in developing the dry, "just the facts" style that the t.a. thought I needed to master in order to become a valid journalist. The other reason was that the real story for me was not, as everyone supposed, that respectable professional men can be sleazy but simply that an eighteen-year-old girl/woman with Arthur Rackham posters and a stuffed koala bear with a Northwestern garter belt had been in this place and talked to these people and seen what she'd seen, and that she had somehow been changed by having told this story. My problem, in 1976, was that I didn't know of a journalistic form that would allow me to tell it the way it wanted to be told; those new literary journalists were not yet being taught. But neither, I discovered when I switched into creative writing, could it be told in a poem or short story.

Poetry writing was a two-quarter sequence taught by a woman who was writing her doctoral dissertation on the Modernist poets. Each week she had us read several volumes of the poet of the week—Eliot, Pound, Moore, Bogan, Stevens, Williams, and others—and then write two poems, the first a "pastiche" for which we obviously stole not only the poet's technical bag of tricks but his or her material as well, and the other an "imitation" for which we borrowed a technique but still tried to write our own poem. By the end of the first semester, whatever "voice" we'd all had before had been consumed by the tones and postures of our Modernist mentors. We would call each other on the phone and say, "How do you write a poem?"

The summer after that workshop I went to Wesleyan College and attended my first writers' conference. My workshop teacher read my poems and was kind enough to point out the origins of each line in my work. "That's from Shakespeare's Sonnet 18," he said, "and that's from 'Love Song of J. Alfred Prufrock,'" and "that's one of Louise Bogan's metaphors for depression. Where are you in these poems?"

A year or so later I went to one of my old poetry teacher's readings. She closed with a poem about the town where she'd grown up, which was some-where—I couldn't believe it—in the South. I'd always assumed, given her diction, that she'd spent much of her life in English boarding schools. Maybe she had. Then it dawned on me. On a certain level, my teacher's aspirations to literary academia may have been spawned by a profound self-hatred. As mine had. Along with the dreams of countless other girl-women I knew skulking around miserably in the library. If my teacher had exerted so much energy trying to transform herself from the "down home" girl to the Oxford poet scholar, then how could she help me go deep into myself to find my authentic voice and material and story? I signed up for fiction writing and hoped for the best.

The fiction writing class was taught by a tall, trim, blue-jeaned, very hip late-thirtyish fellow who was nicknamed "The Marlboro Man" by the circle of female students who had crushes on him. He had a slight Western twang and wore cow-boy boots. When he came to our parties he smoked pot with us and told humor-ous anecdotes about the famous writers he'd met. His class was entertaining and lively. We got to write about subjects closer to our own life, but there was still a lot of stigma against being "self-indulgent" and "autobiographical." Style was more important than content—you had to be slick and exude a certain daring razzmatazz. You couldn't be political or direct. Processing personal experience was only okay if you applied heavy irony. Think of the times. It was now 1978, and people everywhere were trying to numb their pain from the previous decade by wearing shiny half-buttoned shirts and jumping into vats of hot water with near-strangers to the beat of the Bee Gees.

Although there was some lip service paid to original voice and place in my writing training, the fashionable voices were usually male back then: Bellow, Nabokov, Gass, excerpts from Pynchon, and a smattering of Ishmael Reed for color. I felt pressure to rev up my narrative engine, just as, when the Carver school made the grade soon thereafter, I felt pressure to edit everything back out except for the name brand products. And as far as place was concerned, it seemed to me you had only two choices. You could write about rural New England, of course, or you could write about the gritty "mean streets" of a Chicago, L.A., or New York. But what about a place as modest and chintzy as Cleveland, nicknamed "The Mistake by the Lake?" When I looked out the window I saw not Mt. Monadnock, not the pushers at the subway, but a few scrappy trees and a mechanical crane devouring crushed cars. I wrote stories, back then, set in places I'd never been, like Paris and Barcelona and San Francisco, because, it seemed, my own eyes had never seen anything worth mentioning.

I've heard that when Annie Dillard first began writing what became *Pilgrim at Tinker Creek*, she intended to set it in Acadia National Park in Maine and write it in third person, in the voice of a fifty-year-old male academic metaphysician. After a time she realized that she didn't know Acadia the way she knew her home in Virginia, but it took a great deal of coaxing on the part of an enlightened editor to get her to write it in her own young female voice. This book, published just a year before I started college, points to a problem that women and people of color have always had in this country. Many of us have gotten one too many "Who cares?" written in red ink on our work. I think it is very common for the writer, especially the student writer, to approach a writing project with the feeling I am not worthy, as I am, with what I know now, to tell this story as I see it in my own words. To be an authority on this subject I have to hide behind the voice of someone else, perhaps someone whiter, with more Y chromosomes; to sound like I've been around I have to be from New York, or London, or Paris, or a charming old farm in New England with a ghost in the apple orchard who recites Robert Frost.

It was not until I was nearly thirty—just as memoir and the whole genre of creative nonfiction began to flower—that the stories from my life I'd tried to disguise and romanticize in fiction came exploding, honestly and urgently, onto the page. As a writer, a teacher, and a reader myself, I have come to see that today's readers are hungering for I-as-eye-witness truth, perhaps because we live in an age where it is now commonly known that our political leaders are liars and thieves. People are choosing to learn about Vietnamese war brides, the years of Stalin, and the American 1950s not from the so-called expert historians or the ruling patriarchs who led from inside their offices, but from *real* people whose solitary landscapes and single voices have a power that illuminates the larger humanity we all share—which makes, as the short story once did, the strange familiar and the familiar strange.

Just as readers are hungry to learn the truth in a language that is more lively than they find in the daily papers, our students yearn to tell their own truths and to come to understand themselves and their connection to the world better in the process. Creative nonfiction is a genre in which student writers can use their authentic voices and make no bones about their presence in the work. They can write about places they know well. They can feel that what they have seen with their own eyes is of literary value, and of human value to others.

It is my belief that education should be a nourishing place for the heart and soul as well as the mind, and it should build confidence, not destroy it. How do we help our students draw on their own resources, not just their acquired knowledge? The teaching of creative nonfiction can validate the students' current lives, and strengthen their writing skills. Nonfiction writing in first person teaches the young writer to sharpen her powers of observation and use of memory, to hone his specificity and finesse for naming concrete things, and to create an honest, living voice. For the student writer, the permission to write about something he or she passionately cares about is what motivates that writer to go the extra mile to make the prose vivid and clear, rather than flat, empty, and vague. To write first-person nonfiction well, one must make contact with what

Brenda Ueland calls "our True Self, the very Center, for . . . here lies all original-ity, talent, honor, truthfulness, courage, and cheerfulness."

I suspect that had courses in creative nonfiction been available to me back in Cleveland, I could have saved myself about fifteen years' worth of writ-ing mistakes.

Perhaps one day when encouraging a student to seek her "True Self" in non-fiction prose is a basic component of writing pedagogy and not some retrograde 1960s concept, it will be customary to write "Why do you care about this?" on student essays, instead of "Who cares?" Perhaps helping our students search for "the very Center" right from the start will save them several years of writing mis-takes. Whereas William Gass, in his introduction to *In the Heart of the Heart of Country* advises the aspiring young fiction writer always to "wait five years," the young nonfiction writer who has found his or her voice can often master a par-ticular piece of memoir well enough to create something worthwhile and even publishable right now.

Bricklayer's Boy
Alfred Lubrano

My father and I were college buddies back in the mid-1970s. While I was in class at Columbia, struggling with the esoterica du jour, he was on a bricklayer's scaffold not far up the street, working on a campus building.

Sometimes we'd hook up on the subway going home, he with his tools, I with my books. We didn't chat much about what went on during the day. My father wasn't interested in Dante, I wasn't up on arches. We'd share a *New York Post* and talk about the Mets.

My dad has built lots of places in New York City he can't get into: col-leges, condos, office towers. He makes his living on the outside. Once the walls are up, a place takes on a different feel for him, as if he's not welcome anymore. It doesn't bother him, though. For my father, earning the dough that paid for my entrée into a fancy, bricked-in institution was satisfaction enough, a vicarious access.

We didn't know it then, but those days were the start of a branching off, a redefining of what it means to be a workingman in our family. Related by blood, we're separated by class, my father and I. Being the white-collar son of a blue-collar man means being the hinge on the door between two ways of life.

It's not so smooth jumping from Italian old-world style to U.S. yuppie in a sin-gle generation. Despite the myth of mobility in America, the true rule, experts say, is rags to rags, riches to riches. According to Bucknell University economist and author Charles Sackrey, maybe 10 percent climb from the working to the profes-sional class. My father has had a tough time accepting my decision to become a mere newspaper reporter, a field that pays just a little more than construction does. He wonders why I haven't cashed in on that multi-brick education and taken on some lawyer-lucrative job. After bricklaying for thirty years, my father promised himself I'd never pile bricks and blocks into walls for a living. He figured an education—genielike and benevolent— would somehow rocket me into the consecrated trajectory of the upwardly mobile, and load some serious loot into my pockets. What he didn't count on was his eldest son breaking blue-collar rule No. 1: Make as much money as you can, to pay for as good a life as you can get.

He'd tell me about it when I was 19, my collar already fading to white. I was the college boy who handed him the wrong wrench on help-around-the-house Saturdays. "You better make a lot of money," my blue-collar handy dad wryly warned me as we huddled in front of a disassembled dishwasher I had neither the inclination nor the aptitude to fix. "You're gonna need to hire someone to hammer a nail into a wall for you."

In 1980, after college and graduate school, I was offered my first job, on a now-dead daily paper in Columbus, Ohio. I broke the news in the kitchen, where all the family business is discussed. My mother wept as if it were Vietnam. My father had a few questions: "Ohio? Where the hell is Ohio?"

I said it's somewhere west of New York City, that it was like Pennsylvania, only more so. I told him I wanted to write, and these were the only people who'd take me.

"Why can't you get a good job that pays something, like in advertising in the city, and write on the side?"

"Advertising is lying," I said, smug and sanctimonious, ever the unctuous undergraduate. "I wanna tell the truth."

"The truth?" the old man exploded, his face reddening as it does when he's up twenty stories in high wind. "What's truth?" I said it's real life, and writing about it would make me happy. "You're happy with your family," my father said, spilling blue-collar rule No. 2. "That's what makes you happy. After that, it all comes down to dollars and cents. What gives you comfort besides your family? Money, only money."

During the two weeks before I moved, he reminded me that newspaper journalism is a dying field, and I could do better. Then he pressed advertising again, though neither of us knew anything about it, except that you could work in Manhattan, the borough with the water-beading high gloss, the island polished clean by money. I couldn't explain myself, so I packed, unpopular and confused. No longer was I the good son who studied hard and fumbled endearingly with tools. I was hacking people off.

One night, though, my father brought home some heavy tape and that clear, plastic bubble stuff you pack your mother's second-string dishes in. "You probably couldn't do this right," my father said to me before he sealed the boxes and helped me take them to UPS. "This is what he wants," my father told my mother the day I left for Columbus in my grandfather's eleven-year-old gray Cadillac. "What are you gonna do?" After I said my good-byes, my father took me aside and pressed five $100 bills into my hands. "It's okay," he said over my weak protests. "Don't tell your mother."

When I broke the news about what the paper was paying me, my father suggested I get a part-time job to augment the income. "Maybe you could drive a cab." Once, after I was chewed out by the city editor for something trivial, I made the mistake of telling my father during a visit home. "They pay you nothin', and they push you around too much in that business," he told me, the rage building. "Next time, you gotta grab the guy by the throat and tell him he's a big jerk."

"Dad, I can't talk to the boss like that."

"Tell him. You get results that way. Never take any shit." A few years before, a guy didn't like the retaining wall my father and his partner had built. They tore it down and did it again, but the guy still bitched. My father's partner shoved the guy into the freshly laid bricks. "Pay me off," my father said, and he and his partner took the money and walked. Blue-collar guys have no patience for office politics and corporate bile-swallowing. Just pay me off and I'm gone. Eventually, I moved on to a job in Cleveland, on a paper my father has heard of. I think he looks on it as a sign of progress, because he hasn't mentioned advertising for a while.

When he was my age, my father was already dug in with a trade, a wife, two sons and a house in a neighborhood in Brooklyn not far from where he was born. His workaday, family-centered life has been very much in step with his immigrant father's. I sublet what the real-estate people call a junior one-bedroom in a dormlike condo in a Cleveland suburb. Unmarried and unconnected in an insouciant, perpetual-student kind of way, I rent movies during the week and feed single women in restaurants on Saturday nights. My dad asks me about my dates, but he goes crazy over the word "woman." "A girl," he corrects. "You went out with a girl. Don't say 'woman.' It sounds like you're takin' out your grandmother."

I've often believed blue-collaring is the more genuine of lives, in greater proximity to primordial manhood. My father is provider and protector, concerned only with the basics: food and home, love and progeny. He's also a generation closer to the heritage, a warmer spot nearer the fire that forged and defined us. Does heat dissipate and light fade further from the source? I live for my career, and frequently feel lost and codeless, devoid of the blue-collar rules my father grew up with. With no baby-boomer groomer to show me the way, I've been choreographing my own tentative shuffle across the wax-shined dance floor on the edge of the Great Middle Class, a different rhythm in a whole new ballroom.

I'm sure it's tough on my father, too, because I don't know much about bricklaying, either, except that it's hell on the body, a daily sacrifice. I idealized my dad as a kind of dawn-rising priest of labor, engaged in holy ritual. Up at five every day, my father has made a religion of responsibility. My younger brother, a Wall Street white-collar guy with the sense to make a decent salary, says he always felt safe when he heard Dad stir before him, as if Pop were taming the day for us. My father, 55 years old, but expected to put out as if he were three decades stronger, slips on machine-washable vestments of khaki cotton without waking my mother. He goes into the kitchen and turns on the radio to catch the temperature. Bricklayers have an occupational need to know the weather. And because I am my father's son, I can recite the five-day forecast at any given moment.

My father isn't crazy about this life. He wanted to be a singer and actor when he was young, but that was frivolous doodling to his Italian family, who expected money to be coming in, stoking the stove that kept hearth fires ablaze. Dreams simply were not energy-efficient. My dad learned a trade, as he was supposed to, and settled into a life of pre-scripted routing. He says he can't find the black-and-white publicity glossies he once had made.

Although I see my dad infrequently, my brother, who lives at home, is with the old man every day. Chris has a lot more blue-collar in him than I do, despite his management-level career; for a short time, he wanted to be a construction worker, but my parents persuaded him to go to Columbia. Once in a while he'll bag a lunch and, in a nice wool suit, meet my father at a construction site and share sandwiches of egg salad on semolina bread.

It was Chris who helped my dad most when my father tried to change his life several months ago. My dad wanted a civil-service, bricklayer foreman's job that wouldn't be so physically demanding. There was a written test that included essay questions about construction work. My father hadn't done anything like it in forty years. Why the hell they needed bricklayers to write essays I have no idea, but my father sweated it out. Every morning before sunrise, Chris would be ironing a shirt, bleary-eyed, and my father would sit at the kitchen table and read aloud his practice essays on how to wash down a wall, or how to build a tricky corner. Chris would suggest words and approaches.

It was so hard for my dad. He had to take a Stanley Kaplan-like prep course in a junior high school three nights a week after work for six weeks. At class time, the outside men would come in, twenty-five construction workers squeezing themselves into little desks. Tough blue-collar guys armed with No. 2 pencils leaning over and scratching out their practice essays, cement in their hair, tar on their pants, their work boots too big and clumsy to fit under the desks.

"Is this what finals felt like?" my father would ask me on the phone when I pitched in to help long-distance. "Were you always this nervous?" I told him yes, I told him writing's always difficult. He thanked Chris and me for the coaching, for putting him through school this time. My father thinks he did okay, but he's still awaiting the test results. In the meantime, he takes life the blue-collar way, one brick at a time.

When we see each other these days, my father still asks how the money is. Sometimes he reads my stories; usually he likes them, although he recently criticized one piece as being a bit sentimental: "Too schmaltzy," he said. Some psychologists say that the blue-white-collar gap between fathers and sons leads to alienation, but I tend to agree with Dr. Al Baraff, a clinical psychologist and director of the Men-Center in Washington, D.C. "The core of the relationship is based on emotional and hereditary traits," Baraff says. "Class [distinctions] just get added on. If it's a healthful relationship from when you're a kid, there's a respect back and forth that'll continue."

Nice of the doctor to explain, but I suppose I already knew that. Whatever is between my father and me, whatever keeps us talking and keeps us close, has nothing to do with work and economic class.

During one of my visits to Brooklyn not long ago, he and I were in the car, on our way to buy toiletries, one of my father's weekly routines. "You know, you're not as successful as you could be," he began, blue-collar blunt as usual. "You paid your dues in school. You deserve better restaurants, better clothes." Here we go, I thought, the same old stuff. I'm sure every family has five or six similar big issues that are replayed like well-worn videotapes. I wanted to fast-forward this thing when we stopped at a red light.

Just then my father turned to me, solemn and intense. His knees were aching and his back muscles were throbbing in clockable intervals that registered in his eyes. It was the end of a week of lifting fifty-pound blocks. "I envy you," he said quietly. "For a man to do something he likes and get paid for it—that's fantastic." He smiled at me before the light changed, and we drove on. To thank him for the understanding, I sprang for the deodorant and shampoo. For once, my father let me pay.

Enrique's Journey
Sonia Nazario

Sept. 29–Oct. 7, 2002

Chapter One: The Boy Left Behind

Sept. 29, 2002

*I*n the vast migration that is changing the U.S., thousands of children travel alone, seeking the mothers who went before them. Most are visited by cruelty. Some are touched by kindness. Success comes only to the brave and the lucky.

The boy does not understand.

His mother is not talking to him. She will not even look at him. Enrique has no hint of what she is going to do.

Lourdes knows. She understands, as only a mother can, the terror she is about to inflict, the ache Enrique will feel and finally the emptiness.

What will become of him? Already he will not let anyone else feed or bathe him. He loves her deeply, as only a son can. With Lourdes, he is a chatterbox. *"Mira, Mami."* Look, Mom, he says softly, asking her questions about everything he sees. Without her, he is so shy it is crushing.

Slowly, she walks out onto the porch. Enrique clings to her pant leg. Beside her, he is tiny. Lourdes loves him so much she cannot bring herself to say a word. She cannot carry his picture. It would melt her resolve. She cannot hug him. He is 5 years old.

They live on the outskirts of Tegucigalpa, in Honduras. She can barely afford food for him and his sister, Belky, who is 7. Lourdes, 24, scrubs other people's laundry in a muddy river. She fills a wooden box with gum and crackers and cigarettes, and she finds a spot where she can squat on a dusty sidewalk next to the downtown Pizza Hut and sell the items to passersby. The sidewalk is Enrique's playground.

They have a bleak future. He and Belky are not likely to finish grade school. Lourdes cannot afford uniforms or pencils. Her husband is gone. A good job is out of the question. So she has decided: She will leave. She will go to the United States and make money and send it home. She will be gone for one year, less with luck, or she will bring her children to be with her. It is for them she is leaving, she tells herself, but still, she feels guilty.

She kneels and kisses Belky and hugs her tightly.

Then Lourdes turns to her own sister. If she watches over Belky, she will get a set of gold fingernails from *El Norte*.

But Lourdes cannot face Enrique. He will remember only one thing that she says to him: "Don't forget to go to church this afternoon."

It is Jan. 29, 1989. His mother steps off the porch.

She walks away.

"*¿Donde esta mi mami?*" Enrique cries, over and over. "Where is my mom?"

His mother never returns, and that decides Enrique's fate. As a teenager—indeed, still a child—he will set out for the U.S. on his own to search for her. Virtually unnoticed, he will become one of an estimated 48,000 children who enter the United States from Central America and Mexico each year, illegally and without either of their parents. Roughly two-thirds of them will make it past the U.S. Immigration and Naturalization Service.

Many go north seeking work. Others flee abusive families. Most of the Central Americans go to reunite with a parent, say counselors at a detention center in Texas where the INS houses the largest number of the unaccompanied children it catches. Of those, the counselors say, 75% are looking for their mothers. Some children say they need to find out whether their mothers still love them. A priest at a Texas shelter says they often bring pictures of themselves in their mothers' arms.

The journey is hard for the Mexicans but harder still for Enrique and the others from Central America. They must make an illegal and dangerous trek up the length of Mexico. Counselors and immigration lawyers say only half of them get help from smugglers. The rest travel alone. They are cold, hungry and helpless. They are hunted like animals by corrupt police, bandits and gang members deported from the United States. A University of Houston study found that most are robbed, beaten or raped, usually several times. Some are killed.

They set out with little or no money. Thousands, shelter workers say, make their way through Mexico clinging to the sides and tops of freight trains. Since the 1990s, Mexico and the United States have tried to thwart them. To evade Mexican police and immigration authorities, the children jump on and off the moving train cars. Sometimes they fall, and the wheels tear them apart.

They navigate by word of mouth or by the arc of the sun. Often, they don't know where or when they'll get their next meal. Some go days without eating. If a train stops even briefly, they crouch by the tracks, cup their hands and steal sips of water from shiny puddles tainted with diesel fuel. At night, they huddle together on the train cars or next to the tracks. They sleep in trees, in tall grass or in beds made of leaves.

Some are very young. Mexican rail workers have encountered 7-year-olds on their way to find their mothers. A policeman discovered a 9-year-old boy four years ago near the downtown Los Angeles tracks. "I'm looking for my mother," he said. The youngster had left Puerto Cortes in Honduras three months before, guided only by his cunning and the single thing he knew about her: where she lived. He asked everyone: "How do I get to San Francisco?"

Typically the children are teenagers. Some were babies when their mothers left; they know them only by pictures sent home. Others, a bit older, struggle to hold on to memories: One has slept in her mother's bed; another has smelled her perfume, put on her deodorant, her clothes. One is old enough to remember his mother's face, another her laugh, her favorite shade of lipstick, how her dress felt as she stood at the stove patting tortillas.

Many, including Enrique, begin to idealize their mothers. In their absence, these mothers become larger than life. Although the women struggle to pay rent and eat in the United States, in the imaginations of their children back home they become deliverance itself, the answer to every problem. Finding them becomes the quest for the Holy Grail.

Confusion

Enrique is bewildered. Who will take care of him now that his mother is gone? For two years, he is entrusted to his father, Luis, from whom his mother had been separated for three years.

Enrique clings to his daddy, who dotes on him. A bricklayer, his father takes Enrique to work and lets him help mix mortar. They live with Enrique's grandmother. His father shares a bed with him and brings him apples and clothes. Every month, Enrique misses his mother less, but he does not forget her.

"When is she coming for me?" he says.

Lourdes crosses into the United States in one of the largest immigrant waves in the country's history. She enters through a rat-infested Tijuana sewage tunnel and makes her way to Los Angeles. She moves in with a Beverly Hills couple to take care of their 3-year-old daughter. Every morning as the couple leave for work, the little girl cries for her mother. Lourdes feeds her breakfast and thinks of Enrique and Belky. "I'm giving this girl food," she says to herself, "instead of feeding my own children." After seven months, she cannot take it. She quits and moves to a friend's place in Long Beach.

Boxes arrive in Tegucigalpa bearing clothes, shoes, toy cars, a Robocop doll, a television. Lourdes writes: Do they like the things she is sending? She tells Enrique to behave, to study hard. She has hopes for him: graduation from high school, a white-collar job, maybe as an engineer. She says she loves him.

She will be home soon, his grandmother says.

But his mother does not come. Her disappearance is incomprehensible. Enrique's bewilderment turns to confusion and then to adolescent anger.

When Enrique is 7, his father brings home a woman. To her, Enrique is an economic burden. One morning, she spills hot cocoa and burns him. His father throws her out. But their separation is brief. Enrique's father bathes, dresses, splashes on cologne and follows her. Enrique tags along and begs to stay with him. But his father tells him to go back to his grandmother.

His father begins a new family. Enrique sees him rarely, usually by chance. "He doesn't love me," he tells Belky. "I don't have a dad."

For Belky, their mother's disappearance is just as distressing. She lives with Aunt Rosa Amalia, one of her mother's sisters. On Mother's Day, Belky struggles through a celebration at school. That night she cries quietly, alone in her room. Then she scolds herself. She should thank her mother for leaving; without the money she sends for books and uniforms, Belky could not even attend school. She commiserates with a friend whose mother has also left. They console each other. They know a girl whose mother died of a heart attack. At least, they say, ours are alive.

But Rosa Amalia thinks the separation has caused deep emotional problems. To her, it seems that Belky struggles with an unavoidable question: How can I be worth something if my mother left me?

Confused by all of this, Enrique turns to his grandmother. Alone now, he and his father's elderly mother share a shack 30 feet square. Maria Marcos built it herself of wooden slats. Enrique can see daylight in the cracks. It has four rooms, three without electricity. There is no running water. Gutters carry rain off the patched tin roof into two barrels. A trickle of cloudy white sewage runs past the front gate. On a well-worn rock nearby, Enrique's grandmother washes musty used clothing she sells door to door. Next to the rock is the latrine—a concrete hole. Beside it are buckets for bathing.

The shack is in Carrizal, one of Tegucigalpa's poorest neighborhoods. Sometimes Enrique looks across the rolling hills to the neighborhood where he and his mother had lived and where Belky still lives with their mother's family. They are six miles apart. They hardly ever visit.

Lourdes sends Enrique $50 a month, occasionally $100, sometimes nothing. It is enough for food, but not for school clothes, fees, notebooks or pencils, which are expensive in Honduras. There is never enough for a birthday present. But Grandmother Maria hugs him and wishes him a cheery "*¡Feliz cumpleaños!*"

"Your mom can't send enough," she says, "so we both have to work."

After school, Enrique sells tamales and plastic bags of fruit juice from a bucket hung in the crook of his arm.

"*¡Tamarindo! ¡Piña!*" he shouts.

After he turns 10, he rides buses alone to an outdoor food market.

He stuffs tiny bags with nutmeg, curry and paprika, then seals them with hot wax. He pauses at big black gates in front of the market and calls out, "*¿Va a querer especias?* Who wants spices?" He has no vendor's license, so he keeps moving, darting between wooden carts piled with papayas.

Grandmother Maria cooks plantains, spaghetti and fresh eggs. Now and then, she kills a chicken and prepares it for him. In return, when she is sick, Enrique rubs medicine on her back. He brings water to her in bed.

Every year on Mother's Day, he makes a heart-shaped card at school and presses it into her hand.

"I love you very much, Grandma," he writes.

But she is not his mother. Enrique longs to hear Lourdes' voice. His only way of talking to her is at the home of a cousin, Maria Edelmira Sanchez Mejia, one of the few family members who have a telephone. His mother seldom calls. One year she does not call at all.

"I thought you had died, girl!" Maria Edelmira says.

Better to send money, Lourdes replies, than burn it up on the phone. But there is another reason she hasn't called. A boyfriend from Honduras had joined her in Long Beach. She unintentionally became pregnant, and now he has been deported. She and her new daughter, Diana, 2, are living in a garage, sometimes on emergency welfare. There are good months, though, when she can earn $1,000 to $1,200 cleaning offices and homes. Scrubbing floors bloodies her knees, but she takes extra jobs, one at a candy factory for $2.25 an hour. Besides the cash for Enrique, every month she sends $50 each to her mother and Belky.

It is no substitute for her presence. Belky, now 9, is furious about the new baby. Their mother might lose interest in her and Enrique, and the baby will make it harder to wire money and save so she can bring them north.

For Enrique, each telephone call grows more strained. Because he lives across town, he is not often lucky enough to be at Maria Edelmira's house when his mother phones. When he is, their talk is clipped and anxious.

Quietly, however, one of these conversations plants the seed of an idea. Unwittingly, Lourdes sows it herself.

"When are you coming home?" Enrique asks.

She avoids an answer. Instead, she promises to send for him very soon.

It had never occurred to him: If she will not come home, then maybe he can go to her. Neither he nor his mother realizes it, but this kernel of an idea will take root. From now on, whenever Enrique speaks to her, he ends by saying, "I want to be with you."

On the telephone, Lourdes' own mother begs her, "Come home."

Pride forbids it. How can she justify leaving her children if she returns empty-handed? Four blocks from her mother's place is a white house with purple trim. It takes up half a block behind black iron gates. The house belongs to a woman whose children went to Washington, D.C., and sent her the money to build it. Lourdes cannot afford such a house for her mother, much less herself.

But she develops a plan. She will become a resident and bring her children to the United States legally. Three times, she hires storefront immigration counselors who promise help. She pays them a total of $3,850. A woman in Long Beach, whose house she cleans, agrees to sponsor her residency. But the counselors never deliver.

"I'll be back next Christmas," she tells Enrique.

Christmas arrives, and he waits by the door. She does not come. Every year, she promises. Each year, he is disappointed. Confusion finally grows into anger. "I need her. I miss her," he tells his sister. "I want to be with my mother. I see so many children with mothers. I want that."

One day, he asks his grandmother, "How did my mom get to the United States?"

Years later, Enrique will remember his grandmother's reply—and how another seed was planted: "Maybe," Maria said, "she went on the trains."

"What are the trains like?"

"They are very, very dangerous," his grandmother said. "Many people die on the trains."

When Enrique is 12, Lourdes tells him yet again that she will come home.

"Sí," he replies. "Va, pues. Sure. Sure."

Enrique senses a truth: Very few mothers ever return. He tells her that he doesn't think she is coming back. To himself, he says, "It's all one big lie."

Lourdes does consider hiring a smuggler to bring the children but fears the danger. The coyotes, as they are called, are often alcoholics or drug addicts. Sometimes they abandon their charges. "Do I want to have them with me so badly," she asks herself, "that I'm willing to risk their losing their lives?" Besides, she does not want Enrique to come to California. There are too many gangs, drugs and crimes.

In any event, she has not saved enough. The cheapest coyote, immigrant advocates say, charges $3,000 per child. Female coyotes want up to $6,000. A top smuggler will bring a child by commercial flight for $10,000.

Enrique despairs. He will simply have to do it himself. He will go find her. He will ride the trains.

"I want to come," he tells her.

Don't even joke about it, she says. It is too dangerous. Be patient.

Rebellion

Now Enrique's anger boils over. He refuses to make his Mother's Day card at school. He begins hitting other kids. He lifts the teacher's skirt.

He stands on top of the teacher's desk and bellows, "Who is Enrique?"

"You!" the class replies.

Three times, he is suspended. Twice he repeats a grade. But Enrique never abandons his promise to study. Unlike half the children from his neighborhood, he completes elementary school. There is a small ceremony. A teacher hugs him and mutters, "Thank God, Enrique's out of here."

He stands proud in a blue gown and mortarboard. But nobody from his mother's family comes to the graduation.

Now he is 14, a teenager. He spends more time on the streets of Carrizal, which is quickly becoming one of Tegucigalpa's toughest neighborhoods. His grandmother tells him to come home early. But he plays soccer until midnight. He refuses to sell spices. It is embarrassing when girls see him peddle fruit cups or when they hear someone call him "the tamale man."

He stops going to church.

"Don't hang out with bad boys," Grandmother Maria says.

"You can't pick my friends!" Enrique replies. She is not his mother, he tells her, and she has no right to tell him what to do.

He stays out all night.

His grandmother waits up for him, crying. "Why are you doing this to me?" she asks. "Don't you love me? I am going to send you away."

"Send me! No one loves me."

But she says she does love him. She only wants him to work and to be honorable, so that he can hold his head up high.

He replies that he will do what he wants.

Enrique has become her youngest child. "Please bury me," she says. "Stay with me. If you do, all this is yours." She prays that she can hold on to him until his mother sends for him. But her own children say Enrique has to go: She is 70, and he will bury her all right, by sending her to the grave.

Sadly, she writes to Lourdes: You must find him another home.

To Enrique, it is another rejection. First his mother, then his father and now his grandmother.

Lourdes arranges for a brother, Marco Antonio Zablah, to take him in.

Her gifts arrive steadily. She is proud that her money pays Belky's tuition at a private high school and eventually a college, to study accounting. Kids from poor neighborhoods almost never go to college.

Money from Lourdes helps Enrique too, and he realizes it. If she were here, he knows where he might well be: scavenging in the trash dump across town. Lourdes knows it too; as a girl, she herself worked the dump. Enrique knows children as young as 6 or 7 whose single mothers have stayed at home and who have had to root through the waste in order to eat.

Truck after truck rumbles onto the hilltop. Dozens of adults and children fight for position. Each truck dumps its load. Feverishly, the scavengers reach up into the sliding ooze to pluck out bits of plastic, wood and tin. The trash squishes beneath their feet, moistened by loads from hospitals, full of blood and placentas. Occasionally a child, with hands blackened by garbage, picks up a piece of stale bread and eats it. As the youngsters sort through the stinking stew, thousands of sleek, black buzzards soar in a dark, swirling cloud.

A year after Enrique goes to live with his uncle, Lourdes calls—this time from North Carolina. "California is too hard," she says. "There are too many immigrants." Employers pay poorly and treat them badly. Here people are less hostile. Work is plentiful. She works on an assembly line for $9.05 an hour—$13.50 when she works overtime—and waits tables. She has met someone, a house painter from Honduras, and they are moving in together.

Enrique misses her enormously. But Uncle Marco and his girlfriend treat him well. Marco is a money changer on the Honduran border, and his family, including a son, lives in a five-bedroom house in a middle-class neighborhood of Tegucigalpa. Uncle Marco gives Enrique a daily allowance, buys him clothes and sends him to a private military school.

Enrique runs errands for his uncle, washes his five cars, follows him everywhere. His uncle pays as much attention to him as he does his own son, if not more. "*Negrito*," he calls him fondly, because of his dark skin. Although he is in his teens, Enrique is small, just shy of 5 feet, even when he straightens up from a slight stoop. He has a big smile and perfect teeth.

His uncle trusts him, even to make bank deposits. He tells Enrique, "I want you to work with me forever."

One week, as his uncle's security guard returns from trading Honduran lempiras, robbers drag the guard off a bus and kill him. The guard has a son 23 years old, and the slaying impels the young man to go to the United States. He comes back before crossing the Rio Grande and tells Enrique about riding on trains, leaping off rolling freight cars and dodging *la migra*, Mexican immigration agents.

Because of the security guard's murder, Marco swears that he will never change money again. A few months later, though, he gets a call. For a large commission, would he exchange $50,000 in lempiras on the border with El Salvador? Uncle Marco promises that this will be the last time.

Enrique wants to go with him.

But his uncle says he is too young. He takes one of his own brothers instead.

Robbers riddle their car with bullets. Enrique's uncles careen off the road. The thieves shoot Uncle Marco three times in the chest and once in the leg. They shoot his brother in the face. Both die.

Now Uncle Marco is gone.

In nine years, Lourdes has saved $700 toward bringing her children to the United States. Instead, she uses it to help pay for her brothers' funerals.

Within days, Uncle Marco's girlfriend sells Enrique's television, stereo and Nintendo game—all gifts from Marco. Without telling him why, she says, "I don't want you here anymore." She puts his bed out on the street.

Addiction

Enrique, now 15, gathers his clothing and goes to his maternal grandmother.

"Can I stay here?" he asks.

This had been his first home, the small stucco house where he and Lourdes lived until Lourdes stepped off the front porch and left. His second home was the wooden shack where he and his father lived with his father's mother, until his father found a new wife and left. His third home was the comfortable house where he lived with his Uncle Marco.

Now he is back where he began. Seven people live here already: his grandmother, Agueda Amalia Valladares; two divorced aunts; and four young cousins. They are poor. "We need money just for food," says his grandmother, who suffers from cataracts. Nonetheless, she takes him in.

She and the others are consumed by the slayings of the two uncles; they pay little attention to Enrique. He grows quiet, introverted.

He does not return to school.

At first, he shares the front bedroom with an aunt, Mirian Liliana Aguilera, 26. One day she awakens at 2 a.m, Enrique is sobbing quietly in his bed, cradling a picture of Uncle Marco in his arms. Enrique cries off and on for six months. His uncle loved him; without his uncle, he is lost.

Grandmother Agueda sours quickly on Enrique. She grows angry when he comes home late, knocking on her door, rousing the household. About a month later, Aunt Mirian wakes up again in the middle of the night. This time she smells acetone and hears the rustle of plastic. Through the dimness, she sees Enrique in his bed, puffing on a bag. He is sniffing glue.

Enrique is banished to a tiny stone building seven feet behind the house but a world away. It was once a cook shack, where his grandmother prepared food on an open fire. Its walls and ceiling are charred black. It has no electricity. The wooden door pries only partway open, and the single window has no glass, just bars. A few feet beyond is his privy—a hole with a wooden shanty over it.

The stone hut becomes his home.

Now Enrique can do whatever he wants. If he is out all night, no one cares. But to him, it feels like another rejection.

Nearby is a neighborhood called El Infiernito, or Little Hell, controlled by a street gang, the Mara Salvatrucha. Some MS have been U.S. residents, living in Los Angeles until 1996, when a federal law began requiring judges to deport them if they committed serious crimes. Now they are active throughout much of Central America and Mexico. Here in El Infiernito, they carry *chimbas*, guns fashioned from plumbing pipes, and they drink *charamila*, diluted rubbing alcohol. They ride the buses, robbing passengers.

Enrique and a friend, Jose del Carmen Bustamante, 16, venture into El Infiernito to buy marijuana. It is dangerous. On one occasion, Jose is threatened by a man who wraps a chain around his neck. The boys never linger. They take their joints partway up a hill to a billiard hall, where they sit outside smoking and listening to the music that drifts through the open doors.

With them are two other friends. Both have tried to ride freight trains to *El Norte*. One is known as El Gato, the cat. He talks about *migra* agents shooting over his head and how easy it is to be robbed by bandits. In Enrique's marijuana haze, train-riding sounds like an adventure.

He and Jose resolve to try it soon.

Some nights, at 10 or so, they climb a steep, winding path to the top of another hill. Hidden beside a wall scrawled with graffiti, they inhale glue late into the night. One day, Enrique's girlfriend, Maria Isabel Caria Duron, 17, turns a street corner and bumps into him. She is overwhelmed. He smells like an open can of paint.

"What's that?" she asks, reeling away from the fumes. "Are you on drugs?"

"No!" Enrique says.

He tries to hide his habit. He dabs a bit of glue into a plastic bag and stuffs it into a pocket. Alone, he opens the end over his mouth and inhales, pressing the bottom of the bag toward his face, pushing the fumes into his lungs.

Belky notices cloudy yellow fingerprints on Maria Isabel's jeans: glue, a remnant of Enrique's embrace.

Maria Isabel sees him change. His mouth is sweaty and sticky. He is jumpy and nervous. His eyes grow red. Sometimes they are glassy, half-closed. Other times he looks drunk. If she asks a question, the response is delayed. His temper is quick. On a high, he grows quiet, sleepy and distant. When he comes down, he becomes hysterical and insulting.

Drogo. Drug addict, one of his aunts calls him.

Sometimes he hallucinates that someone is chasing him. He imagines gnomes and fixates on ants. He sees a cartoon-like Winnie the Pooh soaring in front of him. He walks, but he cannot feel the ground. Sometimes his legs will not respond. Houses move. Occasionally, the floor falls.

For two particularly bad weeks, he doesn't recognize family members. His hands tremble. He coughs black phlegm.

An Education

Enrique marks his 16th birthday. All he wants is his mother. One Sunday, he and his friend Jose put train-riding to the test. They leave for *El Norte.*

At first, no one notices. They take buses across Guatemala to the Mexican border.

"I have a mom in the U.S.," Enrique tells a guard.

"Go home," the man replies.

They slip past the guard and make their way 12 miles into Mexico to Tapachula. There they approach a freight train near the depot. But before they can reach the tracks, police stop them. The officers rob them, the boys say later, but then let them go—Jose first, Enrique afterward.

They find each other and another train. Now, for the first time, Enrique clambers aboard. The train crawls out of the Tapachula station. From here on, he thinks, nothing bad can happen.

They know nothing about riding the rails.

Jose is terrified. Enrique, who is braver, jumps from car to car on the slow-moving train. He slips and falls—away from the tracks, luckily—and lands on a backpack padded with a shirt and an extra pair of pants.

He scrambles aboard again.

But their odyssey comes to a humiliating halt.

Near Tierra Blanca, a small town in Veracruz state, authorities snatch them from the top of a freight car. The officers take them to a cell filled with MS gangsters, then deport them. Enrique is bruised and limping, and he misses Maria Isabel. They find coconuts to sell for bus fare and go home.

A Decision

Enrique sinks deeper into drugs. By mid-December, he owes his marijuana supplier 6,000 lempiras, about $400. He has only 1,000 lempiras. He promises the rest by midweek, but cannot keep his word. The following weekend, he encounters the dealer on the street.

The supplier accuses Enrique of lying and threatens to kill him.

Enrique pleads with him.

If Enrique doesn't pay up, the dealer vows, he will kill Enrique's sister. The dealer mistakenly thinks that Enrique's cousin, Tania Ninoska Turcios, 18, is his sister. Both girls are finishing high school, and most of the family is away at a Nicaraguan hotel celebrating their graduation.

Enrique pries open the back door to the house where his Uncle Carlos Orlando Turcios Ramos and Aunt Rosa Amalia live. He hesitates. How can he do this to his own family? Three times, he walks up to the door, opens it, closes it and leaves. Each time, he takes another deep hit of glue.

Finally, he enters the house, picks open the lock to a bedroom door, then jimmies the back of his aunt's armoire with a knife. He stuffs 25 pieces of her jewelry into a plastic bag and hides it under a rock near the local lumberyard.

At 10 p.m., the family returns to find the bedroom ransacked.

Neighbors say the dog did not bark.

"It must have been Enrique," Aunt Rosa Amalia says. She calls the police. Uncle Carlos and several officers go to find him.

"Why did you do this? Why?" Aunt Rosa Amalia yells.

"It wasn't me." As soon as he says it, he flushes with shame and guilt. The police handcuff him. In their patrol car, he trembles and begins to cry. "I was drugged. I didn't want to do it." He tells the officers that a dealer wanting money had threatened to kill Tania.

He leads police to the bag of jewelry.

"Do you want us to lock him up?" the police ask.

Uncle Carlos thinks of Lourdes. They cannot do this to her. Instead, he orders Tania to stay indoors indefinitely, for her own safety.

But the robbery finally convinces Uncle Carlos that Enrique needs help. He finds him a $15-a-week job at a tire store. He eats lunch with him every day—chicken and homemade soup. He tells the family they must show him their love.

During the next month, January 2000, Enrique tries to quit drugs. He cuts back, but then he gives in. Every night, he comes home later. He looks at himself in disgust. He is dressing like a slob—his life is unraveling. He is lucid enough to tell Belky that he knows what he has to do.

He simply has to go find his mother.

Aunt Ana Lucia Aguilera agrees. She and Enrique have clashed for months. Ana Lucia is the only breadwinner. Even with his job at the tire store, Enrique is an economic drain.

Worse, he is sullying the only thing her family owns: its good name.

They speak bitter words that both, along with Enrique's Grandmother Agueda, will recall months later. "Where are you coming from, you old bum?" Ana Lucia asks as Enrique walks in the door. "Coming home for food, huh?"

"Be quiet!" he says. "I'm not asking anything of you."

"You are a lazy bum! A drug addict! No one wants you here." All the neighbors can hear. "This isn't your house. Go to your mother!"

Over and over, in a low voice, Enrique says, half pleading, "You better be quiet."

Finally, he snaps. He kicks Ana Lucia twice, squarely in the buttocks.

She shrieks.

His grandmother runs out of the house. She grabs a stick and threatens to club him if he touches Ana Lucia again. Now even his grandmother wishes he would go to the United States. He is hurting the family—and himself. She says, "He'll be better off there."

Goodbye

Maria Isabel, Enrique's girlfriend, finds him sitting on a rock at a street corner, weeping, rejected again. She tries to comfort him. He is high on glue. He tells her he sees a wall of fire that is killing his mother. "*¿Por qué me dejó?*" he cries out. "Why did she leave me?"

He feels shame for what he has done to his family and what he is doing to Maria Isabel, who might be pregnant. He fears he will end up on the streets or dead. Only his mother can help him. She is his salvation. "If you had known my mom, you would know she's a good person," he says to his friend Jose. "I love her."

Enrique has to find her. He sells the few things he owns: his bed, a gift from his mother; his leather jacket, a gift from his dead uncle; his rustic armoire, where he hangs his clothes.

He crosses town to say goodbye to Grandmother Maria. Trudging up the hill to her house, he encounters his father. "I'm leaving," he says. "I'm going to make it to the U.S." He asks him for money.

His father gives him enough for a soda and wishes him luck.

"Grandma, I'm leaving," Enrique says. "I'm going to find my mom."

Don't go, she pleads. She promises to build him a one-room house in the corner of her cramped lot.

But he has made up his mind.

She gives him 100 lempiras, about $7—all the money she has.

"I'm leaving already, Sis," he tells Belky the next morning.

She feels her stomach tighten. They have lived most of their lives apart, but he is the only one who understands her loneliness. Quietly she fixes a special meal: tortillas, a pork cutlet, rice, fried beans with a sprinkling of cheese.

"Don't leave," she says, tears welling in her eyes.

"I have to."

It is hard for him too. Every time he has talked to his mother, she has warned him not to come—it's too dangerous. But if somehow he gets to the U.S. border, he will call her. Being so close, she'll have to welcome him. "If I call her from there," he says to Jose, "how can she not accept me?"

He makes himself one promise: "I'm going to reach the United States, even if it takes one year."

Only after a year passes will he give up, turn on his heel and go back.

Quietly, Enrique, the slight kid with a boyish grin, fond of kites, spaghetti, soccer and break dancing, who likes to play in the mud and watch Mickey Mouse cartoons with his 4-year-old cousin, packs up his belongings: corduroy pants, a T-shirt, a cap, gloves, a toothbrush and toothpaste.

For a long moment, he looks at a picture of his mother, but he does not take it. He might lose it.

He writes her telephone number on a scrap of paper. Just in case, he also scrawls it in ink on the inside waistband of his pants.

He has $57 in his pocket.

On March 2, 2000, he goes to his Grandmother Agueda's house. He stands on the same porch that his mother disappeared from 11 years before.

He hugs Maria Isabel and Aunt Rosa Amalia. Then he steps off.

Around the Corner

Sharon Bryan

*W*hen I was small, maybe seven or eight, I noticed some crinkled leather boots in my mother's closet, some I knew I had never seen her wear. She told me they were for horseback riding, and showed me some funny-shaped pants. "They're called jodhpurs," she said, and spelled it for me. She said she'd ridden when she was in college. She had taken archery, too. She had planned to major in journalism so she could meet with world leaders, and she had interviewed the university president for the student newspaper. She had taken Spanish, and sometimes spoke phrases of it around the house: "You're *loco in la cabeza*," she would say to my father, and she had taught me to count from *uno* to *diez*. She also knew another language: shorthand. Her mother had made her take it because it was practical, and my mother had used it when she worked as a secretary at the truckline. She wrote her Christmas lists in shorthand—and anything else she didn't want me or my father to read, like her diary. It was a little red leather book with gilt-edged pages, and I was most intrigued by its little gold lock. As I remember it, my mother showed it to me, and maybe even read some passages to me. Looking over her shoulder I could see that some parts were in shorthand. When I asked what they said she just laughed and turned the page.

My mother seemed to treat the diary—and the boots and jodhpurs, the glamorous pictures of herself that she had sent to my father overseas, her dreams of becoming a famous journalist— as relics of a distant past that no longer had much to do with her. She had left them all behind for life with my father, and me, and eventually my two brothers. I loved my mother, and thought she was beautiful. I was grateful for the sort of mother she was—she had milk and cookies waiting when I came home from school, packed my lunchbox each morning. Every holiday was full of treats and surprises: a present by my plate on Valentine's Day, eggs hidden all over the house on Easter morning, Kool-Aid in my thermos on my birthday. Yet at the same time that I basked in the attention my mother lavished on me, I was haunted by the image of the person who seemed to have disappeared around the corner just before I arrived.

Clip from a Winter Diary
Kelly Cunnane

*I*n the middle of the morning, she makes slices of herb bread with melted cheese. When they fuss, all day she cuts small squares and hands them to the complaining mouths. Later, she finds black cheese stuck in the rug, on the couch, but she has given, and that is all they want, although she knows it is not food they desire. Sometimes she gives out a story, and they huddle next to her and put her arm around them and fight about who has the most of her body next to them. The four of them are a corral, a fence within which she moves. She may run but not too far or fast. She may do whatever she wishes but inside the fence of them. The movement of them and the way they appear draws her toward them. She offers hot chocolate, a bubble bath, and they bound at her, squeeze her, and she turns on the TV and they disappear into its living color.

With snow on the ground, there is hope, and she bundles them and goes out into the pinched whiteness, its scrunch, scrunch. The noise of them dissipates and falls powdery off the branches of evergreens. She tucks the baby in a box with a blanket, so that only his round eyes show, and tugs him around and around and around the yard, her back hot and her cheeks burning. Anything that requires her mind can only occur in small, indecent intervals. Her body carries on with sweeping, crying, bursting out in laughter, and bends 100 times a day toward a toy, a child, mechanically, rhythmically. The computer, house building plans, articles to write, lie untended, five minutes here, twenty there. The snow and the sleigh bring her to life, and the moon comes up over the trees and when she lifts the baby from the box, he is still warm.

Research and Practice Strategies

1. Write a description of the mother portrayed in Bryan's piece "Around the Corner." What kind of a person is she? What are her qualities? Traits? Can you describe her appearance? Now write a similar description of Chernin's mother in her piece, "Oy, My Enlightenment," included in Chapter 8. How fully do we know each mother? How important is it that we know what a person looks like? Discuss this within the context of these two stories. Be sure to address the powerful presence of each woman in each story.

2. What do you know about your ancestors? Do you know where they come from? What are some of the family stories you've heard about more distant ancestors? Try telling their stories from their perspective. Can you capture a sense of their voice and preoccupations? If this is too challenging, you might tell their story from another family member's perspective. For example, if you are writing about your paternal great-grandmother, try telling it from your grandfather's point of view. This will be his mother's story and the story he tells will reveal aspects of his character as well as his mother's. You may choose to show your grandfather in the present time and weave this "telling" as a way to ground the story in the present, or you may wish to return to the past with him and show him as a young boy. You may choose to do both. The reading from Chernin's *In My Mother's House* will be helpful in doing this exercise. "Oy, My Enlightenment" is told from Chernin's point of view while interacting with her mother as her mother recalls the past.

Pointers and Potential Pitfalls

Remember, it's not just the physical description that is important; it's also the idiosyncrasies of the person whose character you are developing that you will want to draw on.

Be careful with accents and colloquialisms; you don't want to stereotype an individual or group. You are trying to give a flavor of an individual's manner of expressing himself to reveal individuality, not a stereotype.

CHAPTER 7

Narrative Persona: Art, Facts, and the "I" of the Story

Out of the raw material of a writer's own undisguised being a narrator is fashioned whose existence on the page is integral to the tale being told.
—VIVIAN GORNICK

Narrative Persona and Voice

Somewhere between the facts of the story and the art of its remembering, imagining, and constructing stands an "I." And it is the imagination of that "I" that is central to the creative part of creative nonfiction, whether the "I" is explicit or implicit within the storyline.

While **narrative persona** results from a writer's observations and responses to events and situations, it is also arrived at through an honest process of self-exploration. In this way the writer's engagement with self, subject, and situation creates the central **point of view** taken by the writer, a perspective that shapes the story. As such, the narrator takes on a persona just as he offers a point of view. While the narrator in creative nonfiction is not a fictional character, the persona created by the writing self—to some extent—is an artifice. Narrative persona takes shape simultaneously with story, and through the act of composition becomes a version of the self.

"The concept of persona allows us to acknowledge that, just as no written account can tell the whole truth about an event, so no 'I' of a poem, essay, or story is exactly the same as the person who writes," notes Janet Burroway in *Imaginative Writing: The Elements of Craft.* "When you write 'as yourself' in your own voice—in a personal essay or lyric poem, for example—there is nevertheless a certain distance between the person you are as you go about living your daily life and the persona in which you write." She adds, "The version of yourself that you choose to reveal is a part of your meaning."

Many writers describe themselves as being surprised, not only by what finds its way to the page, but also the **voice** through which self-expression takes shape. Still others say that this is why they write—to find out, not only what it is they know, but also a fuller sense of who they are. This speaking self doesn't rise up effortlessly, nor can it be separated from the language through which it is expressed. As meaning takes shape on the page, narrative persona is brought to life. Writing, then, from initial idea to completion, is a way of engaging the heart as well as the mind in various modes of comprehending experience and emotion. It's a wonderful way to understand and share the self. In "The Writer's Journey," book editor, publisher, and literary agent Deborah Levine Herman encourages writers to focus their attention on the process of writing instead of the goal of publishing, noting that "the process of writing is like a wondrous journey that can help you cross a bridge to the treasures hidden within your own subconscious."

Writers of fiction create characters that do the work of enacting the story for them. But writers of narrative nonfiction must orchestrate this dynamic more directly from lived experience, emotional response, and observation. This is especially true of memoir and the personal essay, and to a great extent, literary journalism. Even when the writer is focused outward on an event or another individual (as in the personal profile, or the feature story), literary journalism invites the "I" into the narrative, so the writer's response to the situation is not only relevant, but a significant part of the story. "The defining mark of literary journalism is the personality of the writer, the individual and intimate voice of the whole, candid person . . . . it is the voice of someone naked, without bureaucratic shelter, speaking simply in his or her own right, someone who has illuminated experience with private reflection, but who has not transcended crankiness, wryness, doubtfulness, and who doesn't blank out emotional realities of sadness, glee, excitement, fury, love," writes Mark Kramer, co-editor with Norman Sims of *Literary Journalism: A New Collection of the Best American Nonfiction.*

A vivid example of how voice can reveal the writer's personality and how literary journalism can build on, not erase, emotional realities, is found in the work of columnist Molly Ivins whose "Texas Women: True Grit and All the Rest" (included in Chapter 9) draws on numerous techniques to convey her wry, humorous, and candid cultural commentary. The language is lively, bringing a spirited voice to the columnist's work; the critique is biting, bringing irony and wit to her analysis of gender roles in Texas. Ivins may not identify as feminist, but she certainly indicts the sexism "so deeply ingrained in the culture" that "it's often difficult to distinguish the disgusting from the outrageous or the offensive from the amusing." Direct, unapologetic, Ivins is from Texas, but she never quite fit into the social script.

> *I spent my girlhood as a Clydesdale among thoroughbreds. I clopped along amongst them cheerfully, admiring their grace, but the strange training rituals they went through left me secretly relieved that no one would ever expect me to step on a racetrack. I think it is quite possible to grow up in Texas as an utter failure in flirting, gentility, cheerleading, sexpottery, and manipulation and still be without any permanent scars. Except one. We'd all rather be blond.*

Ivins was ineligible for several reasons, least of which is that she doesn't fit the part, she informs the reader, drawing on the vivid comparison between

Clydesdales and thoroughbreds. She plays with language and creates humor, often at her own expense, but also to convey a sharp wit that cuts through the demure persona expected of the Texas girl or woman. Her critique of domestic violence and even rape jokes in the Texas legislature doesn't derail her from using humor to achieve her goal.

Very little is taken at face value by writers who approach the self—as surely as they would any external situation—as a source of investigation. Indeed, to criticize the mass appeal of contemporary creative nonfiction as a sign of a solipsistic society is to misunderstand the motivation behind the genre. Notice, for example, how Ivins scrutinizes herself even as she analyzes the Texas culture by which she has been shaped. The creative nonfiction piece, as Vivian Gornick so aptly notes in *The Situation and the Story*, "builds only when the narrator is involved not in confession but in this kind of self-investigation, the kind that means to provide motion, purpose, and dramatic tension."

It may seem odd that as writers we would approach the self in the spirit of investigation. After all, don't we come to the act of writing fully knowing ourselves? Perhaps. Perhaps not. But the point is that the relationship that develops between writer and narrator comes from a paradoxical position, from peering into one's self from an intimate, but detached perspective. This act brings the narrator into the story, in effect, as yet another character within the story. The self becomes both "I" and "eye," the one who experiences and the one who responds to that experience, the one who explores the experience and her reactions to it—the one who is, simultaneously, subject and investigator.

Narrative Point of View

We often think of point of view as personal opinion, as in "that's *just* your point of view," which is intended to be dismissive. But **narrative point of view**, when used as a literary technique, links persona and perspective; it situates the level of intimacy on the part of the narrator to scene and situation. As a writer you want to achieve a balance between the overly familiar voice, which has no distance from the experience, and the overly distanced voice, which has a deadening quality on the narrative. If you find that you can't get into a scene or situation from one perspective, try another. Move about and approach things from a variety of points of view until one seems to carry you into the narrative. There is no one way to tell any story, but you will find that some approaches work better than others, so you should keep trying until you find the best one.

Narrative point of view is usually first- or third-person (the second person "you" is used less frequently) and may be **limited** (the reader views the story through the consciousness of the narrator or one character), **unlimited** (the reader is permitted to move in and out of the consciousness of several characters and be made aware of their perceptions and thoughts), or **omniscient** (the reader views the story through an all-knowing narrator who may move among different scenes, situations, and characters' consciousnesses simultaneously).

First-person singular ("I")

The narrator is an integral part of the story, even when employing scenes, dialogue, and other individuals as characters.

Second-person ("you")

Use this point of view sparingly; it assumes identification with the narrator on the part of the reader and may alienate a reader for this very reason.

Third-person singular ("he" or "she")

Provides a bit more distance; the reader doesn't necessarily view everything directly through the consciousness of the narrator.

The "I" in Imagination

> *If we stick only to facts, our past is as skeletal as black-and-white line drawings in a coloring book. We must color it in.*
> — MIMI SCHWARTZ, *"Memoir? Fiction? Where's the Line?"*

Memory is selective. What we remember tends to take on the quality of our own personal truth over time, remaining—practically speaking—unconscious, until some smell, sound, bit of music, taste, brings it all back in full color, rich with the detail of sensuous experience. "If I approach writing from memory with the assumption that I know what I wish to say, I assume that intentionality is running the show. Things are not that simple," writes Patricia Hampl in "Memory and Imagination" (included in Chapter 4). "The heart, the guardian of intuition with its secret, often fearful intentions, is the boss, its commands are what a writer obeys—often without knowing it."

Distinguishing between the narrative self (who invents) and the reflective self (who wants to understand and make sense of what is half-remembered), Hampl advises writers to give the story authority over its own trajectory, proposing that first drafts are "mysteries" that "drop clues."

> *By writing about that first piano lesson, I've come to know things I could not know otherwise. But I only know these things as a result of reading this first draft. While I was writing, I was following the images, letting the details fill the room of the page and use the furniture as they wished. I was their dutiful servant—or thought I was. In fact I was the faithful retainer of my hidden feelings which were giving the commands.*

If we are willing to let just about anything happen in our first drafts we can make some surprising discoveries. Later, as we shuttle back and forth between our narrative and reflection on that narrative, a narrative persona—a kind of hybrid self—is born; it is that self who gives us the gift of story.

Art, Imagination, and Truth

While most narrative nonfiction writers would agree that their task is not simply to capture the facts, but to make something of those facts, there is a great deal of disagreement about where to draw the line in "making something" of the facts. Some insist that it is the emotional truths of a given experience that we must rely on if we are to discover what our experience really means. Others say that even that is going too far. Peter Ives explores this complicated issue in his essay, "The Whole Truth" (included in this chapter), drawing on his own and a range of other writers' thoughts on the subject of where the line should be drawn between truth and imagination, memory and verifiable fact, in narrative nonfiction. All writers must struggle with this and the issue is far from resolved. As you work with nonfiction, you need to find a comfortable balance between memory and imagination, observation and interpretation, fact and personal point of view.

Say, for example, that you have many shared experiences with a sibling; this doesn't mean your feelings about those experiences will be the same. You will probably experience some things that are similar, but there will be nuances to your perceptions as well as your responses to those experiences. If you and a sibling remember family vacations of childhood, you will likely remember different aspects of those vacations. This doesn't have to mean that one is right and the other wrong. It is just an example of how we each hold within ourselves a personal archive of emotional truths, which live somewhere in that murky substratum beneath fact and fiction. It is this emotional truth that Annie Dillard describes as a "covenant" between the nonfiction writer and the reader. And Peter Ives puts his faith, not in objectivity, but what he considers to be "the greater witness"—*subjectivity*.

Lee Gutkind writes in *Creative Nonfiction* that "the importance of providing accurate information cannot be overemphasized: names, dates, places, descriptions, quotations may not be created or altered for any reason, at any time." And Philip Gerard, author and editor of numerous texts on creative nonfiction, offers the following advice: "You're stuck with what really happened—you can't make it up."

This doesn't stop creative nonfiction writers from being as metaphorical as any poet, as adept with dramatic action as any fiction writer, as nimble with dialogue as any playwright. However, nonfiction is about real people, real events, real life. Of course, postmodernist philosophers may refute notions like "real" and "truth"; but, simply stated, such terms are meant to differentiate fact from fiction—to denote the sincere *intention* to get as close to what really happened as possible—rather than taking the shortcut of invention. Judith Kitchen and

Mary Paumier Jones, editors of *In Short* and *In Brief: Short Takes on the Personal*, note in their introduction to *In Brief* that "nonfiction writers often admit that the places where they were tempted to invent can, if they stick with the scrupulously factual, end up yielding the deepest genuine insight and best writing." Imagination, they conclude, "becomes a way to probe reality. The real world we are lucky enough to live in is revealed as endlessly rich and deep."

Diction, Syntax, and Style

> *A rock is not a stone.*
>
> — MARY OLIVER, *A Poetry Handbook*

The words we choose to use in our narratives not only communicate meaning, they also convey our sensibilities. Erudite or simple, elegant or crude, formal or casual, the gathering of words into meaning carries with it an atmosphere that reveals the writing self. This atmosphere embodies the writer's style. Just as the narrative persona cannot be separated from meaning-making, so language choice isn't separate from voice.

One of your challenges in using the medium that you use every day—language—is to use it intentionally in your creative writing. Selection and arrangement, or **syntax**, carries an individual's personal imprint. No one else uses language in the particular way that you do. The quality of an experience is suggested by **diction**—the words that you choose to convey it. "Diction has several components," poet and essayist Mary Oliver reminds us, "the sound of the word; the accuracy of the word; and its connotation—the atmosphere." Accuracy may mean a number of things. Certainly you want to choose the best words possible, but accuracy also suggests specificity. Try not to settle for the general term—a tree, a flower, a bird. Your work will be more evocative if you use the more specific descriptor—hemlock, astilbe, goldfinch. This is as true for verbs as it is for nouns: rather than walked, try sauntered, or strolled, or even strutted. The active verb becomes an image. We *see* the latter, but not the former. Read the following passages from selections in the anthology for a sense of the stylistic distinctiveness of voice as well as its range.

Ivins uses satire to excellent effect:

> *As has been noted elsewhere, there are several strains of Texan culture: They are all rotten for women. There is the Southern belle nonsense of our Confederate heritage, that little-woman-on-a-pedestal, flirtatious, "you're so cute when you're mad," Scarlett O'Hara myth that leads, quite naturally, to the equally pernicious legend of the Iron Magnolia. Then there's the machismo of our Latin heritage, which affects not only our Chicana sisters, but has been integrated into Texas culture quite as thoroughly as barbecue, rodeo, and Tex-Mex food.*

Kirk Read draws on irony in "How I Learned to Snap" (included in this chapter), when he links the firing of the school bus driver with a student's sense of dignity in the face of homophobia, a complication that becomes understood within the particular circumstances of the scene.

> *Jesse Fowler was the gay Rosa Parks of Lexington, Virginia. In a way, he one-upped her. He got the bus driver fired. Much of what I know about dignity came from him.*
>
> *Jesse was a senior when I was a freshman. . . . He had a different hairstyle every two weeks and often chided me for my "boy hair." He sometimes crimped my bangs, prompting the Colonel to ask if I'd been hanging out with the Fowler boy again.*
>
> *"Yes," I replied at supper. "And child, he's fierce."*

Active and Passive Voice

Lively narrative relies more on active, rather than passive voice. Concrete nouns, vigorous verbs, more verbs than adjectives, fewer adverbs, even.

Passive

The fiat was driven recklessly by George. (My grammar check just told me to change this to the active voice.)

Active

George drove his new fiat in a reckless manner. (Even among active verbs, some are more vigorous than others.)

Vigorous and Active

George careened around the corner, his new fiat's tires squealing.

Parts of Speech

Novice writers fill their writing with adjectives and adverbs, thinking they strengthen their writing. They don't. Such efforts slow the reader down, clutter the language, and weaken the narrative. Adverbs are nickels, adjectives are quarters; but strong verbs are worth a silver dollar.

Rhythm in Sentences

Vary your sentence structure, its length, and get rid of inert words that stop the sentence.

While a prison inmate, Jerome Washington received a grant from the New York Foundation for the Arts for his collection of shorts, *Iron House: from the Yard*, from which "The Blues Merchant" is taken (included in Chapter 8). It's about a blues band performance inside the prison where a thousand inmates have gathered to listen. Pay attention to the rhythm.

> *The Blues Merchant leans forward and mumbles, "Listen. Listen here, you all" into the microphone. "I want to tell you about Fancy Foxy Brown and Mean Lean Green. They is the slickest couple in the East Coast scene."*
>
> *Thump. Thump. The drummer plays. Boom-chicka-chicka-boom. He slams his tubs. The show is on. Toes tap. Hands clap. Fingers pop. The audience vibrates. Long Tongue finds his groove. He leans back. He moans. He shouts. His message is picked up, translated and understood. With his soul he releases us from bondage, puts us in tune with tomorrow, and the memories of the cold steel cells—our iron houses— evaporate.*

Read the excerpt above out loud. Count the number of words in each sentence and write them down in a single column. Notice the number of words, the number of syllables, and the sentence structure Washington uses to create rhythm. Notice the rhyme as well as the rhythm in the following two sentences: "I want to tell you about Fancy Foxy Brown and Mean Lean Green. They is the slickest couple in the East Coast scene." Notice, too, his choice of words. Washington's verbs are active: "He leans back. He moans. He shouts." We *see* the action even as we hear the music. The rhythm of the music infuses the story and we are there. Consider how much would have been lost if Washington would have written: He moans deeply. He shouts loudly. The power of the verbs and therefore their effect would have been lost. Giving a close reading will help you understand *how* Washington has constructed the musicality and rhythm of the piece.

Readings

Writers on Writing

from *The Situation and the Story*, Vivian Gornik

"The Whole Truth," Peter M. Ives

Memoir

from *Naked*, "A Plague of Tics," David Sedaris

The Short

"How I Learned to Snap," Kirk Read

Prose Poem

from *Winter Hours*, "Three Prose Poems," Mary Oliver

The Situation and the Story
Vivian Gornick

*E*very work of literature has both a situation and a story. The situation is the context or circumstance, sometimes the plot; the story is the emotional experience that preoccupies the writer: the insight, the wisdom, the thing one has come to say. In *An American Tragedy* the situation is Dreiser's America; the story is the pathological nature of hunger for the world. In Edmund Gosse's memoir *Father and Son* the situation is fundamentalist England in the time of Darwin; the story is the betrayal of intimacy necessary to the act of becoming oneself. In a poem called "In the Waiting Room" Elizabeth Bishop describes herself at the age of seven, during the First World War, sitting in a dentist's office, turning the pages of *National Geographic*, listening to the muted cries of pain her timid aunt utters from within. That's the situation. The story is a child's first experience of isolation: her own, her aunt's, and that of the world.

Augustine's *Confessions* remains something of a model for the memoirist. In it, Augustine tells the tale of his conversion to Christianity. That's the situation. In this tale, he moves from an inchoate sense of being to a coherent sense of being, from an idling existence to a purposeful one, from a state of ignorance to one of truth. That's the story. Inevitably, it's a story of self-discovery and self-definition.

The subject of autobiography is always self-definition, but it cannot be self-definition in the void. The memoirist, like the poet and the novelist, must engage with the world, because engagement makes experience, experience makes wisdom, and finally it's the wisdom—or rather the movement toward it—that counts. "Good writing has two characteristics," a gifted teacher of writing once said. "It's alive on the page and the reader is persuaded that the writer is on a voyage of discovery." The poet, the novelist, the memoirist—all must convince the reader they have some wisdom, and are writing as honestly as possible to arrive at what they know. To the bargain, the writer of personal narrative must also persuade the reader that the narrator is reliable. In fiction a narrator may be—and often famously is—unreliable (as in *The Good Soldier*, *The Great Gatsby*, Philip Roth's Zuckerman novels). In nonfiction, never. In nonfiction the reader must believe that the narrator is speaking truth. Invariably, of nonfiction it is asked, "Is this narrator trustworthy? Can I believe what he or she is telling me?"

How do nonfiction narrators make themselves trustworthy? A question perhaps best answered by example.

"In Moulmein, in Lower Burma," George Orwell writes in "Shooting an Elephant," "I was hated by large numbers of people—the only time in my life that I have been important enough for this to happen to me. I was sub-divisional police officer of the town, and in an aimless, petty kind of way anti-European feeling was very bitter. No one had the guts to raise a riot, but if a European woman went through the bazaars alone somebody would probably spit betel juice over her dress. As a police officer I was an obvious target and was baited

whenever it seemed safe to do so. When a nimble Burman tripped me up on the
football field and the referee (another Burman) looked the other way, the crowd
yelled with hideous laughter. This happened more than once. In the end the
sneering yellow faces of young men that met me everywhere, the insults hooted
after me when I was at a safe distance, got badly on my nerves. The young Buddhist
priests were the worst of all. There were several thousands of them in the town
and none of them seemed to have anything to do except stand on street corners
and jeer at Europeans.

"All this was perplexing and upsetting. For at that time I had already made
up my mind that imperialism was an evil thing and the sooner I chucked up my
job and got out of it the better. Theoretically—and secretly, of course—I was all
for the Burmese and all against their oppressors, the British. As for the job I was
doing, I hated it more bitterly than I can perhaps make clear. In a job like that
you see the dirty work of Empire at close quarters. The wretched prisoners hud-
dling in the stinking cages of the lock-ups, the grey, cowed faces of the long-term
convicts, the scarred buttocks of the men who had been flogged with bamboos—
all these oppressed me with an intolerable sense of guilt. But I could get nothing
into perspective. I was young and ill-educated and I had had to think out my
problems in the utter silence that is imposed on every Englishman in the East. I
did not even know that the British Empire is dying, still less did I know that it is
a great deal better than the younger empires that are going to supplant it. All I
knew was that I was stuck between my hatred of the empire I served and my
rage against the evil-spirited little beasts who tried to make my job impossible.
With one part of my mind I thought of the British Raj as an unbreakable tyranny,
as something clamped down, in *saecula saeculorum*, upon the will of prostrate
peoples; with another part I thought that the greatest joy in the world would be
to drive a bayonet into a Buddhist priest's guts. Feelings like these are the normal by-products of imperialism; ask any Anglo-Indian official, if you can catch
him off duty."

The man who speaks those sentences *is* the story being told: a civilized man
made murderous by the situation he finds himself in. We believe this about him
because the writing makes us believe it. Paragraph upon paragraph—composed
in almost equal part of narration, commentary, and analysis—attests to a reflective nature now regarding its own angry passions with a visceral but contained
distaste. The narrator records his rage, yet the writing is not enraged; the narrator hates Empire, yet his hate is not out of control; the narrator shrinks from the
natives, yet his repulsion is tinged with compassion. At all times he is possessed
of a sense of history, proportion, and paradox. In short, a highly respectable intelligence confesses to having been *reduced* in a situation that would uncivilize
anyone, including you the reader.

This man became the Orwell persona in countless books and essays: the
involuntary truth speaker, the one who implicates himself not because he wants
to but because he has no choice. He is the narrator created to demonstrate the
dehumanizing effect of Empire on all within its reach, the one whose presence
alone—"I am the man, I was there"—is an indictment.

It was politics that Orwell was after: the politics of his time. That was the situation into which he interjected this persona: the one who alone could tell the story he wanted told. Orwell himself—in unaesthetic actuality—was a man often at the mercy of his own mean insecurities. In life he could act and sound ugly: revisionist biographies now have him not only a sexist and an obsessed anti-communist but possibly an informer as well. Yet the persona he created in his nonfiction—an essence of democratic decency—was something genuine that he pulled from himself, and then shaped to his writer's purpose. *This* George Orwell is a wholly successful fusion of experience, perspective, and personality that is fully present on the page. Because he *is* so present, we feel that we know who is speaking. The ability to make us believe that we know who is speaking is the trustworthy narrator achieved.

From journalism to the essay to the memoir: the trip being taken by a non-fiction persona deepens, and turns ever more inward.

One of the most interesting memoirists of our time is another Englishman, J. R. Ackerley. When Ackerley died in 1967, at the age of seventy-one, he left behind a remarkable piece of confessional writing he had been working on for the better part of thirty years. It is, ostensibly, a tale of family life. He was the son of Roger Ackerley, a fruit merchant known most of his life as "the banana king." This father was a large, easygoing, generous man, at once expansive and kindly but indirect in his manner, most indirect. Ackerley himself grew up to become literary and homosexual, absorbed by his own interests and secrets, given to hiding his real life from the family. After his father's death in 1929 Ackerley learned that Roger had lived a double life. All the time the Ackerleys were growing up in middle-class comfort in Richmond, the father was keeping a second family on the other side of London: a mistress and three daughters. The disclosure of this "secret orchard," as the Victorian euphemism had it, astounded Joe Ackerley to such a degree that he became obsessed with probing deeper into the obscurity of his father's beginnings. In time he became convinced that in his youth Roger had also been a male whore and that it was through the love of a wealthy man that he had gained his original stake in life.

This is the story J. R. Ackerley set out to tell. Why did it take him thirty years to tell it? Why not three? Because what I've told you was not his story; it was his situation. It was the story that took thirty years to get itself told.

Ackerley was, he thought, only putting together a puzzle of family life. All I have to do, he said to himself, is get the sequence right and the details correct and everything will fall into place. But nothing fell into place. After a while he thought, I'm not describing a presence, I'm describing an absence. This is the tale of an unlived relationship. Who was he? Who was I? Why did we keep missing each other? After another while he realized, I always thought my father didn't want to know me. Now I see I didn't want to know him. And then he realized, it's not him I haven't wanted to know, it's myself.

My Father and Myself is little more than two hundred pages in length. Its prose is simple and lucid, wonderfully inviting from the first, now famous sentence, "I was born in 1896 and my parents were married in 1919." The voice that speaks that sentence will address with grace and candor whatever it is necessary to examine. From it will flow strong feeling and vivid intelligence, original phrasing and a remarkable directness. It's the directness that dazzles, coming as it does—and this is a minor miracle—from the exactly right distance: not too close, not too far. At this distance everyone and everything is made understandable, and therefore interesting. Because everyone and everything is interesting, we believe that the narrator is telling us all he knows.

Ackerley, as I have experienced him in writings *about* him, often seems nasty or pathetic; the Ackerley speaking here in *My Father and Myself* is a wholly engaging man, not because he sets out to be fashionably honest but because the reader feels him actively working to strip down the anxiety till he can get to something hard and true beneath the smooth surface of sentimental self-regard. It took Ackerley thirty years to clarify the voice that could tell his story—thirty years to gain detachment, make an honest man of himself, become a trustworthy narrator. The years are etched in the writing. Incident by incident, paragraph by paragraph, sentence by sentence, we have the glory of an achieved persona. Ackerley may not have the powers of a poet, but in *My Father and Myself* he certainly has the intent.

My trip to Egypt and the book that emerged from it now seem to me an embodiment of my own struggle to clarify, to release from anxiety the narrator who could serve the situation and find the story—a thing I was not then able to do. It was a time when my own psychological wishes were so mixed as to make it impossible for that instinct to be obeyed. I wanted at once both to clarify and to mystify. The compromised intent proved fatal. The problem was not detachment; the problem was I never knew who was telling the story. As a result, I never *had* a story. A dozen years after Egypt I set out to write a memoir about my mother, myself, and a woman who lived next door to us when I was a child. Here, for the first time, I struggled to isolate the story from the situation; here I taught myself what a persona is; and here I began to figure out what they all had to do with one another.

This story—the one about my mother, myself, and the woman next door—was based on an early insight I'd had that these two women between them had made me a woman. Each had been widowed young, each had fallen into despair; one devoted the rest of her life to the worship of lost love, the other became the Whore of Babylon. No matter. In each case the lesson being taught was that a man was the most important thing in a woman's life. I hated the lesson from early on, had resolved to get out and leave both it and the women behind. I did get out, but as time went on I discovered that I couldn't leave any of it behind. Especially not the women. Most especially not my mother. I had determined to separate myself from her theatrical self-absorption, but now, as the years accumulated, I saw that my hot-tempered and cutting ways were, indeed, only another version of her needy dramatics. I saw further that for both of us the self-dramatization was a substitute for action: a piece of Chekhovian unresolve raging in me as well as her. It flashed on me that I could not leave my mother because I had become my mother.

This was the story I wanted to tell without sentiment or cynicism; the one I thought justified speaking hard truths. The flash of insight I'd had—that I could not leave my mother because I'd become my mother—was my wisdom: a tale of psychological embroilment I wanted badly to trace out.

To tell that tale, I soon discovered, I had to find the right tone of voice; the one I habitually lived with wouldn't do at all: it whined, it grated, it accused; above all, it accused. Then there was the matter of syntax: my own ordinary, everyday sentence—fragmented, interjecting, overriding—also wouldn't do; it had to be altered, modified, brought under control. And then I could see, this as soon as I began writing, that I needed to pull back—*way* back—from these people and these events to find the place where the story could draw a deep breath and take its own measure. In short, a useful point of view, one that would permit greater freedom of association—for that of course is what I have been describing—had to be brought along. What I *didn't* see, and that for a long while, was that this point of view could only emerge from a narrator who was me and at the same time not me.

I began to correct for myself. The process was slow, painful, and, to my surprise, riddled with crippling self-doubt. I found a diary I had kept one summer ten years earlier; it contained information that I knew I could use. I opened the diary eagerly but soon turned away from it, stricken. The writing was soaked in a kind of girlish self-pity—"alone again!"—that I found odious. More than odious, threatening. As I read on, I felt myself being sucked back into its atmosphere, unable to hold on to the speaking voice I was working hard to develop. I threw the diary down in a panic, then felt confused and defeated. A few days later I tried again, but again felt myself going under. At last, I put it away.

One day—when I had been looking over an accumulation of pages possessed of what seemed to me the sufficiently right tone, syntax, and perspective—I opened the diary again, read in it a bit, laughed, got interested, even absorbed, and within minutes was making notes. With relief I thought, I'm not losing myself. Suddenly I realized there was no myself to lose. I had a narrator on the page strong enough to do battle for me. The narrator was the me who could not leave her mother because she had become her mother. She was not intimidated by "alone again." Nor, come to think of it, was she much influenced by the me who was a walker in the city, or a divorced middle-aged feminist, or a financially insecure writer. She was, apparently, only her solid, limited self—and she was in control. I saw what I had done: I had created a persona.

Devotion to this narrator—this persona—became, while I was writing the book, an absorption that in time went unequaled. I longed each day to meet up again with her, this other one telling the story that I alone—in my everyday person—would not have been able to tell. I could hardly believe my luck in having found her (that's what it felt like, luck). It was not only that I admired her style, her generosity, her detachment—such a respite from the me that was me!—she had become the instrument of my illumination.

Later, reading and re-reading Edmund Gosse, Geoffrey Wolff, Joan Didion, I went into a trance of recognition from which I don't think I ever emerged. I could see that their writing was "about" something in very much the same way that mine was. In each case the writer was possessed of an insight that organized the writing, and in each case a persona had been created to serve the insight. I became enraptured, tracing out the development of the persona in memoir after essay after memoir (it was out of this rapture that I realized I was a nonfiction writer). I began to read the greats in essay writing—and it wasn't their confessing voices I was responding to, it was their truth-speaking personae. By which

I mean that organic wholeness of being in a narrator that the reader experiences as reliable; the one we can trust will take us on a journey, make the piece arrive, bring us out into a clearing where the sense of things is larger than it was before.

Living as I now did with the idea of the nonfiction persona, I began to think better than I had before about the commonplace need, alive in all of us, to make large sense of things in the very moment, even as experience is overtaking us. Everywhere I turned in those days, I found an excuse for the observation that we pull from ourselves the narrator who will shape better than we alone can the inchoate flow of event into which we are continually being plunged. I remember once my then husband and I, and a friend of ours, went on a rafting trip down the Rio Grande. The river was hot and wild; sad, brilliant, remote; closed in by canyon walls, desert banks, snakes, and flash floods; on one side Texas, the other Mexico: a week after we'd been there, snipers on the Mexico side killed two people also floating on a raft. Later, we each wrote about the trip. My husband focused brightly on the "river rats" who were our guides, our friend soberly on the misery of illegal immigration, I morbidly on what strangers my husband and I had become. Reading these pieces side by side was in itself an experience. We had all used the river, the heat, the remoteness to frame our stories. Beyond that, how alone each of us had been, sitting there side by side on that raft, carving out of our separating anxieties the narrator who, in the midst of all that beauty and oppressiveness, would keep us company—and tell us what we were living through.

I began to see that in the course of daily life when, by my own lights, I act badly—confrontational, challenging, dismissive—I am out there on that raft before I have found the narrator who can bring under control the rushing onslaught of my own internal flux. When I am doing better, I am able to see that the flux is a situation. I stop churning around inside my own defensiveness; adopt a tone, a syntax, a perspective not wholly mine that allows me to focus on. . . . what? the husband? the guides? the illegals? No matter. Any one of them will do. I become interested then in my own existence only as a means of penetrating the situation in hand. I have created a persona who can find the story riding the tide that I, in my unmediated state, am otherwise going to drown in.

The Whole Truth

Peter M. Ives

I

About a year ago, I gave my sister, Kitty, a draft of an essay I'd been working on. Up to that point, I had never shared any of my autobiographical writing with a family member. Part of the essay dealt with the day of our father's death, and I was sincerely interested to see if she could add any details or observations. I spent an anxiety-filled week, second-guessing my decision, before calling her. I was quite surprised by her reaction. It wasn't that she was offended or angry—I had prepared myself for that possibility. No, in fact she was quite generous in her comments about the piece. However, what caught me off guard was the degree to which her memories of that day—April 5, 1969—conflicted substantially with my own recollections.

She remembered the day as being sunny. I remembered a light drizzle with low gray clouds. She remembered being with me in the bedroom when I found my father's body. I remembered only my brother John being there. She remembered the coroner pronouncing my father dead before Father Ramsey came to perform the last rites. I remembered Father Ramsey arriving before the coroner. As we talked, it became clear to me that this event—indisputably the most central instance of my childhood—was subject to conflicting perspectives.

There were other details where our memories conflicted, but in the end it didn't matter whether or not it had been sunny or rainy or whether it was the priest or coroner who arrived first, because one thing has always remained certain: our father died that day, and both of us remembered watching the ambulance attendants carry his body out the front door.

II

Shortly after that revelatory conversation with my sister, I came across an essay written by Anna Quindlen for the *New York Times Book Review*. In her piece, "How Dark? How Stormy? I Can't Recall," Ms. Quindlen questioned the legitimate employment of specific details in memoir. It seems that because the author couldn't remember the name of her kindergarten teacher, she felt compelled to question how Frank McCourt—the author of *Angela's Ashes*—could remember "the raw, itching sore that erupted between his eyes when he was a boy, or the sight of himself in a mirror on his fourteenth birthday." In support of her incredulity, Ms. Quindlen continued: "I can't remember the spread on my parents' bed. If it was quilted satin, I can't remember running my hand over its smooth surface when I was seven or eight years old. If it was chenille, I can't recall feeling the bobbles beneath my palm as I sat and watched in the mirror as my mother braided my long hair." To be fair, Ms. Quindlen reminds readers that she spent most of her life as a reporter, and that the "strictures of her trade run deep." In this regard, it is completely understandable that Ms. Quindlen is, by nature, suspicious of anything as unverifiable as memoir.

As for me, I know very little about quilted satin, and—to the best of my knowledge—my mother never braided my hair. But I do remember the oil stains on my father's callused hands, how his finger nails were bitten down almost to the cuticles; I remember how he used to wear an oversized, fluorescent, orange raincoat to my JV football games—rain or shine—so I could see him as he pranced up and down the sidelines shouting instructions; I remember the doilies my grandmother used to keep on the mahogany dresser in her bedroom, the Jell-O-like flesh that drooped below her upper arms; I remember my mother singing in the kitchen on school mornings; I remember the first time I had the wind knocked out of me; I remember my grandfather on his death bed, rolling imaginary Bull Durham cigarettes and offering them to my grandmother (who'd been dead for eight years); I remember how my mom used to take her boys out to the back fence, line us up, and give crew cuts, washing us off with the hose afterwards so we wouldn't scatter loose hair in the house; I remember faking a stomachache when I was six and winding up having my appendix taken out; I remember playing in a sand pile and almost being eaten by a pig.

These are vivid, honest memories. But I would never swear to them as facts. They are honest and true only in that this is how I remember them, verifying where I can, letting the reader know whenever I step over the line into uncertainty or even imaginative re-recreation. But within each of these memories is a story loaded with details, dialogue, and imagery. And I've told these stories hundreds of times.

III

"The blurring of reality" is a catchy new phrase proclaimed by a self-appointed few out to rescue a gullible reading public from an ontological meltdown. It reminds me of the old "Twilight Zone" episode where a browbeaten author permanently dispatches his wife by burning the tape recording on which he described (dictated) her into being: she feels woozy, puts the back of her hand to her forehead and slowly dissipates into oblivion. Who are these critics? For the most part, I suspect that they are talented writers, columnists, and intellectuals who regard the imminent collapse of the wall separating fiction and nonfiction as having ominous reverberations for literature and for society as a whole. In many ways, I think their concerns are justified. But are they justified in singling out memoir as the prime component of a world slipping into virtual reality?

Turn on the TV and you'll get John Wayne pitching beer commercials or Humphrey Bogart drinking Diet Coke or Fred Astaire dancing with an Electrolux. Watch any broadcast of the national political news then pick up a video of *Wag the Dog* or *Primary Colors*. An article in a recent issue of *Harper's* describes how digital technology calls into question the legitimacy of still photography. Our ability to manipulate images has become so sophisticated that it is now nearly impossible to tell whether an image is a representation of the real world or the product of a hard drive. We are now told that Ansel Adams, the patron saint of nature photography, played around in his dark room "Making little circles with [a] wand over the area he wanted lightened," laughing in "crazy, nasal, Mephistophelean" glee.

Nevertheless, critics continue to blame memoir for a disproportionate share of this blurring of reality. No less a writer than Joyce Carol Oates has jumped into the fray. In a recent article for the *New York Times*, Ms. Oates suggested that "Memoir testifies, perhaps, to our desperate wish that some truth of the spirit be presented to us, though we know it's probably invented. We want to believe! We are a species who clamors to be lied to." I am not going to address, at least directly, what I consider to be the depressingly elitist, cynical, and patronizing tone of Ms. Oates' observations. Rather, I would like to suggest that what people desperately want, what they've always wanted, is not to be lied to, but to be told a story. And if nonfiction is burning up the best seller lists, it's not because memoirists have learned to become better liars than fiction writers; maybe it's because they're just telling a better story.

In a 1997 interview, fiction writer and essayist Bob Shacochis commented upon the underlying hostility within the literary community over the "appropriation" of traditional fiction techniques—dialogue, scene construction, vividly recollected detail—into today's nonfiction. The real issue, he says, is the quality of storytelling, not whether it's invented or remembered, and "beyond that the arguments become uninteresting, and they get precious. If someone tells you that the memoir or essay is this certain thing, they're really not telling you what they know so much as they're telling you what they've read. It doesn't address the magnitude and diversity of what's been done, or being done out there. They try to tell you that 'objectivity' is the rule in nonfiction, where I regard subjectivity as the greater witness."

For all I know, all of my memories could be inaccurate. But as I write, I am not consciously dissembling, creating instances and scenes to fit the awkward angles of a story line. My past is not inhabited by a cast of stick figures awkwardly dramatizing a plodding, unimaginative plot line. And just because I can't remember everything doesn't—or shouldn't—mean I have to let my past evaporate, or say that it wasn't real. I am not ready to surrender my past, my life, to fiction. The world is a strange enough place as it is.

I don't remember what my father wore under his orange raincoat during my JV football games. But if I wrote about it, I'd tell the reader he had on an open collared, red plaid shirt, with black suspenders fastened to dark green cotton trousers—the kind school janitors used to wear. Oh yes! He'd also have on an old, frayed T-shirt, his thick, dark, chest hair curling over the neckband. I'd write all this because it was a standard outfit for my father, because his wearing it beneath his raincoat was both probable and possible. In my mind, when he opens his raincoat, he's not naked. I'm not being "flashed" while my imagination rummages around in wardrobe.

Mary McCarthy, in her memoir *Memories of a Catholic Girlhood*, directly confronted the difficulty of writing from memory. In her foreword, "To the Reader," she wrote: "Many a time, in the course of doing these memoirs, I have wished I were writing fiction. The temptation to invent has been very strong, particularly where recollection is hazy . . . Sometimes I have yielded, as in the case of conversations. My memory is good, but I cannot obviously recall whole passages of dialogue that took place years ago." McCarthy's discussion of the difference between memory and technical reproduction applies not only to dialogue, but to all the other facets of storytelling. A writer must deal honestly with whatever facts he or she has at hand, limited as the facts may be. This requires enormous storytelling skill, because the past is a moving image, requiring almost constant readjustment of the viewing lens. And the images we retrieve arrive in different ways. What transports me back to the past varies greatly: sometimes it's the way my son drops his head when I'm angry; sometimes it's an old Beatles song, a photo album, or a receipt I found in the pocket of a coat I haven't worn in years.

IV

So I would like to challenge the nature of memory, to question the notion that all must be known before an event can be rendered truthfully as story. Indeed, because a large part of our lives can never be retrieved, it is a storyteller's duty to use whatever tools are at hand.

In *How Proust Can Change Your Life*, Alain De Botton discusses Proust's concept of *voluntary* and *involuntary* memory. Voluntary memory is the memory of multiplication tables, bus schedules, and daily agendas—memories that we intellectually attempt to provoke. Involuntary memory, on the other hand, occurs when a recollection is stirred by "a long forgotten smell or an old glove." Something that has remained dormant since childhood and "therefore remains uncorrupted by later associations." These instances of almost epiphanic intensity are also known as *Proustian moments*.

In a letter, the essayist and critic Sven Birkerts elaborates on just such a distinction when he writes: "What we outwardly regard as important—the big events, the key moves, the prominent characters—may have nothing to do with the story that needs to be written. We can banish the idea of telling the story of our life and concentrate on evoking its mystery." He suggests following the patterns of memory, even if that means you "devote six pages to writing about a grandfather's cigar box, then jump to the memory of burning ants with a magnifying glass, and then recall the braid of a girl you sat behind in third grade." Birkerts suggests letting the force of memory, not public concerns, be the measure of an event's importance. As he puts it: "You may leave out entirely—or consign to the margins—the fact that your house was burned down or that your grandfather was George Bush. . . . [W]hat makes this kind of writing stick is the level of absorption. And if in your writer's soul you remember the smell of wool mittens more than you remember climbing Everest with your father, you may have to write the wool mittens." Involuntary memory—what is called up from deep emotional experience and of its own accord—is immensely valuable to writers of any genre. It is far more complicated than fact—the bus schedules of voluntary memory. It is where the heart and soul of our past resides.

V

To Virginia Woolf, the present was a platform for viewing the past, the string of experiences we drag behind us like a bedraggled train. We are not imagined. Our past is real, but it is not static. Like the cosmos, it moves unceasingly away from us, and what a memoirist captures is but a glimpse of its receding illumination, a recollective red shift that can only be adjusted through re-creation. Can we change the past? No. But we can change how it is remembered because we grow, change, and (hopefully) learn from our experiences. Or, as Tomás Eloy Martínez writes in his novel *Santa Evita*: "Every story is by definition, unfaithful. Reality, as I've said, can't be told or repeated. The only thing that can be done with reality is to invent it all over again."

So it comes back to what is real—the rightness of a memory or experience—because in order to make a claim on legitimacy, any story, with the possible exception of parable and allegory, must have a basis in reality. That is, what we read—whether fiction or nonfiction—must in some way correlate to our experience, to our sense of what is real. How many times have you put down a novel or story because the plot or characterizations or details seemed implausible? As Aristotle wrote in his *Poetics*: "It is not the poet's function to describe what actually happened, but the kind of things that might happen, that is, that could happen because they are, in the circumstances, either probable or necessary. . . . Even if the poet writes about things that have actually happened, that does not make him any less a poet, for there is nothing to prevent some of the things that have happened from being in accordance with the laws of possibility and probability, and thus he will be a poet in writing about them."

Or, as author Sherwood Anderson put it: "While art is distinct from real life, the imagination must constantly feed upon reality or starve." But sometimes, in order that the real story may be told, the ineluctable passage of time is a necessity. In his magisterial short story "A Death in the Woods," Anderson describes the death of an old woman during a violent Midwestern snowstorm, a story based on an actual event in his childhood. In the following passage, Anderson's narrator, now an adult, reflects: "The whole thing, the story of the old woman's death, was to me, as I grew older, like music heard from far off. The notes had to be picked up slowly one at a time. Something had to be understood. . . . " What is essential, the narrator realizes, is the perspective of distance and age. As children, he and his brother were too young to understand the point of the story. "A thing so complete has its own beauty. . . . I shall not try to emphasize the point. I am only explaining why I was dissatisfied then and have been ever since. I speak of that only that you may understand why I have been impelled to try to tell the simple story over again."

This same act of remembering and telling in order to arrive at an understanding is the basic premise of memoir: thinking out loud, retelling a story over and over again, using imagination to understand and reconcile a past where reality served as the background music. We recall it only with the greatest difficulty, following the tune as best we can, using our imaginations to improvise notes where the score goes blank. How many truths are there to an event? How much music have we failed to hear? And when the melody finally comes—a sense of longing, a sudden unexplained feeling of joy or sadness—the best we can do is whistle along, staying as close to the original melody as we can.

William Maxwell's *So Long, See You Tomorrow*, an almost perfect novel, is written in the form of a memoir in which an aging narrator reflects upon his

Midwestern childhood. It is an evocative elegy to youth, centered on a fictional murder in a small Illinois farming town around World War I. Like his Midwestern literary predecessor, Sherwood Anderson, Maxwell uses simple and unadorned language that masks an uncompromisingly complex and richly detailed narrative. The genesis for this novel, published in 1980, can be found in another book he wrote nine years earlier: *Ancestors*, a memoir.

It is generally not wise to read a piece of fiction as though it were autobiography. But for anyone who has read both books, the comparisons cannot be avoided: each narrator had an older and younger brother; each lost a mother to the 1919 influenza epidemic; each had a businessman father who ultimately relocated the family to Chicago and remarried a much younger woman. Even some of the scenes are the same: the fictional and nonfictional boy with his arm wrapped around the father's waist as they paced the floor in the days after the mother's death, and the father blowing pipe smoke into the fictional and nonfictional boy's ear to cure an earache. Both books examine the ways in which memory can best interrogate the past. But on this last point they differ. In *Ancestors*, the earlier book, Maxwell writes: "I have to get out an imaginary lens and fiddle with the lens until I see something that interests me, preferably something small and unimportant." But in *So Long, See You Tomorrow*, Maxwell's approach to memory is more circumspect as he repeatedly and directly confronts the complexity and unverifiability of memory: "What we, or at any rate what I, refer to as memory—meaning a moment, a scene, a fact that has been subjected to a fixative and thereby rescued from oblivion—is really a form of storytelling that goes on continually in the mind and often changes with the telling. Too many conflicting emotional interests are involved for life ever to be wholly acceptable, and possibly it is the work of a storyteller to arrange things so that they conform to this end. In any case, in talking about the past, we lie with every breath we draw."

Is Maxwell suggesting that we are incapable of truth? That is not my reading of the passage. Rather, I believe he is speaking in phenomenological terms, suggesting that because of "conflicting emotions" and shifting circumstances everything we witness is but an illusion, representative of a deeper, underlying reality. In this way of thinking, fiction is a play upon illusion, and memoir is the illusion itself. So, in the end, neither is real. Or, put another way, both are equally real.

VI

It has been my experience that we do not perceive or write about things as they are, but, rather, we perceive or write about them as *we* are. What a memoirist describes is often confined to the perspective of an immediate and unfinished circumstance. But between what we remember and what really happened are the shadows from which the truth will ultimately reassert itself.

Vladimir Nabokov, in his memoir *Speak Memory*, addresses one of the most luminous aspects of memory: the conflict that arises when a child's experience is at odds with empirical reality. In one of the early chapters, Nabokov describes a scene in which his aristocratic father is pitched into the air by a group of celebratory villagers. Nabokov writes: "From my place at table I would suddenly see through one of the west windows a marvelous case of levitation. There, for an instant, the figure of my father in his windrippled white summer suit would be displayed, gloriously sprawling in midair, his limbs in a curiously casual attitude, his handsome, imperturbable features turned to the sky . . . and then there he would be, on his last and loftiest flight, reclining, as if for good, against the cobalt blue of the summer noon. . . . " The final sentence of this recollection runs for 127 words, during which the child's vision evolves into an extended metaphysical presentiment of his father's death. Could a child have perceived all this? Probably not. But the pristine truth of Nabokov's numinous image serves as the framework for an extended, mature meditation. It is a vision of first things.

VII

There is a story about my father I'd like to write: My father. Forty-five years ago. I have yet to be born. He's flying a single-engine plane above the old house on Franklin Street. My mother is in the back yard hanging out laundry. There are only two children—Holley and John—whom Mom sends in the house when she looks up to see my father swooping low over the neighborhood. It's a beautiful summer evening—a Friday, so she knows that he's already made a quick tour of the city's gin mills.

He's done these fly-bys before, screaming down from above the tree tops in the plane he borrows from Jimmy Durr, a childhood pal. They both earned their wings eight years earlier, flying sub reconnaissance in the South Pacific. But tonight my father has decided to push his fly-by game to the limit. My mother tries to wave him off, but my father thinks she's calling him in closer, and he obliges her, eventually buzzing the whole block. It doesn't take long for Chief of Police Leo LeBeau and the fire trucks to come barreling in, sirens blaring, lights flashing. From the air it looks like a carnival.

Taking the hint, my father gently rolls the plane and heads north, crossing the mile-wide Saint Lawrence River in order to follow the Ontario shoreline. Every now and then he sweeps down to dip his wings to the ocean freighters, their giant hulls lumbering down the Seaway. The ships flash their running lights in salute as he rolls south, heading back, descending to just above the water as he comes into the mouth of the Oswegatchie, the last light of the day shooting like flames along the fuselage as he hot dogs it home under the Lafayette Street bridge.

I write about my father because there is no one else to write about him. Because he was real and vital and flawed. Because I loved him. Because I want to imagine him as a man close to my own age now. I no longer seek my father's understanding, I seek, through re-creation, to understand him. And so I return to the beginning—April 5, 1969—where, I suppose, the only accurate written history about my father's death can be found in a copy of his obituary. But my hometown newspaper got a couple of the facts wrong. It printed his date of birth as October 25, 1916 when, according to his birth certificate, he was actually born in 1915. The obituary also misrepresented his military service and the ages of two of my siblings. But these are only details.

So much for the first rough draft of history.

A Plague of Tics
David Sedaris

*W*hen the teacher asked if she might visit with my mother, I touched my nose eight times to the surface of my desk.

"May I take that as a 'yes'?" she asked.

According to her calculations, I had left my chair twenty-eight times that day. "You're up and down like a flea. I turn my back for two minutes and there you are with your tongue pressed against that light switch. Maybe they do that where you come from, but here in my classroom we don't leave our seats and lick things whenever we please. That is Miss Chestnut's light switch, and she likes to keep it dry. Would you like me to come over to your house and put my tongue on *your* light switches? Well, would you?"

I tried to picture her in action, but my shoe was calling. *Take me off,* it whispered. *Tap my heel against your forehead three times. Do it now, quick, no one will notice,*

"Well?" Miss Chestnut raised her faint, penciled eyebrows. "I'm asking you a question. Would you or would you not want me licking the light switches in your house?"

I slipped off my shoe, pretending to examine the imprint on the heel.

"You're going to hit yourself over the head with that shoe, aren't you?"

It wasn't "hitting," it was tapping; but still, how had she known what I was about to do?

"Heel marks all over your forehead," she said, answering my silent question.

"You should take a look in the mirror sometime. Shoes are dirty things. We wear them on our feet to protect ourselves against the soil. It's not healthy to hit ourselves over the head with shoes, is it?"

I guessed that it was not.

"Guess? This is not a game to be guessed at. I don't 'guess' that it's dangerous to run into traffic with a paper sack over my head. There's no guesswork involved. These things are facts, not riddles." She sat at her desk, continuing her lecture as she penned a brief letter. "I'd like to have a word with your mother. You do have one, don't you? I'm assuming you weren't raised by animals. Is she blind, your mother? Can she see the way you behave, or do you reserve your antics exclusively for Miss Chestnut?" She handed me the folded slip of paper. "You may go now, and on your way out the door I'm asking you please not to bathe my light switch with your germ-ridden tongue. It's had a long day; we both have."

It was a short distance from the school to our rented house, no more than six hundred and thirty-seven steps, and on a good day I could make the trip in an hour, pausing every few feet to tongue a mailbox or touch whichever single leaf or blade of grass demanded my attention. If I were to lose count of my steps, I'd have to return to the school and begin again. "Back so soon?" the janitor would ask. "You just can't get enough of this place, can you?"

He had it all wrong. I wanted to be at home more than anything, it was getting there that was the problem. I might touch the telephone pole at step three hundred and fourteen and then, fifteen paces later, worry that I hadn't touched it in exactly the right spot. It needed to be touched again. I'd let my mind wander for one brief moment and then doubt had set in, causing me to question not just the telephone pole but also the lawn ornament back at step two hundred and nineteen. I'd have to go back and lick that concrete mushroom one more time, hoping its guardian wouldn't once again rush from her house shouting, "Get your face out of my toadstool!" It might be raining or maybe I had to go to the bathroom, but running home was not an option. This was a long and complicated process that demanded an oppressive attention to detail. It wasn't that I enjoyed pressing my nose against the scalding hood of a parked car—pleasure had nothing to do with it. A person *had* to do these things because nothing was worse than the anguish of not doing them. Bypass that mailbox and my brain would never for one moment let me forget it. I might be sitting at the dinner table, daring myself not to think about it, and the thought would revisit my mind. *Don't think about it.* But it would already be too late and I knew then exactly what I had to do. Excusing myself to go to the bathroom, I'd walk out the front door and return to that mailbox, not just touching but jabbing, practically pounding on the thing because I thought I hated it so much. What I really hated, of course, was my mind. There must have been an off switch somewhere, but I was damned if I could find it.

I didn't remember things being this way back north. Our family had been transferred from Endicott, New York, to Raleigh, North Carolina. That was the word used by the people at IBM, *transferred*. A new home was under construction, but until it was finished we were confined to a rental property built to resemble a plantation house. The building sat in a treeless, balding yard, its white columns promising a majesty the interior failed to deliver. The front door opened onto a dark, narrow hallway lined with bedrooms not much larger than the mattresses that furnished them. Our kitchen was located on the second floor, alongside the living room, its picture window offering a view of the cinder-block wall built to hold back the tide of mud generated by the neighboring dirt mound.

"Our own little corner of hell," my mother said, fanning herself with one of the shingles littering the front yard.

Depressing as it was, arriving at the front stoop of the house meant that I had completed the first leg of that bitter-tasting journey to my bedroom. Once home I would touch the front door seven times with each elbow, a task made more difficult if there was someone else around. "Why don't you try the knob," my sister Lisa would say. "That's what the rest of us do, and it seems to work for us." Inside the house there were switches and doorstops to be acknowledged. My bedroom was right there off the hallway, but first I had business to tend to. After kissing the fourth, eighth, and twelfth carpeted stair, I wiped the cat hair off my lips and proceeded to the kitchen, where I was commanded to stroke the burners of the stove, press my nose against the refrigerator door, and arrange the percolator, toaster, and blender into a straight row. After making my rounds of the living room, it was time to kneel beside the banister and blindly jab a butter knife in the direction of my favorite electrical socket. There were bulbs to lick and bathroom faucets to test before finally I was free to enter my bedroom, where I would carefully align the objects on my dresser, lick the corners of my metal desk, and lie upon my bed, rocking back and forth and thinking of what an odd woman she was, my third-grade teacher, Miss Chestnut. Why come here and lick my switches when she never used the one she had? Maybe she was drunk.

Her note had asked if she might visit our home in order to discuss what she referred to as my "special problems."

"Have you been leaving your seat to lick the light switch?" my mother asked. She placed the letter upon the table and lit a cigarette.

"Once or twice," I said.

"Once or twice what? Every half hour? Every ten minutes?"

"I don't know," I lied. "Who's counting?"

"Well, your goddamned math teacher, for one. That's her *job*, to count. What, do you think she's not going to notice?"

"Notice what?" It never failed to amaze me that people might notice these things. Because my actions were so intensely private, I had always assumed they were somehow invisible. When cornered, I demanded that the witness had been mistaken.

"What do you mean, 'notice what?' I got a phone call just this afternoon from that lady up the street, that Mrs. Keening, the one with the twins. She says she caught you in her front yard, down on your hands and knees kissing the evening edition of her newspaper."

"I wasn't kissing it. I was just trying to read the headline."

"And you had to get that close? Maybe we need to get you some stronger glasses."

"Well, maybe we do," I said.

"And I suppose this Miss . . ." My mother unfolded the letter and studied the signature. "This Miss Chestnut is mistaken, too? Is that what you're trying to tell me? Maybe she has you confused with the other boy who leaves his seat to lick the pencil sharpener or touch the flag or whatever the hell it is you do the moment her back is turned?"

"That's very likely," I said. "She's old. There are spots on her hands."

"How many?" my mother asked.

On the afternoon that Miss Chestnut arrived for her visit, I was in my bedroom, rocking. Unlike the obsessive counting and touching, rocking was not a mandatory duty but a voluntary and highly pleasurable exercise. It was my hobby, and there was nothing else I would rather do. The point was not to rock oneself to sleep: This was not a step toward some greater goal. It was the goal itself. The perpetual movement freed my mind, allowing me to mull things over and construct elaborately detailed fantasies. Toss in a radio, and I was content to rock until three or four o'clock in the morning, listening to the hit parade and discovering that each and every song was about me. I might have to listen two or three hundred times to the same song, but sooner or later its private message would reveal itself. Because it was pleasant and relaxing, my rocking was bound to be tripped up, most often by my brain, which refused to allow me more than ten consecutive minutes of happiness. At the opening chords of my current favorite song, a voice would whisper, *Shouldn't you be upstairs making sure there are really one hundred and fourteen peppercorns left in that small ceramic jar? And, hey, while you're up there, you might want to check the iron and make sure it's not setting fire to the baby's bedroom.* The list of demands would grow by the moment. *What about that television antenna? Is it still set into that perfect V, or has one of your sisters destroyed its integrity. You know, I was just wondering how tightly the lid is screwed onto that mayonnaise jar. Let's have a look, shall we?*

I would be just on the edge of truly enjoying myself, this close to breaking the song's complex code, when my thoughts would get in the way. The trick was to bide my time until the record was no longer my favorite, to wait until it had slipped from its number-one position on the charts and fool my mind into believing I no longer cared.

I was coming to terms with "The Shadow of Your Smile" when Miss Chestnut arrived. She rang the bell, and I cracked open my bedroom door, watching as my mother invited her in.

"You'll have to forgive me for these boxes." My mother flicked her cigarette out the door and into the littered yard. "They're filled with crap, every last one of them, but God forbid we throw anything away. Oh no, we can't do that! My husband's saved it all: every last Green Stamp and coupon, every outgrown bathing suit and scrap of linoleum, it's all right here along with the rocks and knotted sticks he swears look just like his old department head or associate district manager or some goddamned thing." She mopped at her forehead with a wadded paper towel. "Anyway, to hell with it. You look like I need a drink, scotch all right?"

Miss Chestnut's eyes brightened. "I really shouldn't but, oh, why not?" She followed my mother up the stairs. "Just a drop with ice, no water."

I tried rocking in bed, but the sound of laughter drew me to the top of the landing, where from my vantage point behind an oversized wardrobe box, I watched the two women discuss my behavior.

"Oh, you mean the touching," my mother said. She studied the ashtray that sat before her on the table, narrowing her eyes much like a cat catching sight of a squirrel. Her look of fixed concentration suggested that nothing else mattered.

Time had stopped, and she was deaf to the sounds of the rattling fan and my sisters' squabbling out in the driveway. She opened her mouth just slightly, running her tongue over her upper lip, and then she inched forward, her index finger prodding the ashtray as though it were a sleeping thing she was trying to wake. I had never seen myself in action, but a sharp, stinging sense of recognition told me that my mother's impersonation had been accurate.

"Priceless!" Miss Chestnut laughed, clasping her hands in delight. "Oh, that's very good, you've captured him perfectly. Bravo, I give you an A-plus."

"God only knows where he gets it from," my mother said. "He's probably down in his room right this minute, counting his eyelashes or gnawing at the pulls on his dresser. One, two o'clock in the morning and he'll still be at it, rattling around the house to poke the laundry hamper or press his face against the refrigerator door. The kid's wound too tight, but he'll come out of it. So, what do you say, another scotch, Katherine?"

Now she was Katherine. Another few drinks and she'd probably be joining us for our summer vacation. How easy it was for adults to bond over a second round of cocktails. I returned to my bed, cranking up the radio so as not to be distracted by the sound of their cackling. Because Miss Chestnut was here in my home, I knew it was only a matter of time before the voices would order me to enter the kitchen and make a spectacle of myself. Maybe I'd have to suck on the broom handle or stand on the table to touch the overhead light fixture, but whatever was demanded of me, I had no choice but to do it. The song that played on the radio posed no challenge whatsoever, the lyric as clear as if I'd written it myself. "Well, I think I'm going out of my head," the man sang, "yes, I think I'm going out of my head."

Following Miss Chestnut's visit, my father attempted to cure me with a series of threats. "You touch your nose to that windshield one more time and I'll guarantee you'll wish you hadn't," he said driving home from the grocery store with a lapful of rejected, out-of-state coupons. It was virtually impossible for me to ride in the passenger seat of a car and not press my nose against the windshield, and now that the activity had been forbidden, I wanted it more than anything. I tried closing my eyes, hoping that might eliminate my desire, but found myself thinking that perhaps *he* was the one who should close his eyes. So what if I wanted to touch my nose to the windshield? Who was it hurting? Why was it that he could repeatedly worry his change and bite his lower lip without the threat of punishment? My mother smoked and Miss Chestnut massaged her waist twenty, thirty times a day—and here *I* couldn't press my nose against the windshield of a car? I opened my eyes, defiant, but when he caught me moving toward my target, my father slammed on the brakes.

"You like that, did you?" He handed me a golf towel to wipe the blood from my nose. "Did you like the feel of that?"

Like was too feeble for what I felt. I loved it. If mashed with the right amount of force, a blow to the nose can be positively narcotic. Touching objects satisfied a mental itch, but the task involved a great deal of movement: run upstairs, cross the room, remove a shoe. I soon found those same urges could be fulfilled within the confines of my own body. Punching myself in the nose was a good place to start, but the practice was dropped when I began rolling my eyes deep in their sockets, an exercise that produced quick jolts of dull, intoxicating pain.

"I know exactly what you're talking about," my mother said to Mrs. Shatz, my visiting fourth-grade teacher. "The eyes rolling every which way, it's like talking to a slot machine. Hopefully, one day he'll pay off, but until then, what do you say we have ourselves another glass of wine?"

"Hey, sport," my father said, "if you're trying to get a good look at the contents of your skull, I can tell you right now that you're wasting your time. There's nothing there to look at, and these report cards prove it."

He was right. I had my nose pressed to the door, the carpet, and the windshield but not, apparently, to the grindstone. School held no interest whatsoever. I spent my days waiting to return to the dark bedroom of our new house, where I could roll my eyes, listen to the radio, and rock in peace.

I took to violently shaking my head, startled by the feel of my brain slamming against the confines of my skull. It felt so good and took so little time; just a few quick jerks and I was satisfied for up to forty-five seconds at a time.

"Have a seat and let me get you something cool to drink." My mother would leave my fifth- and then my sixth-grade teachers standing in the breakfast nook while she stepped into the kitchen to crack open a tray of ice. "I'm guessing you're here about the head-shaking, am I right?" she'd shout. "That's my boy, all right, no flies on him." She suggested my teachers interpret my jerking head as a nod of agreement. "That's what I do, and now I've got him washing the dishes for the next five years. I ask, he yanks his head, and it's settled. Do me a favor, though, and just don't hold him after five o'clock. I need him at home to straighten up and make the beds before his father gets home."

This was part of my mother's act. She played the ringleader, blowing the whistle and charming the crowd with her jokes and exaggerated stories. When company came, she often pretended to forget the names of her six children. "Hey, George, or Agnes, whatever your name is, how about running into the bedroom and finding my cigarette lighter." She noticed my tics and habits but was never shamed or seriously bothered by any of them. Her observations would be collected and delivered as part of a routine that bore little resemblance to our lives.

"It's a real stretch, but I'm betting you're here about the tiny voices," she said, offering a glass of sherry to my visiting seventh-grade teacher. "I'm thinking of either taking him to an exorcist or buying him a doll so he can bring home some money as a ventriloquist."

It had come out of nowhere, my desperate urge to summon high-pitched noises from the back of my throat. These were not words, but sounds that satisfied an urge I'd never before realized. The sounds were delivered not in my voice but in that of a thimble-sized, temperamental diva clinging to the base of my uvula. "Eeeeeeee—ummmmmmmmmmm—ahhhh—ahhh—meeeeeeee." I was a host to these wailings but lacked the ability to control them. When I cried out in class, the teachers would turn from their blackboards with increasingly troubled expressions. "Is someone rubbing a balloon? Who's making that noise?"

I tried making up excuses, but everything sounded implausible. "There's a bee living in my throat." Or "If I don't exercise my vocal cords every three minutes, there's a good chance I'll never swallow again." The noise-making didn't replace any of my earlier habits, it was just another addition to what had become a freakish collection of tics. Worse than the constant yelps and twitchings was the fear that tomorrow might bring something even worse, that I would wake up with the urge to jerk other people's heads. I might go for days without rolling my eyes, but it would all come back the moment my father said, "See, I knew you could quit if you just put your mind to it. Now, if you can just keep your head still and stop making those noises, you'll be set."

Set for what? I wondered. Often while rocking, I would imagine my career as a movie star. There I was attending the premiere beneath a floodlit sky, a satin scarf tied just so around my throat. I understood that most actors probably didn't interrupt a love scene to press their noses against the camera or wail a quick "Eeeeeee—ahhhhhhh" during a dramatic monologue, but in my case the world would be willing to make an exception. "This is a moving and touching film," the papers would report. "An electrifying eye-popping performance that has audiences squealing and the critics nodding, 'Oscar, Oscar, Oscar.'"

I'd like to think that some of my nervous habits faded during high school, but my class pictures tell a different story. "Draw in the missing eyeballs and this one might not be so bad," my mother would say. In group shots I was easily identified as the blur in the back row. For a time I thought that if I accompanied my habits with an outlandish wardrobe, I might be viewed as eccentric rather than just plain retarded. I was wrong. Only a confirmed idiot would wander the halls of my high school dressed in a floor-length caftan; as for the countless medallions that hung from around my neck, I might as well have worn a cowbell. They clanged and jangled with every jerk of my head, calling attention when without them I might have passed unnoticed. My oversized glasses did nothing but provide a clearer view of my rolling, twitching eyes, and the clunky platform shoes left lumps when used to discreetly tap my forehead. I was a mess.

I could be wrong, but according to my calculations, I got exactly fourteen minutes of sleep during my entire first year of college. I'd always had my own bedroom, a meticulously clean and well-ordered place where I could practice my habits in private. Now I would have a roommate, some complete stranger spoiling my routine with his God-given right to exist. The idea was mortifying, and I arrived at the university in full tilt.

"The doctors tell me that if I knock it around hard enough, there's a good chance the brain tumor will shrink to the point where they won't have to operate," I said the first time my roommate caught me jerking my head. "Meanwhile, these other specialists have me doing these eye exercises to strengthen what they call the 'corneal fibers,' whatever that means. They've got me coming and going, but what can you do, right? Anyway, you go ahead and settle in. I think I'll just test this electrical socket with a butter knife and re-arrange a few of the items on my dresser. Eeeee-sy does it. That's what I always s-ahhhhhhh."

It was hard enough coming up with excuses, but the real agony came when I was forced to give up rocking.

"Give it a rest, Romeo," my roommate moaned the first night he heard my bedsprings creak. He thought I was masturbating, and while I wanted to set the record straight, something told me I wouldn't score any points by telling him that I was simply rocking in bed, just like any other eighteen-year-old college student. It was torture to lie there doing nothing. Even with a portable radio and earphones, there was no point listening to music unless I could sway back and forth with my head on a pillow. Rocking is basically dancing in a horizontal position, and it allowed me to practice in private what I detested in public. With my jerking head, rolling eyes, and rapid stabbing gestures, I might have been a sensation if I'd left my bed and put my tics to work on the dance floor. I should have told my roommate that I was an epileptic and left it at that. He might have charged across the room every so often to ram a Popsicle stick down my throat, but so what? I was used to picking splinters out of my tongue. *What* I wondered, *was an average person expected to do while stretched out in a darkened room?* It felt pointless to lie there motionless and imagine a brighter life. Squinting across the cramped, cinder-block cell, I realized that an entire lifetime of wishful thinking had gotten me no further than this. There would be no cheering crowds or esteemed movie directors shouting into their bullhorns. I might have to take this harsh reality lying down, but while attempting to do so, couldn't I rock back and forth just a little bit?

Having memorized my roommate's course schedule, I took to rushing back to the room between classes, rocking in fitful spurts but never really enjoying it for fear he might return at any moment. Perhaps he might feel ill or decide to cut class at the last minute. I'd hear his key in the door and jump up from my bed, mashing down my wadded hair and grabbing one of the textbooks I kept on my prop table. "I'm just studying for that pottery test," I'd say. "That's all I've been up to, just sitting in this chair reading about the history of jugs." Hard as I tried, it always wound up sounding as if I were guilty of something secretive or perverse. *He* never acted in the least bit embarrassed when caught listening to one of his many heavy-metal albums, a practice far more shameful than anything I have yet to imagine. There was no other solution: I had to think of a way to get rid of this guy.

His biggest weakness appeared to be his girlfriend, whose photograph he had tacked in a place of honor above the stereo. They'd been dating since tenth grade, and while he had gone off to college, she'd stayed behind to attend a two-year nursing school in their hometown. A history of listening to Top 40 radio had left me with a ridiculous and clichéd notion of love. I had never entertained the feeling myself but knew that it meant never having to say you're sorry. It was a many-splendored thing. Love was a rose *and* a hammer. Both blind and all-seeing, it made the world go round.

My roommate thought that he and his girlfriend were strong enough to make it through the month without seeing each other, but I wasn't so sure. "I don't know that I'd trust her around all those doctors," I said. "Love fades when left untended, especially in a hospital environment. Absence might make the heart grow fonder, but love is a two-way street. Think about it."

When my roommate went out of town, I would spend the entire weekend rocking in bed and fantasizing about his tragic car accident. I envisioned him wrapped tight as a mummy, his arms and legs suspended by pulleys. "Time is a great healer," his mother would say, packing the last of his albums into a milk crate. "Two years of bed rest and he'll be as good as new. Once he gets out of the hospital, I figure I'll set him up in the living room. He likes it there."

Sometimes I would allow him to leave in one piece, imagining his joining the army or marrying his girlfriend and moving someplace warm and sunny, like Peru or Ethiopia. The important thing was that he leave this room and never come back. I'd get rid of him and then move on to the next person, and the one after that, until it was just me, rocking and jerking in private.

Two months into the semester, my roommate broke up with his girlfriend. "And I'm going to spend every day and night sitting right here in this room until I figure out where I went wrong." He dabbed his moist eyes with the sleeve of his flannel shirt. "You and me, little buddy. It's just you and me and Jethro Tull from here on out. Say, what's with your head? The old tumor acting up again?"

"College is the best thing that can ever happen to you," my father used to say, and he was right, for it was there that I discovered drugs, drinking, and smoking. I'm unsure of the scientific aspects, but for some reason, my nervous habits faded about the same time I took up with cigarettes. Maybe it was coincidental or perhaps the tics retreated in the face of an adversary that, despite its health risks, is much more socially acceptable than crying out in tiny voices. Were I not smoking, I'd probably be on some sort of medication that would cost the same amount of money but deny me the accoutrements: the lighters I can thoughtlessly open and close, the ashtrays that provide me with a legitimate reason to leave my chair, and the cigarettes that calm me down while giving me something to do with my hands and mouth. It's as if I had been born to smoke, and until I realized it, my limbs were left to search for some alternative. Everything's fine as long as I know there's a cigarette in my immediate future. The people who ask me not to smoke in their cars have no idea what they're in for.

"Remember when you used to roll your eyes?" my sisters ask. "Remember the time you shook your head so hard, your glasses fell into the barbeque pit?"

At their mention I sometimes attempt to revisit my former tics and habits. Returning to my apartment late at night, I'll dare myself to press my nose against the doorknob or roll my eyes to achieve that once-satisfying ache. Maybe I'll start counting the napkins sandwiched in their plastic holder, but the exercise lacks its old urgency and I soon lose interest. I would no sooner rock in bed than play "Up, Up, and Away" sixty times straight on my record player. I could easily listen to something else an equal number of times while seated in a rocking chair, but the earlier, bedridden method fails to comfort me, as I've forgotten the code, the twitching trick needed to decipher the lyrics to that particular song.

I remember only that at one time the story involved the citizens of Raleigh, North Carolina, being herded into a test balloon of my own design and making. It was rigged to explode once it reached the city limits, but the passengers were unaware of that fact. The sun shone on their faces as they lifted their heads toward the bright blue sky, giddy with excitement.

"Beautiful balloon!" they all said, gripping the handrails and climbing the staircase to their fiery destiny. "Wouldn't you like to ride?"

"Sorry, folks," I'd say, pressing my nose against the surface of my ticket booth. "But I've got other duties."

How I Learned to Snap
Kirk Read

Jesse Fowler was the gay Rosa Parks of Lexington, Virginia. In a way, he one-upped her. He got the bus driver fired. Much of what I know about dignity came from him.

Jesse was a senior when I was a freshman. After we became friends, we walked home from school together. Upon parting, I'd run home to write down everything he said. I worked feverishly to make his vocabulary my own. From him I learned to properly use the words *tragic, fierce*, and *drama*. I learned to begin, whenever possible, all sentences with *Child*. . . .

He had a different hairstyle every two weeks and often chided me for my "boy hair." He sometimes crimped my bangs, prompting the Colonel to ask if I'd been hanging out with the Fowler boy again.

"Yes," I replied at supper. "And *child*, he's *fierce*."

One day, as we neared the corner of McDaniel Street where he walked east and I walked west, a school bus came to a rolling stop beside us. The bus was full of elementary school children. Dozens of them stuck their heads out the windows and screamed "Faggot!"

Jesse held his middle finger in the air for a solid minute. It felt like a lifetime. "I don't have enough middle fingers for these children," he said.

Finally, the bus sped off. Kids were hanging their heads out the windows, giving him the finger and screaming.

I asked him where they learned that word. "The bus driver tells them to call me that," he said. "It happens every day. I'm just trying to get from point A to point B."

"Every day?" I asked, wondering if they would start slowing down for me.

"Come with me," he said, lighting a cigarette.

We walked to his house. I felt like I was going backstage. He'd painted his entire room black. Besides the phase in which he dressed as Boy George, Jesse had done a stint as Robert Smith of the Cure, but that day he was looking one hell of a lot like Siouxsie Sioux. Throughout each transformation, he was unequivocally Jesse.

Jewelry and clothing was scattered everywhere. He had bottles of Sun-In. When I picked one up to look at it, he grabbed it from me.

"You've got brown hair like mine. Save yourself the pleasure of turning a very vivid orange, because you *so* will."

Jesse took several silver rings from his fingers and put them on his dresser.

He sat me on the bed and said, "Pay attention." He put the stereo needle down on Bronski Beat's *Smalltown Boy* and watched my face change as I heard Jimmy Somerville's voice for the first time. *The love that you need will never be found at home*, Jimmy sang. My soul already knew the song.

"*Run away, turn away, run away, turn away, run away.*"

Jesse danced in the mirror. He'd taught the entire school to dance. The only problem was that our high school's soundtrack was a bluegrass ditty, his was a twelve-inch remix. He had a brand of soul that had eluded me altogether. His dancing was a joyful explosion, the genesis of which is authentic pain. He danced so well with black girls because their dancing was also about escaping. It was about showing people they wouldn't let the world win.

One of his signature expressions was "I am not afraid." That day, after being called faggot by dozens of screaming children, Jesse positioned me in front of the mirror. He taught me to make wide circles with my arm. Three circles and a snap, he said. Snap on the word *not*. "I am *not* (snap) afraid."

I practiced over and over.

"Let the children hear you," he said.

When I went home, I stood in front of my mirror. I snapped and snapped and snapped. I snapped for my parents, who thought it was a beatnik thing. I snapped for my white friends, who thought it was funny. I snapped for my black friends, who gave me advice on how to snap even louder—how to really scare people when I snapped. Because that was the purpose.

Later, Jesse went to the school board office and filed a complaint that eventually got that bus driver fired.

"I hope the bitch gets her food stamps," he said. It was the sweetest vengeance a small town queer could imagine in the late-eighties.

When all was said and done, Jesse just wanted to walk home in peace. The bravest of angels often travel with dignity as their only weapon. Jesse also packed a knife throughout high school, just in case.

Later that year, when Jesse graduated, people cheered as he crossed the stage. He'd put up with their shit for four long years. His chemically damaged hair poked out from under his scarlet cap. His pointy black boots carried him across that stage, each step eliciting another audience member's howl.

It was the end of my ninth-grade year. I still had three more to go. How in the world was I going to get from point A to point B? I am *not* afraid, I said out loud.

As he received his diploma, I could hear the angels snapping.

Three Prose Poems

Mary Oliver

1

Oh, yesterday that one, we all cry out. *Oh, that one!* How rich and possible every-thing was! How ripe, ready, lavish, and filled with excitement—how hopeful we were on those summer days, under the clean, white racing clouds. *Oh, yesterday!*

2

I was in the old burn-dump—no longer used—where the honeysuckle all summer is in a moist rage, willing it would seem to be enough to decorate the whole world. Here a pair of hummingbirds lived every summer, as if the only ones of their kind, in their own paradise at the side of the high road. On hot afternoons, beside the blackberry canes that rose thickly from that wrecked place, I strolled, and was almost always sure to see the male hummingbird on his favorite high perch, near the top of a wild cherry tree, looking out across his kingdom with bright eye and even brighter throat. And then, on the afternoon I am telling about, as he swung his head, there came out of the heavens an immense growl, of metal and energy, shoving and shrilling, boring through the air. And a plane, a black triangle, flew screaming from the horizon, heavy talons clenched and lumpy on its underside. Immediately: a suffering in the head, through the narrow-channeled ears. And I saw the small bird, in the sparkle of its tree, fling its green head sideways for the eye to see this hawk-bird, this nightmare pressing overhead. And, lo, the hum-mingbird cringed, it hugged itself to the limb, it hunkered, it quivered. It was God's gorgeous, flashing jewel: afraid.

All narrative is metaphor.

3

After the storm the ocean returned without fanfare to its old offices; the tide climbed onto the snow-covered shore and then receded; so there was the world: sky, water, the pale sand and, where the tide had reached that day's destination, the snow.

And this detail: the body of a duck, a golden-eye; and beside it one black-backed gull. In the body of the duck, among the breast feathers, a hole perhaps an inch across; the color within the hole a shouting red. And bend it as you might, nothing was to blame: storms must toss, and the great black-backed gawker must eat, and so on. It was merely a moment. The sun, angling out from the bunched clouds, cast one could easily imagine tenderly over the landscape its extraordinary light.

Research and Practice Strategies

1. You may want to draw from memories of times spent with others. Or you might choose to return to an earlier exercise where you focused more on a solitary experience. In any case, you will want to re-enter the earlier draft or exercise with an eye to working with issues surrounding narrative point of view. If you choose the current exercise of moments spent with others, you'll write a series of narratives comprised of segments. Each segment will represent a different individual's story of the shared memory and will capture their point of view, voice, memory. Draw on all that you've learned thus far about character revelation, dialogue specific to a character, descriptive details that reveal the teller, including gestures, word choice and such. You're not describing the act of, for example, John telling his version in this exercise; you're writing John's version of the story, actively, but in his voice. Draw on his memories to recreate the moment. You will then shift to a third individual's recollection of the same event. And so on. Be sure to include a paragraph of your own reconstruction of the memory. *How* does John's version tell us about him? *How* does the difference between his version and another friend's version create tension for you as a writer? Should their points of view and recollections simply stand side by side or can you make something of the differences? Once you have at least three versions of a shared experience, you will want to begin working with it as a whole. Do the various points of view need to be interwoven, providing texture and dimension to the piece, or do you need to work with distinct segments so that the versions are juxtaposed, perhaps even contradicting one another?

2. One way to deal with a painful subject or experience is to go ahead and push the envelope, as David Sedaris is known for doing and which he so masterfully does in "A Plague of Tics," (included at the end of this chapter). Sometimes telling the raw truth on ourselves, or on others, or on society, is the best way to provide an effective critique. Take a moment in your life that was particularly hurtful or embarrassing and push it to its limits. See if you can find the point at which humor and pain meet. This brand of humor can give voice to the unspeakable, providing a cultural critique while also making us laugh, perhaps even uncomfortably. This doesn't mean the experience is trivialized; on the contrary, often it is more fully understood because you have gained perspective on it. And it is narrative perspective that can render the experience fully human, while also making us smile, or laugh, or cry—perhaps all at once.

3. Take a piece you have written earlier in the course and rewrite it, shifting your point of view somewhat. Write a brief reflection on how this changes, not only the story, but your own narrative persona.

Pointers and Potential Pitfalls

A cautionary note on humor: be careful whom you skewer.

Chapter 8

Finding Story in Situation: Resonance and Theme

Sit-u-a-tion

The way in which something is positioned with regard to its surroundings. Position with regard to surrounding conditions and attendant circumstances. A critical or problematic combination of circumstances.

— Websters II New College Dictionary

Every story has a **situation**. "The situation is the context or circumstance, sometimes the plot," notes memoirist and essayist, Vivian Gornick, in her aptly titled book on the subject, *The Situation and the Story*. "The story is the emotional experience that preoccupies the writer: the insight, the wisdom, the thing one has come to say."

One way to approach a discussion of situation and story is to think of narrative nonfiction as having four dimensions: what is happening (**action**), how it is happening (**plot**), what it means to the individual or individuals involved (**personal theme**), and what it means in a larger sense in terms of human experience (**universal theme**). Another way would be: the immediacy of experience, the personal significance of experience, and the human relevance of experience. **Narrative**—the story itself—may seem like fiction, although in its guise of narrative nonfiction it is *not* fiction. Rather than relying entirely on **exposition**— writing *about* a particular experience—the creative writer relies sparingly on exposition, perhaps to set up the situation, or to reflect on a memory, or to summarize, but usually not to *unfold* the central events of the story. More likely, the creative writer works within the parameters of the story and situation to generate the story's theme.

"The Blues Merchant," by Jerome Washington (included in this chapter), does this by writing *through* narrative action to get at theme. As readers we are left to interpret the story, without thematic explanation on the part of the writer. Even so, Washington adeptly turns the tables on the prison guards, allowing the story's action to set the prisoners free, if only for a short time.

The notion that a story has only one "truth," is addressed by Laura Wexler in her essay, "Once Upon a Time," or Implementing Postmodernism in Creative Nonfiction (included in this chapter). Noting that "we tell different stories about the same events," Wexler's essay emphasizes the importance of recognizing the illusion created by the story—that there exists a single, true, and knowable version of "What Happened." Does this mean we should avoid writing the kinds of narratives that deal with subjectivity and point of view? "Absolutely not," she stresses. In fact, one of the strengths of narrative nonfiction is its mediating power—its depiction of point of view.

A piece like Kim Chernin's "Oy, My Enlightenment" (included in this chapter) reflects this approach, for example, by recreating a bed-making scene between Chernin's mother, herself, and her daughter. The scene represents decidedly different experiences and philosophies about what it means to make a bed.

Relying more on narrative than the reflective dimension that is prevalent in the personal essay, Chernin draws on literary strategies traditionally associated with the short story, novel, poem, play: image, scene, setting, situation, action, dialogue. When theme arises organically from scene and situation the writer refrains from extensive *telling*, constructing the scene in such a way that it *shows*, while leaving most of the unfolding action's thematic interpretation up to the reader.

But, What Does it *Mean*?

Narratives that convey literal meaning only, that recount events but fail to go beyond them to work metaphorically, lack the complexity and texture that suggests meaning beyond the particular. Narratives that come alive literarily carry within them larger meanings, allow for ambiguity, and engage their readers in interpretation. For example, in describing the process of writing his play, *The Cryptogram*, playwright David Mamet said that around the "billionth draft" he realized that he "had all this stuff about the kid not going to sleep,"and it finally occurred to him that the play was not about an inability to fall asleep, but about "why." "It was not *that* the kid can't sleep, but *why* can't the kid sleep?" When readers ask what a story is about, they are not simply asking *what happened*, but also *what does it mean?*

The events of a story—action, descriptive details, dialogue—are so significant that there is no story without them. At the same time, to be more than reportage—to be a *story*—the narrative must exceed the facts of the situation in which the story finds itself. The story is organized in such a way that the dynamic interaction among the scenes and imagery creates resonance that sets up an interpretive dimension to the story. This dimension, which I refer to as **thematic resonance**, is larger than **situation**, but it arises directly from situation.

The Point of the Story—Thematic Resonance

> What's happening (action/scene) + How it is happening
> (plot/complication) = What it means (theme)

The mathematical principle—the whole is greater than the sum of its parts—is a helpful concept for grasping what writers mean when they talk about thematic resonance.

While prewriting welcomes a profusion of disorder, and early drafts often focus on *what is happening*—scene, situation, and summary—thus constructing effective infrastructure for a story, it is not yet a story. To bring a story to fruition is to re-enter it and ask that it do something more. It is to ask that the parts— situation, scene, imagery, character, setting—interact suggestively, generating a larger meaning that resonates beyond the particularity of its parts. When there is resonance, as readers we are interested. There is life here, something to be struggled over, wrestled with, understood. If we think of a subject or situation as a stone dropped into a still lake, theme can be likened to the ripples that flow out and away. Subject and theme are different things, interdependent, interactive, but different.

Theme isn't something the writer explains to the reader, it's embedded within the story—found in the situation and revealed through dramatic and metaphoric effect. Since the reader will become the owner of the story's theme, once the narrative is written and sent out into the world, as a writer you want to provide as many cues and clues as possible along the way to move your readers in the interpretive direction you want them to go.

Whether it is an internal situation, which opens out into external action and resolution, or an external situation, which moves inward toward realization or insight, the **situation** at hand is a major driving force within the creative nonfic- tion story—but it is not the story, "the story is the emotional experience that preoccupies the writer"; it reverberates as theme. Consider "The Clan of One- Breasted Women" by Terry Tempest Williams (included in this chapter). Writing about generations of women in her family who have had breast cancer, the land- scape of the Utah desert, and the cancer-causing effects from nuclear testing in Utah in the 1950s, Williams explores the internal situation while recounting the external. In fact, the two realms merge in a single key scene. In conversation with her father about a recurring dream she has about a "flash of light in the night in the desert," Williams comes face to face with a stark reality. Her father explains that this isn't just a dream image, but an event she actually witnessed as a small child, riding on her mother's lap in the car—the atomic bomb mushroom cloud "rising from the desert floor." In the following passage, notice how the external and internal come together for Williams:

> *I stared at my father.*
> *It was at this moment that I realized the deceit I had been living under. Children growing up in the American Southwest, drinking conta- minated milk from contaminated cows, even from the contaminated breasts of their mothers, my mother—members, years later, of the Clan of One-Breasted Women.*

The "situation" here is the effect nuclear testing had on those who lived in this region, and the cancer the women of Williams's family suffered as a result.

It is this that moves the story along. But the nuclear testing (and its effect) is not entirely the story. The "story" is the larger theme—Williams' grappling with her anger, grief, and her determination to reclaim what has been lost.

Scene and Situation—Story and Theme

Literary Journalism, like other forms of narrative nonfiction, is based solidly on fact. However, even literary journalism works with thematic resonance (ergo the term, "literary"). Take another look at the excerpt from Sonia Nazario's "Enrique's Journey"—a Pulitzer Prize-winning feature story published in the *Los Angeles Times* (included in Chapter 6). The scenes Nazario portrays are particularly compelling in their descriptive details coupled with the tension that is present in the situation. Even within the small space of scenes, thematic resonance exists. For example, look carefully at the opening and closing scenes of Nazario's piece. Notice how they mirror one another, creating the suggestion of a cycle that goes well beyond the acts of leave-taking. While readers may have differing interpretations of what each seemingly simple step off the porch means, its resonance reaches us, bringing with it enlarged meaning.

Shorter work is also capable of achieving thematic resonance through effective scenes constructed within a situation. You might review Judith Ortiz Cofer's memoir piece, "Volar," included in Chapter 1. It's a fine example of a story that focuses on a specific situation to achieve thematic resonance. Volar's 715 carefully selected words taken from Cofer's experience, are organized and connected in such a way that the dynamic interaction among the scenes and imagery creates emotional and imaginative resonance, setting up an interpretive dimension to the story. This dimension is larger than the situation in which Cofer and her mother and father find themselves, but it arises from that situation.

The story's situation shows a family that would like to return home to Puerto Rico, but cannot afford to. The young Cofer's situation parallels her family's; she would like to escape her childhood identity and her feelings of entrapment in her adolescent self.

Cofer's desire for transformation from childhood to superwoman, which she achieves through her dreams and a vivid imagination developed from reading comic books about super heroes, takes on thematic resonance as it echoes and resolves (for the child) the family's plight. Thus, the desire to "fly" takes on larger meaning by the story's conclusion, when Cofer hears her mother's familiar refrain: "Ay, si yo pudiera volar (Oh, if I could fly)."

Another fine example of a short whose theme is embedded within the narrative, rather than explained, is Brian Doyle's "Two Hearts" (also in Chapter 1). The title itself, "Two Hearts," resonates with ambiguous possibilities. Certainly it represents the two hearts of the twin boys: Joseph's healthy heart, Liam's unhealthy heart. But, the title also gestures toward the narrator's dual and dueling positions on the issue: he is angry, he is grateful; he loves, he hates. Yes, life denotes inevitable death, but not like this! Doyle, both writer and father, experiences his own heart as broken in two.

Readings

Writers on Writing

"Saying Good-Bye to 'Once Upon a Time,' or Implementing Postmodernism in Creative Nonfiction," Laura Wexler

Memoir

"Oy, My Enlightenment," Kim Chernin

Lyric Essay

"The Clan of One-Breasted Women," Terry Tempest Williams

Prose Poem

"The Blues Merchant," Jerome Washington

Saying Good-Bye to "Once Upon a Time," or Implementing Postmodernism in Creative Nonfiction

Laura Wexler

*O*nce upon a time is the most seductive line in literature.

Hearing it, we're immediately tantalized and calmed. Tantalized, because we know the story that follows will involve heroes and villains engaged in a fierce struggle. Calmed, because we know the heroes will prevail and live "happily ever after." The particulars may be different, but such a cocktail of excitement and ease can be found in nearly every fairy tale . . . and, for that matter, in every Hollywood blockbuster.

And yet, the fantasy of fairy tales has less to do with made-up characters and plot than with an illusion created about storytelling itself: the illusion that there always exists a single, true, and knowable version of What Happened.

Let's say that you, an aspiring creative nonfiction writer, decide to write about one of the most controversial events of the final decade of the twentieth century, the beating of Rodney King. Would it be possible for you to tell the story with the same calm omniscience as those who tell fairy tales? Would you be able to write the single, true version of What Happened, with a clear and certain idea of who did what to whom, and when and why?

Would your story paint the baton-wielding police officers as the villains and Rodney King the hero/victim—or would you cite the flawed use-of-force policies in the Los Angeles Police Department as a mitigating factor? And would you mention that Rodney King had been driving drunk and led the police on a chase? Would you tell the beating of Reginald Denney, a white man, by black men in the aftermath of the King trial, as a story about uncontrolled black anger—despite the fact those who rescued Denney were also black?

And how would you account for the fact that, in the rioting that followed the original not-guilty verdict of the officers, a conflict painted as a black-white thing, Korean businesspeople suffered the brunt of the property destruction? And what about the fact that one of the officers who beat Rodney King made a comment about *Gorillas in the Mist* several hours before the beating—does that mean he beat Rodney King because King was black, or because he (incorrectly) thought King was on the drug PCP? And what of the motives of the judge, the jury, the media, the citizens?

These questions make it clear that the Rodney King beating cannot be told as a fairy tale. There is no single, true version of What Happened. Because everything about it is up for grabs, everything is unstable: motives, actions, and interpretations. It seems we cannot, despite Rodney King's famous plea, "all get along"—because we tell different stories about the same events.

We always do.

An event like the Rodney King beating is simply a "hot spot" that brings our various and conflicting stories into high relief. It, like so many stories that reflect and perpetuate our national obsession with race, is a palimpsest. It is a particular story, certainly, but one that is freighted with all the conflicting stories about lynching, police brutality, and racism in the criminal justice system that have been told before. It is an event that occurred at a fixed point in time; nonetheless, it seems to exist more as an arrow, reaching into the past.

So as nonfiction writers, should we shy away from stories like this, stories that thwart our methods of researching and writing, our every effort to learn and record Truth? Absolutely not. Rather, we should recognize that the genre of creative nonfiction—with its emphasis on stories—is perfectly suited to deal with contested terrain, both in the past and present. We'll get tangled up, that's certain. But it can't be any other way.

A Brief and Reductive Definition of Postmodernism

The bedrock principle of postmodernism is *subjectivity*, the idea that the world looks different depending where you stand, both literally and figuratively. The fancy name for this is *positionality*; a variety of things—race, class, gender, sexual orientation, cultural background, educational level, experiences—combine to produce your positionality.

Your positionality affects your perceptions of the world and, at the same time, your perceptions of the world affect your positionality. Certainly there's a lot more to postmodernism, but for our purposes, it's important to acknowledge that different people almost always have different interpretations of the same event, and these different interpretations are illustrative of a whole range of interesting phenomena. The other thing that's crucial to realize is that seeing the world in a postmodern way makes it impossible—irresponsible at worst, uninteresting at best—to write any story like a fairy tale. Postmodernism shows us the impossibility of the existence of one true version of anything that matters.

Think about these ideas in terms of our nation's history. The Boston Tea Party—was it the act of patriots or insurgents? Depends whether you talk to the people who chucked the tea or the man who wore the British crown. The Civil War (or the War of Northern Aggression)—was it fought largely over slavery or states' rights? Depends whether you talk to a self-righteous Yankee or a devotee of the Lost Cause.

Then think about more recent events: The O.J. Simpson trial—was it long-denied justice finally served, or a travesty? The Elian Gonzalez brouhaha—was it a conflict over core politics or child rearing?

Or consider more run-of-the-mill events. A friend recently told me that several of her colleagues, who were Chinese men newly arrived to the United States, were asked to relocate to a different bureau to fill in a gap in their company's operations. The men perceived the relocation as a message that they were not performing well. Despite every attempt to convince them that the relocation was for logistical reasons, the men felt that they had dishonored the company, and themselves, and they resigned. Same action, different interpretations.

In an even more troubling—and thus illuminating—incident, a friend's wife, who is white, was waiting in line at the airport in Atlanta. It was crowded, and she stepped back to let a person pass through. That person—who was a black man—interpreted her stepping back as a sign of fear or distaste, and he told her so. She felt it was a gesture of consideration and politeness. Again, same action, different interpretations.

All of these cases deal with points of conflict. That's what makes them challenging to write about; that's also what makes them compelling. And certainly any journalist writing about events like these would seek out different people with different opinions in an effort to be objective. That's standard operating procedure. But implementing the principles of postmodernism in creative nonfiction means taking standard journalistic operating procedure further. It means creating literary structures and techniques that are the formal embodiment of these principles, such that readers have not only a cerebral, but also a visceral, experience.

Stopping to Consider

As writers, it's easy to go about our business without much consideration to the theoretical implications of what we do. But think about it. What is really the main goal of the creative nonfiction writer? To use research methods and literary techniques to re-create actual events and people on the page, you might say. And that's a good answer. Certainly there are many instances in which re-creating what happened—a ship going down in a storm, a climbing team perishing on Everest, a synagogue exploding in Atlanta—is an amazing reportorial and artistic enterprise, one that requires prodigious talent and skill. To borrow from Shakespeare, sometimes the play really *is* the thing.

But sometimes it isn't the *only* thing. Some stories are so contested that creative nonfiction writers must be as concerned with representing interpretations of those events as they are with re-creating the events themselves. In general, these are events that concern national hot spots, or secrets, or taboos; in the United States, the national taboo is, of course, race.

Consider one of the most fascinating history-made-current-affair stories to surface in the last few years: the question of whether Thomas Jefferson's sexual relationship with his slave Sally Heming led to a set of descendants that has never been recognized. "Jefferson's Blood," a documentary that aired on PBS's *Frontline*, dealt with this question by alternating scenes about life in Monticello during Jefferson's era with scenes from the current day, as people step forward claiming to be the secret descendants of Jefferson, and other people, in turn, deny those claims.

Again, the story is a palimpsest, a story whose modern chapters cannot be understood without understanding the history of race in America, as well as

Thomas Jefferson's previously uncriticized place in that history. The documentary, at its end, does not solve the mystery. Rather, it provides insight into both our past and present by allowing us to see and hear clashing answers to the same question.

When I began writing my own book about the lynching of two black men and two black women in Walton County, Georgia, in 1946, my initial goal was to uncover who had fired the shots that killed the four victims—it was a lynching by bullet rather than by rope—and then re-create the story of the lynching on the page. I set out to do this in the same way I'd chased all the stories I'd ever written: I talked to people.

I talked to relatives of the victims, as well as white and black people who were living in Walton County at the time. I talked to people who were interviewed during the six-month FBI investigation in 1946 and others who had testified at the grand jury held in Athens, Georgia. After twenty or so interviews, I scanned my notebooks, looking to see what facts I'd collected, what I knew. I realized I had a lot of what people *thought* had happened, but very little I could confirm, very little that looked like truth.

Looking hard at my notebooks, I began to see that my hopes of re-creating a truthful and whole account of the lynching—much less solving it—would never be fulfilled. There was nobody living who could tell the story straight; there was, like with the Jefferson-Heming story, simply too much at stake for people. It was then I began to see that re-creating the lynching would be only part of my job. The other part was to investigate and represent the legacy of the lynching, which was the gossip, rumors, and beliefs I'd begun scribbling in my notebook. As soon as the last shot rang out that afternoon at the Moore's Ford Bridge in Walton County, the set of facts that was the lynching disappeared, and the lynching could, from that moment, live on only in stories.

People told, and tell, stories to deal with the surprise of the lynching. They tell stories to help themselves imagine the lynching even after it has occurred, a phenomenon Philip Gourevitch discusses in terms of the Rwandan genocide in his book *We Wish to Inform You That Tomorrow We Will Be Killed With Our Families*. They tell stories to serve their political, and their psychic, needs. Most of the stories aren't whole, and many can't be considered reliable. But their fragmentation, their unreliability, is the basis of their truth. People's stories about the lynching reveal as much about life in Georgia in 1946—and now—as the lynching itself. And the same holds true for any story that touches on a national taboo, secret, mystery, any event that's gone unstudied, undiscussed, unacknowledged.

And so, embracing the principles of postmodernism allows us to do several things as writers of creative nonfiction. It allows us, on both a theoretical and a practical level, to see the events we're writing about as refracted through a prism. And it allows us to see that even the most unreachable stories—the stories in which truth seems to purposely hide in the shadows—can be written as nonfiction by focusing as much on interpretation as event. In fact, it is these very stories that most need to be written as nonfiction.

Using Interviews to Enact the Principles of Postmodernism

Remember that standard journalism legend in which two cars crash in an intersection, five people witness it, and, minutes later, all five people tell different stories about what happened? This exercise doesn't tell us anything we didn't know already: people lie, memory fails. But it does confront us with choices. Do we quit asking people for their stories because they're often inaccurate, or do we examine the unreliability, inspect the diverging stories for what they reveal?

When, during interviews or conversation, we ask people, "What happened?"; "Why did this happen?"; "Who was responsible?"; "What does it mean?"—we're asking them to connect cause and effect in a meaningful narrative. We're asking them to construct and create stories. In doing so, they usually tell us less than a transcription of events would—but often they tell us more.

One afternoon, after I'd spent about a year conducting interviews with black people who were living in Walton County, Georgia, at the time of the 1946 lynching, I was driving on a country road when I spotted an older white woman in her front yard raking leaves, and stopped to chat with her.

"What do you remember about the summer of 1946?" I asked after we'd dispensed with introductions.

"I remember that black man stabbed Barney," she said. "That was awful."

The woman remembered accurately; a black man had stabbed a white farmer named Barney Hester during the summer of 1946. And two weeks later, that black man, along with three other black people, was lynched. The lynching of four black people was what most people I'd talked to remember as the tragedy of the summer of 1946; this woman remembers the stabbing of the white man (who later recovered). Standing there that afternoon, I was struck by the profound gap in what people remember as important or surprising or tragic. That gap is the truth; set alongside all the conflicting stories, it offers an accurate portrait of the legacy of racial violence, both in 1946 and today.

The recognition that stories are subjective does not, then, negate the value of the interview, the cornerstone tool of creative nonfiction. Rather, it requires that we view interviewing as a critical—rather than simply a documentary—endeavor. We don't have to interrogate people or accuse them of lying, though both are sometimes necessary. But we have to consider that everybody tells the story "slant." On the one hand, this is unavoidable. Different people see the world differently. On the other hand, people often consciously tell a story a certain way in order to convey a message about themselves/their family/their political party. As creative nonfiction writers, we must bring all sorts of journalistic research—court documents, newspapers, crime reports, and other sources—to bear. Again, recognizing that the truth is subjective doesn't mean that it's OK to print lies. It means that in addition to pointing out inaccuracies in a particular version of a story, the creative nonfiction writer investigates the possible reasons for these inaccuracies.

This opens up fertile and exciting ground. A book about a controversial event—anything that travels contested terrain—then becomes a kind of oral historiography of that event, an examination of the ways people tell that event.

Forging A Structure

When I began my book on the quadruple lynching in Walton County, Georgia, I had in mind a nice, neat narrative structure in which a single main character would serve as a kind of guide, leading readers through the chaos of the lynching. But once I began to come to terms with the uncertainty that had to be a part of my account of the lynching, I came to terms with the fact that my structural plan for the book did not reflect the multiplicity and uncertainty that was at the heart of the content.

When I looked around for structural models that could allow for multiplicity and conflict, I found several. In some ways, the most obvious possibility is to fashion yourself—the writer/reporter—as the recipient of all the conflicting stories. In his book *The Other Side of the River: A Story of Two Towns, a Death, and America's Dilemma*, author Alex Kotlowitz positions himself as a stand-in for the reader. He listens closely to people's stories and theories about the death of a black teenager in Michigan, and attempts to arrive at an account of what likely happened. This is not objectivity; it's informed subjectivity. The most famous example of this in nonfiction is, of course, James Agee and Walker Evans's *Let Us Now Praise Famous Men*, in which Agee's struggle to represent the lives of the three tenant farm families becomes the central struggle of the book.

But there are possibilities in other genres. Certainly Akira Kurosawa's film *Rashomon*, which replays the same event four times, each narrated by four different characters, offers interesting possibilities. Translating that to creative nonfiction, the idea would be to place conflicting accounts next to each other, without authorial interpretation, and let the reader puzzle it out.

Documentary theater, as practiced most famously by Anna Deveare Smith, also offers interesting structural ideas. For her pieces—which include works on the Crown Heights, Brooklyn, racial riots; the L.A. riots; and the Clinton White House—she interviews hundreds of people. Then, she edits the transcripts of select interviews to create monologues that she acts out onstage in the character of the interviewee. The effect of the monologues, coming one after another, and clashing with one another, is disorienting—which, of course, is the point.

There are, of course, all sorts of other possibilities. The important thing is to create a structure for your article or book that translates content into form, that allows the structure of a story to serve as a metaphor for the story itself. This struggle to find the literary tools—structure, language, character—is what distinguishes creative nonfiction from purely documentary endeavors, such as oral history or cultural anthropology.

In terms of implementing the principles of postmodernism, the goal is to forge a structure that allows for multiple viewpoints and fragmentation, and a bit of complication and messiness. It would be nice to tell a clean, straight narrative about a highly-charged event, just as it would be nice to be a kid again. But simple stories are for demagogues and their followers. The rest of us need reality, which is that no one has a monopoly on truth.

A Naked Appeal to Creative Nonfiction Writers

When I first divulged that I planned to write a book about a lynching that happened more than a half-century ago, some people counseled me to reconsider. It's not a story that can be written as creative nonfiction, they said. All the victims are dead; the members of the lynch mob are either dead or silent; and other people can't be relied upon. There simply aren't enough provable facts. You can never be sure what exactly happened, or who exactly did it. Why not write the story as a novel? others asked.

Every nonfiction writer dreams of the flexibility of fiction at one time or another. Not sure if a person wore a hat on the day he died? Make it up. Not sure what someone thought when she stepped off the bus? Put some thoughts into her head yourself. But, in the end, it was not a suggestion I could consider seriously. So many lynchings—like other instances of violence, like other taboos—have been denied, ignored, and veiled in secrecy. That leaves the victims and their loved ones not only with their loss, but also without any official or public acknowledgment of their loss.

Creative nonfiction writers are in an ideal position to be one-person "truth and reconciliation" commissions, to uncover "the small stories that have gone missing," as one writer put it. Rooted as it is in telling people's stories, creative nonfiction is a particularly well-equipped genre to deal with events that have been forgotten or understudied by official histories, and to unearth lives at the margin of bigger events. Seek out these stories. Listen to them critically. Try to learn as much as possible about what it is to live in this fragmented, contradictory, often incomprehensible world. Then write.

Oy, My Enlightenment
Kim Chernin

*M*y mother's face is the face of a child. It refuses to give up its sense of the marvelous. She looks up, as if she could still see that light coming from the ceiling. Her white hair is curled and tousled. Her head tilted to one side, she seems to be listening to the echo of her own voice. And then, without warning, something happens to her face. To me, it seems that a great convulsion passes over her features. She does not move, even her breathing seems to have stopped and now, very slowly, a single tear moves down her cheek. She lifts her hand, wipes impatiently at this tear, and suddenly she is an old woman again.

But I cannot escape so easily from the past. I imagine myself walking through muddy streets. I carry heavy books beneath my arm; around the corner is a study house. And she says, interrupting my thoughts, "You are a woman. Don't you understand? In that world, you think you would have become a scholar?"

When I glance down I notice that my hands are taut, stretched out, straining. But something elusive is passing away from us. We cannot hold it, we are being driven into the present. I sense that something irretrievable has been lost. My mother wipes crumbs from the table into an ashtray. Gertrude, without saying a word, gets up and walks from the room. I shake myself past the feeling of desolation that tries to settle on me. And Larissa stretches out her legs, uncurling from the story's rapture. "Mama, I'm tired," she says, with a trace of irritation in her voice. And now my mother and I, uneasy, guilty mothers both of us, because we do not make our children the center of our lives, bustle into activity.

And so we enter the present together, making up the couch into a bed for Larissa and me to sleep in. My mother, invigorated by the story she has been telling, has regained that self I remember from my childhood, making this work into a game, organizing everything, going out of the room and returning with Larissa beside her, their arms piled high with pillows and sheets and blankets, marching as my mother chants, *"Raz, dva, tre, cheteri, piat, vwishel seitchik pagulyat,"* correcting Larissa's pronounciation, calling out to me, "Translate. Translate for your daughter."

"One, two, three, four," I shout, obedient to her high spirits, "the hunter went out hunting for a hare."

Now we are making the bed together, smoothing the sheet and tucking it with careful folds at the corners, while my mother discourses upon women and the making of beds. Listening, half-listening to her, I observe the way she never loses an opportunity for giving instruction. "My own mother," she says, "told me not to learn to cook or to sew. 'You'll marry a rich man? then you won't need it. If he's a poor man, better you don't know how to become his slave.'"

Now she is telling us, as the blanket flaps up into the air, and, laughing, we take hold of the corners and spread it out, the way the world is ordered by these smoothings and tuckings. The way, as I remind her, I needed her there at night when I was a child because no one else could tuck me in tightly enough. How, when she was arrested during the McCarthy time and went to jail, it seemed that my father, no matter how hard he tried, could not make the bed covers smooth, and could not braid my hair so that the braids were tight enough. The way, without her, things always seemed to come undone.

Now we pull the corners taut and slip them under the mattress. My mother passes her hand over the blanket and I recall how much I loved this gesture when I was a girl, believing it made sleep possible and kept it peaceful.

Larissa has been eager to join this conversation. She turns her head from me to my mother, watching our lips, waiting for an opportunity. The moment she begins to talk I restrain an impulse to reach out and clap my hand over her mouth.

"Grandma," she is saying, "Grandma, you know what Mama used to say?" My mother looks over at her with a heartbreaking eagerness, delighted that this reserved child is now so willing to confide in her. "It was a hot day," says Larissa. "Mama was helping me make my bed. But I didn't want to. I hated it, didn't I,

Mama? And Mama said, 'Larissa, when I have to do something I don't like, I tell myself that if I take the right care with this work, and do it patiently, even this humble task could show me the way to enlightenment.'"

She looks up at us, her eyes full of the knowledge that she has become a storyteller for the first time in her life.

But my mother does not smile down at her as Larissa has expected. Instead, a silence comes up and we all fidget and feel uncomfortable. That word *enlightenment!* And I am embarrassed, too, by the way I am like and not like my mother, always seeking opportunity for instruction but drawing from it such different morals.

Larissa is growing angry. She looks up at me—I should take her side. And I realize just how hard it is to become a daughter of this family, never knowing when some chance word or expression will suddenly transform a happy mood and create this terrible abyss, the silence.

My mother says, "So this is the way you are raising your daughter?" But she does not wait for me to answer. Leaving us now with a quick kiss good-night, eager to avoid any friction between us, any disagreement, however slight.

Larissa is sitting straight up in bed. She is hurt and angry, I can tell, as she tugs on her red nightgown and turns her back to me, socking the pillows into place beneath her head. But when I sit down next to her I see that deep look in her eyes, which at such times are so much like the eyes of my mother. "Mama," she says, forgiving me, "do you think she was strange?"

"Who?" I ask, knowing perfectly well whom she means.

And then, because of this dishonesty, she casts a baleful look at me. "You know," she says, the judgment implacable, "who I mean."

These eyes run in our family. In the older world, my mother says, they were known as the eyes of the *macheschaefe*, the witch. But then, I suspect, the word was never used lightly and I wonder what it means that my grandmother used it of my own mother, who has frequently used it of me.

"Well, do you?" she insists as if this were a simple question. Was my grandmother peculiar already in the old country? Is that why her husband left her and went to America? Is that why she stayed so close to her father and never really wanted to leave home?

"It's not so easy," I say finally, hearing even more in this question than she asks. "When I was a little girl, growing up in the Bronx, I used to look for her every day on the park bench even though I knew she was already dead. You see what I mean? There was, in that woman's life, some feeling about the world that our own time has lost."

I watch her face as the words settle. She does not at first know what they mean, but she is comforted by the fact that I am being philosophical. Then, the words seem to reach a place where her understanding is larger than she is. For an instant she glances again into my eyes, touching a carefully guarded place few people are able to reach. And then something closes inside her, locking the words away. Later, they will become her conscious knowledge. For now they are simply the guarantee that understanding is possible.

She shakes herself, swallows once or twice, and begins to hum. She is folding a small piece of paper, her hands skillful the way the hands of my mother and myself have never been. She seems to have forgotten completely about me and looks up surprised at my gasp of astonishment as she unfolds a perfect bird from the scrap of newspaper with which she has been working. It is a skill her great-grandmother might have taught her, sitting next to the tiled stove in that vanished house in the little village, telling her how the windows must be left open at night so that the restless evil spirits can escape.

These old stories, which she has never heard, live in her eyes. Looking at her I understand why I must have frightened my mother when I was a child. We all have eyes that see into the far side of things which people prefer to keep hidden.

Absorbed in her folding and tearing, Larissa moves her lips silently as she creates these elusive paper beings who have made a menagerie of our bed. The bird with its bemused, quizzical expression; the grave innocence of this angel who seems to know everything although he has experienced nothing; the little house that stands at the edge of a crease that stands for a river. Is she creating a little shtetl on our bed, into which we ourselves can now enter, so that I shall not have to continue to feel this loneliness, this futile nostalgia, this sense of loss?

She lifts her head. For an instant I see my mother's face, turned to the ceiling, beholding light. "Not yet, not yet," I whisper absurdly to myself, afraid that she will wake up from her reverie and become an old woman. But she does not reach up impatiently to cast away her childhood. Very carefully, setting down a rocking chair next to the little house wobbling on her bed, she says to me, "Tell me, Mama," with precisely the tone and expression I used as a child. "Tell me," she repeats, musing so deeply, "could someone living now do something as great as Einstein did?"

"Well," I say, "yes, I suppose so." But suddenly her question impresses me through its urgency.

"Could I, Mama? Is it still possible? Could I, do you think?"

This girl sleeps with a picture of Einstein over her bed; riding his bicycle through the stone courtyard at the California Institute of Technology.

And so I think, urgently now, does one feel in this girl that capacity she asks of? And then I give up trying to reach this knowledge. I let something in myself which knows these things answer her. "Yes," I say to her, "it is possible for you." And I see, in the look she casts into me now, that a lie here, the slightest failure to know or to report truly, would have cost me this closeness with her forever.

"Good," she says, reaching out to smooth a village square in front of the synagogue where the angel rests haphazardly. "I hoped it would be."

It is one of those moments between people, and I have known them frequently, when something is asked, something tested, a barrier falls and one passes or fails, is deemed worthy, or is closed out from this sort of vulnerable communion forever. That is the kind of girl she is. And I am the same sort of woman.

She puts her head on my lap. "Perle," she says in that dreamy voice she has not used for years. "And after Perle came Rochele. And after Rochele, Elke. And then came Larissa."

She stretches out, turning over the little house in the shtetl, crushing the innocent angel, pinching the wing of the quizzical bird I have wanted to keep forever, out of the reach of this sort of holocaust. And now, satisfied that her future will be large enough to accommodate the forces she feels stirring inside her, she reaches out and flattens the rocking chair, wiping away a past that has always refused to belong to me. But I understand her. I put my hand on her head and in a moment she is asleep.

But now, of course, my mother comes back down the hall. The door opens, she peeks in and nods vigorously, pleased that I, too, have not been able to sleep. She sits down next to me on the bed, careful not to disturb Larissa. "My mother," she says and then drops her voice to a whisper, "my mother used to start first thing in the morning with the beds." The memory, pushing against some obstacle I cannot see, passes furiously over her face. She gazes around her absently for a moment or two and then picks up the crumpled pieces of paper that so recently were a world. Very carefully now she begins to smooth them out, unfolding them, returning them to their state of pure potential.

"That," she says, her voice rising, "was after we left the shtetl. So forgive me, I am ahead of my story. Then, when we were living in Waterbury, she had not only our beds, and Lillian's bed, but she had also the beds from the boarders. So think. What would it mean to this woman if you would say to her, Do every little task in that certain way which makes it perfect? Of course, maybe I don't know what you mean by enlightened,"she says, interrupting herself and looking at me with an expression intended to leave no doubt she knows perfectly well what this word means to me. "But I can tell you," she continues, "just what an oppression this would be to my mother, who was still working on those beds when we got home from school. And maybe she tried to cook dinner for us, maybe she tried to clean the house, and of course it was hard for her, she never liked it and now she was always confused. And so those beds, I tell you, were always there . . ."

Larissa ceases to pretend that she is still asleep. She sits up in bed, throws her arms around my mother, and begins to rock her in her arms. My mother looks down at her, startled, suspicious and then, as she takes in the expression on her face, triumphant. "Ha," she says and picks up a corner of the blanket. She holds it up in the air and gazes at it reverently. "Oy, my enlightenment," she chants, winking at my daughter, "how shall I fold you so that you will never come out from your fold again?"

Larissa loves it. Ignoring me, she shakes the pillow out of its case and wags her head at my mother. "Oy, my enlightenment," she chokes out, bent double with laughter.

I sit here, waiting to argue for my point of view, wanting to keep my mother from winning over my daughter, but knowing if I remain serious now, I shall look even smaller, more absurd. And finally, it does not seem to matter so much as I watch them undoing this bed we made up so carefully an hour ago. It was, after all, for this I brought her to visit my mother, was it not? This girl who, less than a year ago, did not know her grandmother was born in a shtetl.

"Oy, my enlightenment," Larissa is chanting wildly to herself, shaking a pillow over her head. And now, glancing quickly from my mother to me, she picks up her cue. "Grandma,"she says, in a voice grown fully conscious of the part it is to play; "Grandma, tell me a story," she shouts, lost to all memory of reserve and caution, as we settle down together in the fine disorder of the bed.

The Clan of One-Breasted Women
Terry Tempest Williams

I belong to a Clan of One-Breasted Women. My mother, my grandmothers, and six aunts have all had mastectomies. Seven are dead. The two who survive have just completed rounds of chemotherapy and radiation.

I've had my own problems: two biopsies for breast cancer and a small tumor between my ribs diagnosed as a "borderline malignancy."

This is my family history.

Most statistics tell us breast cancer is genetic, hereditary, with rising per-centages attached to fatty diets, childlessness, or becoming pregnant after thirty. What they don't say is living in Utah may be the greatest hazard of all.

We are a Mormon family with roots in Utah since 1847. The "word of wisdom" in my family aligned us with good foods—no coffee, no tea, tobacco, or alcohol. For the most part, our women were finished having their babies by the time they were thirty. And only one faced breast cancer prior to 1960. Tradition-ally, as a group of people, Mormons have a low rate of cancer.

Is our family a cultural anomaly? The truth is, we didn't think about it. Those who did, usually the men, simply said, "bad genes." The women's attitude was stoic. Cancer was part of life. On February 16, 1971, the eve of my mother's surgery, I accidentally picked up the telephone and overheard her ask my grand-mother what she could expect.

"Diane, it is one of the most spiritual experiences you will ever encounter."

I quietly put down the receiver.

Two days later, my father took my brothers and me to the hospital to visit her. She met us in the lobby in a wheelchair. No bandages were visible. I'll never forget her radiance, the way she held herself in a purple velvet robe, and how she gathered us around her.

"Children, I am fine. I want you to know I felt the arms of God around me.

We believed her. My father cried. Our mother, his wife, was thirty-eight years old.

A little over a year after Mother's death, Dad and I were having dinner together. He had just returned from St. George, where the Tempest Company was completing the gas lines that would service southern Utah. He spoke of his love for the country, the sandstoned landscape, bare-boned and beautiful.

He had just finished hiking the Kolob trail in Zion National Park. We got caught up in reminiscing, recalling with fondness our walk up Angel's Landing on his fiftieth birthday and the years our family had vacationed there.

Over dessert, I shared a recurring dream of mine. I told my father that for years, as long as I could remember, I saw this flash of light in the night in the desert—that this image had so permeated my being that I could not venture south without seeing it again, on the horizon, illuminating buttes and mesas.

"You did see it," he said.

"Saw what?"

"The bomb. The cloud. We were driving home from Riverside, California. You were sitting on Diane's lap. She was pregnant. In fact, I remember the day, September 7, 1957. We had just gotten out of the Service. We were driving north, past Las Vegas. It was an hour or so before dawn, when this explosion went off. We not only heard it, but felt it. I thought the oil tanker in front of us had blown up. We pulled over and suddenly, rising from the desert floor, we saw it, clearly, this golden-stemmed cloud, the mushroom. The sky seemed to vibrate with an eerie pink glow. Within a few minutes, a light ash was raining on the car."

I stared at my father.

"I thought you knew that," he said. "It was a common occurrence in the fifties."

It was at this moment that I realized the deceit I had been living under. Children growing up in the American Southwest, drinking contaminated milk from contaminated cows, even from the contaminated breasts of their mothers, my mother—members, years later, of the Clan of One-Breasted Women.

It is a well-known story in the Desert West, "The Day We Bombed Utah," or more accurately, the years we bombed Utah: above ground atomic testing in Nevada took place from January 27, 1951 through July 11, 1962. Not only were the winds blowing north covering "low-use segments of the population" with fallout and leaving sheep dead in their tracks, but the climate was right. The United States of the 1950s was red, white, and blue. The Korean War was raging. McCarthyism was rampant. Ike was it, and the cold war was hot. If you were against nuclear testing, you were for a communist regime.

Much has been written about this "American nuclear tragedy." Public health was secondary to national security. The Atomic Energy Commissioner, Thomas Murray, said, "Gentlemen, we must not let anything interfere with this series of tests, nothing."

Again and again, the American public was told by its government, in spite of burns, blisters, and nausea, "It has been found that the tests may be conducted with adequate assurance of safety under conditions prevailing at the bombing reservations." Assuaging public fears was simply a matter of public relations. "Your best action," an Atomic Energy Commission booklet read, "is not to be worried about fallout." A news release typical of the times stated, "We find no basis for concluding that harm to any individual has resulted from radioactive fallout."

On August 30, 1979, during Jimmy Carter's presidency, a suit was filed, *Irene Allen v. The United States of America*. Mrs. Allen's case was the first on an alphabetical list of twenty-four test cases, representative of nearly twelve hundred plaintiffs seeking compensation from the United States government for cancers caused by nuclear testing in Nevada.

Irene Allen lived in Hurricane, Utah. She was the mother of five children and had been widowed twice. Her first husband, with their two oldest boys, had watched the tests from the roof of the local high school. He died of leukemia in 1956. Her second husband died of pancreatic cancer in 1978.

In a town meeting conducted by Utah Senator Orrin Hatch, shortly before the suit was filed, Mrs. Allen said, "I am not blaming the government, I want you to know that, Senator Hatch. But I thought if my testimony could help in any way so this wouldn't happen again to any of the generations coming up after us . . . I am happy to be here this day to bear testimony of this."

God-fearing people. This is just one story in an anthology of thousands.

On May 10, 1984, Judge Bruce S. Jenkins handed down his opinion. Ten of the plaintiffs were awarded damages. It was the first time a federal court had determined that nuclear tests had been the cause of cancers. For the remaining fourteen test cases, the proof of causation was not sufficient. In spite of the split decision, it was considered a landmark ruling. It was not to remain so for long.

In April 1987, the Tenth Circuit Court of Appeals overturned Judge Jenkins's ruling on the ground that the United States was protected from suit by the legal doctrine of sovereign immunity, a centuries-old idea from England in the days of absolute monarchs.

In January 1988, the Supreme Court refused to review the Appeals Court decision. To our court system it does not matter whether the United States government was irresponsible, whether it lied to its citizens, or even that citizens died from the fallout of nuclear testing. What matters is that our government is immune: "The King can do no wrong."

In Mormon culture, authority is respected, obedience is revered, and independent thinking is not. I was taught as a young girl not to "make waves" or "rock the boat."

"Just let it go," Mother would say. "You know how you feel, that's what counts."

For many years, I have done just that—listened, observed, and quietly formed my own opinions, in a culture that rarely asks questions because it has all the answers. But one by one, I have watched the women in my family die common, heroic deaths. We sat in waiting rooms hoping for good news, but always receiving the bad. I cared for them, bathed their scarred bodies, and kept their secrets. I watched beautiful women become bald as Cytoxan, cisplatin, and Adriamycin were injected into their veins. I held their foreheads as they vomited green-black bile, and I shot them with morphine when the pain became inhuman. In the end, I witnessed their last peaceful breaths, becoming a midwife to the rebirth of their souls.

The price of obedience has become too high.

The fear and inability to question authority that ultimately killed rural communities in Utah during atmospheric testing of atomic weapons is the same fear I saw in my mother's body. Sheep. Dead sheep. The evidence is buried.

I cannot prove that my mother, Diane Dixon Tempest, or my grandmothers, Lettie Romney Dixon and Kathryn Blackett Tempest, along with my aunts developed cancer from nuclear fallout in Utah. But I can't prove they didn't.

My father's memory was correct. The September blast we drove through in 1957 was part of Operation Plumbbob, one of the most intensive series of bomb tests to be initiated. The flash of light in the night in the desert, which I had always thought was a dream, developed into a family nightmare. It took fourteen years, from 1957 to 1971, for cancer to manifest in my mother—the same time, Howard L. Andrews, an authority in radioactive fallout at the National Institutes of Health, says radiation cancer requires to become evident. The more I learn about what it means to be a "downwinder," the more questions I drown in.

What I do know, however, is that as a Mormon woman of the fifth generation of Latter-day Saints, I must question everything, even if it means losing my faith, even if it means becoming a member of a border tribe among my own people. Tolerating blind obedience in the name of patriotism or religion ultimately takes our lives.

When the Atomic Energy Commission described the country north of the Nevada Test Site as "virtually uninhabited desert terrain," my family and the birds at Great Salt Lake were some of the "virtual uninhabitants."

One night, I dreamed women from all over the world circled a blazing fire in the desert. They spoke of change, how they hold the moon in their bellies and wax and wane with its phases. They mocked the presumption of even-tempered beings and made promises that they would never fear the witch inside themselves. The women danced wildly as sparks broke away from the flames and entered the night sky as stars.

And they sang a song given to them by Shoshone grandmothers:

Ah ne nah, nah	Consider the rabbits
nin nah nah—	How gently they walk on the earth—
ah ne nah, nah	Consider the rabbits
nin nah nah—	How gently they walk on the earth—
Nyaga mutzi	We remember them
oh ne nay—	We can walk gently also—
Nyaga mutzi	We remember them
oh ne nay—	We can walk gently also—

The women danced and drummed and sang for weeks, preparing themselves for what was to come. They would reclaim the desert for the sake of their children, for the sake of the land.

A few miles downwind from the fire circle, bombs were being tested. Rabbits felt the tremors. Their soft leather pads on paws and feet recognized the shaking sands, while the roots of mesquite and sage were smoldering. Rocks were hot from the inside out and dust devils hummed unnaturally. And each time there was another nuclear test, ravens watched the desert heave. Stretch marks appeared. The land was losing its muscle.

The women couldn't bear it any longer. They were mothers. They had suffered labor pains but always under the promise of birth. The red hot pains beneath the desert promised death only, as each bomb became a stillborn. A contract had been made and broken between human beings and the land. A new contract was being drawn by the women, who understood the fate of the earth as their own.

Under the cover of darkness, ten women slipped under a barbed-wire fence and entered the contaminated country. They were trespassing. They walked toward the town of Mercury, in moonlight, taking their cues from coyote, kit fox, antelope squirrel, and quail. They moved quietly and deliberately through the maze of Joshua trees. When a hint of daylight appeared they rested, drinking tea and sharing their rations of food. The women closed their eyes. The time had come to protest with the heart, that to deny one's genealogy with the earth was to commit treason against one's soul.

At dawn, the women draped themselves in mylar, wrapping long streamers of silver plastic around their arms to blow in the breeze. They wore clear masks, that became the faces of humanity. And when they arrived at the edge of Mercury, they carried all the butterflies of a summer day in their wombs. They paused to allow their courage to settle.

The town that forbids pregnant women and children to enter because of radiation risks was asleep. The women moved through the streets as winged messengers, twirling around each other in slow motion, peeking inside homes and watching the easy sleep of men and women. They were astonished by each stillness and periodically would utter a shrill note or low cry just to verify life.

The residents finally awoke to these strange apparitions. Some simply stared. Others called authorities, and in time the women were apprehended by wary soldiers dressed in desert fatigues. They were taken to a white, square building on the other edge of Mercury. When asked who they were and why they were there, the women replied, "We are mothers and we have come to reclaim the desert for our children."

The soldiers arrested them. As the ten women were blindfolded and handcuffed, they began singing:

> You can't forbid us everything
> You can't forbid us to think—
> You can't forbid our tears to flow
> And you can't stop the songs that we sing.

The women continued to sing louder and louder, until they heard the voices of their sisters moving across the mesa:

> *Ah ne nah,nah*
> *nin nah nah—*
> *Ah ne nah, nah*
> *nin nah nah—*

Nyaga mutzi
oh ne nay—
Nyaga mutzi
oh ne nay—

"Call for reinforcements," one soldier said.

"We have," interrupted one woman, "we have—and you have no idea of our numbers."

I crossed the line at the Nevada Test Site and was arrested with nine other Utahns for trespassing on military lands. They are still conducting nuclear tests in the desert. Ours was an act of civil disobedience. But as I walked toward the town of Mercury, it was more than a gesture of peace. It was a gesture on behalf of the Clan of One-Breasted Women.

As one officer cinched the handcuffs around my wrists, another frisked my body. She found a pen and a pad of paper tucked inside my left boot.

"And these?" she asked sternly.

"Weapons," I replied.

Our eyes met. I smiled. She pulled the leg of my trousers back over my boot.

"Step forward, please," she said as she took my arm.

We were booked under an afternoon sun and bused to Tonopah, Nevada. It was a two-hour ride. This was familiar country. The Joshua trees standing their ground had been named by my ancestors, who believed they looked like prophets pointing west to the Promised Land. These were the same trees that bloomed each spring, flowers appearing like white flames in the Mojave. And I recalled a full moon in May, when Mother and I had walked among them, flushing out mourning doves and owls.

The bus stopped short of town. We were released.

The officials thought it was a cruel joke to leave us stranded in the desert with no way to get home. What they didn't realize was that we were home, soul-centered and strong, women who recognized the sweet smell of sage as fuel for our spirits.

The Blues Merchant

Jerome Washington

*L*ong Tongue, The Blues Merchant, strolls on stage. His guitar rides side-saddle against his hip. The drummer slides onto the tripod seat behind the drums, adjusts the high-hat cymbal, and runs a quick, off-beat tattoo on the tom-tom, then relaxes. The bass player plugs into the amplifier, checks the settings on the control panel and nods his okay. Three horn players stand off to one side, clustered, lurking like brilliant sorcerer-wizards waiting to do magic with their musical instruments.

The auditorium is packed. A thousand inmates face the stage; all anticipate a few minutes of musical escape. The tear gas canisters recessed in the ceiling remind us that everything is for real.

The house lights go down and the stage lights come up. Reds and greens and blues slide into pinks and ambers and yellows and play over the six poised musicians.

The Blues Merchant leans forward and mumbles, "Listen. Listen here, you all," into the microphone. "I want to tell you about Fancy Foxy Brown and Mean Lean Green. They is the slickest couple in the East Coast scene."

Thump. Thump. The drummer plays. Boom-chicka-chicka-boom. He slams his tubs. The show is on. Toes tap. Hands clap. Fingers pop. The audience vibrates. Long Tongue finds his groove. He leans back. He moans. He shouts. His message is picked up, translated and understood. With his soul he releases us from bondage, puts us in tune with tomorrow, and the memories of the cold steel cells—our iron houses—evaporate.

Off to one side, a blue coated guard nods to the rhythm. On the up-beat his eyes meet the guard sergeant's frown. The message is clear: "You are not supposed to enjoy the blues. You get paid to watch, not be human." The message is instantaneously received. The guard jerks himself still and looks meaner than ever.

Long Tongue, The Blues Merchant, wails on. He gets funky. He gets rough. He gets raunchy. His blues are primeval. He takes everybody, except the guards, on a trip. The guards remain trapped behind the prison's walls while, if only for a short time, we are free.

Research and Practice Strategies

1. After reading "Oy, My Enlightenment," highlight those sentences or phrases where you find effective use of the senses—sight, sound, touch, smell, perhaps even taste—particularly descriptive. From your selections make a list of the words that you find most evocative. Now return to the various settings in the story and identify those words, passages, ideas, and images that convey larger meaning. Finally, look at the passages, sentences, phrases you have chosen thus far, both those with descriptive value and those conveying the larger meaning for which you are striving. Are there overlaps between your two sets of selections? This exercise is intended to help you make connections between descriptive settings and scenes and the thematic meaning conveyed in a story. So, as you find overlaps you will want to consider how you might heighten such connections so that meaning is enlarged, becoming more thematically resonant.

2. In Jerome Washington's "The Blues Merchant," the prison is transformed into a musical concert and takes on a life of its own, shifting power from guards to inmates, who for a few brief moments are set free. For this exercise you might return to a particular place where setting is as important as event, and where setting and situation are intertwined. Remember as you write the piece that you are not only bringing in descriptive details about setting, you are using such description to move the story forward and to organically weave theme into narrative. In addition to Washington's "The Blues Merchant," you might revisit Joan Nestle's "A Restricted Country" in Chapter 5.

3. Here is a suggestion for an exercise closer to literary journalism, but with the same goal of illuminating how setting and scene interact with contextual meaning: Think about an issue that concerns you. It might be the high cost of textbooks, the losing streak of a college's athletic team, fan behavior, the college dating scene, the face of a homeless person you pass daily, the increasingly distracted atmosphere of public cell phone conversations and ears plugged with headphones. Go to a place where you can observe the issue you are addressing being "lived." Note the setting, as well as what you see, hear, and smell. Pay attention to how people interact, what they say to one another, and how they say it. Watch their body language. Think about how these people and your observations of them might contribute to the *issue* of your piece.

   For example, you might go to the campus bookstore and eavesdrop on a student in the aisles as she reacts to the price of the textbook she's just selected from a shelf. Listen to the crunch of rows of cash registers ringing up sales and the comments student buyers make as they pay. Don't forget visuals: the light in the store, security cameras, wandering students carrying lists. You're doing "eye search," research based on observations. For now, don't bother expanding your research to anything more than this. Forget statistics that might work well in a longer, more thorough story.

   Now write what you know. Don't write the words "the high cost of textbooks." Readers should be able to figure this out through your descriptions. Write the setting or settings, the scenes showing action, while using descriptive details sufficiently to give the reader a sense of the issue at hand.

   Don't worry about getting the story perfect in the first draft; just focus on setting, scene, and the larger issue that will begin to make its way into the story.

4. Select a significant scene from an earlier piece and summarize it. Read your summary carefully and comparatively to see if the scene

has all the elements of your summary. Is anything missing from the descriptive scene that you have included in your summary? Are there details you might add to the scene to fully dramatize aspects of your summary?

5. Divide a piece of paper into three columns. In the left column, write: "What is happening and how is it happening?" In the middle column write: "What does it mean to me?" In the right column write: "What is the universal meaning of this?" Now, think of a significant event in your life—moving to a new town, parents' divorce or remarriage, a birth, making a new and lifelong friend, a travel experience. Think of a scene or two that occurred within that situation. Write everything you can about it in the left column. Don't forget everything we've discussed—imagery as in "Restricted Country," action as in "Clip from a Winter Diary," dialogue and culture as in "Bricklayer's Boy," rhythm as in "The Blue's Merchant." In the middle column jot down how this impacted your day, your life, note the meaning *you* assigned to it. Were you amused? Sympathetic? Angry? Did the situation reveal something larger to you about yourself or others? In the right column, jot down what you think this means for us all. Can we all find some relevance for this in our lives? Is the larger meaning a universal? Now put pen to paper, or fingers to the keyboard, and write a nonfiction short story, emulating one of your favorite writers, possibly one you've read in this book. Let it be rough, messy, confused, sappy, and whatever else it wants to be at first. Just get it down. In subsequent drafts you can work with the structure of the story, metaphors, symbols, shaping beginning and ending, while discovering and developing thematic resonance.

CHAPTER 9

Bringing Research to the Process

I have often been able to construct a news story around just a few facts,
but even simple feature stories require a multitude.

— JAMES B. STEWART

Research and Creative Nonfiction

We must strike a balance between allowing the facts of a situation to paralyze our imaginative capacities and riding roughshod over those facts. As Gail Godwin illustrates in "Watcher at the Gate" (included in Chapter 3), the rush to research can serve to extinguish creativity, just as it can feed the flame. Research can become an excuse for procrastination, especially in the early stages of a writing project when we may be hesitant to move from research and prewriting into getting a first draft onto the page. It is also "the most vital and irreplaceable aspect of all, the reason we are attempting to be creative: the non-fiction part" of the narrative, as Lee Gutkind so aptly notes in *The Art of Creative Nonfiction*. He states, "Even the most personal essays are full of substantive detail about a subject that affects or concerns a writer and the people about whom he or she is writing. Read the books and essays of the most renowned nonfiction writers of this century and you will read about a writer engaged in a quest for information and discovery." Rick Bragg corroborates this in his memoir, *All Over but the Shoutin'*. He writes: "I spent a year just talking to the people close to me, filling in the holes in my memory."

In her collection of essays titled *Small Wonder*, Barbara Kingsolver makes a case for diligence in research, noting that she has found herself tossing aside stories because of "botched Spanish or French phrases uttered by putative native speakers who were not supposed to be toddlers or illiterates." Kingsolver refuses to continue reading a narrative when birds sing on the wrong continents or full moons appear two weeks apart. "Literature should inform as well as enlighten," she advises, and playing fast and loose with facts not only destroys the writer's credibility as a nonfiction writer, it is a disservice to readers as well as the public interest.

252

Bill Roorbach suggests in *Writing Life Stories* that in addition to scheduling writing time and reading time, writers should schedule research time. This is an excellent suggestion for several reasons, one being that research seems to calm our inner critics who forever fret that we will get it wrong. I soothe my inner critic's concerns about these matters by jotting in my research log those questions that pop up in the middle of writing, but which will take me away from writing and into research mode. I always note where the well-researched or fact-checked information will go once I've found it from a reputable source. This way I don't have to drop everything and rush out to get an answer in the middle of my writing time, as Godwin's critic tells her she must. This seems to release my inner critic from its meticulous eye for detail and fact-finding fury, because that part of the project will be done on, say Thursday afternoon, when we (my inner critic and I) will either head out to the library, schedule an interview, or spend time in cyberspace.

"I" and "Eye"

The play on "I" and "eye" refers to turning inward *and* outward (the memoir as "I" and the feature story, for example, emphasizing the "eye"). But there is another way to think about "I" and "eye," and that is to apply the "eye" to the "I." In "Researching Your Own Life" (included in this chapter), Michael Pearson writes: "All memoir is a process of researching one's own life." As a "diligent and systematic inquiry into a subject," Pearson suggests that we "look for evidence," not just to confirm our memory of things, "but to stimulate it and to provide a larger context" for those childhood experiences about which we want to write. In Pearson's case, research about the period in which he grew up—the 1960s—led him to read newspapers, magazines, and books about the Vietnam War, the Kennedy assassination, Woodstock, and to watch films and listen to the music of that era. His research became a catalyst for memories and this led him to revisit landmarks of his youth, which in turn ignited new recollections. "Memory is an archive like any other and can be used as such," Pearson points out.

N. Scott Momaday agrees with this approach. In his memoir, *The Way to Rainy Mountain* (included in this chapter), he writes of returning to the place of his childhood, which is the home of his beloved grandmother who has died recently. This is the land the Kiowa tribe holds sacred. Weaving history, legend, and sacred story with the narrative of his return, Momaday enlarges his own story with the story of his people. As does Harriet Doerr in "Low Tide at Four" (also included in this chapter), where she returns to an extended moment from her past and recaptures a scene that reveals her and her family at an idyllic time. Equally important, in this Short, however, is the context within which the scene takes shape, a context that foreshadows a dramatic change in the course of history. As you read "Low Tide at Four" be sure to peruse it for those elements that required research for accuracy and detail.

Immersion Journalism

(handwritten margin notes: real life, reflection, research, reading, writing)

In "The Five Rs of Creative Nonfiction" (included in Chapter 5), Gutkind introduces us to one of the journalist's primary tools of research—an immersion experience. In his essay, Gutkind is "standing on a stool in the operating room at the University of Pittsburgh Medical Center." It is 3 a.m. and he is in scrubs, "peering over the hunched shoulders of four surgeons and a scrub nurse as a dying woman's heart and lungs are being removed from her chest." As the essay so beautifully exemplifies, immersion journalism is just that—complete involvement in the lives of those about whom we are writing so that we may bring our readers into that world in an immediate way. Immersion journalism is in-depth research, often to the point of literally living among the subjects of one's study.

Preparing for the Interview

Interviewing people can be your best source for information, whether you are interviewing your mother for family history, a politician, a corporate executive, an expert on the mating rituals of penguins. An effective interview begins long before the actual questioning.

- Research the subject. You need to have some knowledge about the issue or individual you are exploring.
- Look at family photo albums, read old family diaries or journals.
- Read newspaper accounts of the person or issue on which you're focusing.
- Research the topic via the Web, using reliable Web sites.
- Write your questions ahead of time and review them so that you don't have to work from them in a rote manner.
- Ask a few neutral questions to break the ice and settle in together; don't ask the most difficult questions first.
- Ask open-ended questions, not "yes" or "no" questions.
- Ask even those questions that you think have obvious answers. The answers are often a surprise.
- Be an active listener; let your interest show. When you don't get a response to an important question move on and come back to that question later, but ask it in a different way.
- Listen for nuggets of information that will take you well beyond the surface of the story.
- Remain open; the direction of your story may change as you gather more information. Don't stick rigidly to your list of questions; be willing to move about based on your interviewee's narrative.
- Always leave time at the end for asking if there's anything else that your interviewee would like to tell you.
- Ask if you may call with any additional questions you might have; you will. The interview usually isn't finished until the story has gone through its final revision.

Getting It Right

Whether you're writing memoir, biography, a profile, travel writing, or literary journalism, the World Wide Web is a promising resource as you do your research. Government Web sites often provide public access to information. Using any search engine, type in the name of the city or town and state that you want to search and you'll find their "official Web site." Once you move into the Web site, you'll discover plenty, such as the policies, town and city demographic information, links to law enforcement and court sites, as well as sites for the legislative bodies. Some courts are even considering making requests for court records available through electronic access. There may be a small fee associated with some however. Vital statistic records, birth and death records are often only available in person at the town or city office or appropriate court.

Watch out for those Web sites whose reliability might be questioned. The ones associated with known organizations, colleges or universities and the electronic databases their libraries subscribe to, or those Web sites that provide the same information as the more reputable ones, can be trusted without too much concern.

Police and Court Records

Most court records are public information. Don't be intimidated by the process of walking into a courthouse in search of a criminal or civil case file, or the death certificate of a relative. It's easier than one might imagine.

For instance, if I wanted to look at a court docket folder for a civil law suit that happened in Anyplace County, I'd go to that county's courthouse where the office for the clerk of Civil Court is located. I'd politely tell the clerk what I needed. She would probably point out a computer on the counter where I would fill in the fields on the screen with any names of parties involved in the suit. The computer would search for the docket number. If one was found, I'd give that to the clerk and she would get the docket folder for me. I would then stand at the counter and spend as much time as I need looking through the documents in the folder. I would ask to make any copies.

The same system exists in most Criminal Court clerk's offices as well as Probate Court clerk's offices (where records of matters of marriage, divorce, wills, death certificates and various other personal business and family matters are held). If the case is an older one, before the advent of computers, you might have to search an alphabetical card catalogue for the docket number. The clerks are busy, but helpful. Use them if you need to.

Police records are another story. Police departments are required to make available a daily log of their activity—calls they responded to, any criminal activity, any reports they took. Some police departments make this available on their Web site. Others provide the log upon request in person. Public access to police reports varies. If the police report makes it to court, however, it usually becomes a public record. There are some exceptions such as matters involving juveniles.

If you have questions about what information is open to the public and what is available through the Freedom of Information Act (FOIA) go to the Web site (*www.firstamendmentcenter.org*). There will be a link for directions on how to request information that falls under the FOIA.

Ethics and Narrative Nonfiction

The following discussion is not intended to be a complete discussion of the legal implications of reporting. However, I would be derelict in my duty, as they say in courtroom drama, if I did not bring up a few "must knows." So, take a deep breath and read patiently and attentively through this section, as the information may serve to keep you out of the courtroom one day.

Whether it is investigative journalism, a feature article, a literary essay, or a profile, there is nothing more important than getting the facts right. If you are embarking on a journalism story, there are a few key points that address your responsibility to the truth and to practicing ethical journalism.

The code of ethics adopted by the Society of Professional Journalists and published in the text, *Doing Ethics in Journalism*, and on the Web site (http://www.spj.org/ethics.asp), provides guidelines for journalists in pursuit of a story. The following excerpt lists the four overarching principles of the code of ethics:

- **Seek Truth and Report It:** Journalists should be honest, fair, and courageous in gathering, reporting, and interpreting information.
- **Minimize Harm:** Ethical journalists treat sources, subjects, and colleagues as human beings deserving of respect.
- **Act Independently:** Journalists should be free of obligation to any interest other than the public's right to know.
- **Be Accountable:** Journalists are accountable to their readers, listeners, viewers, and each other.

Under these principles exist the standards of practice to which every journalist should adhere, such as verifying the accuracy and credibility of your sources, understanding the impact your story has on others, avoiding conflicts of interest and associations that may compromise your integrity and credibility, and admitting mistakes and correcting them. Read the Code of Ethics for a more detailed outline of the four principles.

Legal Concerns and Lawsuits

The privilege of using your gifts in the exercise of your First Amendment rights does not come without a cost. In some cases, this cost can be measured in having to defend against a frivolous lawsuit, or in facing the prospect of jail time for defying the illegal order of an abusive

judge. However, if writers refuse to fight these battles and succumb to self-censorship, the real cost to society will be measured in the gradual loss of our liberties and freedoms, which will have withered like a useless appendage from apathy and disuse.
    —NICHOLAS S. HENTOFF AND HARVEY A. SILVERGLATE, "AVOIDING SELF-CENSORSHIP: A GUIDE TO THE DETECTION OF LEGAL LANDMINES"

Consider this scenario. You've just spent the last three months researching and interviewing sources for a high profile literary journalism story. You've verified the veracity of your sources and all the information you've gathered. You've written a strong story and it's published. You receive a letter from a high-powered law firm that intends to sue you on behalf of one of their clients who alleges that you committed libel against him—or published a falsehood that caused him harm. Was there any way you could have seen this coming? Did you step over the line? If you could have seen this coming, would you have changed your story in any way?

In "Avoiding Self-Censorship: A Guide to the Detection of Legal Landmines," attorneys Nicholas S. Hentoff and Harvey A. Silverglate argue that "the self-imposed obstacle of self-censorship is perhaps the greatest pitfall nonfiction writers face" when confronted with a scenario similar to the one above. "Nothing can put a damper on a work in progress faster than a threat from a law firm with half a dozen names on its letterhead." Hentoff and Silverglate provide excellent advice to the nonfiction writer on how to recognize when you've moved into troublesome terrain that could result in tort claims. Just so you understand the term, a "tort" is defined by *Webster's II New College Dictionary* as "a wrongful act, damage, or injury done willfully, negligently, or in circumstances involving strict liability, but not involving breach of contract, for which a civil suit can be brought."

Hentoff and Silverglate lay out the basics of the privacy torts that journalists could face. That is, what **libel and slander** amount to, what constitutes **intrusion,** what placing someone in a **false light** means, the tort of **public disclosure of embarrassing private facts,** and **appropriation.** While there are myriad circumstances specific to individual cases of tort claims, here are brief summaries of the terms I just mentioned, drawn from Hentoff and Silverglate's essay:

Libel

A published falsehood that harms somebody. **Slander** is the same except that it is applied to the spoken word as opposed to the written. Libel and slander are collectively referred to as *defamation.*

To be sued for libel, you must have done four things:

- made a false defamatory statement about
- an identifiable person that is
- published to a third party and
- caused injury to his or her reputation.

Libel laws vary somewhat from state to state, but this is a good general definition. Also, it is important to note the distinction in the standard of proof between the *public figure* who alleges libel and a *private individual*.

The public figure that sues you, the mayor, for example, has to work harder to prove that you committed libel against him. In addition to those four elements of libel listed above, the public figure must also prove that you acted with what is legally called *actual malice*. This basically means that you "knew or had actual knowledge that the published statement was false" OR that you "had a reckless disregard for the truth or falsity of the statement."

Intrusion

This applies to three scenarios.

- illegally accessing real property (houses, buildings, etc., that are private) or electronic property or files (access without consent)
- tape-recording phone conversations without consent
- intrusion by fraud

Have you ever heard the story of the determined reporter who climbs the wall of a celebrity's property and lies in wait in the bushes beside the front door of the house in order to get a surprise interview from the unsuspecting star? Well . . . when that reporter's feet hit the ground on the other side of the wall, she opened herself up for a tort claim for intrusion. Of course, this is a slight exaggeration, but the point is, every person, even that celebrity, has a right to be secure from intrusion within his private space or solitude. If you trespass or otherwise intrude into a person's reasonable realm of privacy, without first getting the person's consent to enter, you're probably vulnerable to a lawsuit for intrusion.

Intrusion is *not* limited to actual real estate "property." It also applies to electronic spaces, like email and voice mail, or computer files. You cannot enter these without the consent of the person legally able to give it. If you gain unauthorized access into these accounts or files, not only could you be subject to a civil lawsuit alleging *intrusion*, you could be criminally charged with either trespassing or breaking and entering, and even larceny if you "walk off" with the files or information that was contained inside those electronic files. This is common sense. After all, would you break into someone's home and steal files from their home office?

Have you ever wondered about recording phone conversations without the consent of those people having the conversation? Intrusion also applies here. If you intend to secretly record a phone conversation, you must first check your state's law regarding this. Hentoff and Silverglate explain that "thirteen states require that *both* parties to the conversation must consent before it can be tape-recorded." Further, if two or more of the parties are in two or more states, you must check the laws of all the states before you record. Hentoff and Silverglate recommend an excellent Web site to check these laws: The Reporters Committee for Freedom of the Press (http://www.rcfp.org).

False Light

So what is this notion of *false light?* Hentoff and Silverglate explain it this way: "False light invasion of privacy occurs when information is published about a person that is false or places the person in a false light, is highly offensive to a reasonable person, and is published with knowledge or in reckless disregard of whether the information was false or would place the person in false light." This is a lot of legal language. A false light claim is similar to a defamation claim, but actually need not be defamatory. They offer the following examples:

- "Publishing a photograph of the plaintiff (the person who is suing as a result) in a legitimate news story in such close proximity to an unrelated article on local child molesters that readers are confused as to which article the photograph relates to."
- "Publishing true facts about a plaintiff while ignoring other facts that would help mitigate (to moderate or make less severe) the harmful impact of the statement, or intentionally deleting portions of a quote that would place a harmful statement in context."

Public Disclosure of Embarrassing Private Facts

Results from publishing facts that are not of public concern and are so intimate that publication outrages the public's sense of decency. In this case, *truth* is not a defense, newsworthiness is. In those cases where the reporter obtains *private* information from *public* sources (such as court records) the plaintiff would have no grounds for a suit. And if the plaintiff had "thrust him or herself into an issue of public concern," he or she would have no grounds for this tort claim, even if "the private facts have nothing to do with the underlying public issue," according to Hentoff and Silverglate.

Appropriation

The unauthorized use of a person's likeness or identity for commercial purposes (also referred to as the Misappropriation Tort). The example given is the case of Vanna White who successfully sued for the unauthorized depiction of a robot turning letters in a set simulating the one on the *Wheel of Fortune* television show.

Hentoff and Silverglate note that courts have generally dismissed those torts when a "person's likeness is used to promote the sales of newspapers or magazines that contain the likeness in a valid news story, as long as the use doesn't imply endorsement."

In the end, what you should take from this is that the truth and the practice of ethical journalism and other forms of nonfiction, including our own stories, are paramount.

Web site help

For information about accessing electronic government databases, First Amendment issues, information on the Freedom of Information Act, access to a Legal Defense Hotline, and much more, including recent court cases, go to the Web site that Hentoff and Silverglate suggest (**http://www.rcfp.org**), which The Reporters Committee for Freedom of the Press maintains.

Readings

Writers on Writing

"*Researching Your Own Life*," Michael Pearson

"*Gathering Information*," James B. Stewart

Memoir

from *The Way to Rainy Mountain*, N. Scott Momaday

Literary Journalism

"*Texas Women: True Grit and All the Rest*," Molly Ivins

The Short

"*Low Tide at Four*," Harriet Doerr

Prose Poem

"*Mass for the Happy Death of Innocence*," Holly Iglesias

Researching Your Own Life

Michael Pearson

As strange as it may sound, all memoir is a process of researching one's own life. By that I mean rethinking, of course. I also mean reimagining and perhaps revising—because to see the past anew is often to view it, even at great distances, more clearly. But in the context of these remarks, I mean the word *research* to imply just that—research, a diligent and systematic inquiry into a subject (in this case yourself) in order, as even the most basic dictionaries will say, "to discover or revise facts, theories, or opinions."

I would venture to guess that many of the best recent memoirs demanded that the writers engage in the wonderfully tedious necessities of research. For instance, Doris Kearns Goodwin, with the instincts of the biographer and historian, surely searched spool after spool of microfilm about the Brooklyn Dodgers' 1951 season for her coming-of-age book, *Wait Till Next Year*. As she said, "If I were to be faithful to my tale, it would be necessary to summon to my own history the tools I had acquired in investigating the history of others. I would look for evidence, not simply to confirm my own memory, but to stimulate it and to provide a larger context for my childhood adventures. Thus I sought out the companions of my youth, finding almost everyone who lived on my block, people I hadn't seen for three or four decades. I explored the streets and shops in which I had spent my days, searched the Rockville Centre archives, and read the local newspapers from the fifties."

The kind of research that Goodwin engaged in was something like reliving the past, and her most interesting insight in describing her research process may be her focusing on her belief that it did not merely confirm the "facts" for her but, more importantly, stimulated her memory of the past. For the memoirist, research can bring the story out of the shadows into the light of the present day. Even in a story like Mary Karr's *The Liars' Club*, a book saturated in the changing stream of memory, the author confirmed the veracity of what she had written by having her sister, Lecia, audit the facts. In addition, Karr's mother answered questions and did information gathering for her. As was the case with Goodwin's narrative, Karr's was most assuredly brought to more vivid life because of the research that she did.

It's probable that even a memoir like *Angela's Ashes* by Frank McCourt benefited from some elements of research. The magic of the book, certainly, is McCourt's ability to transform his voice into the evolving child's. As William Kennedy said, McCourt "inhabits the mind of the child he was with such vital memory that boyhood pain and family suffering become as real as a stab in the heart." But there are many moments that McCourt could not have reasonably recollected without some unearthing of documents—the letters written under the name of Mrs. Brigid Finucane or Philomena Flynn, for example. My guess is that McCourt had notebooks and scrapbooks to sift through much as a scholar of early American history will have diaries and family Bibles.

Memory is an archive like any other and can be used as such. The materials stored there can sometimes be tested against other sources. Your memory, after all, is only one person's opinion, and if you can get some evidence to support that opinion, it will make it more cogent, probably more specific and more complex, as well. But rather than speaking for other writers of memoir, let me use my own experience in writing *Dreaming of Columbus: A Boyhood in the Bronx* as an example that may be either representative or anomalous but certainly indicative of what can be true of the relationship between memoir and research.

When the idea for the narrative of *Dreaming of Columbus* first began to germinate, it took root in my imagination as a novel. It wasn't long, though, before I saw that it was a work of nonfiction. The line between memoir and fiction is often blurred, but I'm fairly sure that I know why I stepped across the line from imagining the invented Bronx of the 1960s to describing the historical place and time. I felt that the story had a meaning that was in the actuality of it, in the solidity of the bricks, the smell of the bus exhaust, the existence beyond words of the characters who lived in the stories in the book.

I sensed that the theme had been given to me by the narrative, that the dreams of escape and return, the longing to go and the desire to stay forever, were part of how the "simple facts" had invented a meaning. And that meaning would be there, speaking in its own true voice, only if the stories of the Bronx were both factual and true. Truth, without question, is the ultimate goal, but sometimes truth is not enough. Sometimes the historical reality, even in our deconstructed new world, provides a shape and substance that would otherwise not be there.

In order to write *Dreaming of Columbus*, a recollection of the Irish Catholic Bronx of decades ago, I felt compelled to do various kinds of research. Even though I started writing from the premise that all memoir may be a lie, that Steven Millhauser was probably right when he said, "memory is merely one form of imagination," that memory's highest function may not be to recollect what has happened but rather preserve meaning or make meaning, I still felt obligated to get the facts right. If I didn't make sure that the little details were accurate, then on some important level for me the book would not be speaking the truth that it was intended to tell. So, early on in the writing process it became apparent to me that old-fashioned research was going to be an integral part of reconstructing the Bronx of the 1960s. What I didn't realize until I was far into the story was that, as with Goodwin's, my memory was stimulated by my research into my own past, that the story of the past came alive for me as I engaged in the adventure of going back, of once again searching for what had seemingly been lost.

The first form my research took was into books—but not into history books of the period. Rather, I was drawn back to those books that had shaped my view of the world when I was a youngster. Flannery O'Connor once said that "the writer is initially set going by literature more than by life," and although this may not be the case for all writers, it definitely was true for me. As a young boy, I found my place in the world in books. Therefore, rereading some of the stories that had been important to me then—*The Life of Kit Carson, Youngblood*

Hawke, The Catcher in the Rye, Catch-22, The Adventures of Huckleberry Finn—was like slipping back in time.

For instance, in rereading *Kit Carson*, which I hadn't looked at since fifth grade, and *Youngblood Hawke*, which I hadn't read since I was fourteen, I found myself recalling vividly what solace books had given me growing up. Rereading those two books allowed me to place myself back in my childhood: "Books became an escape from the present, in the classroom at St. Philip Neri or in the living room at home. Books were a way to forget the world, what Richard Wright called 'a drug, a dope.' And they were addictive. The more I read, the more I wanted to read. For me Kit Carson was a pathfinder. He led me toward Don Quixote and David Copperfield, Pip and Tom Sawyer, the Joads and the Lilliputians. He also led me back to the world, to see how close I could bring my changing vision of possibility to the rigid nature of things. The stories I read made me feel as if I were threading a needle, squinting through whatever aperture the world would allow."

And even though *Youngblood Hawke* was not the same reading experience for me as an adult that it had been for me as a child, I was able to remember what the book had said to me as an adolescent: ". . . a voice in the book told me then to watch and wait; it suggested that living and creating are one and the same, that writing is an act of faith, that, perhaps, all real adventure begins in the imagination."

My research also took a traditional path into the history of the period, particularly the 1960s. I read newspapers, magazines, and books recounting the events of the Vietnam War, the Kennedy assassination, Woodstock, and any other moments that seemed to me to be watershed points in my own life. I watched videos about the times and listened to music that I might not have heard for years.

I remembered that on the day after President Kennedy was shot, my mother took me to Madison Square Garden to see the New York Knicks play the Detroit Pistons. In order to bring that night back to me more tangibly, I read the newspaper accounts of the day after the assassination and the accounts of the Knicks' victory.

Facts can be a catalyst for remembering: "I don't recall much about the game except a feeling that the whole event was surreal. Jumping Johnny Green of the Knicks flew magically into the air for rebounds while gravity held the seven thousand of us in our seats, and our young president had just been shot. Newspapers strewn about the stadium announced, 'Kennedy Killed by Sniper.' News of the assassination had been played over and over again so many times during the twenty-four hours that the murder seemed little more than a nightmare created by the media."

The last shape that my research took was in the form of something akin to time travel. I went back to the Bronx half a dozen times over the course of a three-year period, revisiting places that were landmarks of my youth—St. Philip Neri Elementary School, Mt. St. Michael High School, Fordham University, Villa Avenue, Harris Field, the bars, the pizza parlors, the subway stations, the apartment buildings, and any other spot that held an important place in my memory.

Along the way, I spoke with many former teachers, old buddies, a few ex-girlfriends, and some present-day residents of the borough.

In the course of reentering my past, I was checking the details of my memory and igniting new recollections. All sorts of questions were answered. What did the pews in the chapel feel like as I slid my hand across the grain of wood? Was the underpass at Bedford Park Boulevard a tunnel of noise, as I remembered it had been? And what of the apartment buildings, the color of the sky in summer as opposed to winter, the sound of the subway rattling along the Grand Concourse, the way the light broke through the stained glass windows of the church?

Returning to the haunts of my youth gave texture and definition to my memories and created a new dimension to my experience. Such research not only gave me another way of seeing the past but another frame for such memories, as well. The present-day Bronx gave me an access to the past that I might not have had otherwise: "As the heavy doors to St. Philip's creak slowly to a close, I see a young woman standing in the frame. Her face could be my sister's at graduation in 1960. The same blue eyes, looking down as if she is ready to raise them at any moment toward an unexpected guest. The same brown hair, a dark wave crashing to her shoulders. The same smile, the lips tugged together and curving toward laughter. Narrow-shouldered, slim as the slant of door light, ready to leave, she is the image of my sister in the Bronx then. With a few inches of light left, she looks up, her eyes clear and patient, and smiles at me as if she regrets my going, our mutual turning into memory."

For me, the act of writing a memoir became an opportunity to travel backward in time. As Joan Didion said, we write to discover what we think. I read and traveled and gathered notes and in the process discovered what the past meant to me. Disparate lines of research twisted into a thickened cord of recollection. You may not be able to repeat the past, as Garsby wished, but you may be able, through research, to reenter it, relive it in your imagination, and re-create it for the future.

Gathering Information

James B. Stewart

*H*owever intense one's curiosity, the time comes when it needs to be satisfied. Information gathering begins in earnest. I often liken the process to prospecting for oil: many wells are drilled, and then I wait to see if oil trickles— or gushes—out.

When I first began teaching my writing course at Columbia, I spent very little time discussing the reporting and information-gathering process. This was a writing course, I explained, and I assumed my students learned reporting somewhere else. It was, in any case, too vast a subject to cover in just one or two classes. I should have known better. For no story is any better than the facts within it. No writer can cover a paucity of information with a veneer of brilliant prose (though many try.) The writing process itself is often a function of the success of information gathering. Reporting is dictated by knowing what kind of writing will result. Writing and reporting are, in sum, inextricable.

An entire book could easily be written on the subject of reporting. In this chapter I will concentrate on aspects of reporting that are especially important for successful feature writing, especially narrative articles or books. Many of my students assume, erroneously, that it is news stories that rely most heavily on facts and information gathering. In reality, the opposite is true. I have often been able to construct a news story around just a few facts, but even simple feature stories require a multitude. Many also assume that anything written in the first person, in the nature of a memoir, requires no reporting or information gathering that extends beyond the writer's own memories. That, too, is a mistake, in my experience.

Reporting can be an immensely pleasurable process, once anxiety is overcome. Almost every writer I know experiences at least some anxiety at the outset of reporting, rooted in the suspicion that no one will talk. In extreme cases, I have seen people become all but paralyzed. I find it soothing to contemplate the obvious: If you know nothing when you begin, you have nothing to lose, and everything to gain, by trying. If someone rudely hangs up on you, you are no worse off than you were before you made the call. When you do succeed, you are that much further ahead. Invariably, a point comes where you know that you have enough to write a good story. How you will wrestle that information onto the printed page may yet seem murky but you know it can be done—even if every person you contact from now on shuts you down. Then any remaining anxiety lifts, leaving you, blissfully unencumbered, to satisfy your curiosity. How many ocher people actually get paid to so indulge themselves?

The vast majority of my information gathering has taken the form of interviewing witnesses and participants in the events that are the subjects of my stories. Since I have written primarily about contemporary events, traditional research—the kind most people learn in college and graduate school—hasn't figured prominently in my own work. Nor have other published and written sources, though they have been important to some stories and I obtain them whenever I can. Interviewing is at the heart of most nonfiction reporting, and it is usually essential if a story is to be vivid and true-to-life.

Probably the question I hear more than any other is "How do you get people to talk?" In fact, I don't feel that I "get" people to talk. Writers don't have the subpoena power—which, in any event, doesn't ensure you're going to get the truth. Reluctant or recalcitrant sources are rarely of much value, even if they are forced to talk by the legal process. People talk because they want to talk. The best I can do is to create a conducive environment.

I often tell my students that what continues to surprise me in my work is not what people don't tell me. It's what they *do* tell. Perhaps that's because I am by nature somewhat shy and often cannot imagine myself answering the questions I ask other people, usually virtual strangers. I have had the most extraordinary telephone conversations with people I have never met. While working on the David Schwartz story, I spoke to a professor who confided that, though he had been married for over twenty years and had five children, he was gay; that no one else knew; and that he was growing increasingly desperate as he saw life passing him by. People have told me about their most intimate marital problems, their children's drug habits, their crises of religious and political faith. Several sources mused that they had come to think of me as their psychiatrist, a notion I tried to dispel by gently reminding them that my primary professional responsibility is to readers.

I have learned that no matter how hopeless the prospect might seem, it is always a mistake to assume that someone will not talk. Probably the most tedious but common exercise I went through as an editor was to ask reporters if they had called someone to get his or her side of the story. "No," the reporter would say. "Why not?" The answer, invariably, was "I know they won't answer," or "They never return my call." Just as invariably, I had to say, "Make the call and then tell me they didn't return it." Predictably, at least half the time the supposedly reclusive source did make a comment. In their anxiety that sources won't talk, reporters often all but guarantee the failure they fear.

Over the years I have often paused to reflect on why so many people talk to reporters. The main reason, I believe, is that no one else ever listens. Just as we live in an age of know-it-alls, we live in an age of talkers. Radio and TV talk shows are filled with people who talk, shout, and scream, often at the same time. Talking all the time, yet feeling that no one listens, paradoxically increases feelings of isolation. The supposed cure—more talking—only makes things worse. Many people, as a result, are lonely. They are waiting for you to call.

I believe that nothing is so important in my own efforts to get people to reveal information than a willingness to listen without judging. I constantly remind my students that in reporting, our only goal is to learn. It is not to browbeat, to argue, or to proselytize. Yet I have seen reporters lose control and engage in all of those tactics, which are invariably counterproductive. I know firsthand that the degree of self-control required can be immense. I have had sources say outrageous things to me; offer opinions, for example, with which I violently disagree, make factual assertions that border on lunacy, present wild theories concerning conspiracies in which I am alleged to be a participant. Yet I bite my tongue. I remind myself that I should be grateful they're talking. No matter what the source says, it is likely to enhance my story.

On many occasions, I have assumed that someone is unlikely to talk, or might do so only reluctantly, and have prepared a detailed argument about my planned story and its importance to the public interest, or some other high-minded appeal to civic virtue. In fact, most such speeches go unsaid. Surprisingly often, people simply begin talking, evidently having already resolved whatever qualms they may have harbored.

That said, there are any number of things I can say or do to try to improve the odds that someone will talk to me. There are as many styles of reporting as there are reporters. I tell my students that there is no one model for success, and therefore they should be themselves. Steve Brill once took me along on an interview, and his performance was mesmerizing. He pounded the source with hostile questions and left him reduced to a quivering bowl of Jell-O. This was effective for Steve, but I couldn't do it. I prefer a quiet, understated, nonjudgmental if not sympathetic approach. Unlike many reporters I know, I tend to say little about myself. This doesn't mean that I don't engage in the usual pleasantries, or mention biographical facts the source and I may have in common, such as where we grew up or went to college. But beyond that, I tend to be very cautious. This allows my potential sources to project onto me whatever qualities they want, and indeed, they have often done so. I don't believe it is my obligation to affirm or contradict their projections. Sometimes sources ask me questions about myself point-blank, most often about my political views. While working on *Blood Sport* I was asked by almost every source whether I voted for Bill Clinton in 1992. I almost always refused to answer. On more than one occasion, I have gone so far as to curtail such questioning by reminding the source, as politely as possible, that as a journalist, I'm the one who's supposed to ask the questions, and to assure my interlocutor that whatever my own views, they will have as little effect as is humanly possible on my work. My political views, consequently are irrelevant. As far as I can tell, no one has taken offense.

While I avoid personal subjects, I am willing to discuss, at whatever length a potential source wants, qualities of mine that I believe are relevant. Indeed, I invite such questions because they give me the opportunity to stress something that may reassure sources and encourage them to talk: my commitment to fairness and thoroughness. To make this clear can also be effective at defusing potential disappointment once a story appears. In this connection, I have learned over the years that it is always best to be honest about what I believe the story will be like. Almost everyone asks, "What kind of story is this going to be?" and, more directly, "Is this story going to be positive or negative?" I generally answer, truthfully, that I don't know. But when I approached Chris Whittle about my story on his crumbling empire, I was candid about what had triggered my interest. Conversely, when I asked lawyers at Cravath, Swaine & Moore about writing a chapter on the firm's work for IBM in the government's long-running antitrust case, I said I didn't know how the firm would be portrayed but that it would be impossible for me to ignore the fact that IBM had won, and surely that was positive for the firm.

Beginning reporters seem to have trouble being honest about their interest in a story, evidently because they fear they might alienate potential sources. Like most forms of dishonesty, this is invariably a mistake. At the very least, being misled can enrage a source or subject when the story appears. And, although I could be wrong, I believe candor enhances a subject's respect for a writer and therefore makes him or her more likely to cooperate.

This was much on my mind when I met with Hillary Clinton to discuss hers and the president's cooperation in what became *Blood Sport*. After we had discussed the vexing Whitewater affair at some length, I asked Mrs. Clinton whether she had any questions for me. Expecting the usual queries about how I thought the book would turn out, what scope it would have, how I would approach my work, and so on, I was surprised when she didn't immediately respond. She even seemed somewhat baffled by my suggestion. So I told her that while I wasn't a public relations expert, I thought there were some things she should consider. Among them, I said, was this: I would approach this story as I would any other; there was no predicting where my research would lead me, what I would uncover, and whether she would in the end be pleased with what I wrote. I stressed that neither she nor the president would have any control over what I wrote, nor would they be permitted to review the manuscript in advance of publication.

It was not easy for me to say these things. Meeting a first lady for the first time, I wanted to make a positive impression, and on some level, as I've said, I hoped she would like me. Though it might seem paradoxical, I made these points in the context of a discussion I hoped would persuade the Clintons to carry out their promise of unprecedented candor and cooperation. I emphasized the positive elements of these conditions, stressing that if the final work was to have credibility with the public at large, the Clintons could not receive any special treatment. I said that if they had something to hide, this venture was a mistake—but I quickly added that if they did not, then they had nothing to fear from my investigation. As for me, I didn't want to drop all else that I was working on and embark on this project only to have the Clintons later change their mind, and I said so explicitly. I recognized that there were certain risks in my approach, but I wanted to respond in keeping with the spirit of candor with which the Clintons themselves had set this project in motion.

Did I succeed? I suppose only Mrs. Clinton could answer that. At the time I thought I had, for I subsequently received encouragement to proceed, if not from Mrs. Clinton herself, then from her chief of staff, Maggie Williams. But the cooperation I was led to expect never did materialize. Someone working in the White House during that period later told me that despite my protests of independence, the Clintons had believed that I would write something favorable to them; immersed in a political world where everyone is partisan no matter what they say, the president and first lady cynically assumed that my comments were just window dressing. In that they were mistaken.

Just as being candid about the nature of one's work helps, so does stressing— without being embarrassingly immodest—whatever positive attributes you bring to a project. I do not recite a list of journalism prizes I have won, nor do I mention my education and related distinctions and awards. I do stress that I try to be fair and thorough, and I refer people to published work, including some of my investigative pieces. I have been fortunate enough to write for publications such as *The Wall Street Journal*, *The New Yorker*, and *Smart Money*, and stressing their virtues has often persuaded people to talk. (I can't tell you how often someone would agree to speak to me after commenting of *The Wall Street Journal*, "I just love your editorials." This was never the time, in my view, to launch into a lengthy explanation of the separation between the paper's news and editorial staffs.) Indeed, a publication's reputation is often crucial, as some reporters, accustomed to routine access to everyone in positions of power and authority, discover when they quit the institution and go out on their own: their phones suddenly stop ringing. But no one who writes for less famous publications should be discouraged. When I began writing for *American Lawyer*, the magazine hadn't even published its first regular issue and was all but unknown. People talked anyway.

In every writer's career, with persistence and a modicum of success, the time comes when his or her reputation is more important than any other factor. By then, one hopes, the quality of the work speaks for itself. There is no doubt in my mind that the more well-known I have become, the more willingly people seem to talk to me, even though my reputation largely rests on my books and my magazine, and newspaper articles, which have been investigative and have described some prominent cases of wrongdoing. People seem to be, at the very least, curious to meet me.

I hope others attest to my fairness, objectivity, willingness to listen and consider various points of view, even though I am not so naïve to believe that my work has left no disgruntled participants in its wake. Not infrequently, prospective sources talk to other subjects of my work, which is a point worth remembering by journalists who take a "scorched earth" approach, assuming that once a story is done, they'll never need to talk to a source again. In this connection, I sometimes think of the commencement speech given at the University of Arkansas by Vince Foster, Clinton's deputy White House counsel, shortly before Foster committed suicide in 1993: "There is no victory, no advantage, no fee, no favor, which is worth even a blemish on your reputation for intellect and integrity."

I emphasize not only my character and reputation, but also the practical benefits of cooperating with a reporter. The best position is one of strength: "I already know so much that I'm going to write this story whether you cooperate or not." This argument demolishes what is often the strongest deterrent to a prospective source's opening up: the belief that if he or she simply remains silent, you and the contemplated story will go away. It is important to try to deflect this thinking in any event, but you'll be far more persuasive if you can demonstrate some knowledge of crucial elements of the story. Then you can argue that a source can only enhance how he or she is treated by granting an interview, avoiding errors, rebutting the impressions of others, and putting the information you have in the most favorable light. Nine times out of ten, I find this approach works. In many cases, I need reveal only a few key details, and then the source assumes, sometimes in error, that I know virtually everything. Sometimes, I admit, what I purport to know is actually something I have inferred.

As I hope I've already made clear, I don't find threats very effective, because a good source cooperates not under duress, but voluntarily. Still, one admonition that, *if true*, is sometimes effective is the pledge that you will write the story whether the source cooperates or not. I stress "if true," because someone who threatens this repeatedly and never follows through will soon lose credibility. I can recall just one instance when I made such a claim and then didn't write the promised story, but that was because another story intervened, not because I gave up due to a source's lack of cooperation. Almost anyone can be profiled, almost any story can be written, without the subject's cooperation. Indeed, the story may be better off, for an uncooperative subject forces the writer to report much more thoroughly. And as word reaches the subject that others are talking, cooperation often ensues.

I sometimes further enhance the argument that someone should cooperate by mentioning that I myself have been the subject of quite a few articles, and that with only one exception, I have always followed my own advice and cooperated. I note that even though the resulting articles have not always been what I'd hoped for, I considered the time well spent. Although it may seem self-serving, since I'm a reporter trying to persuade people to talk, this claim has the virtue of being true. I recall spending hours with a reporter from *Institutional Investor* who was writing a cover story on me after the publication of *Den of Thieves*. I began to suspect this would not necessarily be a flattering article when the photographer went to great lengths to get me to pose behind the bars of a stair railing and used a filter on the lens that was so dark it looked as if I hadn't shaved in days. The reporter was nothing if not persistent; I remember at least five in-person interviews. She later told me that the editor had insisted that the theme of the article be that I had succumbed to the same deadly sins as the characters in my book—namely greed, gluttony, and conspicuous consumption. The absence of a new home or a new car, and my failure to take exotic vacations or spend lavishly in any way, came as a great disappointment to her, I could tell. That didn't eliminate the negative article's slant, but I can only imagine what it would have said if I hadn't invested the countless hours with the reporter.

The only time I refused an interview was with the author of a book on *The Wall Street Journal*. The book's catalogue description had already appeared by the time the author called me, and it said that the *Journal* had actually been scooped by others on the insider-trading scandal; that I had stolen my material on Michael Milken from writer Connie Bruck (who happens to be a close friend of mine and whose help I acknowledged in my book); and that *Den of Thieves* was, in any event, biased and inaccurate. I asked the writer, whom I had never met, whether he would grant an interview if our roles were reversed. He acknowledged that he would not. Looking back now, I feel I was mistaken. I should have suppressed my indignation and spoken to him. For the book itself contained some inaccurate comments about me that had nothing to do with Milken or insider trading, and perhaps I might have warded those off.

So when I tell sources that it's in their interest to talk to me, I believe this to be true. I know it's not what many PR agents advise their clients. The conventional wisdom, for example, is that someone should not talk about matters under investigation or subject to litigation, although the O. J. Simpson case seems to have stood that notion on its head. I now sometimes cite that case to emphasize the point that talking to the press has become an inextricable part of any successful lawsuit, for better or worse. And I'm not sure the conventional wisdom ever made much sense, as many lawyers recognized long before the Simpson case.

The one exception to my own belief that it's always in a source's interest to speak to the press is the very rare case where without that cooperation, the story would be impossible. I once sought to write about a deposed head of a Hollywood studio. My goal was to write a very detailed and personal account of the experience of suddenly being deprived of power in Hollywood. After initially being interested, and despite my efforts at persuasion, the subject of the story declined to cooperate. It's true I could have gone ahead and done a story *about* him, and maybe he would have changed his mind as he realized others were talking. But the heart of the story had to be his experiences, feelings, and reactions, as only he could describe them. So I saw no point in going ahead without him. On the other hand, the Sheinberg family managed to silence almost everyone involved in the Jonathan Sheinberg insider-trading case. This—in itself, an interesting measure of Sidney Sheinberg's power in Hollywood—did not stop me from reporting and writing a very detailed story. While I was ultimately indifferent to whether the Sheinbergs cooperated, I continue to believe their silence was a mistake.

If I sense that a potential source is hesitating, I may make two further points. I will often say something to the effect that "I want to assure you that whether you do or don't talk with me I will not let that decision affect how you are portrayed in the story, to the best of my ability." I sometimes add that I respect people's right to remain silent as much as I do their right to talk. These assertions also have the virtue of being true. I myself have been offended by reporters who demand that I answer their questions, as if, being a reporter myself, I have an obligation to talk about everything they may chose to ask, no matter how irrelevant, personal, or private. I try to state, politely but firmly, that I won't answer those questions, which is an approach I respect when the roles are reversed and I'm the reporter. What annoys me is when sources hide behind some irrelevant claim of grand jury secrecy, or claim not to know or remember something, when it's patently obvious that's not true. They simply don't want to answer, which is their right. Still, even as I'm trying to defuse a source's anxiety and be reassuring, I recognize that in saying that someone's refusal to cooperate won't affect his or her portrayal, I am planting the idea that it might. However, most sources seem pleasantly surprised that I'm not out to retaliate, and the statement buttresses my argument that I try to be fair.

Another point I sometimes make is that the earlier someone cooperates, the more influence he or she ultimately has over the scope of the story. I've realized, over the years, that inevitably the course of reporting and the final story are disproportionately influenced by the people who are interviewed first. This isn't because I'm trying to favor these people, or because I'm grateful for their early cooperation (though I may well be); it's inherent in the process. By the time a reporter approaches a subject with a final round of questions, the story is probably all but written; in many cases, it is written, awaiting only specific responses. By then it is too late for that set of answers to make much difference to the structure of the story. I made this point to Mrs. Clinton and her staff on several occasions, and it obviously had no effect. But I'm confident that sophisticated PR advisers and sources know it to be true. Chris Whittle responded to my interest in writing about him by all but overwhelming me with cooperation, using the opportunity to try to shift my interest away from his earlier business ventures to his newer Edison project of for-profit schools. It was a shrewd approach, though I'm not sure it had much effect on the final story. In *Den of Thieves*, Martin Siegel was by far the most cooperative of the major characters. As a result, he emerged as the book's central figure, not because I favored him but because he gave me by far the most material to work with. I didn't minimize his criminal culpability, but his early and uninhibited cooperation made it possible to put those actions in a much broader, and ultimately more sympathetic, context.

This is a point that I find many reviewers of nonfiction fail to understand. They seem peeved if they detect that someone who cooperated ended up being treated more sympathetically than someone who did not. To some extent, that result is inevitable, as I've already explained. But it has nothing to do with rewarding or punishing anyone. And for examples to the contrary, I would refer them to the Whittle story, in which Whittle did cooperate, or to the Sheinberg story, where no one cooperated, yet Sid Sheinberg emerged in a sympathetic light, at least from my perspective.

I will briefly mention one common tactic: flattery. I have often heard reporters lavishing praise on a potential source to a degree that makes me cringe. All I can say is that insincerity is usually quite transparent and rarely effective. If I like someone, and I often do, I assume that becomes apparent one way or another. If I don't, I figure there's little point in pretending otherwise.

Finally, I cannot stress enough the virtue of persistence. Our natural tendency is not to be rude and, once rebuffed, to stop trying. But I myself have often found myself talking to reporters I had hoped to avoid, simply to get them to stop calling. Persistence is effective. It took me months of trying to finally make contact with Susan McDougal, who was the Clintons' partner in Whitewater and is a central character in *Blood Sport*. Susan had fallen on difficult times; she was moving from place to place, and she was difficult to track down, let alone persuade to talk, given that she was under investigation and was soon to be indicted. But finally we spoke on the phone (she returned one of my calls) and she agreed to an interview. She was living in California at the time, and said that if I flew out there, she'd meet with me. Hoping for a specific appointment, I asked where and when; she said—in a maddening way that I often encountered in Arkansas— "Oh, just give me a call when you get here." I told her the day I expected to arrive and the approximate time of my call. Imagine my frustration when I flew to California, checked into a hotel, and called the number she'd given me, only to get the answering machine of someone she was then living with. I called constantly for two days, trying to control my mounting panic, when the friend finally called me to say that Susan had gone back to Arkansas and didn't know when she'd return. I flew back to New York dejected and empty-handed.

I was angry and disappointed at being stood up, and I'm not sure why I persisted. But I kept calling, and finally one day Susan returned another call. She admitted she'd gotten cold feet, but said she was now prepared to meet me. I asked for an appointment, but she demurred, again insisting that I simply call upon my arrival. I flew to California as soon as I could. This time she was at home and she answered the phone. And the next morning she did show up at my hotel—wearing, I will always remember, a purple cocktail dress.

Early discussions with potential sources inevitably cover the terms on which the interview will be conducted. Even relatively unsophisticated sources are now familiar with the notion of "off the record" and will usually bring it up. If they don't, I consider it my obligation to discuss such terms and explain what I mean by them.

One reason this subject almost always arises is that sources are understandably apprehensive about what the consequences to them might be if they talk. We should always remember that candor is not necessarily viewed as a virtue in America—especially if it clashes with loyalty. Indeed, I am often struck by what seems to be a quality inherent in human nature: people frequently want to tell the truth even when it is not in their narrow self-interest to do so. It may well take considerable courage for someone to talk.

The three basic terms I use are "on the record," "not for attribution," and "off the record." Some reporters insist on putting all interviews on the record, which in my view is often a mistake. I only want a source to be on the record if he or she is comfortable enough with the idea that I am likely to get the whole story. Especially early in the information-gathering process, the important thing is to learn what happened; who can be quoted and identified as a source is a subsidiary question. So, in the early stages of a story, I will sometimes ask a source willing to speak on the record if he or she might not be more comfortable speaking "not for attribution."

Most sources assume that "off the record" accords them the highest degree of protection, but I have not always found this to be the case. By "off the record," I mean that what a source tells me cannot be used in my story or book, whether or not it is attributed to anyone. But it *can* be used—and this is crucial—in gathering information. So sometimes I will call another source, ask a question, and realize that the person is obviously omitting some crucial details. Then I might say, "But someone else already told me that. . ." and proceed to provide a detailed account. While I have honored my off-the-record commitment, it is often quite obvious who the source was, usually because the universe of possibilities is quite small.

And in the overwhelming majority of instances, only a very small number of people care who a source is—and they are usually contacted in the research phase of my work. I usually try to explain these risks if a source insists on speaking off the record.

I find that "not for attribution" provides most of the protection that sources want while giving me the flexibility I need to use material. By "not for attribution" I mean that I can use the information, but not by attributing it through direct quotation and not in a way that allows others to deduce the source's identity. "Not for attribution" actually provides a higher degree of protection in some ways than "off the record" does, because in using "not for attribution" information in the reporting process, I consider it part of my obligation to protect the identity of my source. So if there is only one possible source for information that contradicts what another source is telling me, I don't mention it. In the narrative writing that I prefer, direct quotations are rarely necessary anyway, and the facts imparted can be used. On the other hand, I always make it clear to sources that narrative quotations and the thoughts of the source can be stated as fact in my writing. In other words, if a source says he felt sick at a certain time and place, the story might say So-and-so "felt sick," but without attributing that information. Even though the identity of a source of unattributed information often seems obvious in the completed piece, I have never had someone decline an interview because I reserved the right to use the information they imparted, including their statements and thoughts.

I should mention the "confidential source," who seems to be surfacing with increasing frequency. So far, the only sources who have demanded such protection from me are lawyers, which suggests that this development is emanating from the legal profession. A "confidential source" is one who may not be identified in any way, either in a story or in the reporting process, and, most important, may not be identified in litigation, even if under a direct court order to do so. In other words, this is the kind of source a reporter is expected to go to jail to protect. I am not entirely sure what the point of this level of protection is, since I would refuse to disclose the names of unidentified sources whether or not they were accorded "confidential" status. On the other hand, I know that many news organizations are in fact disclosing sources to protect themselves from libel suits, so perhaps this is a legitimate concern.

I have found that many of my students are reluctant to conduct interviews on any but an on-the-record basis. While this is understandable, and in some ways admirable, given the media's frequent abuse of unattributed quotes, it isn't necessarily conducive to the level and depth of reporting needed for feature writing. I remind my students that the reporter's goal is to obtain information, not to enforce a moral code. Often sources of mine will speak only after being given some assurance of protection. In many cases, a degree of trust develops, after which they agree to abandon such constraints. Or they agree to let me quote specific statements I later find I want to use.

Whatever the arrangement, it needs to be taken seriously. I don't know that it needs to be treated as a contract, enforceable in court, as at least one judge has ruled. But the potential for disputes between reporter and source is vastly reduced if such agreements are honored.

Once someone has agreed to an interview, the first meeting is crucial. I say "meeting" because, in my experience, the level of detail required for a successful narrative requires a relationship that, with rare exceptions, can only be established in person. Witnessing firsthand a source's demeanor is also essential to assessing credibility (which is one reason I believe even presidents should be made to testify in court, in person, rather than on videotape). I will go anywhere at any time for an initial interview, a willingness that I think underscores the importance I place on our interview and my willingness to accommodate a source.

Perhaps the most peculiar such occasion came when someone who was a potentially valuable source for *Den of Thieves* agreed to meet me at the University Club in Manhattan. It was an eminently respectable venue that gave rise to no apprehension on my part. But when I arrived, he told me that he had booked side-by-side massages for us, and that I would be allowed to ask questions while the massage was in progress. Odd? Perhaps, but it seemed harmless enough. I had already agreed that this would be a "background" interview but this unorthodox configuration—we were both on our stomachs, clad only in towels—certainly guaranteed that I would not be taking notes.

I have gone to Paris, the Costa del Sol, and Australia just to interview people in person; I once waited for Adnan Khashoggi while he had his hair and nails done in his penthouse suite at a Honolulu luxury hotel (he had his hair cut every day, I was told). If you think this kind of travel is glamorous, I should mention that I have also gone to Mamou, Louisiana, where the hotel—the *only* hotel—turned out to be a brothel, and I have driven over what seems like every paved road in the state of Arkansas. I believe I would draw the line at anything that seemed to put me in physical danger. But a friend of mine, a woman, once agreed to meet a potential source alone at midnight in Central Park. As I recall, the source used the occasion to make an amorous advance; with benefit of hindsight, my friend agreed she'd been foolhardy to agree to the meeting.

I rarely come to a first interview armed with an elaborate script, the way lawyers often do when they take a deposition in a lawsuit. It's an ominous sign when a source begins, "What are your questions?" Such interviews require you to know almost everything already, which certainly gets in the way of learning something new. I usually respond by saying that I'm there to listen and learn, and that I will probably only occasionally interrupt to ask questions. My goal is to get sources to narrate—to simply tell their stories in their own ways, in their words. It's often fascinating, for example, to see where a source begins a story— often much further in the past than I might have guessed. Most people soon relax and come to enjoy this approach, which is so much less adversarial than most seem to expect. And let's face it: most people find themselves interesting, and are pleased when you do, too.

Some people are born storytellers, and others, I'm sorry to say, are the opposite. It's often impossible to predict which category a source will fall into. Martin Siegel and Robert Wilkis, two characters in *Den of Thieves*, are probably two of the best narrators I have ever encountered. They can think chronologically, they have fantastic memories, they have a visual sense, and they intuitively discard irrelevancies. These skills and sensibilities rarely coalesce in one person, but when they do, it is relatively easy to bring such characters to life on the page. By contrast, one of the worst narrators I have ever met was Fred Joseph, the former chief executive of Drexel Burnham Lambert and another character in *Den of Thieves*. Let me hasten to say that I like Fred very much and don't hold this against him; he wasn't deliberately concealing information or, worse, trying to deceive me. Simply, his mind is analytical, and he seemed unable to put events into a chronology. Rather, he would move from concept to concept without any regard for time sequence or cause and effect. There was a logic to his narration, but it was of scant use to me. When I reread portions of *Den of Thieves*, I still lament how flat some of the narrative is because I couldn't get more from Fred.

One of the most taxing interviews I ever experienced—I should say, several of the most taxing—involved Ron Woods, the electrician at Chrysler who protested the company's policies toward gays. I flew to Detroit for our initial interview and met him at his well-kept home in a nearby suburb. We spent five or six hours together—and only got as far as Ron's performance evaluations during his first year at Chrysler, of which there were many, each and every one of which he had saved and each of which he insisted I review with him. I heard in excruciating detail about his early years, his parents and family, his elementary school education . . . virtually none of which, I knew, would make it into any story. Woods, too, would often stray from the chronology, one incident reminding him of another, sometimes separated from the first by years. He often apologized, and told me everyone told him he talked too much. I can only guess at how many hours I spent with Ron before his debriefing was complete—hundreds. I can honestly say I have never had an interviewing experience that even remotely compares to this. I could easily have filled a book on his life.

How do I handle such situations? As gently as possible, I interrupt and try to bring the speaker back to a specific date or event, in some cases all but forcing him or her to focus on chronology. In Woods's case, I had to be as blunt as I've ever been, sometimes telling him point-blank that a story he'd embarked on was irrelevant or boring or both. But a great deal of patience is often required. The expenditure of time may be inefficient, but I usually consider it a small price to pay for someone's heartfelt cooperation.

It may seem that allowing someone to talk with little interruption, especially if the narrator is a good one, leaves the interviewer without much to do, but the opposite is true. Listening is hard work, and I find I don't have the stamina for much more than three or four hours at a time. Particularly in early interviews, I'm looking for clues that go well beyond the surface of what someone has to say. What emphasis does someone place on certain events? What details are remembered? What does this signify? I am often asked by some readers and my students why I chose certain events to illustrate in great detail, while all but ignoring others. In most cases, I chose events because a source, while narrating, emphasized them by dwelling on them, without any prompting from me. Similarly with remembered conversations: sources usually narrate them; I don't have to interrupt and ask, "And what did you say then?"

Another important goal I have in early interviews is to identify other potential sources, including people or documents that might corroborate what someone is telling me. So perhaps my most frequent reason for interrupting is to ask for other people's names and find out where they might be reached, even get their phone numbers if these are readily at a source's disposal.

Especially for important sources, I find it is helpful to conduct a series of interviews, which gives them time to react and absorb the experience of the first interview. This is an advantage of working on a longer-term project, whether a book or an article. Many times in my experience, sources come to second and third interviews more relaxed and talkative. I suspect that, having approached the initial interview with some apprehension, they found the experience less onerous than they expected; furthermore, no adverse consequences ensued. Since I hadn't yet written anything, the consequences of talking weren't yet apparent. Indeed, on occasion I have come to the end of a lengthy series of interviews, only to hear the source express surprise that what he or she said was going to appear in print.

These follow-up interviews can often be conducted on the phone, or, I suppose, by e-mail, though I haven't yet tried that. I find that once a level of familiarity is established in the initial interview, most sources are quite comfortable on the phone, sometimes more so than in person. Only for the most important sources, usually major characters in a book or story, do I try to conduct all, or at least most, of the interviews in person. There is no substitute for personal contact, and for the ability to see and sense a source's reactions.

As interviews progress, they tend to become less narrative in style, and my questions may become somewhat more pointed. I never consider the interviewing completed until a story or book is published. Invariably, the process of writing triggers additional questions, and I often find myself typing a source's answers right into a manuscript. This is particularly true of the kinds of details that bring a scene to life, for it is often only in the writing that the need for such a level of description becomes clear. (Obviously, if the weather, say, was reported for every day that figured in a story, the reporting might never end.)

It is a common practice to save the most sensitive questions until the end, in case they will cause the source to stop cooperating. In my experience this is a legitimate concern, and I have on occasion saved the "hard" questions until a story is nearly complete. But sometimes that isn't an option. It's essential, in my view, that a source be given the time and opportunity to respond to such questions, outside of a last-minute "ambush" situation. That's not only because it seems the fair and decent thing to do, but because incorporating a source's responses to such questions invariably improves a story. And in most instances, if the hard questions are handled forthrightly, the source doesn't stop cooperating, even when it's clear the story is going to raise some troubling issues and may be far from flattering. This was the case with the Chris Whittle story I described earlier, and I remember my interviews with him toward the end of my reporting as some of the toughest I've ever conducted. Yet we remained in contact until the end. Even though the story was a highly unflattering account of his business practices—it detailed questionable accounting practices and a failure to pay state taxes—and no doubt caused serious disruptions in his career, we remained on cordial terms, at least as I saw it. Whatever else I had to say about Whittle, my description of him as a gentleman proved to be correct.

The last phase of reporting usually comes in the context of fact-checking, which is usually done after a story is written. I cannot stress how valuable this process can be, whether it is performed by a professional fact-checker, as is often the case at magazines, or whether you do it yourself. Knowledge that particular information is actually going to appear in print almost invariably triggers an outpouring of additional information. Many writers I know are reluctant to fact-check, for fear that knowledge of impending publication will alienate sources or give them reason to retract what they said. Surprisingly, though the concern is understandable, I've never known it to be borne out. For both *Blood Sport* and *Den of Thieves*, I hired fact-checkers to work with me. Fact-checkers have contributed greatly to the quality of my work for *The New Yorker*. At *The Wall Street Journal*, as at most newspapers, there were no fact-checkers, so I did my own checking. The benefit was twofold: not only was additional information uncovered, but my work became more accurate. Nothing makes a story more vulnerable to attack than a factual error, even if minor. Something that is demonstrably wrong can undermine the credibility of an entire story or book. I have sometimes been amazed at how errors crept into my work, despite my diligence and care. Fact-checking helps minimize this possibility, though it can never eradicate it entirely.

While I have emphasized in-person interviewing, I don't mean to ignore documentary sources. Computer search mechanisms, especially Nexis, have been a godsend to researchers, and I have used them extensively. While many reporters and writers disdain any reliance on anyone else's work, I have no qualms about doing so, and am flattered and pleased when others use mine, as long as it is acknowledged. I have often incorporated the publication of other stories into my own narratives, especially *Blood Sport*, in which other members of the press, especially Jeff Gerth of *The New York Times*, figure prominently as characters. Obviously, I wasn't going to pretend to have discovered Whitewater, a story broken by Gerth.

Originality is an important virtue, and any story worth writing should include an abundance of new information. But while other journalists and editors often obsess about who was first to report a particular fact and what is "new" in an article or book, I find that readers rarely do. Indeed, they tend to extend credit to the writer even when something is attributed to someone else. An enthusiastic reader of *Blood Sport* came up to me after one of my bookstore appearances to praise a section of the book about Lisa Foster, Vince Foster's wife. As graciously as I tried to accept the compliment, I pointed out that I had attributed that passage to an article by Peter Boyer in *The New Yorker*. Sometimes I've gotten misplaced credit for my own work. Someone complimented me on a revelation in *Den of Thieves* that had actually appeared years before in one of my articles for *The Wall Street Journal*.

Besides published material, original documents are often a treasure trove. Letters, diaries, financial records, engagement calendars—any written, contemporaneous evidence—is invaluable and, I might add, usually far more dramatic and persuasive than verbal summaries. Whenever a source refers to a written record of some sort, I try to get the original document. Sources who are cooperative will usually try to oblige. For *Blood Sport*, after strenuous efforts, I was able to get from First Ozark National Bank in Flippin, Arkansas, the original Whitewater lender, the file containing correspondence between Hillary Clinton and the bank's officers. Far more persuasively than anything Jim or Susan McDougal might have said, it established that Mrs. Clinton was effectively handling White-water's affairs and thus undercut her public statement that she and the president were just passive investors. I found those letters so significant that I included photocopies of them as an appendix to the book. Such documents often go a long way toward corroborating sources' accounts, and thereby establishing their honesty and reliability, or conversely, undercutting them. Many writers shy away from "document" stories, evidently finding documents tedious to pore over. I find this is a mistake, for they sometimes reveal rich dramatic material.

In the case of the Sheinberg story I mentioned earlier, almost the entire narrative was constructed from the paper trail—transcripts and documents from the SEC investigation into insider trading in the MCA deal. The fact is that almost no one was willing to speak with me on any basis after the Sheinberg family apparently put out the word that they wanted no one to talk. I could never have written the story on the basis of my interviews. But I made a successful Freedom of Information Act request for transcripts of all the depositions taken in the case before it was settled. They were a trove of revealing, dramatic material. The testimony had the added virtue of having been given under oath.

The Sheinberg story is a good illustration of why I love lawsuits—at least, lawsuits in which I'm not a defendant. Lawsuits spawn an avalanche of material, much of it tedious and irrelevant, but much of it immensely valuable to a reporter. It was enormously helpful to me that many of the events described in *Den of Thieves* were the subject of both civil and criminal litigation. I would go so far as to say that any lawsuit is worth considering as a story simply because it yields so much information. I should point out that I am hardly the only person to have recognized this; lawyers themselves have become increasingly aware of the publicity their efforts can yield, and so have been moving to place court materials under seal, which prevents their disclosure to the public. Judges seem to be all too willing to grant such requests, both because no one is ever in court to speak on behalf of the public interest (most litigants are happy to keep materials in confidence, so they don't object) and because judges, like society at large, seem to be developing a growing disdain for the press and the public's right to know. (Judge Susan Webber Wright's opinions in the Paula Jones lawsuit against President Clinton displayed a barely concealed hostility toward the press, and she made numerous rulings placing materials under seal.)

As I mentioned earlier, I don't consider my reporting to be finished until a story or book is published. (Even then, I have occasionally had people call with even more information—which, in a few cases, led to sequels.) But a point invariably comes when I know it is time to start writing my story. How do I know? Generally it's because the curiosity that drove the story in the first place has been satisfied, or, in other words, the mystery has been solved. This doesn't mean that every loose end has been pinned down, just that, overall, I have a sense that I know what happened and why, at least as far as such things can be determined. At this point, I go over a mental checklist: Have I interviewed or tried to interview all possible sources, particularly those likely to appear as major characters?

Even if I don't have everything that is to be known, do I have a critical mass of information that I find interesting? If, for some reason, I can't answer the questions that triggered the story, do I have a good reason why not, and can I still alert readers to some interesting new information? Sometimes I have begun to write too early in the reporting, which is a harrowing experience—the major cause, I believe, of so-called writer's block. The solution for me is simply to stop, clear my head, throw away whatever I've written, and go back to reporting.

At some point well into my research I develop something like impatience to get to the keyboard. Standing in the shower, going for a run in Central Park, I find myself fantasizing about possible leads. My friends find me preoccupied and absent-minded. That's generally a sure sign that it's time to write.

The Way to Rainy Mountain

N. Scott Momaday

A single knoll rises out of the plain in Oklahoma, north and west of the Wichita Range. For my people, the Kiowas, it is an old landmark, and they gave it the name Rainy Mountain. The hardest weather in the world is there. Winter brings blizzards, hot tornadic winds arise in the spring, and in summer the prairie is an anvil's edge. The grass turns brittle and brown, and it cracks beneath your feet. There are green belts along the rivers and creeks, linear groves of hickory and pecan, willow and witch hazel. At a distance in July or August the steaming foliage seems almost to writhe in fire. Great green and yellow grasshoppers are everywhere in the tall grass, popping up like corn to sting the flesh, and tortoises crawl about on the red earth, going nowhere in the plenty of time. Loneliness is an aspect of the land. All things in the plain are isolated; there is no confusion of objects in the eye, but *one* hill or *one* tree or *one* man. To look upon that landscape in the early morning, with the sun at your back, is to lose the sense of proportion. Your imagination comes to life, and this, you think, is where Creation was begun.

I returned to Rainy Mountain in July. My grandmother had died in the spring, and I wanted to be at her grave. She had lived to be very old and at last infirm. Her only living daughter was with her when she died, and I was told that in death her face was that of a child.

I like to think of her as a child. When she was born, the Kiowas were living the last great moment of their history. For more than a hundred years they had controlled the open range from the Smoky Hill River to the Red, from the headwaters of the Canadian to the fork of the Arkansas and Cimarron. In alliance with the Comanches, they had ruled the whole of the southern Plains. War was their sacred business, and they were among the finest horsemen the world has ever known. But warfare for the Kiowas was preeminently a matter of disposition rather than of survival, and they never understood the grim, unrelenting advance of the U.S. Cavalry. When at last, divided and ill-provisioned, they were driven onto the Staked Plains in the cold rains of autumn, they fell into panic. In Palo Duro Canyon they abandoned their crucial stores to pillage and had nothing then but their lives. In order to save themselves, they surrendered to the soldiers at Fort Sill and were imprisoned in the old stone corral that now stands as a military museum. My grandmother was spared the humiliation of those high gray walls by eight or ten years, but she must have known from birth the affliction of defeat, the dark brooding of old warriors.

Her name was Aho, and she belonged to the last culture to evolve in North America. Her forebears came down from the high country in western Montana nearly three centuries ago. They were a mountain people, a mysterious tribe of hunters whose language has never been positively classified in any major group. In the late seventeenth century they began a long migration to the south and east. It was a journey toward the dawn, and it led to a golden age. Along the way the Kiowas were befriended by the Crows, who gave them the culture and religion of the Plains. They acquired horses, and their ancient nomadic spirit was suddenly free of the ground. They acquired Tai-me, the sacred Sun Dance doll, from that moment the object and symbol of their worship, and so shared in the divinity of the sun. Not least, they acquired the sense of destiny, therefore courage and pride. When they entered upon the southern Plains they had been transformed. No longer were they slaves to the simple necessity of survival; they were a lordly and dangerous society of fighters and thieves, hunters and priests of the sun. According to their origin myth, they entered the world through a hollow log. From one point of view, their migration was the fruit of an old prophecy, for indeed they emerged from a sunless world.

Although my grandmother lived out her long life in the shadow of Rainy Mountain, the immense landscape of the continental interior lay like memory in her blood. She could tell of the Crows, whom she had never seen, and of the Black Hills, where she had never been. I wanted to see in reality what she had seen more perfectly in the mind's eye, and traveled fifteen hundred miles to begin my pilgrimage.

Yellowstone, it seemed to me, was the top of the world, a region of deep lakes and dark timber, canyons and waterfalls. But, beautiful as it is, one might have the sense of confinement there. The skyline in all directions is close at hand, the high wall of the woods and deep cleavages of shade. There is a perfect freedom in the mountains, but it belongs to the eagle and the elk, the badger and the bear. The Kiowas reckoned their stature by the distance they could see, and they were bent and blind in the wilderness.

Descending eastward, the highland meadows are a stairway to the plain. In July the inland slope of the Rockies is luxuriant with flax and buckwheat, stonecrop and larkspur. The earth unfolds and the limit of the land recedes. Clusters of trees, and animals grazing far in the distance, cause the vision to reach away and wonder to build upon the mind. The sun follows a longer course in the day, and the sky is immense beyond all comparison. The great billowing clouds that sail upon it are shadows that move upon the grain like water, dividing light. Farther down, in the land of the Crows and Blackfeet, the plain is yellow. Sweet clover takes hold of the hills and bends upon itself to cover and seal the soil. There the Kiowas paused on their way; they had come to the place where they must change their lives. The sun is at home on the plains. Precisely there does it have the certain character of a god. When the Kiowas came to the land of the crows, they could see the dark lees of the hills at dawn across the Bighorn River, the profusion of light on the grain shelves, the oldest deity ranging after the solstices. Not yet would they veer southward to the caldron of the land that lay below; they must wean their blood from the northern winter and hold the mountains a while longer in their view. They bore Tai-me in procession to the east.

A dark mist lay over the Black Hills, and the land was like iron. At the top of a ridge I caught sight of Devil's Tower upthrust against the gray sky as if in the birth of time the core of the earth had broken through its crust and the motion of the world was begun. There are things in nature that engender an awful quiet in the heart of man; Devil's Tower is one of them. Two centuries ago, because they could not do otherwise, the Kiowas made a legend at the base of the rock. My grandmother said:

> *Eight children were there at play, seven sisters and their brother. Suddenly the boy was struck dumb; he trembled and began to run upon his hands and feet. His fingers became claws, and his body was covered with fur. Directly there was a bear where the boy had been. The sisters were terrified; they ran, and the bear after them. They came to the stump of a great tree, and the tree spoke to them. It bade them climb upon it, and as they did so it began to rise into the air. The bear came to kill them, but they were just beyond its reach. It reared against the tree and scored the bark all around with its claws. The seven sisters were borne into the sky, and they became the stars of the Big Dipper.*

From that moment, and so long as the legend lives, the Kiowas have kinsmen in the night sky. Whatever they were in the mountains, they could be no more. However tenuous their well-being, however much they had suffered and would suffer again, they had found a way out of the wilderness.

My grandmother had a reverence for the sun, a holy regard that now is all but gone out of mankind. There was a wariness in her, and an ancient awe. She was a Christian in her later years, but she had come a long way about, and she never forgot her birthright. As a child she had been to the Sun Dances; she had taken part in those annual rites, and by them she had learned the restoration of her people in the presence of Tai-me. She was about seven when the last Kiowa Sun Dance was held in 1887 on the Washita River above Rainy Mountain Creek. The buffalo were gone. In order to consummate the ancient sacrifice—to impale the head of a buffalo bull upon the medicine tree—a delegation of old men journeyed into Texas, there to beg and barter for an animal from the Goodnight herd.

She was ten when the Kiowas came together for the last time as a living Sun Dance culture. They could find no buffalo; they had to hang an old hide from the sacred tree. Before the dance could begin, a company of soldiers rode out from Fort Sill under orders to disperse the tribe. Forbidden without cause the essential act of their faith, having seen the wild herds slaughtered and left to rot upon the ground, the Kiowas backed away forever from the medicine tree. That was July 20, 1890, at the great bend of the Washita. My grandmother was there. Without bitterness, and for as long as she lived, she bore a vision of deicide.

Now that I can have her only in memory, I see my grandmother in the several postures that were peculiar to her: standing at the wood stove on a winter morning and turning meat in a great iron skillet; sitting at the south window, bent above her beadwork, and afterwards, when her vision failed, looking down for a long time into the fold of her hands; going out upon a cane, very slowly as she did when the weight of age came upon her; praying. I remember her most often at prayer. She made long, rambling prayers out of suffering and hope, having seen many things. I was never sure that I had the right to hear, so exclusive were they of all mere custom and company. The last time I saw her she prayed standing by the side of her bed at night, naked to the waist, the light of a kerosene lamp moving upon her dark skin. Her long, black hair, always drawn and braided in the day, lay upon her shoulders and against her breasts like a shawl. I do not speak Kiowa, and I never understood her prayers, but there was something inherently sad in the sound, some merest hesitation upon the syllables of sorrow. She began in a high and descending pitch, exhausting her breath to silence; then again and again—and always the same intensity of effort, of something that is, and is not, like urgency in the human voice. Transported so in the dancing light among the shadows of her room, she seemed beyond the reach of time. But that was illusion; I think I knew then that I should not see her again.

Houses are like sentinels in the plain, old keepers of the weather watch. There, in a very little while, wood takes on the appearance of great age. All colors wear soon away in the wind and rain, and then the wood is burned gray and the grain appears and the nails turn red with rust. The windowpanes are black and opaque; you imagine there is nothing within, and indeed there are many ghosts, bones given up to the land. They stand here and there against the sky, and you approach them for a longer time than you expect. They belong in the distance; it is their domain.

Once there was a lot of sound in my grandmother's house, a lot of coming and going, feasting and talk. The summers there were full of excitement and reunion. The Kiowas are a summer people; they abide the cold and keep to themselves, but when the season turns and the land becomes warm and vital they cannot hold still; an old love of going returns upon them. The aged visitors who came to my grandmother's house when I was a child were made of lean and leather, and they bore themselves upright. They wore great black hats and bright ample shirts that shook in the wind. They rubbed fat upon their hair and wound their braids with strips of colored cloth. Some of them painted their faces and carried the scars of old and cherished enmities. They were an old council of warlords, come to remind and be reminded of who they were. Their wives and daughters served them well. The women might indulge themselves; gossip was at once the mark and compensation of their servitude. They made loud and elaborate talk among themselves, full of jest and gesture, fright and false alarm. They went abroad in fringed and flowered shawls, bright beadwork and German silver. They were at home in the kitchen, and they prepared meals that were banquets.

There were frequent prayer meetings, and great nocturnal feasts. When I was a child I played with my cousins outside, where the lamplight fell upon the ground and the singing of the old people rose up around us and carried away into the darkness. There were a lot of good things to eat, a lot of laughter and surprise. And afterwards, when the quiet returned, I lay down with my grandmother and could hear the frogs away by the river and feel the motion of the air.

Now there is a funeral silence in the rooms, the endless wake of some final word. The walls have closed in upon my grandmother's house. When I returned to it in mourning, I saw for the first time in my life how small it was. It was late at night, and there was a white moon, nearly full. I sat for a long time on the stone steps by the kitchen door. From there I could see out across the land; I could see the long row of trees by the creek, the low light upon the rolling plains, and the stars of the Big Dipper. Once I looked at the moon and caught sight of a strange thing. A cricket had perched upon the handrail, only a few inches away from me. My line of vision was such that the creature filled the moon like a fossil. It had gone there, I thought, to live and die, for there, of all places, was its small definition made whole and eternal. A warm wind rose up and purled like the longing within me.

The next morning I awoke at dawn and went out on the dirt road to Rainy Mountain. It was already hot, and the grasshoppers began to fill the air. Still, it was early in the morning, and the birds sang out of the shadows. The Long yellow grass on the mountain shone in the bright light, and a scissortail hied above the land. There, where it ought to be, at the end of a long and legendary way, was my grandmother's grave. Here and there on the dark stones were ancestral names. Looking back once, I saw the mountain and came away.

Texas Women: True Grit and All the Rest
Molly Ivins

*T*hey used to say that Texas was hell on women and horses—I don't know why they stopped. Surely not because much of the citizenry has had its consciousness raised, as they say in the jargon of the women's movement, on the issue of sexism. Just a few months ago one of our state representatives felt moved to compare women and horses—it was the similarity he wanted to emphasize.

Of course some Texas legislator can be found to say any fool thing, but this guy's comments met with general agreement from his colleagues. One can always dismiss the entire Legislature as a particularly deplorable set of Texans, but as Sen. Carl Parker observes, if you took all the fools out of the Lege, it wouldn't be a representative body anymore.

I should confess that I've always been more of an observer than a participant in Texas Womanhood: the spirit was willing but I was declared ineligible on grounds of size early. You can't be six feet tall and cute, both. I think I was first named captain of the basketball team when I was four and that's what I've been ever since. I spent my girlhood as a Clydesdale among thoroughbreds. I clopped along amongst them cheerfully, admiring their grace, but the strange training rituals they went through left me secretly relieved that no one would ever expect me to step on a racetrack. I think it is quite possible to grow up in Texas as an utter failure in flirting, gentility, cheerleading, sexpottery, and manipulation and still be without any permanent scars. Except one. We'd all rather be blonde.

Please understand I'm not whining when I point out that Texas sexism is of an especially rank and noxious variety—this is more a Texas brag. It is my belief that it is virulence of Texas sexism that accounts for the strength of Texas women. It's what we have to overcome that makes us formidable survivors, say I with some complacency.

As has been noted elsewhere, there are several strains of Texan culture: They are all rotten for women. There is the Southern belle nonsense of our Confederate heritage, that little-woman-on-a-pedestal, flirtatious, "you're so cute when you're mad," Scarlett O'Hara myth that leads, quite naturally, to the equally pernicious legend of the Iron Magnolia. Then there's the machismo of our Latin heritage, which affects not only our Chicana sisters, but has been integrated into Texas culture quite as thoroughly as barbecue, rodeo, and Tex-Mex food.

Next up is the pervasive good-ol'-boyism of the *Redneckus texensis*, that remarkable tribe that has made the pickup truck with the gun rack across the back window and the beer cans flying out the window a synonym for Texans worldwide. Country music is a good place to investigate and find reflected the attitudes of kickers toward women (never ask what a kicker kicks). It's your basic, familiar virgin/whore dichotomy—either your "Good-Hearted Woman" or "Your Cheatin' Heart," with the emphasis on the honky-tonk angels. Nor is the jock idolatry that permeates the state helpful to our gender: Football is not a game here, it's a matter of blood and death. Woman's role in the state's national game is limited, significantly, to cheerleading. In this regard, 1 can say with great confidence that Texas changeth not—the hopelessly intense, heartbreaking longing with which most Texas girls still want to be cheerleader can be observed at every high school, every September.°

° In February 1991, a woman in Channelview, Texas, was indicted for plotting the murder of the mother of her own daughter's chief rival for the cheerleading squad.

Last but not least in the litany of cultures that help make the lives of Texas women so challenging is the legacy of the frontier—not the frontier that Texas women lived on, but the one John Wayne lived on. Anyone who knows the real history of the frontier knows it is a saga of the strength of women. They worked as hard as men, they fought as hard as men, they suffered as much as men. But in the cowboy movies that most contemporary Texans grew up on, the big, strong man always protects "the little lady" or "the gals" from whatever peril threatens. Such nonsense. Mary Ann Goodnight was often left alone at the JA Ranch near the Palo Duro Canyon. One day in 1877, a cowboy rode into her camp with three chickens in a sack as a present for her. He naturally expected her to cook and eat the fowl, but Goodnight kept them as pets. She wrote in her diary, "No one can ever know how much company they were." Life for farm and ranch wives didn't improve much over the next 100 years. Ruth White raised nine children on a farm near High, Texas, in the 1920s and thirties. She used to say, "Everything on this farm is either hungry or heavy."

All of these strains lead to a form of sexism so deeply ingrained in the culture that it's often difficult to distinguish the disgusting from the outrageous or the offensive from the amusing. One not infrequently sees cars or trucks sporting the bumper sticker HAVE FUN—BEAT THE HELL OUT OF SOMEONE YOU LOVE. Another is: IF YOU LOVE SOMETHING, SET IT FREE. IF IT DOESN'T COME BACK, TRACK IT DOWN AND KILL IT. I once heard a legislator order a lobbyist, "Get me two sweathogs for tonight." At a benefit "roast" for the battered women's shelter in El Paso early in 1985, a couple of the male politicians told rape jokes to amuse the crowd. Most Texas sexism is not intended to be offensive—it's entirely unconscious. A colleague of mine was touring the new death chamber in Huntsville last year with a group of other reporters. Their guide called to warn those inside they were coming through, saying, "I'm coming over with eight reporters and one woman." Stuff like that happens to you four or five times a day for long enough, it will wear you down some.

Other forms of the phenomenon are, of course, less delightsome. Women everywhere are victims of violence with depressing regularity. Texas is a more violent place than most of the rest of America, for reasons having to do with guns, machismo, frontier traditions, and the heterogeneous population. While the law theoretically applies to male and female alike, by unspoken convention, a man who offs his wife or girl friend is seldom charged with murder one: we wind up filed under the misnomer manslaughter.

That's the bad news for Texas women—the good news is that all this adversity has certainly made us a bodacious bunch of overcomers. And rather pleasant as a group, I always think, since having a sense of humor about men is not a luxury here; it's a necessity. The feminists often carry on about the importance of role models and how little girls need positive role models. When I was a kid, my choice of Texas role models went from Ma Ferguson to the Kilgore Rangerettes. Of course I wanted to be a Rangerette: Ever seen a picture of Ma? Not that we haven't got real women heroes, of course, just that we were never taught anything about them. You used to have to take Texas history two or three times in order to get a high school diploma in this state: The Yellow Rose of Texas and Belle Starr were the only women in our history books. Kaye Northcott notes that all the big cities in the state have men's last names—Houston, Austin, Dallas. All women got was some small towns called after their front names: Alice, Electra, Marfa. This is probably because, as Eleanor Brackenridge of San Antonio (1837–1924) so elegantly put it, "Foolish modesty lags behind while brazen impudence goes forth and eats the pudding." Brackenridge did her part to correct the lag by founding the Texas Woman Suffrage Association in 1913.

It is astonishing how recently Texas women have achieved equal legal rights. I guess you could say we made steady progress even before we could vote—the state did raise the age of consent for a woman from 7 to 10 in 1890—but it went a little smoother after we got some say in it. Until June 26, 1918, all Texans could vote except "idiots, imbeciles, aliens, the insane and women." The battle over woman's suffrage in Texas was long and fierce. Contempt and ridicule were the favored weapons against women. Women earned the right to vote through years of struggle; the precious victory was not something handed to us by generous men. From that struggle emerged a generation of Texas women whose political skills and leadership abilities have affected Texas politics for decades. Even so, Texas women were not permitted to serve on juries until 1954. As late as 1969, married women did not have full property rights. And until 1972, under Article 1220 of the Texas Penal Code, a man could murder his wife and her lover if he found them "in a compromising position" and get away with it as "justifiable homicide." Women, you understand, did not have equal shooting rights. Although Texas was one of the first states to ratify the Equal Rights Amendment, which has been part of the Texas Constitution since 1972, we continue to work for fairer laws concerning problems such as divorce, rape, child custody, and access to credit.

Texas women are just as divided by race, class, age, and educational level as are other varieties of human beings. There's a pat description of "what every Texas woman wants" that varies a bit from city to city, but the formula that Dallas females have been labeled with goes something like this: "Be a Pi Phi at Texas or SMU, marry a man who'll buy you a house in Highland Park, hold the wedding at Highland Park Methodist (flowers by Kendall Bailey), join the Junior League, send the kids to St. Mark's and Hockaday in the winter and Camps Longhorn and Waldemar in the summer, plus cotillion lessons at the Dallas Country Club, have an unlimited charge account at Neiman's as a birthright but buy almost all your clothes at Highland Park Village from Harold's or the Polo Shop, get your hair done at Paul Neinast's or Lou's and drive a Jeep Wagoneer for carpooling and a Mercedes for fun." There is a kicker equivalent of this scenario that starts, "Every Texas girl's dream is a double-wide in a Lubbock trailer park. . . ." But I personally believe it is unwise ever to be funny at the expense of kicker women. I once met a kicker lady who was wearing a blouse of such a vivid pink you could close your eyes and still see the color; this confection was perked up with some big rhinestone buttons and a lot of ruffles across an impressive bosom. "My," said I, "where did you get that blouse?" She gave me a level look and drawled. "Honey, it come from mah coutouri-ay, Jay Cee Penn-ay." And if that ain't class, you *can* kiss my grits.

To my partisan eye, it seems that Texas women are more animated and friendly than those from, say, Nebraska. I suspect this comes from early training: Girls in Texas high schools are expected to walk through the halls smiling and saying "Hi" to everyone they meet. Being enthusiastic is bred into us, as is a certain amount of obligatory social hypocrisy stemming from the Southern tradition of manners, which does rather tend to emphasize pleasantness more than honesty in social situations. Many Texas women have an odd greeting call—when they haven't seen a good friend for a long time, the first glimpse will provoke the cry, "Oooooooo—honey, how good to see yew again!" It sounds sort of like the "Soooooey, pig" call.

Mostly Texas women are tough in some very fundamental ways. Not unfeminine, nor necessarily unladylike, just tough. It may be possible for a little girl to grow to womanhood in this state entirely sheltered from the rampant sexism all around her—but it's damned difficult. The result is that Texas women tend to know how to cope. We can cope with put-downs and come-ons, with preachers and hustlers, with drunks and cowboys. And when it's all over, if we stick together and work, we'll come out better than the sister who's buried in a grave near Marble Falls under a stone that says, "Rudolph Richter, 1822–1915, and Wife."

Low Tide at Four
Harriet Doerr

*W*hat I remember of those summers at the beach is that every afternoon there was a low tide at four.

I am wrong, of course. Memory has outstripped reality. But before me as I write, in all its original colors, is a scene I painted and framed and now, almost fifty years later, bring to light.

Here, then, is a California beach in summer, with children, surfers, fishermen, and gulls. The children are seven and three. We are on the sand, a whole family—father, mother, a boy and a girl. The year is 1939. It is noon. There will be a low tide at four.

Days at the beach are all the same. It is hard to tell one from another. We walk down from our house on the side of the hill and stop on the bluff to count the fishermen (five) on the pier and the surfers (three), riding the swells, waiting for their waves. We turn into Mrs. Tustin's pergola restaurant for hamburgers. Though we recognize them as the best in the world, we never eat them under the matted honeysuckle of the pergola. Instead, we carry them, along with towels, buckets, shovels, books, and an umbrella, down the perilous, tilting wooden stairs to the beach. Later we go back to the pergola for chocolate and vanilla cones.

"Ice cream special, cherry mint ripple," says Mrs. Tustin on this particular day, and we watch a fat man lick a scoop of it from his cone. We wait for him to say, "Not bad," or"I'll try anything once," but he has no comment. A long freight train rattles by on the tracks behind the pergola. As we turn away, Mrs. Tustin says, "The world's in big trouble," and the fat man says, "You can say that again. How about that paperhanger, Adolf?" But it's hard to hear because of the train.

Back on the beach, our heads under the umbrella, we lie at compass points like a four-pointed star. The sun hangs hot and high. Small gusts of wind lift the children's corn-straw hair. We taste salt. Face down, arms wide, we cling to the revolving earth.

Now Mr. Bray, the station agent, a middle-aged Mercury in a shiny suit, crosses the dry sand in his brown oxford shoes. He is delivering a telegram. Everyone listens while I read the message from our best and oldest friends. Sorry, they can't come next weekend after all. Good, we say to ourselves, without shame.

I invite Mr. Bray to join us under the umbrella. "Can't you stay on the beach for a while?" He pauses with sand sifting into his shoes. Oh, no, he has to get back to his trains. He left his wife in charge, and the new diesel streamliner will be coming through.

At this moment a single-seated fighter plane from the navy base north of us bursts into sight along the shore, flying so low it has to climb to miss the pier. The children jump into the air and wave. The pilot, who looks too young for his job, waves back.

"Look at that," says Mr. Bray. "He could get himself killed."

Time and the afternoon are running out. A fisherman reels in a corbina. Three gulls ride the swells under the pier. The children, streaked with wet sand, dig a series of parallel and intersecting trenches into the ebb tide. Their father walks to the end of the pier, dives into a swell, rides in on a wave, and walks out to the end of the pier again. I swim and come back to my towel to read. I swim and read again.

Winesburg, Ohio; Sister Carrie; Absalom, Absalom!; Ethan Frome; The Magic Mountain; Studs Lonigan; A Handful of Dust; A Room with a View. There are never books enough or days enough to read them.

I look up from my page. Here is old Mrs. Winfield's car being parked at the top of the bluff. It must be almost four. Her combination driver, gardener, and general manager, Tom Yoshimura, helps her into a canvas chair he has set up in front of the view. His wife, Hatsu, new from Japan, is stringing beans for dinner in Mrs. Winfield's shingled house on the hill. Hatsu can't speak English. She bows good morning and good afternoon.

Mrs. Winfield has survived everything: her husband's death and the death of a child, earthquakes, floods, and fires, surgical operations and dental work, the accidents and occasional arrests of her grandchildren. All these, as well as intervals of a joy so intense it can no longer be remembered. I watch Tom Yoshimura bring her an ice cream cone from the pergola.

It is four o'clock. We are standing in shallow water at low tide. The children dig with their toes and let the waves wash in and out over their feet. They are sinking deeper and deeper. During the summer, their skins have turned every shade of honey: wildflower, orange, buckwheat, clover. Now they are sage. I look into my husband's face. He reaches over their heads to touch my arm.

At this time on this August day in 1939, I call up my interior reserves and gather strength from my blood and bones. Exerting the full force of my will, I command the earth to leave off circling long enough to hold up the sun, hold back the wave. Long enough for me to paint and frame low tide.

Mass for the Happy Death of Innocence
Holly Iglesias

*G*irls sashaying to the candy store for smokes, to the drug store for violet pastilles and betadyne, ladies at the soda fountain sucking their teeth, dabbing sweat from their lips with lavender handkerchiefs, pouring more chicory for Father Poché, poor soul, too late for communion, too early for scotch. *Candy man has come and gone, oh my candy man has come and gone.* Boys hide in the trees, in trees that never shed leaves, boys with beers, boys who jeer and flirt, who whisper nasties into the hats of passersby. A girl presses the small of her back into a thick trunk, cocks one foot behind the ankle of the other, the air an invitation to spoil, and carnival just a place between the legs. Air, the air that rarely moves, damp as anything in the mouth, and leaves that never fall. A single blossom of tea olive, white, the size of the fingernail on a pinkie, gives off a scent that can buckle a grown man's knees, plant the idea of sex *right now* behind his eyes. Shoes melting into the mud, the tar on the street, odors evolving with progress up or down Canal Street, Annunciation, Calliope. Standing in the shade, heels sunk in the soft soil of the neutral ground, a woman fingers a token, her friend rolling crisp white paper down the length of a baguette, offering a bite as the trolley approaches, its wheels clacking, sparks flying high and low.

Like a scar from a thousand whippings, the levee rises between river and peril, young men high on the swell of it taking their leisure. Stuck with school-yard names—Bobby, Baby, Jimmy D—they consider themselves boys, always will, even when lifting the skirt of a wife, a mistress, a forbidden young thing. Everything that sloshes in a bottle of pink chablis smiles on them, gives the nod to their antics as sun bronzes the water. Come dusk, they depart, gallants on the prowl, aiming for cocktails studded with cherries and girls who straddle stools like they can't get enough of anything, who booze with boys through an eternal childhood of damp air and the tropical imperative to couple. The only breeze enters the bar from a tiny window to the street, where pedestrians buy pints of Crown Royal and rye. Clinging to the vinyl bumper, a weathered woman goes for the record, six Skip 'n' Go Nakeds, college kids who smell like roast beef po' boys gawking at the local color, and the one who never eats, who never comes inside, stumbles into a metal cart, the vendor yelling, *Red Hots! Get 'em while they're red hot!* from clouds of steam. Eventually one day becomes the next and truth squats at the curb, blue as a bruise, as Jesuits move from *lait chaude* in the refectory to desks piled with scholarship and arcana, waiting till lunch to switch to the hard stuff.

River like a slug in June, mud and more mud passing by, silt for the delta, memory scoured from banks upriver, from territories once French and Indian, St. Louis regent of the upper valley, New Orleans the queen below. Imagine then the moment of purchase, the swift exchange of documents and flags, Toussaint and Napoleon menacing the freshly minted borders, the snits and snares of surrender to the bawdy boy of a nation set on conquest. Amateur naturalists, cartographers, dispatched to measure mountains, to gather pelts and seed pods, to list the names of tribes on the journey west, slow-tongued mercenaries sent to translate the nuances of fealty, front men for speculators who reduced the filigree of creole society to knots on a surveyor's rope. The tourist is to believe that what remains of this plot is a mere flair for gracious living, nostalgic tidbits of burnt sugar served on doilies in the Quarter, though each mansion, shotgun and housing project holds a secret, some hoodoo against the invader scrawled on wallpaper, silver spoons stashed beneath a floor board, tisanes for misery locked in the pantry. The city itself settles deeper into that great bowl where all worlds—the new, the old, the first, the third—splash about.

Point your shoes where you want to go. Only in this way will you know direction in a land that sloughs itself off, where tiny territories slip between your toes and seasons exceed meaning, just bloom and rain, no gap between Carnival and Lent, Lent and Carnival, where up river and down are the cardinal points until the storm comes that changes the destiny of water, the current reversed like an infant who refuses birth, aching back toward the warm and murky middle. Bend down and touch the imprint of lovers in the sodden grass, a heel here, a knee there, the weight of their ardor in the aftermath. Watch as the bodies of August wash by and know your turn will come. Pray now for those on foot, that they make the bridge by dark, that they cross over, mercy! cross over for good.

Research and Practice Strategies

1. In "Researching Your Own Life," Pearson writes: "Memory is an archive like any other and can be used as such." Memories can also be set within the context of other sources. You might, for example, explore letters, diaries, scrapbooks, and photo albums. Newspapers from the time and region of the remembered event can shed light on your subject as well. Or, like Pearson, you may want to read some of the books, watch films, and listen to music that was important to you at the time, allowing yourself to slip back into the world that had a role in shaping your imagination. In any case, you will want to write two different pieces: the first from an older, perhaps adult perspective, remembering, similar to Ivin's essay in this chapter. The second may be written similarly to Sedaris (in Chapter 7), re-entering your childhood point of view. Recreate the scenes as vividly as you can from memory, while also bringing to bear those elements you have gathered from other sources. Be sure to develop your scenes and provide a sense of your character. This exercise is about revealing character and point of view within the context of scene and situation. Once you've written the two pieces, read them and ask yourself: Do I prefer one piece over the other? Might one be enhanced by the other? Do I need to return to any of my other sources to sharpen any details that may have become blurred over the years? You will want to complete this piece with the intent of bringing two voices and points of view into an interactive relationship. This interaction should carry some of the thematic weight.

2. After reading Pearson's "Researching Your Own Life," you might want to create a timeline of significant events and emotional experiences in your life. A timeline can help you not only see the bigger picture, it can help you focus on specific experiences, some that may have been turning points in your life. Timelines also are helpful in making patterns apparent. My timeline revealed that my family moved every year in the middle of the school year from second through sixth grade, something I had forgotten about my formative years. There are numerous ways I could explore this, not least of which is how such moves were disruptive to developing long-term friendships, for example, but also how frequent moves affected my sense of home. In any case, your timeline will bring many potential stories to the foreground for consideration. Your timeline can be elaborate or simple, creative or merely informative; it can take the form of sentences or word clusters. It doesn't matter. The point is to include important events from your life, such as the following:

   - Significant births and deaths
   - Developmental stages in your life

- Moves
- Beginnings of key relationships (and endings, if relevant): friends, teachers, lovers, animals, professional relationships, mentors
- Schools and the dates you attended them, degrees
- Work, service, activism, community or organizational involvement
- Health concerns
- Turning points

The above categories can go across the top of a landscape-oriented, legal-sized page, or it can go down the left side of a portrait-oriented, legal-sized page. This next list will go on the opposite side (below or to the right) of the same page. Or, if you need more room, simply line up legal pages side-by-side.

Now, let's bring research into this. Include historical and cultural events that line up chronologically with your timeline. These might include, for example:

- major news stories of the time,
- wars and assassinations of public figures,
- space travel and even the Challenger explosion,
- economic up- and down-turns,
- social movements,
- epidemics,
- major world changes, and so on.

You might include:

- the music popular during specific eras,
- popular culture and its social echoes.

You may find it helpful to talk with friends and family after you've completed your version of the timeline. They may recall events that you've forgotten or dismissed as unimportant. Ask them how *they* would describe the important events of *your* life; this will help you pull back and get others' perspectives on your life. Keep this timeline in your journal or notebook and refer to it from time to time. You may find yourself using it for story ideas, or you may use it to refresh your memory as you develop a story already in progress.

3. If you are writing a profile or biography, you can create a similar timeline to work from. You can do this with your research source, and begin it in your initial interview, or after you have developed a bit of rapport together. In any case, it should be done early in the process of gathering information so that you begin to see which experiences had the

greatest impact on your interviewee. And don't make the mistake of thinking the goal is to get the timeline done; it isn't. The point is to generate conversation, realizations, and to draw out of the individual those memories and moments that are most important to her. Have her bring out photographs, memorabilia, newspaper articles, scrapbooks, even old yearbooks.

4. If you are interested in immersion journalism you will need to be willing to dedicate some time to the endeavor. You may want to join a club or organization. You may want to volunteer at a community center or serve at a soup kitchen. Perhaps you will become a Big Brother or Big Sister. You don't have to give months or years to the project, but you do need to get to know your subject intimately so that you can write about him from an insider's perspective. You will want to move well beyond an intellectual response and include sensory data, even your own emotional responses when relevant. The point of immersion journalism is to bring your reader there; to do that you must go there yourself, and you must keep careful notes of your experiences and observations.

Appendix

A Guide to Avoiding Plagiarism

Plagiarism is using someone else's work—words, ideas, or illustrations, published or unpublished—without giving the creator of that work sufficient credit. A serious breach of scholarly ethics, plagiarism can have severe consequences. Students risk a failing grade or disciplinary action ranging from suspension to expulsion. A record of such action can adversely affect professional opportunities in the future as well as graduate school admission.

Documentation: The Key to Avoiding Unintentional Plagiarism

It can be difficult to tell when you have unintentionally plagiarized something. The legal doctrine of **fair use** allows writers to use a limited amount of another's work in their own papers and books. However, to make sure that they are not plagiarizing that work, writers need to take care to credit the source accurately and clearly for *every* use. **Documentation** is the method writers employ to give credit to the creators of material they use. It involves providing essential information about the source of the material, which enables readers to find the material for themselves. It requires two elements: (1) a list of sources used in the paper and (2) citations in the text to items in that list. To use documentation and avoid unintentionally plagiarizing from a source, you need to know how to

- Identify sources and information that need to be documented.
- Document sources in a Works Cited list.
- Use material gathered from sources: in summary, paraphrase, and quotation.
- Create in-text references.
- Use correct grammar and punctuation to blend quotations into a paper.

Identifying Sources and Information That Need to be Documented

Whenever you use information from **outside sources,** you need to identify the source of that material. Major outside sources include books, newspapers, magazines, government sources, radio and television programs, material from electronic databases, correspondence, films, plays, interviews, speeches, and information from Web sites. Virtually all the information you find in outside sources requires documentation. The one major exception to this guideline is that you do not have to document common knowledge. **Common knowledge** is widely known information about current events, famous people, geographical facts, or familiar history. However, when in doubt, the safest strategy is to provide documentation.

Documenting Sources in a Works Cited List

You need to choose the documentation style that is dominant in your field or required by your instructor. Take care to use only one documentation style in any one paper and to follow its documentation formats consistently. The most widely used style manuals are *MLA Handbook for Writers of Research Papers*, published by the **Modern Language Association (MLA)**, which is popular in the fields of English language and literature; the *Publication Manual of the American Psychological Association (APA)*, which is favored in the social sciences; and *The Chicago Manual of Style*, published by the **University of Chicago Press (CMS)**, which is preferred in other humanities and sometimes business. Other, more specialized style manuals are used in various fields. Certain information is included in citation formats in all styles:

- Author or other creative individual or entity
- Source of the work
- Relevant identifying numbers or letters
- Title of the work
- Publisher or distributor
- Relevant dates

Constructing a Works Cited List in MLA Style

As an accompaniment to your English text, this guide explores MLA style. MLA lists are alphabetized by authors' last names. When no author is given, an item can be alphabetized by title, by editor, or by the name of the sponsoring organization. MLA style spells out names in full, inverts only the first author's name, and separates elements with a period. In the MLA Works Cited list below, note the use of punctuation such as commas, colons, and angle brackets to separate and introduce material within elements.

Books

Chernow, Ron. *Alexander Hamilton*. New York: Penguin, 2004.

Maupassant, Guy de. "The Necklace." Trans. Marjorie Laurie. *An Introduction to Fiction*. Ed. X. J. Kennedy and Dana Gioia. 7th ed. New York: Longman, 1999. 160–66.

Claiborne, Robert. *Our Marvelous Native Tongue: The Life and Times of the English Language*. New York: New York Times, 1983.

Periodicals

"Living on Borrowed Time." *Economist* 25 Feb.–3 Mar. 2006: 34–37.
"Restoring the Right to Vote." Editorial. *New York Times* 10 Jan. 2006, late ed., sec. A: 24.
Ulrich, Lars. "It's Our Property." *Newsweek* 5 June 2000: 54.
Williams, N. R., M. Davey, and K. Klock-Powell. "Rising from the Ashes: Stories of Recovery, Adaptation, and Resiliency in Burn Survivors." *Social Work Health Care* 36.4 (2003): 53–77.
Zobenica, Jon. "You Might As Well Live." Rev. of *A Long Way Down* by Nick Hornby. *Atlantic* July–Aug. 2005: 148.

Electronic Sources

Glanz, William. "Colleges Offer Students Music Downloads." *Washington Times* 25 Aug. 2004. 17 Oct. 2004 <http://washingtontimes.com/business/20040824-103654-1570r.htm>.
McNichol, Elizabeth C., and Iris J. Lav. "State Revenues and Services Remain below Pre-Recession Levels." *Center on Budget Policy Priorities*. 6 Dec. 2005. 10 Mar. 2006 <http://www.cbpp.org/12-6-05sfp2.html>.
Reporters Without Borders. "Worldwide Press Freedom Index 2005." *Reporters Without Borders*. 2005. 28 Feb. 2006 <http://www.rsf.org/article.php3?id_article=15331>.

Using Material Gathered From Sources: Summary, Paraphrase, Quotation

You can integrate material into your paper in three ways—by summarizing, paraphrasing, and quoting. A quotation, paraphrase, or summary must be used in a manner that accurately conveys the meaning of the source.

A **summary** is a brief restatement in your own words of the source's main ideas. Summary is used to convey the general meaning of the ideas in a source, without giving specific details or examples that may appear in the original. A summary is always much shorter than the work it treats. Take care to give the essential information as clearly and succinctly as possible in your own language.

Rules to Remember

1. Write the summary using your own words.
2. Indicate clearly where the summary begins and ends.
3. Use attribution and parenthetical reference to tell the reader where the material came from.
4. Make sure your summary is an accurate restatement of the source's main ideas.
5. Check that the summary is clearly separated from your own contribution.

A **paraphrase** is a restatement, in your own words and using your own sentence structure, of specific ideas or information from a source. The chief purpose of a paraphrase is *to maintain your own writing style* throughout your paper. A paraphrase can be about as long as the original passage.

Rules to Remember

1. Use your own words and sentence structure. Do not duplicate the source's words or phrases.
2. Use quotation marks within your paraphrase to indicate words and phrases you do quote.
3. Make sure your readers know where the paraphrase begins and ends.
4. Check that your paraphrase is an accurate and objective restatement of the source's specific ideas.
5. Immediately follow your paraphrase with a parenthetical reference indicating the source.

A **quotation** reproduces an actual part of a source, word for word, to support a statement or idea, to provide an example, to advance an argument, or to add interest or color to a discussion. The length of a quotation can range from a word or a phrase to several paragraphs. In general, quote the least amount possible that gets your point across to the reader.

Rules to Remember

1. Copy the words from your source to your paper exactly as they appear in the original. Do not alter the spelling, capitalization, or punctuation of the original. If a quotation contains an obvious error, you may insert [sic], which is Latin for "so" or "thus," to show that the error is in the original.
2. Enclose short quotations (four or fewer lines of text) in quotation marks, and set off longer quotations as block quotations.
3. Immediately follow each quotation with a parenthetical reference that gives the specific source information required.

Creating In-Text References

In-text references need to supply enough information to enable a reader to find the correct source listing in the Works Cited list. To cite a source properly in the text of your report, you generally need to provide some or all of the following information for each use of the source:

- Name of the person or organization that authored the source.
- Title of the source (if there is more than one source by the same author or if no author is given).
- Page, paragraph, or line number, if the source has one.

These items can appear as an attribution in the text ("According to Smith . . . ") or in a parenthetical reference placed directly after the summary, paraphrase, or quotation. The examples that follow are in MLA style.

Using An Introductory Attribution and a Parenthetical Reference

The author, the publication, or a generalized reference can introduce source material. Remaining identifiers (title, page number) can go in the parenthetical reference at the end, as in the first sentence of the example below. If a source, such as a Web site, does not have page numbers, it may be possible to put all the necessary information into the in-text attribution, as in the second sentence of the example below.

> *The Economist* noted that since 2004, "state tax revenues have come roaring back across the country" ("Living" 34). However, McNichol and Lav, writing for the Center on Budget and Policy Priorities, claim that recent gains are not sufficient to make up for the losses suffered.

Identifying Material by an Author of More Than One Work Used in Your Paper

The attribution and the parenthetical reference combined must provide the title of the work, the author, and the page number of the citation.

> Describing the testing of the first atom bomb, Jennet Conant says, "The test had originally been scheduled for 4:00 A.M. on July 16, when most of the surrounding population would be sound asleep and there would be the least number of witnesses" (*109 East Palace* 304–05).

Identifying Material That the Source Is Quoting

To use material that has been quoted in your cited source, add *qtd. in*, for "quoted in."

> The weather was worrisome, but procrastination was even more problematic. General Groves was concerned that "every hour of delay would increase the possibility of someone's attempting to sabotage the tests" (qtd. in Conant, *109 East Palace* 305).

Using Correct Grammar and Punctuation to Blend Quotations into a Paper

Quotations must blend seamlessly into the writer's original sentence, with the proper punctuation, so that the resulting sentence is neither ungrammatical nor awkward.

Using a Full-Sentence Quotation of Fewer Than Four Lines

A quotation of one or more complete sentences can be enclosed in double quotation marks and introduced with a verb, usually in the present tense and followed by a comma. Omit a period at the close of a quoted sentence, but keep any question mark or exclamation mark. Insert the parenthetical reference, then a period.

> One commentator asks, "What accounts for the government's ineptitude in safeguarding our privacy rights?" (Spinello 9).
> "The test had originally been scheduled for 4:00 A.M. on July 16," Jennet Conant writes, "when most of the surrounding population would be sound asleep" (*109 East Palace* 304–05).

Introducing a Quotation with a Full Sentence

Use a colon after a full sentence that introduces a quotation.

> Spinello asks an important question: "What accounts for the government's ineptitude in safeguarding our privacy rights?" (9).

Introducing a Quotation with "That"

A single complete sentence can be introduced with a *that* construction.

> Chernow suggests that "the creation of New York's first bank was a formative moment in the city's rise as a world financial center" (199–200).

Quoting Part of a Sentence

Make sure that quoted material blends grammatically into the new sentence.

> McNichol and Lav assert that during that period, state governments were helped by "an array of fiscal gimmicks."

Using a Quotation That Contains Another Quotation

Replace the internal double quotation marks with single quotation marks.

> Lowell was "famous as a 'confessional' writer, but he scorned the term," according to Bidart (vii).

Adding Information to a Quotation

Any addition for clarity or any change for grammatical reasons should be placed in square brackets.

> Describing how the weather would affect the testing of the first atom bomb, Jennet Conant says, "The test had originally been scheduled for 4:00 A.M. on July 16, [1945,] when most of the surrounding population would be sound asleep" (*109 East Palace* 304–05).

Omitting Information From Source Sentences

Indicate an omission with ellipsis marks (three spaced dots).

> Describing how the weather would affect the testing of the first atom bomb, Jennet Conant says, "The test had originally been scheduled for 4:00 A.M. on July 16, when . . . there would be the least number of witnesses" (304–05).

Using a Quotation of More Than Four Lines

Begin a long quotation on a new line and set off the quotation by indenting it one inch from the left margin and double spacing it throughout. Do not enclose it in quotation marks. Put the parenthetical reference *after* the period at the end of the quotation.

Human Rights Watch recently documented the repression of women's rights in Libya:

> The government of Libya is arbitrarily detaining women and girls in "social rehabilitation" facilities, . . . locking them up indefinitely without due process. Portrayed as "protective" homes for wayward women and girls, . . . these facilities are de facto prisons . . . [where] the government routinely violates women's and girls' human rights, including those to due process, liberty, freedom of movement, personal dignity, and privacy. (Human)

Is It Plagiarism? Test Yourself On In-Text References

Read the Original Source excerpt. Can you spot the plagiarism in the examples that follow it?

Original Source

To begin with, language is a system of communication. I make this rather obvious point because to some people nowadays it isn't obvious: they see language as above all a means of "self-expression." Of course, language is one way that we express our personal feelings and thoughts—but so, if it comes to that, are dancing, cooking and making music. Language does much more: it enables us to convey to others what we think, feel and want. Language-as-communication is the prime means of organizing the cooperative activities that enable us to accomplish as groups things we could not possibly do as individuals. Some other species also engage in cooperative activities, but these are either quite simple (as among baboons and wolves) or exceedingly stereotyped (as among bees, ants and termites). Not surprisingly, the communicative systems used by these animals are also simple or stereotypes. Language, our uniquely flexible and intricate system of communication, makes possible our equally flexible and intricate ways of coping with the world around us: in a very real sense, it is what makes us human. (Claiborne 8)

Works Cited entry:

Claiborne, Robert. *Our Marvelous Native Tongue: The Life and Times of the English Language.* New York: New York Times, 1983.

Plagiarism Example 1

One commentator makes a distinction between language used as a **means of self-expression** and **language-as-communication.** It is the latter that distinguishes human interaction from that of other species and allows humans to work cooperatively on complex tasks (8).

What's wrong? The source's name is not given, and there are no quotation marks around words taken directly from the source (in **boldface** in the example).

Plagiarism Example 2

Claiborne notes that language "is the prime means of organizing the cooperative activities." Without language, we would, consequently, not have civilization.

What's wrong? The page number of the source is missing. A parenthetical reference should immediately follow the material being quoted, paraphrased, or summarized. You may omit a parenthetical reference only if the information that you have included in your attribution is sufficient to identify the source in your Works Cited list and no page number is needed.

Plagiarism Example 3

Other animals also **engage in cooperative activities.** However, these actions are not very complex. Rather they are either the very **simple** activities of, for example, **baboons and wolves** or the **stereotyped** activities of animals such as **bees, ants and termites** (Claiborne 8).

What's wrong? A paraphrase should capture a specific idea from a source but must not duplicate the writer's phrases and words (in **boldface** in the example). In the example, the wording and sentence structure follow the source too closely.

Evaluating Sources

It's very important to evaluate critically every source you consult, especially sources on the Internet, where it can be difficult to separate reliable sources from questionable ones. Ask these questions to help evaluate your sources:

- Is the material relevant to your topic?
- Is the source well respected?
- Is the material accurate?
- Is the information current?
- Is the material from a primary source or a secondary source?

Avoiding Plagiarism: Note-Taking Tips

The most effective way to avoid unintentional plagiarism is to follow a systematic method of note taking and writing.

- **Keep copies of your documentation information.** For all sources that you use, keep photocopies of the title and copyright pages and the pages with quotations you need. Highlight the relevant citation information in color. Keep these materials until you've completed your paper.
- **Quotation or paraphrase?** Assume that all the material in your notes is direct quotation unless you indicated otherwise. Double-check any paraphrase for quoted phrases, and insert the necessary quotation marks.
- **Create the Works Cited or References list *first*.** Before you start writing your paper, your list is a **working bibliography,** a list of possible sources to which you add source entries as you discover them. As you finalize your list, you can delete the items you decided not to use in your paper.

—Linda Stern,
Publishing School of Continuing and
Professional Studies, New York University

Notes on the Contributors

Diane Ackerman was born in Waukegan, Illinois. Her nonfiction works include her bestseller *A Natural History of the Senses*, as well as *An Alchemy of Mind, Cultivating Delight: A Natural History of My Garden*, and *A Natural History of Love; On Extended Wings*, and most recently, *The Zookeeper's Wife*. Her essays about nature and human nature have appeared in *The New York Times, Smithsonian, Parade, The New Yorker, National Geographic*, and many other journals. Ackerman holds a doctorate of literature from Kenyon College and has received a Guggenheim Fellowship. She has taught at a variety of universities.

Marjorie Agosín grew up in Chile, although born in Maryland. Agosín has authored numerous books including a memoir of her mother, *A Cross and a Star: Memoirs of a Jewish Girl In Chile*; a memoir of her father, *Always from Somewhere Else: A Memoir of My Chilean Jewish Father*; and several collections of poetry and literary criticism. In her narrative nonfiction book, *Cartographies: Meditations on Travel*, Agosín recreates meaningful moments from her voyages across four continents. She was awarded the 1995 Latino Literature Prize for Poetry for her book *Toward the Splendid City*. In 1995 she received the Letras de Oro prize for poetry. Agosín is a professor at Wellesley College where she teaches courses in Spanish language and Latin American literature.

Dorothy Allison grew up in Greenville, South Carolina, and Florida. She is a poet, novelist, memoirist, and essayist, and has won numerous literary awards. Her memoir, *Two or Three Things I Know for Sure*, was selected as a Notable Book of the Year by the *New York Times Book Review*. Allison's autobiographical novel, *Bastard Out of Carolina*, won the Lambda Award and was nominated for the National Book Award. Her short story collection, *Trash*, won two Lambda Literary Awards and the American Library Association Prize for Lesbian and Gay Writing and has recently been republished in an expanded edition. Her second novel, *Cavedweller*, became a national bestseller, *New York Times* Notable Book of the Year finalist for the Lillian Smith prize, and was an American Library Association prize winner. Recipient of the 2007 Robert Penn Warren Award for Fiction, Allison is a member of the Fellowship of Southern Writers. She lives in Northern California with her partner and their son.

Jane Bernstein was born in Brooklyn, New York, and educated at New York University and Columbia University. She is the author of five books, *Loving Rachel, Bereft—A Sister's Story, Seven Minutes in Heaven, Departures*, and most recently *Rachel in the World*. Her essays and articles have appeared widely in such places as *The New York Times Magazine*, *Ms.*, *Creative Nonfiction*, the *Massachusetts Review*, and *Glamour*. She is a professor of English and creative writing at *Carnegie Mellon University* and lives in Pittsburgh, Pennsylvania.

Madeleine Blais, professor at the University of Massachusetts Amherst, earned a bachelor's degree at the College of New Rochelle and a master's from the School of Journalism at Columbia University. She was a reporter for the *Boston Globe*, the *Trenton Times*, and *Tropic Magazine* of the *Miami Herald* from 1979 to 1987. She won the Pulitzer Prize for Feature Writing while at the *Miami Herald*. Blais was a Nieman Fellow at Harvard University. She has written for the *Washington Post*, *Chicago Tribune*, *Northeast Magazine* in the *Hartford Courant*, *Philadelphia Inquirer*, *Newsday*, *Nieman Reports*, *Detroit Free Press*, *Boston Globe*, and *San Jose Mercury News*. She is the author of *In These Girls, Hope is a Muscle*, which was a National Book Critics Circle Award finalist in nonfiction and named one of the top 100 sports books of the twentieth century by ESPN; *The Heart is an Instrument: Portraits in Journalism*; and *Uphill Walkers: Memoir of a Family*, honored with a Massachusetts Book Award. She is a member of the advisory board for Goucher College's MFA program in creative nonfiction, and she serves on the editorial boards of *Riverteeth* and *Doubletake: Points of Entry*.

Jane Brox grew up on a farm in the Merrimack Valley of Massachusetts. Her first memoir, *Here and Nowhere Else: Late Seasons of a Farm and Its Family*, won the L. L. Winship/PEN New England Award. Her second book, *Five Thousand Days Like This One*, was a 1999 finalist for the National Book Critics Circle Award in nonfiction. Brox's most recent book is *Clearing Land: Legacies of the American Farm*. Her essays have appeared in *The Georgia Review* and other journals and magazines, and have been selected for inclusion in many anthologies, including *Best American Essays*, *The Norton Book of Nature Writing*, and the *Pushcart Prize Anthology*. She has received grants from the National Endowment for the Arts and the Massachusetts Cultural Council. She teaches nonfiction writing at Lesley University and lives in Maine.

Sharon Bryan is the author of three books of poems: *Flying Blind*, *Objects of Affection*, and *Salt Air*. She edited *Where We Stand: Women on Literary Tradition*, and co-edited, with William Olsen, *Planet on the Table: Poets on the Reading Life*. She has recently completed her fourth collection of poems, *Stardust*, BOA Editions, 2009. She is currently working on a book of poems and a memoir, *Searching for Andras*. Bryan teaches as a visiting poet at universities around the country.

Kim Chernin has a body of work that spans numerous genres, including memoir, autobiography, narrative nonfiction, autobiographical fiction, mythic fiction, and poetry. Her work includes a series of books about girls' development, among them, *The Hungry Self: Women, Eating, and Identity* and *The Obsession: Reflections on the Tyranny of Slenderness*. *Reinventing Eve: Modern Woman in Search of Herself* traces Chernin's own psychological and spiritual journey, as does *A Different Kind* of Listening: My Psychoanalysis and Its Shadow. Crossing the Border: An Erotic Journey not only explores life on a kibbutz in Israel, but also memory and experience, and the frequent disjunction between the two. Her mythic novel, The Flame Bearers, takes the reader into the realm of an ancient sect of Jewish women whose gift and burden is to pass the flame of secret knowledge from generation to generation. A twentieth anniversary edition of Chernin's memoir, In My Mother's House: A Daughter's Story, has been recently released. The Girl Who Went and Saw and Came Back is her most recent novel. Chernin lives in Northern California with Renate Stendhal, her life companion.

Judith Ortiz Cofer, poet, novelist, and essayist, was born in Puerto Rico. Her many works include A Love Story Beginning in Spanish: Poems; Silent Dancing, a collection of essays and poetry; Woman in Front of the Sun: On Becoming a Writer, a collection of essays; and The Latin Deli: Prose and Poetry. Her work has appeared in The Georgia Review, Kenyon Review, Southern Review, and Glamour. She has been anthologized in Best American Essays 1991, The Norton Book of Women's Lives, The Norton Introduction to Literature, The Norton Introduction to Poetry. Cofer is the Regents' and Franklin Professor of English and creative writing at the University of Georgia.

Kelly Cunnane is the author of the award-winning children's book, For You Are a Kenyan Child, winner of Chicago Public Library's Best of the Best, Ezra Jack Keats New Writer Award, among numerous other awards. Her essays have been published by The Christian Science Monitor. Cunnane teaches literature and writing at the University of Maine Machias.

Joan Didion was born in California. She is the author of five novels and seven books of nonfiction. Didion began her career at Vogue magazine and later became a political reporter. Her nonfiction works include, among others, We Tell Ourselves Stories in Order to Live: Collected Nonfiction, Slouching Towards Bethlehem, After Henry, and most recently, Where I Was From and The Year of Magical Thinking. Her awards include the Edward MacDowell Medal for outstanding contributions to the arts, and the Columbia Journalism Award. Didion is a contributor to The New Yorker magazine and The New York Review of Books. She lives in New York City.

Harriet Doerr was born in 1910 in Pasadena, California, where she lived much of her life. In 1930, she left Stanford University after her junior year to marry. At the age of 67 she completed her B.A. in European History, having returned to Stanford after her husband's death. In 1983, at the age of 73, Doerr published her first novel, Stones for Ibarra, which went on to win a 1984 National Book Award for First Work of Fiction. Doerr's second book, Consider This, Senora, was published in 1993 and became a best seller. The Tiger in the Grass, a collection of essays and short stories, was published in 1995. Doerr died in 2002.

Brian Doyle is the editor of *Portland Magazine* at the University of Portland, and the author of nine books of essays and poems, most recently *Epiphanies & Elegies*. His work has appeared in the annual *Best American Essays*, *Best American Science and Nature Writing*, and *Best Spiritual Writing* anthologies. As a dad he is now inundated by teenagers, suitable punishment for having once been a teenager himself.

K. Gregg Elliott was first inspired to start writing when she went birdwatching at the beach in northern California and wound up witnessing the effects of an oil spill in progress. Eighteen years of conservation work, including stints with The Nature Conservancy and the Point Reyes Bird Observatory, provide the perspective for much of her freelance writing. She has been published in numerous magazines, including *Bay Nature*, *California Coast & Ocean*, *Wild Earth*, and most recently *BARk*. Her story in *Best Women Travel Writers 2007* marks her debut in book format.

Gail Godwin was born in Alabama and grew up in North Carolina. She worked briefly as a general assignment reporter for the *Miami Herald* after graduating from the University of North Carolina at Chapel Hill. She has completed two works of nonfiction, *Heart: A Personal Journey Through Its Myths and Meanings*, and her most recent book, *The Making of a Writer: Journals, 1961–1963*. Her other works include 12 novels and two short story collections. Godwin's essays have appeared in *Antaeus*, *The Washington Post Book World*, and *The Writing Life: a Collection of Essays and Interviews by National Book Award Authors*. Along with the late composer Robert Starer, she wrote ten musical works. Godwin earned an M.A. and Ph.D. in English from the University of Iowa. She has taught at the Iowa Writers' Workshop, Vassar College, and Columbia University. Godwin lives in Woodstock, New York.

Vivian Gornick was born and raised in New York. She is the author of eight books, among them her most recent, *The Solitude of Self: Thinking About Elizabeth Cady Stanton*; her memoir, *Fierce Attachments*; *The Situation and the Story: The Art of Personal Narrative*; and two collections of essays, *Approaching Eye Level* and *The End of the Novel of Love*, a finalist for the National Book Critics Circle Award. For many years Gornick wrote for the *Village Voice*. She currently teaches at The New School in Greenwich Village.

Lee Gutkind is founder and editor of the journal, *Creative Nonfiction*, the first literary journal to exclusively publish nonfiction, now in its fourteenth year of publication, and editor of *The Best Creative Nonfiction*, a new annual anthology. He has appeared on National Public Radio's *Talk of the Nation*, the BBC World, *Wired.com*, and *The Daily Show*. Gutkind's new book, *Almost Human: Making Robots Think*, is a portrait of the robotics subculture and the scientific quest for robot autonomy.

Patricia Hampl first won recognition for *A Romantic Education*, her memoir about her Czech heritage. Other publications include *Virgin Time*, a memoir about her Catholic upbringing and an inquiry into contemplative life; *Blue Arabesque: A Search for the Sublime*; and her most recent memoir, *The Florist's Daughter*. Her book, *I Could Tell You Stories: Sojourns in the Land of Memory*, was a finalist in the National Book Critics Circle Awards for General Nonfiction. Hampl's fiction, poems, reviews, essays, and travel pieces have appeared in *The New Yorker*, *Paris Review*, *The New York Times*, *Los Angeles Times*, *Best American Short Stories*, *Best American Essays*, and *The Best Spiritual Writing*. Hampl is Regents Professor and also McKnight Distinguished Professor at the University of Minnesota in Minneapolis where she teaches in the MFA program.

Holly Iglesias, a poet and translator, has been awarded fellowships by the Massachusetts Cultural Council and the Edward Albee Foundation. She is the author of two chapbooks, *Hands-on Saint*, and *Good Long Enough*, as well as a critical work, *Boxing Inside the Box: Women's Prose Poetry*. Her most recent project is a collection of poems focused on the 1904 World's Fair. She teaches at the University of North Carolina-Asheville and Warren Wilson College.

Peter Ives has published essays, reviews, and criticism in numerous journals and anthologies. He directs the Writing Center at Rollins College in Winter Park, Florida, and was a creative writing teacher at Trinity Preparatory School. His work has appeared in a number of anthologies and literary journals, including *Gettysburg Review*, *Laurel Review*, *Florida Review*, and *Fourth Genre*. Ives lives in Winter Park, Florida.

Molly Ivins, a Texas columnist known for her strong liberal views and populist humor, began her journalism career in the complaint department at the *Houston Chronicle* in the late 1960s. She edited the *Texas Observer* and reported for *The New York Times*. She was a columnist for the *Fort Worth Star-Telegram*, then went on to become an independent journalist, with her columns syndicated in approximately 400 newspapers. Ivins's bestselling books include, *Shrub: The Short but Happy Political Life of George W. Bush* and *BUSHWHACKED: Life in George W. Bush's America*, co-authored with Lou Dubose. Ivins died of breast cancer in 2007.

Yusef Komunyakaa was born in Bogalusa, Louisiana, in 1947. His nonfiction works include *Blue Notes: Essays, Interviews and Commentaries*, and numerous collections of poetry including, *Thieves of Paradise*, a finalist for the National Book Critics Circle Award; *Neon Vernacular: New & Selected Poems 1977–1989*, which won the Pulitzer Prize and the Kingsley Tufts Poetry Award. In 1999 Komunyakaa was elected a chancellor of the Academy of American Poets. He is a professor in the Council of Humanities and Creative Writing Program at Princeton University and the Distinguished Senior Poet at New York University's graduate creative writing program.

Phillip Lopate was born in Brooklyn, New York. His published works include the essay collections, *Bachelorhood*, *Against Joie de Vivre*, and *Portrait of My Body*; two novels, *Confessions of Summer* and *The Rug Merchant*; two poetry collections, *The Eyes Don't Always Want to Stay Open* and *The Daily Round*; and a memoir, *Being With Children*, about his teaching experiences, in addition to his collection, *Getting Personal: Selected Writings*. His essays, fiction, poetry, film, and architectural criticism have appeared in several anthologies and national journals. He holds the John Cranford Adams Chair at Hofstra University, and teaches in the MFA graduate programs at Columbia, The New School, and Bennington.

Audre Lorde was born in New York to West Indian immigrants. In 1991 she was named New York State's Poet Laureate. Lorde's works include prose writings, *Sister Outsider*, *Burst of Light*, which won a National Book Award, and the autobiographical *Zami: A New Spelling of My Name*. Her poetry publications include *The First Cities*, *The Black Unicorn*, and *Undersong: Chosen Poems Old and New*. With Barbara Smith, Lorde founded Kitchen Table: Women of Color Press. She was a poet in residence at Tougaloo College, Mississippi, and a visiting lecturer throughout the United States. Lorde died of breast cancer in 1992. Her battle with the disease is chronicled in her book *The Cancer Journals*.

Alfred Lubrano, a New York City native and a reporter for the *Philadelphia Inquirer*, has written for newspapers since 1980. He is the author of *Limbo: Blue-Collar Roots, White-Collar Dreams* and has been a commentator for National Public Radio since 1992. His work has appeared in various national magazines and anthologies. He lives with his daughter in South Jersey.

Karen Salyer McElmurray has an MFA in fiction writing from the University of Virginia, an M.A. in creative writing from Hollins University, and a Ph.D. from the University of Georgia. Her first novel, *Strange Birds in the Tree of Heaven*, received the 2001 Lillie D. Chaffin Award for Appalachian Writing. Most recently, McElmurray has published a memoir, *Surrendered Child: A Birth Mother's Journey*, winner of the AWP Award Series for Creative Nonfiction. The memoir was a National Book Critics Circle Notable Book selected as winner of the Georgia Author of the Year Award for memoir. McElmurray has received numerous grants, including the National Endowment for the Arts, the North Carolina Arts Council, and the Kentucky Foundation for Women. She is assistant professor of English at Georgia College and State University where she teaches creative writing courses. McElmurray and her husband divide their time between Georgia and North Dakota.

Pamela Michael has been writing about education, community, the arts, and travel for over 25 years. She is the co-founder, with former U.S. Poet Laureate Robert Hass, of *River of Words*, a nonprofit organization that helps children around the world combine poetry, art, and environmental education. Michael is the former director of the United Nations-sponsored Media/Education Task

Force and a member of Wild Writing Women, whose anthology by the same name won Best Book of the Year in 2002 from the North American Travel Journalists Association. Michael teaches writing workshops around the world and hosts an interview program on KPFA-FM, the nation's first listener-supported public radio station. Her books include, *River of Words: Images and Poetry in Praise of Water*, *The Gift of Rivers*, *A Woman's Passion for Travel*, and *River of Words: Young Poets on the Nature of Things*.

N. Scott Momaday grew up on the Navajo, Apache, and Pueblo reservations of the American Southwest. A scholar of the work of nineteenth century poet Frederick Goddard Tuckerman, as well as of Indian oral traditions, Momaday is the author of 13 books, including novels, poetry collections, literary criticism, and works on Native American culture. His first novel, *House Made of Dawn*, won the 1969 Pulitzer Prize for fiction; *The Way to Rainy Mountain* is a collection of Kiowa tales illustrated by his father, Al Momaday. Momaday earned his M.A. and Ph.D. degrees from Stanford University. He is Regents Professor Emeritus of English at the University of Arizona.

Sonia Nazario grew up in Kansas and Argentina. She reported for the *Wall Street Journal* before joining the *Los Angeles Times*, where she reports and writes on social issues. Nazario has written extensively from Latin America and about Latinos in the United States. The *Los Angeles Times* newspaper series upon which her book, *Enrique's Journey*, is based won more than a dozen awards, among them the 2003 Pulitzer Prize for feature writing. In 1998 she was a Pulitzer Prize finalist for a series on children of drug-addicted parents. Nazario is a graduate of Williams College and has a master's degree in Latin American studies from the University of California, Berkeley. She lives in Los Angeles with her husband.

Joan Nestle is the author of *A Restricted Country*, which received the Gay, Lesbian, & Bisexual Book Award from the American Library Association, *A Fragile Union*, and editor of *The Persistent Desire: A Femme-Butch Reader*. She co-founded the New York-based Lesbian Herstory Archives. Along with Naomi Holoch, she has edited three volumes of *Women on Women* anthologies. In 1996 she was awarded the Bill Whitehead Award for Lifetime Achievement in Lesbian and Gay Literature by the Publishing Triangle. For close to 30 years she taught writing in the SEEK Program at Queens College, CUNY until cancer forced her to retire in 1995.

Mary Oliver is the author of more than ten volumes of poetry and prose, including *American Primitive*, for which she was awarded the Pulitzer Prize; *New and Selected Poems*, which won the National Book Award; and *House of Light*, which won the Christopher Award and the L. L. Winship/PEN New England Award. Oliver attended Ohio State University and Vassar College. She taught literature at Bennington College in Vermont. She lives in Provincetown, Massachusetts.

Michael Pearson has published four nonfiction books, *Imagined Places: Journeys into Literary America*, *A Place That's Known*, *John McPhee*, *Dreaming of Columbus: A Boyhood in the Bronx*, and a novel, *Shohola Falls*. He directed the MFA program in creative writing at Old Dominion University in Virginia for a decade and now is professor of creative writing.

Leila Philip lived in New York City until the age of 15 when her family moved to the Hudson Valley to save a family farm. She is the author of *The Road Through Miyama*, for which she received the Martha Albrand Citation for Nonfiction; *Hidden Dialogue; A Discussion Between Women in Japan and the United States*; and her most recent book, the award-winning memoir, *A Family Place: A Hudson Valley Farm, Three Centuries, Five Wars, One Family*. Her work has been anthologized in a number of books, among them: *Family Travels: The Farther You Go the Closer You Get*, *Japan: True Stories of Life on the Road*, and *A Woman's Passion for Travel*. She is the author of numerous articles and reviews. Philip is the acting director of the creative writing program at the College of the Holy Cross and teaches creative writing and literature. She lives in Woodstock, Connecticut with her husband and son.

Kirk Read is the author of *How I Learned to Snap*, a memoir about growing up in the Reagan-era south. He lives in San Francisco where he co-hosts two open mics, *K'vetsh* and *Smack Dab*. He has worked for many years at the St. James Infirmary, a free health care clinic for sex workers where he has been an HIV counselor. He has toured widely as a storyteller and can be found online at kirkread.com.

David Sedaris is the author of *Barrel Fever* and *Holidays on Ice*, as well as personal essays *Naked*, *Me Talk Pretty One Day*, and *Dress Your Family in Corduroy and Denim*. He is a Grammy Award-nominated humorist and contributor to Public Radio International's *This American Life*. Sedaris has co-authored several plays with his sister Amy Sedaris, which have been produced at La Mama and Lincoln Center in New York City. In 2001 Sedaris became the third recipient of the Thurber Prize for American Humor and was named Humorist of the Year by *Time* magazine. Raised in Raleigh, North Carolina, Sedaris lives in France with his partner.

Natalia Rachel Singer is the author of *Scraping by in the Big Eighties*, a memoir in the *American Lives* series edited by Tobias Wolff. She is co-editor, with Neal Burdick, of *Living North Country: Essays on Life and Landscapes in Northern New York*. Her works of nonfiction and fiction have been published in numerous major magazines and literary journals, and anthologized in a number of books, among them *Collateral Language*, *Rooted in Rock*, *The Mammoth Book of Short Short Stories*, *The Best Writing on Writing*, and *Reading Seattle: The City in Prose*. She has won several national awards for her writing, including first prize in the Best Short Short Story contest and second prize in the Annie Dillard Award for Nonfiction, and has been a recipient of a grant from the

New York Foundation for the Arts for nonfiction literature. Singer is a professor of English at St. Lawrence University in upstate New York.

Alice Steinbach was awarded the Pulitzer Prize for Feature Writing in 1985 for her work at the *Baltimore Sun*, "A Boy of Unusual Vision." Her books include *Without Reservations: The Travels of An Independent Woman*, which chronicles her European journey of self-discovery; and *Educating Alice: Adventures of a Curious Woman*. Her work as a freelance journalist has appeared in many magazines and newspapers, including *Glamour*, *McCall's*, *The Washington Post*, *The Philadelphia Inquirer*, and *Boston Globe*. Steinbach lives in her native Baltimore. She has two grown sons.

James B. Stewart, lawyer, journalist, and writer, is the author of eight books, including the recent national bestseller, *Disney War*, an account of Michael Eisner's tumultuous reign at America's best known entertainment company. In 1988, he won the Pulitzer Prize for Explanatory Journalism for his articles in *The Wall Street Journal* about the 1987 dramatic upheaval in the stock market and insider trading. He is also the author of national bestsellers *Den of Thieves*, about Wall Street in the 1980s; *Blind Eye*, an investigation of the medical profession, which won the 2000 Edgar Allan Poe Award given by the Mystery Writers of America; and *Blood Sport*, about the Clinton White House. *Follow the Story: How to Write Successful Nonfiction*, was inspired by his classes at Columbia University. Stewart writes *Common Sense*, a column in *SmartMoney* and *SmartMoney.com*, which also appears in the *Wall Street Journal*. He contributes regularly to *The New Yorker*. Stewart is the Bloomberg professor of business journalism at Columbia University Graduate School of Journalism.

Jerome Washington was born in Trenton, New Jersey. He attended Columbia University and then served in the Army for three years in Vietnam and in Europe. He later became involved with the civil rights and peace movements. He wrote and published books, poems, and a play about his experiences in New York prisons, where he spent 16 years following his conviction in 1973 for the murder of a bartender and the attempted murder of the bar owner. Washington was founder and editor of the *Auburn Collective*, an award-winning prison newspaper that chronicled prisoner's struggles. As a result, he was abruptly moved from Auburn prison to Attica prison and his typewriter and manuscripts were confiscated. He filed a lawsuit and won the first prisoner amendment for the "Right to Write." Washington led campaigns to allow prisoners free access to books. Washington was released from prison in 1988 and his charges were dropped. In 1995 he was living in Fort Bragg, California, organizing writing workshops for the elderly, and working with at-risk teenagers. He published two books, *A Bright Spot in the Yard* and *Iron House: Stories from the Yard*.

Laura Wexler is the author of the nonfiction book, *Fire in a Canebrake: The Last Mass Lynching in America*. She is senior editor of *Baltimore Style Magazine* and founder, producer, and co-host of *The Stoop Storytelling Series, an open mic program.* She is on the faculty of the MFA program in creative nonfiction at Goucher College. Wexler lives in Baltimore.

Terry Tempest Williams, a native of Utah, is the author of *Refuge: An Unnatural History of Family and Place*; a collection of essays, *An Unspoken Hunger: Stories from the Field*; *Desert Quartet: An Erotic Landscape*; *Leap*; *Red: Patience and Passion in the Desert*; and *The Open Space of Democracy*, among others. She is the author of two children's books: *Secret Language of Snow* and *Between Cattails*. Her writing has appeared in *The New Yorker*, *The New York Times*, *Orion Magazine*, *The Iowa Review*, and *The New England Review*, among other national and international publications. She divides her time between Castle Valley, Utah, and Moose, Wyoming, where her husband Brooke Williams is the executive director of The Murie Center, which promotes the value of wild nature and its connection to the human spirit.

Credits

Diane Ackerman, "Courting the Muse" from *A Natural History of the Senses*. Copyright © 1990 by Diane Ackerman. Reprinted with permission of Random House, Inc.

Marjorie Agosín, "Traces" from *Cartographies*. Copyright © 2004 by Marjorie Agosín. Reprinted with permission of The University of Georgia Press.

Marjorie Agosín, "A Map of My Face" from *Cartographies*. Copyright © 2004 by Marjorie Agosín. Reprinted with permission of The University of Georgia Press.

Dorothy Allison, "Hypertext" from *Two or Three Things I Know for Sure*. Copyright © 1995 by Dorothy Allison. Reprinted with permission of Dutton, a division of Penguin Group (USA) Inc.

Jane Bernstein, "How and Why" originally appeared in *Creative Nonfiction*. Also appeared in *The Essayist at Work*. Copyright © 1996 by Jane Bernstein. Reprinted by permission of Brandt & Hochman Literary Agents, Inc.

Madeleine Blais, "Serviam" from *Uphill Walkers: Portrait of a Family*. Copyright © 2001 by Madeleine Blais. Reprinted with permission of Grove/Atlantic, Inc.

Jane Brox, "The Quality of Mercy" from *Five Thousand Days Like This One*. Copyright © 1999 by Jane Brox. Reprinted with permission of Beacon Press, Boston.

Sharon Bryan, "Around the Corner" originally published in *In Short: A Collection of Brief Creative Nonfiction* edited by Judith Kitchen and Mary Paumier Jones. Copyright © 1996 by Sharon Bryan. Reprinted with permission of the author.

Kim Chernin, "Oy, My Enlightenment" from *In My Mother's House*. Copyright © 1983, 2003 by Kim Chernin. Reprinted with permission of MacAdam/Cage Publishing.

Judith Ortiz Cofer, "Volar" from *Year of Our Revolution*. Copyright © 1998 by Judith Ortiz Cofer. Reprinted with permission of Arte Público Press University of Houston.

Kelly Cunnane, "Clip from a Winter Diary" originally published in *In Brief: Short Takes on the Personal* edited by Judith Kitchen and Mary Paumier Jones. Copyright © 1999 by Kelly Cunnane. Reprinted with permission of the author.

Joan Didion, "On Keeping a Notebook" from *Slouching Towards Bethlehem*. Copyright © 1966, 1968, renewed 1996 by Joan Didion. Reprinted with permission of Farrar, Straus and Giroux, LLC.

Harriet Doerr, "Low Tide at Four" from *The Tiger in the Grass*. Copyright © 1995 by Harriet Doerr. Reprinted with permission of Viking Penguin, a division of Penguin Group (USA) Inc.

Brian Doyle, "Two Hearts" originally appeared in *Portland Magazine*. Copyright © 1995 by Brian Doyle. Reprinted with permission of the author.

K. Gregg Elliott, "What Can't Be Spoken" from *The Best Women's Travel Writing 2007: True Stories From Around the World*, edited by Lucy McCauley, published by Traveler's Tales, an imprint of Solas House, Inc. Copyright © 2007 by K. Gregg Elliott. Reprinted with permission of Travelers' Tales and the author.

Gail Godwin, "Watcher at the Gate" from *The Spirit of Writing: Classic and Contemporary Essays Celebrating the Writing Life*, edited by Mark Robert Waldman. Copyright © 1995 by Gail Godwin. Reprinted with permission of John Hawkins & Associates, Inc.

Vivian Gornick, "On the Street: Nobody Watches, Everyone Performs" from *Approaching Eye Level*. Copyright © 1996 by Vivian Gornick. Reprinted with permission of Beacon Press, Boston.

Vivian Gornick, from *The Situation and the Story* by Vivian Gornick. Copyright © 2001 by Vivian Gornick. Reprinted with permission of Farrar, Straus and Giroux, LLC.

Index

317